CRITICAL
REASONING
IN
CONTEMPORARY
CULTURE

SUNY Series in the
Philosophy of
the Social Sciences
Lenore Langsdorf, EDITOR

CRITICAL REASONING in CONTEMPORARY CULTURE

Edited by Richard A. Talaska

State University
of New York Press

Published by
State University of New York Press, Albany

Production by Bernadine Dawes
Marketing by Bernadette LaManna

For information, address the State University of New York Press,
State University Plaza, Albany, NY 12246

Library of Congress Cataloging-in-Publication Data

Critical reasoning in contemporary culture / Richard A. Talaska,
    editor.
        p.   cm.—(SUNY series in the philosophy of the social
sciences)
    Includes bibliographical references and indexes.
    ISBN 0-7914-0979-1 (alk. paper) : $59.50. — ISBN 0-7914-0980-5
(pbk. : alk. paper) : $19.95
        1. Critical thinking.   2. Reasoning.   3. Critical thinking—Study
and teaching.   4. Reasoning—Study and teaching.   I. Talaska,
Richard A., 1953- .   II. Series.
BC177.C755   1992
160—dc20   91-27680
                                                                      CIP

10   9   8   7   6   5   4   3   2   1

CONTENTS

v

Acknowledgments

The idea for this volume arose as a result of a speaker series put on by the Department of Philosophy of Xavier University in the 1987–1988 academic year entitled "Teaching Critical Thinking: Three Divergent Approaches."

Special thanks are due to my colleague (at that time chair of Xavier's philosophy department) Richard Bonvillain for securing funds to send me to the 1986 critical thinking conference at Christopher Newport College where I met Ralph H. Johnson, Lenore Langsdorf, and John E. McPeck, who agreed to be the featured speakers in our series on critical thinking. The series itself was funded by Xavier University, and for that I thank Robert J. Murray of the Department of Classics, then acting academic vice president, and Joan Connell, who became academic vice president in the year the series took place. Stanley E. Hedeen, Dean of the College of Arts and Sciences, and E. Paul Colella, Chair of the Department of Philosophy, allowed me a teaching load reduction in the Spring of 1990, and the dean provided some funds to cover the preparation of the volume. In preparing the typescript, I was lucky to have the excellent services of Darleen Frickman and

Eunice J. Staples of Xavier. I am also grateful to Rosalie M. Robertson, editor at the State University of New York Press, for her ever constructive advice, encouragement, and willingness always to be available to explain technical production details. Finally, if not for the help of Lenore Langsdorf in every aspect of this project from the beginning, this book would never have been possible.

Six of the papers contained in this volume originally appeared elsewhere. Four of these have been revised especially for this volume. Chapter 1, Robert H. Ennis's article "Conflicting Views on Teaching Critical Reasoning" originally appeared as "Critical Thinking and Subject Specificity: Clarification and Needed Research" in *Educational Researcher* 18 (3)(April 1989), pp. 4–10. It is reprinted by permission of the publisher, the American Educational Research Association.

Chapter 2, John E. McPeck's article "Teaching Critical Reasoning through the Disciplines: Content versus Process" originally appeared as chapter 3, "Teaching Critical Thinking Through the Disciplines," in McPeck's *Teaching Critical Thinking: Dialogue and Dialectic* (New York: Routledge, 1990), pp. 34–47. It is reprinted with slight revisions by permission of the author and the publisher, Routledge, Chapman, and Hall, Inc.

Chapter 5, Harvey Siegel's article "Education and the Fostering of Rationality" is a revised version of his paper "The Role of Reasons in (Science) Education," which appeared in William Hare's collection *Reason in Teaching and Education* (Halifax: Dalhousie University School of Education, 1989), pp. 5–21. It is reprinted with revisions by permission of the publisher.

Chapter 7, Richard W. Paul's essay "Teaching Critical Reasoning in the Strong Sense: Getting Behind Worldviews" is an extensively revised version of his article "Teaching Critical Thinking in the 'Strong' Sense: A Focus on Self-Deception, World Views, and a Dialectical Mode of Analysis," which appeared in *Informal Logic Newsletter* 4 (2)(1982), pp. 2–7. It is reprinted with revisions by permission of the author and the publisher.

Chapter 9, Gerald Graff's article "Taking Cover in Coverage: Critical Reasoning and the Conflict of Theories" is an extensive revision of his article "Taking Cover in Coverage," which appeared in *Profession 1986* (1986), pp. 41–45. It is reprinted by permission of the Modern Language Association of America.

Chapter 11, Stanley Rosen's essay "Postmodernism and the Possibility of Critical Reasoning" originally appeared as "Postmodernism and the End of Philosophy" in the *Canadian Journal of Political and Social Theory* 9 (3)(1985), pp. 90–101. It is reprinted with alterations by permission of the publisher.

Finally, it should be noted that earlier versions of the articles by Ralph H. Johnson, Lenore Langsdorf, and John E. McPeck were given as part of the above-mentioned speaker series, "Teaching Critical Thinking: Three Divergent Approaches," given at Xavier University, and that Michael J. Buckley's article is a revision of his keynote address given at the inauguration of Le Moyne College's eighth president, Kevin G. O'Connell, SJ, on April 16, 1988.

As an endnote, I should like to thank three people who were most helpful in the final stages of the production process: Bernadine E. Dawes, for her careful work as production editor; Christian J. Cashman, for his work on the index; and Hoang M. Phan, for his help with the proofreading.

Introduction

There has been much talk about "critical thinking" in recent years[1], but the idea is old, at least as old as philosophy. It has, therefore, been treated before, and in different ways. Why should the time be ripe for a book which claims to give diverse theoretical perspectives on the idea of critical reasoning? How is such a project in any way new?

The theoretical answer to this question is that, if the relatively recent discovery of the historical nature of human understanding is real and not counterfeit, then each age must reconsider the issue of critical reasoning. For the Greeks, critical reasoning meant the active engagement in questioning their nonphilosophical culture, the established, foundational, nonphilosophical beliefs of the various cities. Classical Greek philosophy began a tradition that may be properly said to include medieval philosophy insofar as the latter is parasitic, in its School Tradition of commentary upon Greek philosophy, upon the former. Early Modern philosophers questioned the Classical tradition of philosophy itself and accused its practitioners of merely accepting its fundamental concepts on the authority of Aristotle and his great Scholastic commentators. They cast doubt upon the whole system of theoretical concepts through which philosophers for nearly two millennia had explained and viewed their world, and did so in the same way that the Greeks had questioned their nonphilosophic world. Thanks to work in this century by students of the history of science and philosophy, of phenomenology, and of hermeneutics, and because of efforts made to understand the concept of scientific revolution, we have come to appreciate how whole systems of science, or whole epochal traditions in philosophy, operate as systems of preestablished and unexamined assumptions. Within those systems or traditions, people think without necessarily questioning the assumptions themselves. In other words, the fundamental ideas of these systems or traditions typically are not themselves made thematic but through them everything else is brought into focus. That insight has led to the recognition that, if critical reasoning is to be possible, the basic assumptions of the systems or traditions within which we do science or philosophy must themselves be put to the test, in the same way that the Greeks questioned the beliefs of their nonphilosophical predecessors, and in the way the early Moderns doubted the Classical tradition in philosophy that had begun with the Greeks. Unless questioning is done at the radical level, Heidegger and others tell us, what goes by the name of "science" ends up being a kind of "tinkering within established procedures"—the activity Kuhn calls "normal science." Thus, critical reasoning is not simply the same for us as it was for the Greeks, it is both the same and different. It is the same in that it presupposes the examination of established beliefs. It is different in that the established beliefs that are to be questioned include the fundamental principles of the various traditions of philosophy and of the various paradigms of science—including our own. The difference makes a reconsideration of critical reasoning necessary for contemporary culture. This book brings together both theoretical papers and papers that one might call practice-oriented theory, all of which treat the meaning of critical reasoning in contemporary culture.

There is also a practical answer to the question about why this volume is needed. Many scholars have been focusing of late on practical educational reforms intended to teach critical reasoning. But no one volume has yet brought together a sampling of attitudes and proposals representing diverse contemporary theoretical views of critical reasoning. This volume does so by collecting a number of essays by scholars that have been focusing on the problem of critical reasoning and practical educational reform. But it is also an attempt to open that discussion up to a wider circle by including articles by scholars who in one way or another raise serious problems for theory of critical reasoning from perspectives quite alien to those of the educational theorists.

Why use the term *critical reasoning* rather than *critical thinking* in the title of the volume? First, the term *critical thinking* is often used as part of the name of a movement with many distinguished members, several of whom are contributors to this volume. But there are other contributors who have written for the volume who do not associate themselves with the so-called critical thinking movement but are nevertheless clearly interested in the problem of what makes up critical, rational thought. Second, because the idea of teaching critical thinking has recently become popular, many educators, not all with equal amounts of professional expertise, claim to teach and discuss critical thinking. Many reputable scholars have become wary of reform proposals that go under the name of critical thinking. Surely the critical thinking movement ought not be misjudged because some unworthy practitioners have associated themselves with it and engendered suspicions in the minds of some who are unfamiliar with the work of its most capable proponents. Yet since some writers have given whatever goes by the name a questionable reputation (as Socrates says of philosophy), it may be best to avoid the term, especially since there are suitable alternatives (as there are not in the case of philosophy). Third, one wonders how there could be such a thing as critical thinking that does not consist in the process of reasoning. According to traditional Scholastic logic, reasoning is the orderly process by which the mind proceeds *ordinate et faciliter et sine errore* ("with order, ease, and correctness")[2] in propositional discourse or judgments. The term *critical* (from *krinein*, "to judge"), used in this logical sense, implies the making of unbiased—if not necessarily true, or at least probable—judgments. The term *thinking* implies the process of constructing connected patterns of judgments, or inferences; the process traditionally called "reasoning." For these three reasons, then, it seems advisable to use the term *critical reasoning* as more accurately descriptive than *critical thinking*.

There is also some need to explain the term *culture*. The term has a broad sociological significance: it means the beliefs and behavioral patterns of any group, widely or narrowly construed. In this sense, one might say that there is such a thing as a community of those engaged in the life of the intellect, and that, given the kinds of debates engaged in by that community, certain patterns of thinking, certain modes of criticism, certain intellectual perspectives, have developed that characterize our age—in the West, at least. Some call our contemporary intellectual culture "postmodern culture." If we are squeamish about this term because we do not see any significant novelty in postmodernism, but rather only the logical conclusions of the early modern project, we may prefer to speak of "later modern culture." In either case, contemporary Western intellectual culture can be associated with a certain range of theoretical as well as moral and political ideas that cannot help exerting an influence on the idea of critical reasoning. Thus, this book asks the question, "What is critical reasoning in the climate of contemporary intellectual culture with all that its theoretical, moral, and political attitudes entails?" Such an investigation properly belongs to a series on the philosophy of social science.

But this is a philosophical book with much emphasis on education. The term *culture* is therefore also used here in its stronger educational sense that is perhaps best reflected in the Greek term *paideia*, the Latin *cultura*, and the German *Bildung*. What these terms intend is the formation of the soul of an individual in accordance with a particular view of a complete human life or a particular model of what a complete human being should be.[3] The essays in this volume engender questions about what that end, and the means to it, should be, at least in the context of the contemporary Western world.[4]

Description of the Contents of This Volume

Common to all the contributors to this volume is a primarily speculative rather than merely practical approach to critical reasoning. Some papers might more properly be described as theory pure and simple; others, more as practice-oriented theory. In any case, any theoretical discussion of education and critical reasoning has a natural practical *telos*. Each essay attempts to develop a unified theoretical slant on critical reasoning. Each in some way proposes a position on the meaning, conditions, and goals of critical reasoning.

Part I deals with theories of critical reasoning and education, and is especially concerned with the problem of the relationship between critical reasoning skills and the learning of the content of the various disciplines. Part II focuses on various crucial theoretical problems at the heart of theory of critical reasoning.

Part I: Theories of Critical Reasoning and Education

At least eight chapters deal in some way with the complex problem of the relationship between learning the content of disciplines or subject areas and learning critical reasoning abilities. There has been much debate on this issue, often construed as a debate on whether priority ought to be given in education to reasoning skills or to content. There are many ways of construing this content/skills relationship, as Robert H. Ennis writes in chapter 1, "Conflicting Views on Teaching Critical Reasoning." Ennis organizes the various theoretical views taken by the participants in the debate and notes that specific kinds of research are required to test the claims of the proponents of the various views. He also indicates the still early stage of discussion of the problem and the need for much rigorous work to sort through the issues, in spite of the fact that educators have been taking positions and changing curricula accordingly for years. Ennis's chapter provides a fine introduction to the several chapters on this issue because he has succinctly organized the diverse theoretical views of the skills/content issue.

Ennis distinguishes several approaches to the teaching of critical thinking. The most prevalent, the "general" approach, is the attempt "to teach critical thinking abilities and dispositions separately from the presentation of the content of existing subject-matter offerings." The principles of reasoning critically are considered teachable apart from the teaching of the individual disciplines and transferable to these disciplines and to subjects that cross them. The best example of such an approach is the teaching of courses in critical thinking or informal logic. Other approaches to teaching critical reasoning deny that critical reasoning can be taught apart from "deep, thoughtful, well-understood subject-matter instruction." The infusion approach uses standard subject-matter content but makes the general principles of reasoning explicit as the appropriateness of teaching such principles arises in the course of teaching content. The immersion approach takes the position that students become critical reasoners in an area precisely by becoming "deeply immersed in the subject," and that it is not necessary to make general principles explicit. Finally, there is the mixed approach: "These distinctions, though conceptually clear, often reduce to continuums and have borderline cases in practice." Ennis distinguishes various theoretical versions of subject specificity, criticizes the idea by displaying crucial ambiguities in the idea of subject, and points in the direction of needed research to solve some of the crucial problems still at issue, such as, the need for methods of testing that can compare one approach with another.

The section entitled "Theories that Emphasize Content" consists of chapters by authors who tend towards the content side of the skills/content dichotomy. John McPeck, in "Teaching Critical Reasoning Through the Disciplines: Content versus Process," defends the view that critical thinking is not the result of learning general skills, but the result of having a great deal of knowledge in the various subject areas. On Ennis' division, McPeck's view is part of the immersion school. McPeck has long been the nemesis of the members of the critical thinking movement, and rather lively exchanges have occurred between McPeck and prominent members of that movement, both in writing and at conferences.[5] McPeck wishes to "redirect attention away from generic *processes of reasoning*," which he claims the critical thinking movement and the various "thinking skills programs" emphasize, to "consider the proposition that the *content* of various subjects and/or problems determines (i.e., creates) the appropriate *process* of reasoning, and not vice versa." McPeck defends, from the point of view of Wittgenstein's epistemological discussion of the relationship between language and thought, what Hirsch defends from the point of view of his own hermeneutics. For both Hirsch and McPeck, the understanding of particular terms and propositions depends upon the broader understanding of a whole system of terms and propositions—a subject area, or a "form of life," or "language game," in Wittgenstein's terminology. Just as for Hirsch there is no such thing as general reading skill, but rather our reading skill in a particular area depends upon our having specific background knowledge in the area of the reading, so for McPeck, there is no such thing as general critical thinking skill, but rather our critical thinking in any discipline depends upon our having in-depth, specific, background knowledge of that discipline. "This is what renders a general thinking skills approach *implausible* from a theoretical point of view, and *ineffective* from a practical point of view." For

McPeck, critical thinking is a combination of adequate specific background knowledge in an area and the disposition "to engage in an activity or problem with *reflective skepticism.*" Such reflective skepticism is possible only in and through immersion in the various disciplines.

The other paper in this section is Donald Lazere's "Cultural Literacy and Critical Literacy." Although Lazere is an acknowledged member of the political left, his view of critical literacy is dependent upon Hirsch's view of cultural literacy (usually associated with the political right).[6] For according to Lazere, "higher order" critical literacy skills depend upon the "lower order" cultural literacy demanded by Hirsch. Lazere accepts the view that participation in American life (i.e., empowerment) requires, as Hirsch suggests, a knowledge of a certain literate vocabulary, or a kind of repertoire of conceptual tools. Only with such a repertoire can the next step to critical literacy be taken. According to Lazere, cultural literacy consists in such things (without giving his full list) as the ability to unify our personal and academic experience; the ability to follow extended and abstract argument; the ability to engage in moral and aesthetic judgment; the ability to form open-minded, autonomous, sociopolitical opinions. A part of critical literacy upon which Lazere places some emphasis is political literacy. He makes a strong case for the necessity of this kind of political savvy in an age and culture in which the forms of manipulation are hidden, sophisticated, and pervasive. But basic cultural literacy is a necessary condition for critical literacy, which amounts to critical thinking. Lazere describes Richard W. Paul's strong-sense critical thinking (see chapter 7, by Paul in this volume) as an approach that "encourages students' attainment of autonomous thinking through skeptically questioning all inadequately substantiated claims and culturally conditioned assumptions. Strong-sense critical thinking is essentially rhetorical in its insistence that learning takes place most effectively through Socratic dialogue and debates between opposing viewpoints. Obviously the more of Hirsch's cultural literacy students possess, the larger arsenal of information they will have for challenging claims and perceiving diverse viewpoints." Lazere's view is therefore an interesting version of the skills/content problem in that it crosses political ideologies: it requires education in traditional content for the very purpose of liberation.

The following section, "Theories that Emphasize Skills," deals with the other side of the skills/content division. Ralph H. Johnson argues, in "Critical Reasoning and Informal Logic," on behalf of informal logic as part of what, in an ideal academic situation, would be a whole system of attempts at teaching critical thinking. Johnson's view is that generic principles and reasoning skills can be taught, but not all the principles and skills that constitute critical thinking can be taught in a single course in informal logic. "To produce such an individual [the critical thinker], the support of the whole educational system is necessary. No one course at any level can do it." However, "preeminent among the skills in the cognitive repertoire of the critical thinker is the ability to appraise arguments. In helping to achieve this ability, informal logic enters the scene." In defending informal logic as the logic of argumentation, Johnson considers an argument to have two layers or "tiers" in its structure: a "premise-conclusion" part and "dialectical" part. He thus develops a two-tiered theory of argument analysis as necessary for the critical evaluation of arguments. The first tier consists in the usual structural analysis of arguments as found in standard informal logic texts. The second consists in a broader dialectical analysis which addresses alternative positions to the ones we hold, objections to our own arguments, and the wider implications of our arguments. Johnson's informal logic approach would probably be classified in Ennis' scheme as "general" (see chapter 1), although his demand for a systematic development of the curriculum in the direction of critical reasoning would render his overall approach "mixed." The description of his second tier of argument analysis also renders his position much broader than the more narrow approach of many informal logic texts.

Two of the principles Johnson mentions as structural criteria for arguments are that premises must be relevant to the conclusion and that premises must provide sufficient evidence for the conclusion. Harvey Siegel's essay, "Education and the Fostering of Rationality" may be said to be, among other things, the careful development of those two principles. "Critical thinking is thinking which adequately reflects relevant reasons; a critical thinker is one whose thinking is similarly reflective of reasons. We can say, in short, that a critical thinker is one who is *appropriately moved by reasons.*" In Siegel's view, critical thinking is the ability to "assess the degree to which a reason supports or warrants a claim or judgment," and to conform our own beliefs, judgments, and actions to that assessment. Such ability implies an awareness of certain principles. Some of those principles are general and entirely subject-neutral (e.g., formal and informal principles of logic), some are subject-specific (e.g., knowing that yellow skin may be a sign of liver damage). "Critical thinking, consequently, is wrongly construed as entirely subject-neutral or entirely subject-specific." Clearly Siegel's view, in Ennis's scheme, is "mixed." In a particularly instructive example, he shows how critical thinking could be used as an educational ideal in science education. It would include not only a discussion of what relevant reasons in science are but a discussion of philosophy of science (such issues as alternative theories and hypotheses, the nature of verification, etc.). "In all curriculum areas, an education which fosters critical thinking in those areas emphasizes the nature and role of reasons, the active consideration of alternative theoretical and critical perspectives, and the philosophical issues and concerns studied by the philosophy of the relevant discipline," which "informs our understanding of the principles governing the evaluation of reasons in that area." Siegel's view may be understood as a blend of McPeck's view, that each discipline has its own epistemology which ought to be mastered to achieve critical thinking in that area, and the informal logic or "general" view. In effect Siegel is arguing for infusing across the curriculum some of the attitudes proper to philosophy as such. Siegel also argues that skills, while necessary for critical thinking, are not sufficient; they must be supplemented by what he calls the "critical spirit"—a complex of attitudes, dispositions, and character traits that include a respect for reasons and a desire to be guided by them. This aspect of critical thinking makes clear that critical thinking is not simply a matter of skills, but is rather an ideal of a certain sort of person.

Robert J. Sternberg's "Creativity, Critical Reasoning, and the Problem of Content-Oriented Education" (chapter 6), belongs in the same group as chapters 4 and 5. But his focus is not, strictly speaking, on critical as much as on creative reasoning. The article is of a piece with others in this group because Sternberg's general criticism of current educational practice is actually the same as that of many others in the critical thinking movement. It is also one that an informal logician—espousing the "general" approach described by Ennis—might make: over-emphasis upon the imparting of content has tended to stifle crucial skills or abilities to use and manipulate that content, and such skills are, in any case, more important than content. In Sternberg's case, the crucial ability is creativity, which, if not part of critical reasoning broadly construed, is surely complementary to critical reasoning. The ability to construct new criticisms of an old body of ideas and then to construct a new way of thinking about those ideas is an example of thought that is both critical and creative. It is characteristic of thinkers such as Galileo, who had to criticize the whole Classical tradition in natural science in order to, as it were, create a new set of basic concepts through which to view the world.

Sternberg's view of the content issue, contrary to McPeck's, is that the schools at all levels have been doing a fair job of imparting content, but have done "at least as much to undermine creativity as to foster it." He develops, within his six-facet theory of the origins of creative behavior, a theory of creativity as well as a critique of current school practices that inhibit the development of creativity. One of the key ideas behind Sternberg's approach is that intelligence consists, in part, in the ability to

define and redefine problems. (The example of Galileo is sufficient to fill this out, but Sternberg mentions others.) His criticism of the schools is that, "in order to redefine a problem, one
has to have the option of defining a problem in the first place.
Schools only rarely give students this luxury." Even when the advocates of thinking skills have successfully turned a curriculum
from memorization to problem-solving, the structures set up for
problem-solving often discourage rather than encourage creative
thinking. Since "creative individuals are often most renowned
not for their solving of problems but for their posing of the problems in the first place," textbooks, standardized tests, and school
assignments designed to have students solve already structured
problems rather than to structure and solve the problems themselves inhibit rather than encourage creative thinking. This approach, which advocates putting initiative in the hands of the
student and rewarding creativity, is the basic theme of Sternberg's theory and of his critique of current educational practices.

The next section has the title "Beyond Skills and Content,"
because the authors of the papers in this chapter present a view of
teaching critical thinking that transcends the skills/content dichotomy. They focus instead on worldviews, the very matrix
within which logical skills and cultural knowledge operate. Richard W. Paul calls this approach "strong-sense critical thinking."

Paul has, for this volume, revised his seminal 1982 article on
strong-sense critical reasoning. In its revised form, it now appears
under the title, "Teaching Critical Reasoning in the Strong
Sense: Getting Behind Worldviews" (chapter 7). His opening paragraph manifests his disagreement with McPeck. According to
Paul, a general critical thinking course at a college or university
is not only possible but necessary. "The intellectual needs that
instruction in critical thinking is intended to fulfill are so central
to education that they must be given serious attention and central focus in at least one foundational course." He later cites two
letters from students complaining of the overemphasis upon
memorization of content and relative neglect of reasoning skills

in their schooling experience. His view is not, however, that learning general principles of argument analysis is sufficient for critical thinking. Much to the contrary: such learning, he claims can make students less rather than more critical, more rather than less closed-minded, by teaching them how to defend their prejudices. By itself, the ability to understand and use informal and formal principles of argument analysis amounts to "weak-sense" critical thinking. "Strong-sense" critical thinking involves the attempt to see how our analysis of arguments is affected by our often unconscious worldviews and interests. The weakness of what Paul calls the "atomistic" approach to argument analysis (the approach of most formal and informal logic courses) is that it fails to consider the broader systematic views and interests that often unconsciously distort our argument analysis. There is a difference between the worldview we consciously assert and the (often unconscious) one that actually determines our beliefs and behavior. This latter worldview, with its connected interests, can distort our construction and analysis of arguments. "Strong-sense" critical thinking is the attempt to make this worldview explicit and to see how it operates in our argumentation. Paul argues the efficacy of using ethical issues as an exceptionally good means of teaching critical thinking. Ethical issues are multidimensional (i.e., they cross disciplines), involve interests and worldviews directly, and are most apt to open up the difference between the worldview that is presupposed by our behavior and the worldview we think we hold.

In "The Interpretive Focus: A Prerequisite for Critical Reasoning" (chapter 8), Lenore Langsdorf argues that there are interpretive skills needed to approach texts (written or oral) critically even before evaluation and logical analysis of specific arguments can begin. A fundamental shift in focus must first take place. The bringing about of this fundamental shift is what Langsdorf, following Paul, calls "strong-sense" critical thinking. She exemplifies the shift in focus by noting crucial differences between attitudes that operate in conversation and those that operate in reading. In conversation, there are two elements: the living personal communicative event between two or more conversationalists, and the content of the conversation. Reading involves only the latter. In ordinary conversational discourse we attend to particular aspects of the event (such as the personality of our interlocutor and the circumstances of the conversation) as well as to content. On some occasions, we may be so taken up with the content of what the speaker is saying that we seem not to be paying attention to the other person. Our attention has shifted from the real conversational event to the content alone, to the "ideal object." A person who makes this shift is normally considered a bad conversationalist, or may be characterized as "absent-minded," so caught up with ideas as to seem out of touch, as it were. But this being "absent-minded" to the particular event, and attentive to the "ideal" object (the content), is precisely the kind of move that we need to make in order to adopt an interpretive perspective. The interpretive focus is the attitude necessary for critical reasoning to occur. Such a shift in focus is preliminary to the logical and evaluative activities that ought to follow our adopting the interpretive stance. Achieving this fundamental shift in focus is crucial to Langsdorf's understanding of "strong-sense" critical thinking. Her approach to critical thinking, like Paul's, would in Ennis's scheme, be considered "mixed." Like Paul, and unlike McPeck, Langsdorf believes that we need certain generic interpretive skills in order to be critical about texts and the arguments they contain. Thus, she directs attention to certain general reasoning skills that, she believes, need to be learned apart from and even prior to an in-depth immersion into the individual disciplines.

Part II. Problems for Theory of Critical Reasoning

Each of the essays in Part II attempts a kind of Copernican revolution in the understanding of the problems attending critical thinking. They focus upon topics normally considered peripheral (or not considered at all), and turn those topics into central issues affecting critical reasoning. The chapters focus on methodology, history, the unity of source for critical reasoning, and values.

The section entitled "The Problem of Methodology" contains two papers that critique the methodological framework within which critical reasoning is supposed to occur. In Gerald Graff's case, this framework is the organization of the place that has traditionally institutionalized critical reasoning: the university. Ralph Sleeper raises the question of conflicting ideas of rationality itself and what counts as knowledge within the framework of such ideas.

In "Taking Cover in Coverage: Critical Reasoning and the Conflict of Theories" (chapter 9), Graff suggests that the very administrative organization of departments in the university, and not individual teaching practices, has done the greatest harm to students' critical thinking abilities. Graff takes English departments as an example, although his criticisms are applicable across disciplines. He argues that debates between the adherents of the various literary theories such as "feminism, Marxism, post-structuralism, and the new historicism," as well as debates between those who advocate teaching only the traditional humanistic canon of Western classics and those who advocate including various minority or multicultural canons or the popular media, have been covered over by the administrative organization of departments in such a way that these debates themselves rarely intrude upon students. The debates rage at specialized conferences or in specialized journals, but hardly ever in the curriculum, the very heart of which should be the place of rational controversy and argument.

Graff uses the term "field-coverage" to describe the organizational structure of departments that has tended to prevent open debate. Departments divide up the disciplines into various systematic or historical areas or "fields" to be covered. Professors specialize in one or several areas, and the job of administration is to ensure that the proper faculty are hired and the proper courses offered so as to cover the fields, and that students majoring in the area cover a sufficient portion of the various fields by taking courses. The creation of a different course offering for each different historical period or systematic topic ensures that the materials are duly covered. But this very compartmentalization discourages faculty holding different theories of literature and criticism from engaging in public argument over differences of principle. Such public argument, to which students should be privy and in which they should participate, ought to be the heart of university life and the arena in which the critical thinking abilities of students are whetted.

"The moral is that if the introduction of literary theory is to make a real difference in encouraging critical thinking in the average literature student, we must find some way to modify the field-coverage model. Otherwise, theory (and perhaps critical thinking itself) will be institutionalized as yet another field, equivalent to literary periods and genres—which is to say, it will become one more option that can safely be ignored. We will lose theory's potential for drawing the disconnected parts of the literature curriculum into relation and providing students with the context needed to develop their critical reasoning capacities." Graff's argument for critical thinking is that, "just as the best way to learn a foreign language is to live in the country in which the language is spoken, the best way to learn critical thinking is to be part of an intellectual community in which such thinking is being practiced (where there will probably be debate over which forms of thinking count as critical, or even as thinking, and which do not)." Thus critical thinking is best brought about by placing in the foreground the central intellectual conflicts of an age and engaging students in the debate over the issues. At present, those issues would include conflict over the canon, various literary theories, and various theories of rationality itself.

The title of Ralph Sleeper's chapter "Whose Reason? Which Canon? Critical Reasoning and Conflicting Ideas of Rationality" (chapter 10), is a reference to Alasdair MacIntyre's *Whose Justice? Which Rationality?* According to Sleeper, MacIntyre is looking, in this time of "the uncertain rationalities of the post-Enlightenment break-up of the tradition," for "an authoritative tradition of agreed-upon canons of rationality that can be counted on to be of use in resolving new problems and controversies as they arise in the ever-changing circumstances of this postmodern world." With this reference to MacIntyre's traditionalist argument serving as a backdrop, Sleeper goes on, citing Emerson and Dewey, to note the antitraditionalist, anti-authoritarian bent of American philosophy. He takes Dewey's criticism of the "epistemological industry" as the starting point for his critique of what he apparently considers the two most misguided camps of educational theorists: the "conservative right," which would include those who believe that "we are wallowing in a swamp of cultural illiteracy and moral relativism" (he later mentions Bloom, Hirsch, Bennett, and Chaney as sharing common ground); and the "conservative left," which would include those who reject the canonical content idea, but appeal to some form of "critical logic of analysis" or "critical reasoning" to "answer to the variety of our human needs in our morals as in our sciences." Sleeper's view is that both the traditionalists like Bloom and the adherents to the various forms of critical thinking start with an ideal of rationality, presupposed and unquestioned, as the end in view, and then proceed to propose a method to achieve the end. This, however, is the true "scandal to philosophy," institutionalized by philosophers since Descartes, who have started by arbitrarily choosing what they mean by legitimate concepts and then simply rejecting as meaningless anything that does not fit their definition. They start by demanding a certain kind of clarity for concepts to be accepted as genuine, and then exclude "all discourse involving the rough-and-ready concepts of natural language in use in the inductive inferences of the everyday world." Thus theology, metaphysics, and most forms of ethics are excluded as unscientific. Sleeper cites Dewey: "We take out of our logical package what we have put into it, and then convert what we draw out to be a literal description of the actual world." Although he does not develop his own proposal at length, Sleeper's discussion suggests that rationality develops through the very process of inquiry (hence his references, at the beginning and end of his essay, to induction).

The section entitled "The Problem of History," raises questions concerning the influence of our own cultural history on interpretations of critical reasoning and its possibility. Stanley Rosen's chapter deals with the problem posed for critical reasoning by postmodernism. My own treats the problem posed for critical reasoning by the historical nature of the understanding.

As Paul's idea of "strong-sense" critical thinking is to make explicit our inexplicit but operative worldviews, Stanley Rosen's attempt in "Postmodernism and the Possibility of Critical Reasoning" is to point out to those who hold doctrines of critical thinking, as well as to those who reject the possibility of critical thinking as it is usually understood, that their views themselves presuppose a much broader scientific or philosophic worldview. He distinguishes between a commonly articulated worldview of our time, that of "postmodernism," with its assumption that both the philosophy of the Classical tradition as well as that of modernity have been overcome, and another worldview that, he claims, operates as the actual basis for our decisions, judgments, and actions. Rosen's attempt is to show that the operative worldview is that of modernity and that the so-called postmodern phenomenon is in fact just another version of that modern worldview. The threat to critical thinking from the postmodern critique is considerable. If that critique is right, the values of "clarity, rationality, and common sense" are actually "outmoded consequences of modernity, or even of metaphysics, or of the former, scientifically articulated, will to power." The proponents of the possibility of critical thinking must face up to the claims and critique of postmodernism, because if postmodernism is right, then philosophy, and with it critical thinking, is at an end. Rosen's paper confronts the postmodern phenomenon by showing that the supporters of the idea of postmodernism have not understood their own worldview correctly. He holds that the worldview is really derivative from, not different from, that of modern philosophy. Rosen's question is fundamental: "In this essay, I am concerned with one question: is the thesis of the end of philosophy, and so of modernity, sound?" If the thesis is sound, there can be no critical thinking. If not, then those who claim that postmodernism is a novel phenomenon have failed to understand themselves and modernity, they have not achieved a critical distance from and understanding of their own worldview—a state of affairs which Paul, Langsdorf, and others demand of any critical thinker.

My own essay, "Critical Reasoning and History" (chapter 12), argues that, given the historical nature of the understanding (that is, the fact that ordinary consciousness always starts with a set of meanings determined by our culture and historical tradition), critical reasoning first and foremost consists in achieving standpoints from which to make thematic the presuppositions guiding our thought and creating our focus on the world. I exemplify the problem of historical prejudice by pointing out that even the best-educated people in the West tend to interpret morality and political events in the East by focusing on them through already uncritically accepted foundational Western beliefs. The idea that individualism, which Hegel calls "the pivot and center of the difference between antiquity and modern times," is one of the key elements of the worldview of the modern liberal West, functions as a key example in my argument. Individualism is so basic to our worldview that we no longer see it, although we see everything else through it. Hence all movements toward individualism in the East are considered progress towards the enlightened true view that lies at the basis of our political views. In the United States these are considered true in part because of the apparent success and stability of our government and society. But if critical reasoning includes freeing ourselves from intellectual prejudice, then this kind of thinking, laden with moral and political presuppositions, is far from critical. The difficulty is learning to

see, and thus in some measure freeing ourselves from, the prejudices of our worldview, our cultural history.

Since individualism, and much else of Western thought, has
its origin in the arguments of great early modern philosophical
writers, the premier way to free ourselves intellectually from
such historical prejudices is to make them thematic by analyzing
the original arguments that gave rise to them. Since these arguments occur in the great texts of the great modern authors, we
must read their texts to uncover the now hidden origins of our
own basic beliefs. Since those authors were rejecting a whole tradition, both in natural science and in morality and politics, in order to understand modern authors, we must also read the texts of
the Classical tradition rejected by modernity. Only by understanding the worldview that modernity originally intended to demolish and for which it substituted new doctrines can we
moderns adequately see the modern worldview for what it is, and
consider it at a sufficient intellectual distance to criticize it rationally. The whole process of reconstituting the Classical tradition and our own foundations by reading great works becomes a
kind of intellectual psychotherapy whereby we uncover the hidden origins of our intellectual prejudices. In some measure, we
free ourselves from them by putting ourselves in a critical stance
toward them. This freeing process is what makes critical reasoning possible. Only by the study of our own cultural history in
foundational historical texts do we free ourselves from that
history and thus achieve the standpoint of critical reasoning.
"Critical reasoning is achieved in the interplay between the
continually acquired content of our cultural history and the continual serious attempt to reach standpoints from which to focus
upon and criticize our historically acquired prejudices. That serious, indispensable attempt is the careful study of foundational
historical texts."

Two articles are contained in the next section, "The Problem
of the Unity Source for Critical Reasoning." They argue from the
perspectives of metaphysics and of theology, each of which has, in

the history of Western thought, been considered ultimate in one way or another. The first chapter is less a prescription for the resolution of conflicts than a proposal for finding and creating difficulties. Eva T. H. Brann's chapter, "Critical Reasoning and The Second Power of Questions: Toward First Questions and First Philosophy" (chapter 13), takes the position that "the insight of critical reasoning . . . seems . . . to show itself almost entirely in the putting of pertinent questions." It is in the displaying rather than resolving of difficulties that critical reasoning is seen most of all. "To give an answer is to make a distinction. But, of course, the discerning answer is solicited and . . . shaped by the question." Critical reasoning begins with the asking of questions, and therefore thinking about critical reasoning ought to begin with thinking about questions. Brann's essay is therefore an inquiry into "the kinds, the forms, the uses, the hierarchies, and also the contemporary fate of questions." Brann offers a synoptic study of questions and the ways they have been treated by key questioners of questions from Plato to Searle—a highly theoretical survey of a primordial issue in critical reasoning. Since answering a question is making a distinction—often a distinction about the way things are—and since the answer is solicited by the question, then inquiry into the nature of the question itself is a "first question"; it belongs to metaphysics. The question about questions is therefore an attempt to get at the unity of source of critical reasoning about the ways things are. Her question, "What is a question?" is thus theoretical in the highest sense.

The second chapter in this section may strike some readers as unusual, because, as Sleeper recognizes in his chapter, we may well hold a hidden but unwarranted assumption about what constitutes the legitimate matrix of scientific rationality. Michael J. Buckley's chapter, "Theology and Critical Reasoning: Ignatius' Understanding of the Jesuit University" (chapter 14), defends theology as a focus of university education and as a means of critical thinking. Buckley's basic idea is that, in accordance with Ignatius' (the writer of the Jesuit constitution with its chapters on education) understanding, theology should function in the Jesuit university as the architectonic discipline which uses the reasoning abilities and content acquired in the other university disciplines, integrates them by putting the disciplines into dialogue with each other and with theology itself on specific issues, and establishes the conditions for a higher form of critical reasoning that leads to, and centers around, ultimate questions. The presupposition of Buckley's argument is that this higher form of critical reasoning could not occur without the preparation received in the study of the other disciplines and the integration of those disciplines in the form of a higher-level dialogue between them. Further, he argues that theology, by raising ultimate questions and putting itself into dialogue with the other disciplines and those into dialogue with each other, furnishes that integration at the highest level. "A Jesuit university institutionalizes critical thinking precisely through, rather than in spite of, theology." Buckley's article on theology provides an unexpected voice in this discussion about critical reasoning. Like Graff's article, it proposes a way of integrating university education by putting conflicting views, and the varied views of the various disciplines, into public dialogue with each other. It implicitly criticizes the fragmentation of contemporary education by seeking unity in theology as the ideal or *pros hen* referent of university education.

The final chapter of this volume focuses on the problem of values. Michael Scriven's chapter, "Evaluation and Critical Reasoning: Logic's Last Frontier?" offers not a different theory of critical reasoning but an argument for the need for a scientific treatment of evaluation, a treatment that presupposes that values can and need to be handled critically and objectively. The logic of evaluation is a part of critical reasoning almost universally ignored by current approaches to philosophy of science, logic, informal logic, and critical thinking, although it has received attention in the social sciences. A science or logic of evaluation charts the multiple complex forms of, and steps in, a properly objective or critical evaluation process. Although human beings engage in evaluation regularly, the process whereby we arrive at critically reasoned, evaluative conclusions has received little attention in philosophy. Such reasoned judgments are made by most of us without much previous practice: important decisions requiring serious methodological evaluation, such as buying a house, choosing a surgeon for serious surgery, etc., occur relatively infrequently. The very idea of a logic or science of evaluation as a part of philosophy of science, logic, informal logic, or critical thinking is as yet new, has yielded no "experts," and certainly is not part of general education. Thus, as a population, we lack rational methods or procedures for making evaluative decisions. Scriven's twofold purpose is "to examine the cultural context" that led to the omission of such a science among philosophers and "take a step towards remedying it by setting out some of the basic logic of practical evaluation." It is perhaps when we have the most at stake (as in the above-mentioned examples) that we are most bereft of a science to help us evaluate critically. Putting all the factors involved in any evaluation together, charting and weighing them in a rational way, finding and applying an appropriate method for generating a conclusion, and making the final evaluation, are the kinds of things involved in a critical evaluation. Scriven argues for the need for a discipline that develops this kind of reasoning. He elucidates the idea of a logic of evaluation through a detailed account of how a methodical, critical evaluation might be carried out. This account covers "enough to indicate the existence of a reasonable procedure for . . . evaluation which avoids a number of serious mistakes" and uncovers "a topic which deserves to be given a place in the logic of science, not discarded into the bin of 'matters of taste.' ".

The above descriptions should make clear that the present volume collects a variety of theoretical perspectives on critical reasoning. Such a diversity of slants, by reason of new problems they raise or interesting new sides of critical reasoning they uncover, suggests the richness of the concept of critical reasoning and the need to open the discussion of critical reasoning to educators beyond the circle of those actively associated with the informal logic and critical thinking movements. These scholars have made the initial contribution by taking the lead in the discussion of critical reasoning and education in recent years. But if the vantage point from which these distinguished thinkers view critical reasoning is not itself to become partial or one-sided, without being recognized as such (as Sleeper suggests that the methodological limitations imposed upon scientific claims to knowledge by early modern philosophy created a kind of unwarranted prejudice about what constitutes scientific knowledge), then the problem of critical reasoning ought to be tackled by the whole spectrum of the academic community to help ensure that no essential aspect of the concept of critical reasoning will be ignored. Perhaps this volume can serve as an introduction and invitation to further, in-depth, cross-disciplinary debate on the theory of critical reasoning in contemporary culture.

Notes

1. See, for example, Hans V. Hansen, "Informal Logic Bibliography," *Informal Logic* 12 (1990): 155–84; Ralph H. Johnson and J. Anthony Blair, "A Bibliography of Recent Work in Informal Logic," *Informal Logic Newsletter* 5 (3) (July 1983): 3–26; Ralph H. Johnson and J. Anthony Blair, "A Bibliography of Recent Work in Informal Logic," in *Informal Logic: The First International Symposium*, eds. Ralph H. Johnson and J. Anthony Blair (Inverness, Cal.: Edgepress, 1980), pp. 163–72; Michael F. Schmidt, "Fallacies—A Bibliography-in-Progress," *Critical Thinking News* 2 (7) (April–May 1984): 11–15, and a later, updated version by the same title in *Informal Logic* 8 (1986): 105–111; John Hoaglund, B. G. Hurdle, Curtis Miles, Philip A. Pecorino, "Bibliographies on Critical Thinking," compiled by Philip A. Pecorino in unpublished typescript, pp. 1–30; "A Partially Annotated Bibliography of Critical Thinking Sources," typescript, 10 pages, distributed at the Conference on Critical Thinking 1986 at Christopher Newport College, Center for Critical Thinking (Newport News, Va.: Christopher Newport College, n.d.)

Critical thinking and informal logic have become valid, professionally recognized areas among the disciplines. In 1980, the *Philosopher's*

Index lists 11 entrys under the title "critical thinking," and 7 under "informal logic," while the 1990 cumulative index reveals 26 under "critical thinking" and 25 under "informal logic." There is now an official association dedicated to the area (The Association for Informal Logic and Critical Thinking), a journal devoted to it (*Informal Logic*), numerous newsletters, such as *Inquiry: Critical Thinking Across the Disciplines*, published by the Institute for Critical Thinking at Montclair State College; an international conference held at Sonoma State University under the auspices of the Center for Critical Thinking and Moral Critique that draws some twelve hundred educators annually, and many other professional organizations, publications, and activities.

2. From Thomas Aquinas' commentary on Aristotle's *Posterior Analytics*, as cited in Jacques Maritain, *Formal Logic* (New York: Sheed and Ward, 1946), p. 1.

3. Cf. Werner Jaegar's *Paedeia: The Ideals of Greek Culture*, trans., Gilbert Highet, vol. 1, *Archaic Greece: The Mind of Athens*, 2d ed. (New York: Oxford University, 1945), introduction, passim, but esp. pp. xvii and xxii–iii, where Jaegar writes, "[The Greeks] were the first to recognize that education means deliberately moulding human character in accordance with an ideal . . . . Only this type of education deserves the name of culture, the type for which Plato uses the physical metaphor of *moulding* character. The German word *Bildung* clearly indicates the essence of education in the Greek, Platonic sense; for it covers the artist's act of plastic formation as well as the guiding pattern present in his imagination, the *idea* or *typos*. Throughout history, whenever this conception reappears, it is always inherited from the Greeks."

4. One might object that contemporary culture is not *paideia* in the Greek sense, since the latter means education to a particular moral form of life, to a particular kind of character with a specific set of moral virtues. This is, of course, true. We in the contemporary West are not in agreement about a set of moral virtues into which to educate our young in the same way that the Greeks were in agreement when they held up Homer as their highest model. But is not the idea that education ought to be in the direction of critical reasoning (or philosophy) for the human person to be liberated and empowered (a view held by some of the contributors to this volume) a moral model, albeit one that has its origin in modern thought? It makes some sense, then, to suggest that one of the

meanings of *culture* in the title points back to the Greek educational sense. But then the very issue of the moral presuppositions behind *our* view of critical reasoning must itself be raised if our approach to critical reasoning itself is to be truly critical.

5. See Richard W. Paul, "McPeck's Mistakes," *Informal Logic* 7 (1985): 35–43, and John McPeck, "Paul's Critique of *Critical Thinking and Education*," *Informal Logic* 7 (1985): 45–54. An example of such an exchange at a conference was the panel discussion entitled "Is Critical Thinking Best Taught in a Separate Course or in the Subject Areas?" which occurred at Conference 86 on Critical Thinking, April 10–12, 1986, at Christopher Newport College. The members of the panel were Richard W. Paul, John E. McPeck, and Ralph H. Johnson.

6. See John Searle, "The Storm over the University," *The New York Review of Books* 37 (19) (December 6, 1990): 34–42, for an informative review of some recent books on education. Searle devotes a good deal of his treatment, as his title implies, to the problem of political polarization in education. To exemplify this very issue of so-called right- and left-wing political stances in regard to education, he discusses the current debate over the canon of literature. To do so, he selects "two books from the current flood, because they take such strong and opposing stands on just this issue" (p. 34). His review is particularly instructive in its neat summary of a timely issue. For a response from those he criticizes, and for Searle's rejoinder, see Gerald Graff, Barbara Herrnstein Smith, George Levine, and John Searle, " 'The Storm over the University': an Exchange," *The New York Review of Books* 38 (4) (February 14, 1991): 48–50.

Part I: THEORIES OF
          CRITICAL REASONING
          AND
          EDUCATION

**||█ The Problem of
Skills versus
Content**

1 Conflicting Views on Teaching Critical Reasoning

ROBERT H. ENNIS

Introduction

Perhaps the most controversial issue within the critical thinking movement these days is whether critical thinking should be taught separately (the general approach), be infused in instruction in existing subject-matter areas (the infusion approach), result from a student's immersion in the subject matter (the immersion approach), or—an oft-neglected possibility—be taught as a combination of the general approach with infusion or immersion (a "mixed-model" approach, to use Robert Sternberg's term[1]). I shall elaborate these approaches after sketching the general plan for this essay, the context of which is this basic issue about which approach to use. This essay will not attempt to resolve the basic issue. Rather, the goal is to make a conceptual contribution to its resolution, both paving the way for more research of the sort needed to help resolve the issue and facilitating interpretation of this research.

In addition to the practical political, economic, and administrative aspects of the basic issue, one significant unresolved theoretical aspect is whether critical thinking is subject-specific, that, is specific to subjects. Subject specificity is a confusing idea that has not received adequate attention and is my principal concern in this essay. I shall attempt to clarify this confusing notion, offer some distinctions, note some pitfalls, and suggest needed research.

There are three principal versions—empirical, epistemological, and conceptual—of the view that critical thinking is subject-specific. (Stephen Norris has introduced a distinction between the first two in his enlightening discussion of criteria for judgments about the existence of abilities—including critical thinking ability.[2]) Distinguishing and elaborating versions of subject specificity is important, because the arguments for them, and the reasonableness and implications of them, differ. To this task I shall devote most of my attention in this essay. But before directly addressing these three versions of subject specificity, I shall offer some preliminary clarification.

Critical Thinking and Thinking

I assume critical thinking to be *reasonable reflective thinking focused on deciding what to believe or do*, a concept I have elaborated elsewhere.[3] The ideas in this essay, however, apply to other concepts of critical thinking, including "the correct assessing of statements"[4] and "the propensity and skill to engage in an activity with reflective scepticism."[5] They also are adaptable to other concepts of thinking, such as higher order thinking, problem solving, and metacognition.

The General Approach

By the *general approach* I mean an approach that attempts to teach critical thinking abilities and dispositions separately from the presentation of the content of existing subject-matter offerings, with the purpose of teaching critical thinking. Examples of the general approach usually do involve content. Local or national political issues, problems in the school cafeteria, or previously learned subject matter, for example, could provide content about which the critical thinking is done, but the primary purpose is to teach students to think critically in nonschool contexts.

However, the concept of the general approach does not require that there be content. For example, logic instruction can be formulated in terms of relationships between variables. The following principle has no content in this sense: *"All As are Bs," implies that if something is not a B, then it is not an A."* Teaching it is like teaching (A × B) = (B × A) in mathematics. Under the general approach, the appropriate balance between emphasis on principles that are applied to content and emphasis on abstract principles depends at least on the nature of the content, the critical thinking dispositions and abilities being promoted, and the students. This balance must be determined empirically.

General critical thinking instruction could take place in separate courses (such as an informal logic course in college, or a critical thinking course in secondary school), in separate instructional units in the elementary school, or as a separate thread in an existing subject-matter sequence (just as writing is a thread in language arts and English). Among the ways of implementing the general approach in secondary schools, the separate critical thinking thread within an existing subject sequence is probably the most feasible politically.

Examples of the pure general approach are described in several summaries, including those of Kruse and Presseisen, Nickerson, Perkins, and Smith, Sternberg, and Sternberg and Kastoor.[6]

Infusion and Immersion

Infusion of critical thinking instruction in subject-matter instruction is deep, thoughtful, well-understood subject-matter instruction in which students are encouraged to think critically in the subject, and in which general principles of critical thinking dispositions and abilities are *made explicit.* On the other hand, *immersion* is a similar thought-provoking kind of subject-matter instruction in which students do get deeply immersed in the subject, but in which general critical thinking principles are *not made explicit.*

Proponents of the infusion approach include Glaser, Resnick, and Swartz.[7] Proponents of the immersion approach include McPeck.[8]

The Mixed Approach

The mixed approach consists of a combination of the general approach with either the infusion or immersion approaches. Under it there is a separate thread or course aimed at teaching general principles of critical thinking, but students are also involved in subject-specific critical thinking instruction. There are many possibilities for such combinations, but presumably the general thread would facilitate articulation among the various efforts and would help fill gaps left as a result of practical exigencies that develop. Proponents of the mixed approach include Ennis, Sternberg, Nickerson, and Perkins and Salomon.[9]

Table 1.1 sets forth the major characteristics of the four basic approaches to teaching critical thinking that provide the context for the subject-specificity issue. These should be viewed as idealized types. In practice, combinations and deviations are not only possible but likely.

A Danger Residing in the Ambiguity of the
Word 'Subject'

It is often noted that critical thinking is always about some subject.[10] This seems obviously true if by the word *subject* one means "topic." But one must beware of slipping back and forth between two significant uses of the word *subject* when considering the implications of the statement that critical thinking is al-

Table 1.1: The General, Mixed, Infusion, and Immersion Approaches
to Teaching Critical Thinking

	Makes general principles explicit?	Uses content?	Uses only standard subject-matter content?	Uses standard subject-matter and other content?
General				
Abstract (only)	Y	N	N	N
Concrete (also)	Y	Y	N	Perhaps both
Mixed	Y	Y	N	Y
Infusion	Y	Y	Y	N
Immersion	N	Y	Y	N

ways about some subject. Sometimes the word *subject* is used to refer to some subject taught in school. Sometimes it refers to the topic under consideration. There are, of course, many topics that are not school subjects and are not included in the study of the school subjects to which a person considering these topics is exposed. For example, the topic "stabbing," which was considered in a murder trial for which I was on the jury, was not part of any school subject that any of us had studied in school or college, yet that was a topic about which we were supposed to think critically.

It is tempting, but a mistake, to infer from the fact that critical thinking is always about some subject (that is, topic) that critical thinking teaching can take place only in school subjects.

Assuming these distinctions and definitions, I shall elaborate the three basic versions of subject specificity.

Domain Specificity: A Popular Empirical View

The use of the word *domain* instead of *subject* tends to avoid the equivocation I have just described, though it suffers from a vagueness problem that I shall discuss presently. Because the word *domain* commonly is used by cognitive scientists in discussing subject specificity, I shall use it as part of the name of an empirically based subject specificity that is characterizable by three principles:

1. *Background knowledge.* Background knowledge is essential for thinking in a given domain.
2. *Transfer.* Simple transfer of critical thinking dispositions and abilities from one domain to another domain is unlikely. However, transfer becomes likely if, but only if, there is sufficient practice in a variety of domains and there is instruction that focuses on transfer.
3. *General instruction.* It is unlikely that any general critical thinking instruction will be effective.

Most cognitive psychologists hold at least the first two principles. All three principles together constitute what I shall call "strong domain specificity," which, if true, would support the infusion-only approach to teaching critical thinking. Proponents appear to include Robert Glaser when he urged:

> abilities to think and reason will be attained when these cognitive activities are taught not as subsequent add-ons to what we have learned, but rather are explicitly developed in the process of acquiring the knowledge and skills that we consider the objectives of education and training.[11]

As I read this statement by Glaser, the general approach would be "add-ons," so he would appear to endorse the third principle.

The first two principles constitute what I shall call "moderate domain specificity." Proponents include Lauren Resnick—who appears to be agnostic about the third principle, but supports an infusion approach, because it assures that at least "something worthwhile will have been learned"[12]—and others who appear to feel that third principle is wrong, including Nickerson, who supports a mixed approach to teaching critical thinking.[13]

I shall consider the three principles of domain specificity, exhibit traps and pitfalls, and urge caution and further research.

Domain-Specificity Principle 1:
Background knowledge is essential for thinking in a given domain.

That knowledge about a topic is ordinarily a necessary condition for thinking critically in the topic seems obvious and is shown by a number of studies, including several cited by Glaser in support of his infusion-only position.[14] We must beware, however, of inferring carelessly from this necessary "conditionship" that subject-matter knowledge is a sufficient condition for good thinking. There are at least three problems with making such an inference.

1. An experienced person can become in a way so well informed about and embedded in an area that he or she stops thinking, becoming inflexible and, for example, unable to conceive of and consider alternatives.

2. Subject-matter knowledge often consists of a mass of rote-memorized subject matter that is not understood deeply enough to enable a student to think critically in the subject. Students are often taught and tested in a way that makes this a likely result. At least the first phases of E. D. Hirsch, Jr.'s cultural literacy, the ones on which he places the most emphasis, appear to be this sort of learning.[15]

3. If the domain-specificity transfer principle is correct, immersion in a subject-matter area, which, let us assume, includes ability to think in the area, probably will not lead to critical thinking in everyday life (except perhaps for gifted students), because immersion is not accompanied by explicit attention to general principles of critical thinking. I am assuming that critical thinking in everyday life is an important goal of the schools, and that explicit attention to general principles of critical thinking is the way to focus on transfer. (Focusing is required by the transfer principle.)

This is not to suggest that anyone would state explicitly that a necessary condition is thereby a sufficient condition and thus risk the difficulties I outlined. Rather, unconsciously doing so is a trap for the unwary.

Domain-Specificity Principle 2: (a) Simple transfer of critical thinking dispositions and abilities from one domain to another domain is unlikely; (b) Transfer becomes likely if, but only if, (i) there is sufficient practice in a variety of domains and (ii) there is instruction that focuses on transfer.

Vagueness of the concept "domain". The application of Parts *a* and *b-i* of the transfer principle requires us to be able to distinguish domains. Otherwise we cannot tell whether we are going from one domain to another instead of staying within the same domain, and we cannot tell whether we are working with a variety of domains or just one. But the concept, *domain*, is vague, because of the ease with which we can draw different boundaries for domains.

To see the vagueness, try to decide which of the following four topics is in the same subject-matter domain as one or more of the others: the degree to which a straight rod will bend (a standard Piagetian topic), the degree to which a spring will stretch, the impact of a sphere that rolls down a ramp, and a person's perception of the credibility of a source of information. Assume that the critical thinking ability involved is judging causal hypotheses in an experimental situation and justifying one's judgment.

All four examples conceivably could be classified under the same domain, science. But science itself is divided into many areas. The first three might come under natural science (or, progressively more narrowly, physical science, or physics, or mechanics: Which should we choose?) and the last under social science (or psychology, or social psychology, or speech communication—Which?). So are the four topics in different domains or the same domain (that is, science)? Why?

Furthermore, within mechanics, the first two might come under statics and the third under dynamics. So the first two could be in different domains from the third, but also could be in the same domain as the third: mechanics (or physics, etc.). Which is it?

Linn, Pulos, and Gans[16] found that there was a content effect for these first three topics in the area of hypothesis judging and justifying—the rods and springs topics were about as distant from each other in tested hypothesis-judging-and-justifying achievement as the springs and ramps topics were from each other. So there is some difference among these three, but whether there is a practical difference among them is not clear. As with most variables involving human beings, there appears to be a continuum.

A possible definition? The only reasonable attempted definition of *domain* by a domain specificist that I have found was offered by Susan Carey; for it she credits Dudley Shapere, a philosopher of science: "He [Shapere] characterized a domain as encompassing a certain set of real-world phenomena, a set of concepts used to represent those phenomena, and the laws and other explanatory mechanisms that constitute an understanding of the domain."[17] This broad definition, if accepted, would probably help us to apply the transfer principle in making predictions about whether learning in the last area will then be applied in the others, because the concepts, laws, and explanatory mechanisms used by scientists in studying the things that affect people's judgment about the credibility of sources are not the ones used in studying rods, springs, and inclined planes. The definition does not tell us, however, whether the first three topics are in different domains from one another. We could put them together under the domain, physics—or mechanics—by starting with a broad set of phenomena and progressing to a broad set of concepts and laws. Or we could even separate rods and springs (as suggested by the Linn et al. research[18]) by noting that the study of springs (if we try to amalgamate it with rods) invokes the concept of a spring's being a spiral rod, a concept not needed in studying rods. It depends on the set of phenomena, concepts, laws, and explanatory mechanisms we choose to associate with a given example.

Another problem with this definition is that it is not at all clear that this is the concept of domain that most cognitive psychologists employ when making statements of domain specificity. So it is not clear that the research that has been done can be applied in terms of this definition.

Research possibilities. To avoid the severe vagueness of the term *domain* in the critical thinking transfer principle, we probably need to reconceive the way the principle works. One possibility is to turn the transfer principle around by using empirically determined nontransfer as one criterion for separate domains (instead of separate domains as the independently determined criterion for nontransfer.) The resulting theory would employ the concept *domain* as a summarizing concept, rather than as an independent variable in the research.

Then we would need much detailed exploratory research (of which the Linn et al. research is a precursor) that investigates the extent to which each of many aspects of critical thinking, when taught to various kinds of students in the context of single pieces or various combinations of pieces of subject matter, is likely to be applied successfully to some other particular piece of subject matter. After a good bit of this sort of exploratory research, some theorizing might well be possible, but the resulting theories would probably be more elaborate than the simple domain-specificity transfer principle.

Until we have much more information, Parts *a* and *b-i* of the transfer principle are too sloganlike. The concept, *domain*, is too vague.

Domain-specificity principle 3: It is unlikely that any general critical thinking instruction will be effective.

For present purposes, a detailed description of the research on the effectiveness of general critical thinking instruction is unnecessary. Instead, the important thing to note about the summaries that have been done is that the results are mixed. On the basis of his review of the literature, Glaser is pessimistic about the possibilities of teaching "the abilities to think and reason . . . as subsequent add-ons to what we have learned,"[19] as are Resnick—though less so—and many others.[20] On the other hand,

Holland, Holyoak, Nisbett, and Thagard; Langley, Simon, Bradshaw, and Zytkow; Nickerson; Nickerson, Perkins, and Smith; Nisbett, Fong, Lehman, and Cheng; Perkins; Perkins and Salomon; and Sternberg and Kastoor[21] are somewhat optimistic and have concluded that some general programs are helpful.

However, most of these more optimistic reviewers express reservations about this overall conclusion because of the difficulties of evaluating the results of the programs that have been studied. Absence of information about what occurred, conflict of interest of those who did the studies, uncertain validity of evaluation devices, vagaries of experimental design, lack of objective information, and differences in conceptual systems and jargon are some of the things that they say make evaluation difficult. But still the reviewers make guarded claims that some general thinking programs (including at least some in critical thinking) were helpful.

Needed research and development. Better evaluation approaches and instruments need to be developed, because our results can be no better than our evaluation devices. Ennis, Arter and Salmon, Ennis and Norris, and Norris and Ennis have descriptions of available critical thinking tests accompanied by discussion of some problems, indicating the need for research on approaches and the development of more, better, and varied instruments.[22] Ennis, a study group chaired by Lamar Alexander, and the Review Committee of the National Academy of Education—Robert Glaser, Chairman, and Resnick have called for such development.[23] Unfortunately, the National Academy of Education review committee has also suggested that we limit our efforts to the development of tests that are specific to school subject-matter areas, a mistake if the transfer of critical thinking instruction to real life is a goal of the schools.[24] School-subject-matter specific tests presumably would not test for transfer.

Large-scale, long-term, school wide (and sometimes school system—wide) use of several variations of each of the four major approaches (general, infusion-only, immersion-only, and mixed) should be compared. Careful records should be kept of the perceived difficulties and successes and of what actually occurs in the schools. The research should be sponsored and carried out by disinterested parties able to make a long-term commitment.

After such research is done, we will have a much better idea of the effectiveness of each of the approaches, including the effectiveness of the controversial general approach, the possibilities of transfer from the infusion and immersion approaches, the advantages and disadvantages of the mixed approach, and of the practical problems involved in implementing each. It is important to know about the practical problems, because it might turn out that even though an approach like the infusion-only approach is the most effective when actually implemented, the coordination, subject-matter coverage, and articulation problems that go with it are overwhelming.

Epistemological Subject Specificity

The epistemological version of subject specificity holds that in different fields different sorts of things count as good reasons, so critical thinking varies from field to field. That only the immersion approach to critical thinking instruction would be appropriate is a conclusion drawn from epistemological subject specificity by John McPeck, who is the version's most influential proponent in education.[25] Resnick also expresses the view that "each discipline has characteristic ways of reasoning," as does Swartz.[26] But they do not draw from it the strong immersion-only conclusion that McPeck does.

Here are three principles of the epistemological subject specificity, which I have abstracted from McPeck.[27]

1. *Background knowledge.* Background knowledge is essential for critical thinking in a given field.

2. *Interfield variation.* Because in different fields different things "constitute good reasons for various beliefs," critical thinking must vary from field to field.

3. *Full understanding.* A full understanding of a field requires the ability to think critically in the field.

The Attractiveness of the Principles
of Epistemological Subject Specificity

The first principle (background knowledge) seems quite acceptable. Though based on an examination of what matters in settling field-specific issues rationally, it is like the first principle of domain specificity, which is based on observation of the difficulties experienced by ignorant people in thinking critically. Being well informed is necessary for critical thinking, no matter which way you look at it.

The following three contrasts show the plausibility of the second principle (interfield variation): (a) Mathematics has different criteria for good reasons from most other fields, because mathematics accepts only deductive proof, whereas most fields do not even seek it for the establishment of a final conclusion; (b) in the social sciences, statistical significance is an important consideration, whereas in many branches of physics it is largely ignored; (c) in the arts, some subjectivity is usually acceptable, whereas in the sciences, it is usually shunned.

The third principle (full understanding) is also acceptable if we take the words "full understanding" to mean much more than memorization of facts and principles and some ability to apply them, and to include the ability to think critically in the field. The principle then becomes true by definition, but it does express a reasonable interpretation of "full understanding" and represents much more than students usually acquire in our schools.

Problems in Using Epistemological Subject Specificity as a Ground
for the Immersion-Only Approach to Critical Thinking Instruction

If one wants to infer from these principles that the only approach to critical thinking instruction is the immersion approach, there are problems.

Vagueness of the concept "field". For one thing, the concept "field" is almost as vague as the concept "domain". For example, is the bending-rods investigation in the same field as the impact-of-the-spheres-rolling-down-the-ramp investigation? They are both in physics and in mechanics, but one is in statics and the other in dynamics. Are they in the same or different fields?

Stephen Toulmin, a philosopher who has inspired McPeck's epistemological subject specificity, has defined *field* in terms of the logical type of argument used: "Two arguments will be said to belong to the same field when the data and conclusions in each of the two arguments are, respectively, of the same logical type."[28] Although it seems clear that arguments in mathematics (which are generally deductive) are of different logical type from arguments in the social and natural sciences, where the form often seems to be best-explanation inference, the concept of logical type seems too loose for us to decide on the basis of it whether the four items considered before come under the same or different logical types. So the claim that critical thinking varies from field to field is not very discriminating.

Interfield commonalities. A second problem is that there are many interfield commonalities in critical thinking, such as agreement that conflict of interest counts against the credibility of a source and agreement on the importance of the distinction between necessary and sufficient conditions. Fields differ, but, as Govier, Resnick, and Weddle[29] have noted, there is also a common core of basic principles that apply in most fields (though not every principle applies in every field). Even Toulmin's book on logic devotes about half its space to general, interfield principles.[30] The three epistemological principles do not exclude such interfield commonalities. Thus the limitation to the immersion approach (or even to the infusion approach) does not follow from the given principles of epistemological subject specificity, which neither imply nor state that there are no general overarching principles that bridge fields.

This is not to say that there is complete agreement about and clarity of these general overarching principles. There are discrepancies in vocabulary (including different meanings for such words as *connotation, theory,* and *assumption*) that cause coordination problems. More seriously, there are some disagreements about the principles themselves, such as the role of the distinction between induction and deduction in argument reconstruction, the fact-opinion distinction, and the meaning of *if.* Weddle, who has provided a helpful untangling of the fact-opinion distinction, exemplifies the sort of work that needs to be done in this area.[31]

Transfer. A third problem is that of transfer. Will the learning in the individual fields transfer to daily life? If the transfer principle of domain specificity is correct, then immersion will not result in transfer to daily life (much of the content of which is not taught in school subjects), because teaching for transfer does not occur in the immersion approach.

Thus the insights of the epistemological view do not imply that we should limit ourselves to the immersion approach. These insights incorporate the vagueness problem of domain specificity and do not rule out interfield commonalities. Furthermore, the transfer principle of domain specificity is inconsistent with the immersion approach, a reason to be leery of the immersion approach.

Research. The extent of interfield commonalities is a topic requiring extensive research. Arguments offered by specialists in a number of different disciplines need to be examined and compared to see how much they have in common. This has never been done thoroughly, so far as I know. In an informal interview study of fellows at the Center for Advanced Study in the Behavioral Sciences in 1984, I found that the behavioral and other social scientists interviewed expressed the view that there are more differences in logical type of data, arguments, and conclusions within individual social science disciplines than between them. But this study dealt only with the social sciences (including history) and was impressionistic. Careful comparative analysis of articles and arguments in these and many other disciplines is needed.

Conceptual Subject Specificity

According to a third version of subject specificity, conceptual subject specificity, it does not even make sense to speak of critical thinking or critical thinking instruction outside of a subject-matter area, and the idea *general critical thinking ability* is meaningless. Hence, general instruction in critical thinking is inconceivable.

As offered by the view's most influential proponent, John McPeck, the argument for the conceptual view starts with the true premise, "Thinking is always thinking *about* something."[32] Mortimer Adler has made a similar statement, though it is not clear that he would take the argument as far as McPeck. McPeck then draws the conclusion that there is nothing general to teach, and so we cannot teach thinking in general. He puts the argument as follows:

> It is a matter of conceptual truth that thinking is always *thinking about X*, and that X can never be "everything in general" but must always be something in particular. Thus the claim "I teach students to think" is at worst false and at best misleading . . . . In isolation from a particular subject, the phrase "critical thinking" neither refers to nor denotes any particular skill. It follows from this that it makes no sense to talk about critical thinking as a distinct subject and that it therefore cannot profitably be taught as such. To the extent that critical thinking is not about a specific subject, X, it is both conceptually and practically empty. The statement "I teach critical thinking," *simpliciter,* is vacuous because there is no generalized skill properly called critical thinking.[33]

This argument assumes that the fact that there can be no examples of critical thinking about nothing (or about everything in general) implies that there can be no general critical thinking skills. But nowhere is this assumption defended. As Richard Paul has suggested, this is like assuming that because, when we write or speak, we are writing or speaking about something, there can be no teaching of general writing or speaking skills.[34] Harvey Seigel and Groarke and Tindale have made a similar point[35].

McPeck replied that writing and speaking are different from critical thinking.[36] So Paul, he urges, has not shown that what holds for writing and speaking also holds for critical thinking.

But McPeck's argument needs more than this. Because it makes the inference—from the proposition that critical thinking is about something—to the conclusion that general critical thinking instruction is impossible, it needs to make explicit and defend the connection between the two propositions. Why should the fact that critical thinking is always about something imply that we cannot have general critical thinking dispositions and abilities (and instruction of them) that can be applied to particular cases?

In his writing, McPeck provides us with an example of what he says is inconceivable. In his treatment of the work of Edward de Bono, McPeck explicitly employs the general principle taught in logic courses that affirming the consequent is a fallacy. He uses the phrase "affirming the consequent" and employs the standard general symbols for explaining the meaning of that phrase "$P \supset Q, Q \therefore P$."[37] To the extent that he learned the principle well and is able to apply it in a number of circumstances, McPeck has acquired a general critical thinking ability, the ability to identify the fallacy of affirming the consequent. Not only is someone's having the ability not inconceivable, but we have evidence that someone has acquired this general ability. We could not have such evidence if it were inconceivable that he could have the ability.

Finally, the conceptual subject-specificity concept, subject, like the concepts domain and field, is too vague. Suppose that within a physics course students study about bending rods, stretching springs, and spheres rolling down inclined planes. Are these in different subjects or the same subject? If they are in different subjects, then no critical thinking ability that can be developed in one of these subjects can conceivably be applied in the other (because that would imply the existence of a general critical thinking ability). If they are in the same subject, then critical thinking instruction in one of these contexts would presumably help in the other. Which is it? Conceptual subject specificity needs a definition of *subject*, but does not provide one.

In summary, conceptual subject specificity appears to have no basis for its basic assumption, is in conflict with the facts, and is too vague.

Summary and Comment

The purposes of this essay are to clarify the confusing topic of subject specificity and to sketch out some needed research. Crucial distinctions include those among the general, infusion, immersion, and mixed approaches to teaching critical thinking; among the empirical, epistemological, and conceptual versions of subject specificity; between the topic and school-subject senses of "subject"; between content as a necessary condition and as a sufficient condition for critical thinking; between deep and shallow knowledge of a subject; between fields having no critical thinking principles in common and having some principles in common; between thinking about a particular subject and having a general ability to do that sort of thing in several subjects; between thinking critically without content (not possible) and teaching content-free principles of critical thinking (possible); and between limiting teaching of critical thinking to subject-matter areas (as is recommended by the infusion and immersion approaches) and limiting testing to subject-specific critical thinking tests (a mistake if we want to test for transfer to daily life). These distinctions, though conceptually clear, often reduce to continuums and have borderline cases in practice.

The three versions of subject specificity differ in their strengths and weaknesses. Conceptual subject specificity has no basis and is too vague, but the other two versions incorporate valuable insights: They share an emphasis on the importance of background knowledge. Epistemological subject specificity notes that there are significant interfield differences in what constitutes a good reason (though its concept, field, is vague). Domain specificity sees the importance of deliberate teaching for transfer combined with frequent application of principles in many different areas, and warns us that a critical thinking aspect demonstrated in one situation will not necessarily be applied in another. But its concept, domain, like its sister concepts, subject and field, is vague.

Needed research includes the following:

- extensive specific studies of the degree of successful application to a topic of a critical-thinking aspect developed in one or more topics, with attention to the variables that affect this degree of success (one result will be giving meaning to the concept domain as used in the transfer principle);

- the study and development of new approaches and instruments for evaluating critical thinking;

- the broad, long-term study in realistic situations of the effectiveness of the four approaches to critical thinking instruction—with attention to the economic, political, and practical articulation problems impinging on their use; and

- the examination of the degree of commonality of the critical thinking aspects found in the different standard existing disciplines and school subjects.

To focus on concepts and interpretations, this discussion of subject specificity leaned on thoughtful research reviews done by others. It assumed a broad conception of critical thinking, but it applies to more restricted conceptions and is adaptable to broader conceptions of thinking, like higher order thinking, problem solving, and metacognition.

Subject specificity is a crucial, frequently confusing aspect of attempts to improve critical thinking and other thinking instruction and assessment. Let us hope that the distinctions and clarification presented in this essay will better enable us to proceed with the needed research and dissemination.[38]

Notes

1. Robert J. Sternberg, "Questions and Answers about the Nature and Teaching of Thinking Skills," in *Teaching Thinking Skills, Theory and Practice*, eds., Joan Boykoff Baron and Robert J. Sternberg (New York: Freeman, 1987), p. 255.

2. Stephen P. Norris, "The Choice of Standard Conditions in Defining Critical Thinking Competence," *Educational Theory* 35 (1)(1985):97–107.

3. Robert H. Ennis, "Critical Thinking and the Curriculum," *National Forum* 65(1)(1985):28–31; Robert H. Ennis, "A Taxonomy of Critical Thinking Dispositions and Abilities," in *Teaching for Thinking*, eds., Joan Boykoff Baron and Robert J. Sternberg (New York: Freeman, 1987), pp. 9–26.

4. Robert H. Ennis, "A Concept of Critical Thinking," *Harvard Educational Review* 32(1962):82.

5. John McPeck, *Critical Thinking and Education* (New York: St. Martin's, 1981), p. 152.

6. Janice Kruse and Barbara Z. Presseisen, *A Catalog of Programs for Teaching Thinking* (Philadelphia: Research for Better Schools, 1987); Raymond S. Nickerson, David N. Perkins, and Edward Smith, *The Teaching of Thinking* (Hillsdale, N.J.: Erlbaum, 1985); Robert J. Sternberg, "How Can We Teach Intelligence?" *Educational Leadership* 42(1)(1984):38–48; Sternberg, "Critical Thinking: Its Nature, Measurement, and Improvement," in *Essays on the Intellect*, ed., F. R. Link (Alexandria, Va.: Association for Supervision and Curriculum Development, 1985), pp. 45–65; Robert J. Sternberg and Kastoor Bhana, "Synthesis of Research on the Effectiveness of Intellectual Skills Pro-

grams: Snake Oil Remedies or Miracle Cures?" *Educational Leadership* 44(2)(1986):60–67.

7. Robert Glaser, "Education and Thinking: the Role of Knowledge," *American Psychologist* 39(1984):93–104; Glaser, "Learning and Instruction: A Letter for a Time Capsule," in *Thinking and Learning Skills*, ed., Susan F. Chipman, Judith W. Segal, and Robert Glaser (Hillsdale, N.J.: Erlbaum, 1985); Lauren B. Resnick, *Education and Learning to Think* (Washington, DC: National Academy Press, 1987); Robert J. Swartz, "Critical Thinking, the Curriculum, and the Problem of Transfer," in *Thinking: Progress in Research and Teaching*, ed., David N. Perkins, Jr. et al. (Hillsdale, N.J.: Erlbaum, 1984), pp. 261–84; Swartz, "Teaching for Thinking: A Developmental Model for the Infusion of Thinking Skills into Mainstream Instruction," in *Teaching Thinking Skills: Theory and Practice*, eds., Joan Boykoff Baron and Robert J. Sternberg (New York: Freeman, 1987), pp. 106–26.

8. McPeck, *Critical Thinking and Education*.

9. Ennis, "Critical Thinking and the Curriculum"; Sternberg, "Questions and Answers"; Raymond S. Nickerson, "On Improving Thinking through Instruction," in *Review of Research in Education*, ed., Ernest Z. Rothkopf (Washington, DC: American Educational Research Association, 1988); David N. Perkins and Gabriel Salomon, "Are Cognitive Skills Context Bound?" *Educational Researcher* 18(1)(1989):16–25.

10. Mortimer Adler, "Why Critical Thinking Programs Won't Work," *Education Week* 6(2)(1986):28; McPeck, *Critical Thinking and Education*.

11. Glaser, "Education and Thinking," p. 93.

12. Resnick, *Education and Learning*, p. 36.

13. Nickerson, "On Improving Thinking."

14. Glaser, "Education and Thinking."

15. E. D. Hirsch, Jr., *Cultural Literacy: What Every American Needs to Know* (Boston: Houghton-Mifflin, 1987).

16. Marcia C. Linn, Steven Pulos, and Adrienne Gans, "Correlates of Formal Reasoning: Content and Problem Effects," *Journal of Research in Science Teaching* 18(5)(1981):443.

17. Susan Carey, "Are Children Fundamentally Different Kinds of Thinkers and Learners Than Adults?" in Chipman et al., *Thinking and Learning Skills*, p. 487.

18. Linn et al., "Correlates of Formal Reasoning," pp. 435–47.

19. Glaser, "Learning and Instruction," p. 93.

20. For Resnick's position, see *Education and Learning.*

21. John Holland et al., *Induction: Processes of Inference, Learning, and Discovery* (Cambridge, Mass.: MIT Press, 1986); Pat Langley et al., *Scientific Discovery: Computational Explorations of the Creative Process* (Cambridge, Mass.: MIT Press, 1987); Raymond S. Nickerson, "Kinds of Thinking Taught in Current Programs," *Educational Leadership* 42(1)(1984); Nickerson, "On Improving Thinking"; Nickerson, et al., *The Teaching of Thinking*; Richard E. Nisbett et al., "Teaching Reasoning," *Science* 238(1987):625–31; David N. Perkins, Jr., "General Cognitive Skills: Why Not?" in Chipman et al., *Thinking and Learning Skills*; Perkins and Salomon, "Cognitive Skills"; Sternberg and Kastoor, "Synthesis of Research."

22. Robert H. Ennis, "Problems in Testing Informal Logic, Critical Thinking, Reasoning Ability," *Informal Logic* 6(1)(1984):3–9; Judith A. Arter and Jennifer R. Salmon, *Assessing Higher Order Thinking Skills, Issues and Practices* (Portland, Oreg.: Northwest Regional Laboratory, 1987); Robert H. Ennis and Stephen P. Norris, "Critical Thinking Testing and Other Critical Thinking Evaluation: Status, Issues, Needs," in *Cognitive Assessment of Language and Math Outcomes*, ed., James Algina and Sue Legg (Norwood, N.J.: Ablex, 1990); Stephen P. Norris and Robert H. Ennis, *Evaluating Critical Thinking* (Pacific Grove, Cal.: Midwest, 1989).

23. Ennis, "Critical Thinking and the Curriculum"; Study Group, Lamar Alexander, chair, in *The Nation's Report Card: Improving the Assessment of Student Achievement*, by P. A. Graham, coordinator (Washington, DC: National Academy of Education, 1987), pp. 3–41; Review Committee of the National Academy of Education, Robert Glaser, chair, "Commentary by the National Academy of Education," in *The Nation's Report Card*; Resnick, *Education and Learning.*

24. Review Committee, p. 54.

25. McPeck, *Critical Thinking and Education.*

26. Resnick, *Education and Learning*, p. 36; Swartz, "Critical Thinking."

27. McPeck, *Critical Thinking and Education*, pp. 22–38.

28. Stephen E. Toulmin, *The Uses of Argument* (Cambridge: Cambridge University Press, 1964), p. 14.

29. Trudy Govier, "Review of *Critical Thinking and Education*," *Dialogue* 22(1983):172; Resnick, *Education and Learning*, p. 45; Perry Weddle, "*Critical Thinking and Education* by John McPeck," *Informal Logic* 6(2)(1984):24.

30. Stephen E. Toulmin, Richard Reike, and Allan Janik, *An Introduction to Reasoning* (New York: Macmillan, 1979).

31. Perry Weddle, "Fact from Opinion," *Informal Logic* 7(1)(1985):19–26.

32. McPeck, *Critical Thinking and Education*, p. 3.

33. Ibid., pp. 4–5.

34. Richard W. Paul, "McPeck's Mistakes," *Informal Logic* 2(1)(1985):36.

35. Harvey Siegel, "Educating Reason: Critical Thinking, Informal Logic, and the Philosophy of Education," *American Philosophical Association Newsletter on Teaching Philosophy* (Spring-Summer 1985):11; Leo Groarke and Christopher Tindale, "Critical Thinking: How to Teach Good Reasoning," *Teaching Philosophy* 9(1986):301–18.

36. John McPeck, "Paul's Critique of *Critical Thinking and Education*," *Informal Logic* 7(1)(1985):49.

37. McPeck, *Critical Thinking and Education*, p. 101.

38. I deeply appreciate the suggestions and encouragement of Sean Ennis, whose frequent careful reading and insights have been especially helpful, Nicholas Burbules, Michelle Commeyras, Delores Gallo, Jana Holt, Robert McKim, Stephen Norris, Edys Quellmalz, William J. Russell, Robert Swartz, Marc Weinstein, Mary Anne Wolff, and the anonymous reviewers of *Educational Researcher;* and the support of the Spencer Foundation, the Center for Advanced Study in the Behavioral Sciences, and the Critical and Creative Thinking Program of the University of Massachusetts in Boston.

Theories That Emphasize Content

2 Teaching Critical Reasoning through the Disciplines: Content versus Process

JOHN E. MCPECK

As my title suggests, I intend to defend the view that the standard (or familiar) disciplines are the most direct route, if not the *only* efficacious route, to teaching critical thinking. A consequence of this view is that most of the so-called thinking skills programs, which are so pervasive today, are importantly misguided. My express purpose here, however, is *not* to criticize thinking skills programs but rather to constructively show the ways in which disciplinary knowledge already contains the major portion of what most people understand by *critical thinking*. In short, I argue that if the disciplines are properly taught, we will get the kind of intelligent thought from students that we normally associate with the phrase *critical thinking*. Thus training and drills in the so-called thinking skills are effectively redundant. I argue that reasoning skill is not something *different from*, or *over and above*, disciplinary thinking (as is implied by the thinking skills movement) but is in fact part and parcel of disciplinary thinking.

Thus, I too call for *reform*, or improvement, in education. We can indeed do much better than at present. But I do not support the revolution that is implicit in the recent thinking skills movement because to construe the problem of critical thinking as a

31

matter of improved "skills and drills" is to misunderstand what is involved in rational thinking in general, and critical thinking in particular.

Although I will not discuss the details of any particular thinking skills program, I will make reference to what I have generally referred to as the thinking skills movement. I mean by this label such programs as Feurstein's *Instructional Enrichment Program*, De Bono's *Cort Thinking Lessons*, the *Productive Thinking Program*, *Odyssey*, typical informal logic courses, and most of the thinking skills programs surveyed in the large two-volume study conducted for the National Institute of Education, edited by Jupoth Segal, Susan Chipman, and Robert Glaser, entitled *Thinking and Learning Skills.*[1] What all of these programs and approaches have in common is a commitment to the view that the *process* of reasoning should take precedence over the *content* of what is being reasoned about. It is not that specific content is irrelevant in the thinking skills view, but rather that teachers should concentrate their attention on the teaching of the reasoning *process*, as such. These programs are thus "how to do it" approaches, and this orientation helps to explain their emphasis on skills and drills of one kind or another.

Before I discuss an alternative *disciplines* approach to all of this, it may be useful to keep in mind several points of agreement between my view and the "thinking skills" approach. To begin with, we agree on ultimate goals and purposes. We all want to produce autonomous thinkers who are not taken in by faulty argument, weak evidence, or trendy opinions, and can face life's problems as people capable of making their own rational decisions about whatever should confront them. These problems and decisions include personal and societal problems, as well as those we might normally think of as academic or cognitive problems. In short, we all want to enable students to become the maximally rational human beings that they are capable of being. Moreover, we agree that this capability can and should be taught to students (whenever possible) since they are not born with the requisite knowledge and skill for attaining this goal. Also, on a more practical instructional level, we agree that the attitude of the teacher, and the learning atmosphere in the class, is likely to have real and important effects on the success of nurturing such autonomous thinking. And, finally, we agree that ignorance, indoctrination, and unreflective conformity are the enemy.

This much agreement is all to the good, and should not be minimized: we agree on our destination, but disagree on the best route for getting there. Similarly, however, we should not minimize the serious consequences of choosing an alternative route, because it might not lead to our destination, despite the best intentions.

The alternative route to our destination begins early on. I wish to redirect attention away from generic *processes of reasoning*, be these logical skills or general strategies, and to have you consider the proposition that the *content* of various subjects and/ or problems determines (i.e., creates) the appropriate *process* of reasoning, and not vice versa. Thus, I would have teachers and researchers consider early on how various kinds of knowledge and understanding of things appropriately shape the way people properly think about those things, rather than have them look for generic "skills" which are alleged to be subject-neutral.

The theoretical underpinning for looking at reasoning from this perspective is to be found in Wittgenstein's insight about the very intimate connection between *thought* and *language*. For Wittgenstein, anything which you or I would recognize as significant thought is fundamentally linguistic in character. (Or more precisely, if the thought is not in words, as such, it will be in some kind of public symbol system—which is most often language.) Thus, to improve people's capacity for thought, you must improve their capacity to use language. The capacity for sophisticated, complex, or subtle thought proportionately requires the sophisticated, complex, or subtle use of a symbol system—which is usually language. And since language can be used for many and diverse purposes, there are many and diverse rules of predication (or "language games") which govern what can and cannot be coherently thought or said. It is not enough, from this point of view, to know that different objects can take different predicates—this is trivially true. We must come to understand what kinds of things in the world can take what kinds of predicates, and what kinds of combinations (or attributions) are and are not coherent ideas. Just as there are different kinds of language games, which stem from what Wittgenstein called different "forms of life" (e.g., mathematics, morality, religion, art, etc.), so there are different rules of predication, or "reasoning," if you will, which govern the different kinds of thought.

To put this very, very crudely, different subjects employ different language games, and different language games have their own peculiar (or unique) rules of predication. How sentences can and cannot be put together constitutes the first level logic of that particular language game. A bit more formally, the actual rules for what is a "well-formed formula" (i.e., an intelligible statement) is determined at the *semantic* level of discourse. Thus, there are almost as many distinguishable logics, or kinds of reasoning, as there are distinguishable kinds of subjects. And there is no way to learn these different logics apart from learning the language (or meanings) of those subjects. This is why I argue that real, honest-to-goodness, everyday reasoning is intimately and permanently connected to the different subjects—more specifically to the language of those subjects. Neil Postman also expresses this view when he points out that:

> As one learns the language of a subject, one is also learning what that subject is. It cannot be said often enough that what we call a subject consists mostly, if not entirely, of its language. If you eliminate all the words of a subject, you have eliminated the subject. Biology is not plants and animals. It is language about plants and animals. History is not events. It is language describing and interpreting events. Astronomy is not planets and stars. It is a way of talking about planets and stars.

He continues:

> If one learns how to speak history or mathematics or literary criticism, one becomes, by definition, a different person. The

point to be stressed is that a subject is a situation in which and through which people conduct themselves, largely in language. You cannot learn a new form of conduct without changing yourself.[2]

I am arguing that this change which comes about is that a person begins to learn how to think and to reason through language. And this becomes progressively more sophisticated, or complex, as one learns more about a subject. In principle, at least, this is what the disciplines attempt to do, or are capable of doing. This is, in effect, an argument for liberal education through the disciplines: it *liberates* one by teaching him or her how to think.

Perhaps I should add here two qualifications, or cautionary notes, about this Wittgensteinian view about the connection between thought and language. First, what Wittgenstein refers to as a "language game," and the rules governing these games, function for thought very similarly to Kant's "categories of the understanding." However, unlike Kant's categories, language games are not fixed and immutable. Rather, Wittgenstein's categories are themselves determined by language and are continually evolving to accommodate new demands brought on by changes in the different "forms of life." Thus categories of understanding are not static (for Wittgenstein); but so long as they are in place at any given time, they are constitutive of coherent thought.

The second feature to be noted about this view of language and thought is that while different language games have their own peculiar rules of predication which are not determined by classical logic, these rules will, by and large, obey classical logic. That is, classical logic can be viewed as a system of metastatements which can be asserted of language games, but language games are not themselves made up of these metastatements. There is, as it were, a primary level of thinking which is governed by the semantic rules of language games. This comprises the bulk of normal thinking behavior. And then there is also classical logic which is *about* that thinking. From the point of view of actual use, however, classical logic, and skill at employing its rules, cannot yield the flesh and blood of everyday rational thought. It cannot do so for the same reasons that the *syntax* of a system cannot yield semantic *meaning*.

Now it might seem that we have moved some distance from our initial discussion about the thinking skills movement versus the disciplinary approach. But really we have not. The distinction between language games and the rules of classical logic is simply a more abstract way of describing the parallel differences between, a content, or disciplinary, approach to thinking and the numerous thinking skills programs. I am arguing that just as different "rules of predication" constitute different language games, so different modes of reasoning constitute what we call "subject areas." Each is a different "category of understanding" (in a Wittgensteinian sense), and each has its own "rules," as it were, of reasoning. This is what renders a general thinking skills approach *implausible* from a theoretical point of view, and *ineffective* from a practical point of view—at least I so submit.

Before I develop the disciplinary (or language-game) approach a bit further, it is helpful to think about some of the factors which may have contributed to the popularity of the thinking skills movement, and some of the things which make it seem plausible to many. You will, of course, have to allow room for what I think is reasonable speculation here, because I cannot know precisely what factors have appealed to whom. But one very clear advantage that the thinking skills movement would appear to offer is relief from the very scary prospect of having to teach every fact about every plausible subject which might confront a student. *That* endeavor would indeed be impossible. Thus, if there *were* a set of general, teachable skills, which could apply across the board, then we could simply arm students with these skills and turn them loose to face the complicated world. And this, indeed, is what the thinking skills movement promises.

However, there seems to be more wish fulfillment at work here than is justifiable. It reminds me in several ways of former President Reagan's fascination with his "Star Wars" scheme: it seemed like a nice technological solution to what is in fact a very thorny political problem. Moreover, it seems to satisfy two quint-essential American traits: (1) the love affair with technology (or gadgets), and (2) the belief that every problem, no matter how complex, is imminently fixable. This "can do" spirit often prompts the familiar saw "If we can land a man on the moon, we can lick the drug problem," or ". . . lick the crime problem," etc. In fact, however, it is not clear that all problems do have accept-able solutions, let alone technological ones. For example, if you believe that reason can construct a technological defense system, then you must have similar faith that reason is capable of crack-ing it—what's good for the goose is good for the gander. What is so powerful about reason is that it can very often tell you what *won't* work, even if it doesn't show you what will.

An additional explanation for the current enthusiasm for thinking skills programs derives from the widely held belief that *reasoning* is a learnable skill in the same way as, say, reading and writing. Indeed, there are numerous articles, and much talk, which explicitly refer to reasoning as the "fourth R," along with "reading, 'riting and 'rithmetic." All are perceived as general, teachable skills—even though reasoning may be acknowledged to be slightly more complex than the other three R's. I think, how-ever, that this widely held belief is as wrong about reading and writing as it is about reasoning. The general mistake stems from a seductive linguistic confusion, namely: that because we have a single word like *reading*, or *writing*, and this word points out, or refers to, a single common property which is common to all cases of reading, or writing, the inference is made that this common property describes a single generic skill. However, all cases of "mending" have a common property also, namely the fixing of whatever needs fixing, but mending a fence requires skills very different from those required to fix an auto engine or a sock. Not all generic skill words denote singular skills, and it is simply a mistake to think that they do.

Prompted by concern about declining reading scores, many researchers have been pointing out that even reading and writing are not general, transferable skills because they are crucially dependent on background knowledge—which varies from task to task. For example, E. D. Hirsch, the distinguished literary critic at the University of Virginia, recently described some of his own empirical studies with college students. He concluded:

> What these experiments demonstrate is that the idea that reading is a general, transferrable skill unrelated to subject matter is essentially wrong, containing only the following grain of truth. Reading is a general skill only with regard to its rather elementary aspects, those involving phonics, parsing strategies, guessing strategies, eye habits, and so on. While these elementary skills are important, normally endowed students, once they acquire the rudiments, need not be continually drilled in them. Such skills are always being used, and every reading task will automatically exercise, improve, and automate them. With that single elementary exception, then, the usual picture of reading as a general skill is wrong. Reading skill varies from task to task, because reading skill depends on specific background knowledge.[3]

This same conclusion about reading was reached by Neil Postman in *Teaching as a Conserving Activity:*

> To put it simply, the question, "how well does one read?" is a bad question, because it is essentially unanswerable. A more proper question is "How well does one read poetry, or history, or religion?" No one I have ever known is so brilliant as to have learned the languages of all fields of knowledge equally well. Most of us do not learn some of them at all. No one is a "good reader," period. There are those, for example, who read the physical sciences well, but not poetry. Each discipline requires of the reader a particular set of abilities, store of knowledge, and frame of mind, so that there must always be great variability in our capacities to read, write, or speak in different subjects.[4]

All of this suggests that there is serious reason to question the extent to which even reading and writing are general skills, let alone reasoning. What phonics, eye habits, and parsing strategies are to *reading,* classical logic is to *reasoning;* both are, indeed, general, but they won't get you through the practical task at hand.

From a more mundane point of view, there has been a tendency to think of reading, writing, and reasoning skills to be like typing, where you do, in fact, have a skill which can be ubiquitously used upon *any* subject matter. Once you can type, then you can type anything and everything. But the crucial difference between typing and the "4 R's" is that in typing you do not have to *understand* what is being typed. Once specific background knowledge is required as part of a skill, however, the *generality* of that skill is seriously restricted.

But let me return to my thesis that the disciplines embody the most efficacious route to critical thinking. Thus far, all I have done is to sketch the ways in which thought or thinking and meaning are connected to *language*. And I have suggested that language development is tantamount to the development of *thought*. Now, I argue that the net effect of *disciplinary knowledge* is to increase a student's capacity to think and to talk in the language of those disciplines. In effect, the disciplines enable one to think and to engage in intelligent conversation, about problems which might fall under disciplinary domains. If we further conceive of the disciplines as more or less structured embodiments of the simple "forms of life" which give rise to them (*à la* Wittgenstein), one will see that much of what we regard as "common knowledge" and "everyday problems" are included within the disciplines. This is not to say that the disciplines have resolved, or provided answers to, the common or everyday problems; but it is to say that this is what they have been *about*, this was their origin, and this is what they have attempted to provide progressively more sophisticated insight into. It is not the case that we have academic or disciplinary knowledge on the one side, and *real* or everyday problems on the other. This is a false dichotomy. It is best to view common or everyday problems as the seeds which have spawned the disciplines. In a very real sense the perennial problems which we now regard as common or everyday problems continue to be embodied within the disciplines. School knowledge is, after all, about the real world.

Again, this is not to suggest that disciplinary knowledge can solve all problems requiring thought. To a large extent, problems and questions that we have will remain problems and questions, despite disciplinary knowledge. But I do want to make two important claims on behalf of the disciplines (and it is not at all clear that the thinking skills approach could make similar claims). First, the disciplines have, over the millennia, provided many answers to important problems which used to perplex mankind. Indeed, many of these are now what constitute our cultural heritage; and this is, by and large, what the schools have been trying to pass on to students. Without this kind of education, each generation would be forced to reinvent the wheel—a highly dubious project. And the great bulk of this education comes via what we now think of as straightforward *content*. Secondly, through the use of their general concepts, and rich language, the disciplines provide a very powerful set of analytic lenses through which students can come to understand problems and to grapple with them in rational ways. Indeed, what it *means* to be rational is to make decisions on the basis of the available evidence. And since people are not born with the knowledge of what might be relevant evidence for a given problem, they must be taught this. This is precisely what the disciplines are about, and what they attempt to do. In short, when the disciplines are effectively taught, they provide the most fundamental (and inescapable) cognitive requirements for being rational.

In recent years, educators have become enamored with the notion of "critical thinking," and all that it might imply. In fact, the critical thinking movement can be seen as the progenitor of the recent thinking skills movement. However, I think that if teachers and administrators would think carefully about what they may wish to achieve, they would see that *normal* rational thinking is more than adequate to meet their needs. Potentially, at least, the disciplines are already suited for the required job.

There is no inherent reason for having to change their original strategy. Why then, we might ask, did the schools feel the need to change their tack and begin introducing these new skills programs? I will answer this question momentarily, but my answer will be better understood in the light of a basic distinction between what I will call "normal correct thinking" (or standard *disciplinary* thinking), and "critical thinking" as such.

Many cognitive tasks, both in life and in school, have well-trodden paths to, or procedures for, their solutions. For example, you might look at a bus schedule, and learn to work your way through its columns of times and numbers—a relatively straightforward procedure. Or if you have a mathematical problem with three unknowns, you might be able to solve it by setting up three equations and then substituting values, one for another. In short, for very many problems which we confront, there often exist rational procedures for their resolution. Some of these problems, of course, are more complex than others, and some require considerable background knowledge even to know how to begin addressing them. Our culture, or more specifically the *disciplines*, have developed entire networks of concepts, methods, and procedures for dealing with an enormous spectrum of life's familiar (and unfamiliar) problems. They have developed tools, as it were, or kinds of tools, for dealing with many different kinds of problems. And even though these procedures may not ultimately be up to the task of solving any given problem, they still constitute the most rational procedure for trying, as a first approximation, to solve a problem. In effect, you should try all the tools in your kit before designing a new one for the particular job at hand. Traditionally, the public schools have been engaged in the business of trying to provide students with the knowledge and understanding contained in these disciplinary networks, concepts, and procedures. And I believe this to be a sensible goal, even if a student's level of understanding may not reach much beyond a beginner's level. At least students are beginners at the most worthwhile tools known to us as a culture. However, all of this knowledge is what I am here calling "normal" thinking or "correct" thinking or "familiar" thinking insofar as its patterns and procedures are more or less well entrenched in the culture. Mind you, to teach these things successfully is no mean achievement! Indeed, this educational outcome is what is normally meant by "rational thinking" *simpliciter.* This fact has let some commentators, specifically Sophie Haroutunian, to argue that this kind of thinking is really the kind of thinking that most educators are probably concerned about; and that the distinction between *this* kind of thinking and critical thinking is therefore a red herring—a difference not worth worrying about.[5] Let me say that I am sympathetic to this view. If the schools could succeed in developing rational thinking, or normal disciplinary thinking, there would be far less talk and worry about critical thinking per se. Rational thinking would give us almost all of what we normally expect from our schools.

But for all this, critical thinking is not an empty concept. It does seem to refer to something which we also regard as worthwhile in people, and our language properly marks this out. I think that this phrase, *critical thinking,* refers to a certain *combination* of what we might think of as a willingness, or disposition (call it an "attitude," if you like), *together with* the appropriate knowledge and skills, to engage in an activity or problem with *reflective skepticism.* Critical thinking consists of the kind of healthy skepticism that we might normally associate with the discipline of philosophy. It is not pernicious skepticism, but rather the kind that we engage in when we have reason to suspect that the normal procedures, or beliefs, leave something to be desired. There might, indeed, be something in the normal procedures or beliefs which is *creating* the problem, rather than helping us solve it. Thus, critical thinking does not come into play on every occasion where rational thought is required, but only on those comparatively rare occasions where we suspect something is amiss. On such occasions it is right and proper to start questioning some of our fundamental assumptions, or beliefs, and to try alternatives: it is this kind of thinking which is properly described as critical thinking—and this is valuable indeed. But there are two characteristics of this kind of thinking which must be borne in mind: (1) it is the exception rather than the rule—normal rational procedures are often adequate for the task; and (2) it presupposes considerable knowledge of the subject area in question.

Thus, the distinction between normal rational thinking, and critical thinking prompts the question of whether or not there has been undue worry about critical thinking as such. Perhaps Sophie Haroutunian is right. But even if one clings to the idea that critical thinking should somehow be woven into the fabric of our school system, because there is, after all, *something* to be said for the idea, there remain two important questions that do not have obvious answers. *When* should it be introduced, and *how*?

These two questions are closely connected, because if you conceive of critical thinking (as I do) as subject-specific, then *when* you introduce such a program is determined in large measure by *what* you are introducing. Since critical thinking is, in my view, parasitic upon the disciplines, it follows that you should not introduce it until students know something about the disciplines. Anything worthy of the name "critical thinking" cannot exist in a subject-matter vacuum. There must first be some substantive content for students to be critical about. Even if we could, in some sense, have young children produce behavior which resembles critical thinking, surely there must be more pressing problems on our educational agendas at this early stage of their education. As the presidential report *A Nation at Risk* dramatically points out, the most fundamental deficiencies in American education are adequate *literacy* on the one hand, and basic information about what makes this culture on the other.[6] Neither my view nor the president's report is a call to stifle independent and creative thought. Far from it. But it is a call to get straight about what needs to be done first. You cannot have creative thought until there is some understanding of what one is being creative about. (You might get *original* thoughts, but that is not sufficient to make them *creative.*) It is simply bad pedagogy to teach exceptions before one understands the rule. Thus, it is unnecessary, and educationally premature, to teach critical thinking to young children. You don't race a pony until its legs are strong enough to take it. I would not, in fact, teach critical thinking before grade ten, or until such time as the disciplines have taken on noticeable shape in the student's mind. *Then* students have something worth sinking their teeth into, and in a way which would have meaningful point. Prior to that, love's labor is largely wasted, if not lost.

There is a commonly heard objection to this view about waiting until high school, which runs something like the following: Once children find out that school is a place where you simply absorb what the teacher says, they become more or less passive receptors of information who are *unable* to think critically because they have never been taught to do so. Thus, when you try to switch gears in high school, students will not be up to the task because they have had no practice, and will be adrift in this new mode of education. In other words, to wait until later, the argument runs, is *too* late.

This argument, plausible as it might appear to some, contains, however, several unsubstantiated assumptions. The first is that most adults, including the authors of various thinking skills programs, have not, in fact, been permanently harmed by their early receptive learning. We made the shift in due course, and are none the worse for it. One often hears the assertion, however, that "I became an autonomous thinker *despite* the system, not because of it." But I am not at all sure about this, and I don't see how anyone else could be either. This assertion about one's educational past reminds me of a line in *Julius Caesar:* "one forgets the base degrees by which he did ascend." I think, to the contrary, that it is not only *necessary* to absorb passively information in the first stage in one's education, but it is also desired and enjoyed by children. Receptive learning of facts, and memorization, have perhaps taken an unjustifiable rap in education. As E. D. Hirsch has argued:

> In early grades, children are fascinated by straightforward information. Our official modern distaste for old-fashioned memorization and rote learning seems more pious than realistic. Young children are eager to master the materials essential for adult life, and if they believe in the materials they will proudly soak them up like sponges and never forget them. . . . Young children have an urge to become acculturated into the adult world by learning the facts of the tribe long before they can make sense out of them.[7]

To this day, one of my most memorable learning experiences comes from fourth-grade geography, where we learned about the great explorers such as Marco Polo, Magellan, Cortez, and Drake. The tests on this material required straightforward memory work, but this did not detract from my interest and excitement in the subject matter. Indeed, most classes in those grades proceeded in the same didactic fashion. It is not at all clear to me that this was particularly harmful, nor that there is a better way to teach at this stage.

That young students might appear passive as a consequence of receptive learning is something to be taken in stride rather than worried about. To passively absorb information is the natural and appropriate way to learn that kind of material. There will be time for analysis and criticism in later grades, but first students must learn the basic information about their culture so that they will have something to be critical about. Possessing basic knowledge and information is a prerequisite for critical thinking, not a deterrent to it.

The contemporary distaste for memorization and receptive learning can, I think, be seen as an overreaction to fears of *indoctrination*. While this fear is understandable, it too is a red herring. No one advocates indoctrination; and there are important differences between indoctrination and receptive learning. To begin with, we are not talking about teaching doctrines as such, but rather the simplest facts about our world. Should some of these facts be regarded as importantly controversial, then, arguably, they could be pushed back to some later age when students are better prepared to cope with them. But, more importantly, there are both conceptual and empirical differences between indoctrination and receptive learning. The purpose and/or effect of indoctrination is that people come to hold a belief so firmly that they cannot change their minds about it even when confronted with counterevidence. However, the purpose and/or effect of *receptive learning* is to teach people what evidence *is*, so that they can learn to use evidence in the formation of their beliefs. While it is at least logically possible that a student *could* come to hold a belief unshakably even though it was not the teacher's intent, the only way to prevent that possibility would be to stop teaching altogether. Surely this would be a draconian solution; and I know of no one seriously advocating this. Moreover, the overwhelming facts are that most people *do not* become indoctrinated as a result of receptive learning. For every student who may have become permanently indoctrinated as a result of early receptive learning, I could show you thousands who have not. A person cannot even start on the path to a rational life without being given information, because information is a logically necessary ingredient of rationality.

Even setting the indoctrination objection aside, it remains worth noticing how the teaching of information and factual knowledge is typically denigrated in modern education as being somehow second class, or not worthy of a serious teacher's efforts. More often than not the teaching of information and factual knowledge is disparagingly predicated with the word *mere*, as in "that's merely factual knowledge," or "mere information." Even Benjamin Bloom relegates this kind of learning to a low station in his taxonomy.[8] But the thinking skills movement has been particularly disdainful of this kind of learning because it is viewed (either tacitly or overtly) as an anathema to what their programs, which focus on the reasoning *process*, are all about. ("You don't want your kid to just know facts, do you?" God forbid!) However, our public understanding of what information and factual knowledge consist in has been conspicuously naive. Our operative notions of information, facts, and factual knowledge are not only amongst the most maligned concepts in education, but they are among the most poorly understood. We have not taken the time to understand or appreciate what is conceptually involved in factual knowledge, nor how far it takes one toward the goal of autonomous thought.

Clearly, some types of information and factual knowledge are, indeed, educationally pointless or trivial. Perhaps learning a page of the encyclopedia (or phone book) by heart would be an example. Moreover, such examples are rhetorically cited, and thought of, by critics as paradigms of what is wrong with teaching facts or information in general. However, it is a serious mistake to regard the teaching and learning of factual information as educationally inferior. Most of the important things that our culture—indeed, humanity—can be said to *know* is of a straightforward factual nature. The mistake that occurs in maligning factual teaching is that we tend to set up, or envisage, a false dichotomy between factual knowledge on the one hand and thinking on the other. We talk as though on one hand there are simple *facts*, which are relatively passive things (like *data*), and on the other there is *thinking*, which is active; hence, the dichotomy. Bloom's taxonomy of educational objectives clearly supports this view of things, and Gilbert Ryle's distinction between "knowing how" and "knowing that" has been interpreted by many educators as supporting it also.[9] No doubt this distinction can sometimes be made, and it is often harmless to do so.

However, there have been, and continue to be, many disastrous consequences in education from reading far too much into this distinction. In most of the interesting cases, and particularly those which are likely to occur in school learning, the distinction between "knowing facts" and "thinking" simply does not hold. Significant thought (i.e., thinking) is required in coming to learn factual knowledge, and to use it. For example, it is a fact that "osmotic pressure increases with the concentration of solution," and to understand this is to have *factual knowledge*. It is a fact that "E = mc^2", and to understand this is to have factual knowledge. Such examples are clearly endless, and in each case the factual knowledge requires thinking. That is, the factual knowledge *itself* requires thinking; there are not two things going on in knowing facts, but one. This is because *knowing* something logically entails understanding it—else we would not say one "knows" it. And understanding requires thinking. The thinking consists in (among other things) coming to see the fact or proposition as part of a network of other facts or propositions which the person already understands. There is an important sense in which people cannot be said to know or understand isolated facts or propositions, but only collections of them; because facts and propositions are composed (logically) of other concepts, or facts, or propositions. Consider, for example, even the relatively trivial piece of factual knowledge that "Albany is the capital of New York." One must first understand what a capital *is*, and that it is not necessarily the largest city, etc. The concept of a capital is itself quasi-sophisticated. This is why second grade students do not understand the proposition "Albany is the capital of New York" but sixth graders *do* understand it. Similarly, sixth graders do not understand the factual proposition about osmotic pressure (above), and college sophomores do. In short, a lot of thinking, and sometimes difficult thinking is required in coming to understand factual information—at least the kind of information that schools have been traditionally concerned to teach. Thus, it is a serious mistake to separate factual knowledge, or information, from thinking. In reality, they cannot be taken apart as easily as our educational talk (and theories) might suggest. And I believe much positive harm is being done by continuing to talk this way, as the "thinking skills" movement does.

Traditionally, initiation into the standard disciplines has never tried to separate the thinking *process* from the information or facts to be thought about. The disciplines have at least tacitly recognized that the way one thinks about something is part of the warp and woof of what is being thought *about:* mathematical questions require mathematical thinking, moral problems, moral thinking, etc. And if some real "everyday" problem involves several of these dimensions (or facts) at once, then several of these different learned dimensions will have to be employed to solve it. There is no getting around this brute fact of intellectual life. Thus, the pedagogical task which lies before our educational institutions is to get on with the business of teaching the disciplines in the most enlightened ways that we know. No available alternative can even come close to producing critical thinkers of the sort we all desire.

Notes

1. Judith W. Segal, Susan F. Chipman, and Robert Glaser, *Thinking and Learning Skills* (Hillsdale, N.J.: Erlbaum, 1985).

2. Neil Postman, *Teaching as a Conserving Activity* (New York: Delacorte, 1979), pp. 165–67.

3. E. D. Hirsch, Jr., "Cultural Literacy in the Schools," *American Educator* (Summer 1985):10.

4. Postman, p. 164.

5. Sophie Haroutunian, "A Response to Testing for 'Critical Thinking,' " *Proceedings of the Philosophy of Education Society* (1985):21–27.

6. United States National Commission on Excellence in Education, *A Nation at Risk: The Imperative for Educational Reform* (Washington, D.C.: The Commission [Supt. of Docs., U.S. G.P.O., Distributor], 1983).

7. Hirsch, p. 13.

8. Benjamin S. Bloom, ed., *Taxonomy of Educational Objectives: The Classification of Educational Goals, Handbook 1: The Cognitive Domain* (New York: David McKay, 1956).

9. For a rich and critical discussion of this distinction as found in the work of Benjamin Bloom, Gilbert Pyle, Peter Geach, and Jane Rolland Martin, see James Gribble, *Introduction to Philosophy of Education* (Boston: Allyn and Bacon, 1969): pp. 59–70.

3 Cultural Literacy and Critical Literacy

DONALD LAZERE

In this paper I will address the relation of critical reasoning to literate culture by first evaluating E. D. Hirsch's conception of cultural literacy and then using it as a point of departure for developing my own conception of "critical literacy."[1]

Many of the harshest critics of Hirsch's *Cultural Literacy* have been Hirsch's colleagues in university English departments. Being an English professor myself, and one who primarily teaches and studies composition, I have on several public occasions found myself in the unpopular position of defending Hirsch. My defense is that, however flawed some of his ideas may be, he deserves great admiration for the example he has set as an established literary scholar at a prestigious university, the University of Virginia, who has asserted the theoretical legitimacy of elementary issues of literacy and culture. He has raised a whole curriculum-full of thorny theoretical issues and obliged other members of the literary critical establishment to join combat on the ground he has staked out. Although I have to agree with some of the criticisms made of Hirsch, I also have to say that many of his most severe critics are literary scholars at elite universities far removed from the grim realities of American education at lower levels,

51

and that many of his strongest supporters are teachers at those lower levels who feel the shock of recognition in his views and are grateful to him for championing their cause.

I am especially wary of Hirsch's critics of the deconstructionist persuasion, the same variety who—although they might not have the remotest acquaintance with the situation of teachers at elementary levels—think it's a fine idea to tell children or college remedial writing students that they don't need to learn to read accurately because all meaning is indeterminate, that they don't need to learn the conventions of written English because they are all arbitrary, and that they don't need to learn to make moral or aesthetic judgments because they are no more than forms of social domination. That way lies madness.

As a leftist, I am more sympathetic to criticisms of Hirsch by American cultural pluralists, but I am also sympathetic to Hirsch's arguments on national language and national culture (Incidentally, these arguments include a thoughtful perspective on the perennial issues in the theory of standard English composition versus nonstandard dialects and students' right to their own languages, as well as a disconcertingly cogent case for the movement to make English the official American language). He acknowledges the need for considerable diversity, flux, and expansion within American culture—he dictates no Bennettite core curriculum or canon of Great Books, no monolithic moral or ideological agenda. He does, however, leave one with the nagging thought that runaway pluralism in all educational sectors of the country is apt to divide the many disfranchised groups in America ever further. Without any strong political organization of the kind that has so far only reached the embryonic stage of Jesse Jackson's Rainbow Coalition, widespread pluralism—even in the legitimate cause of cultural affirmative action—ends up leaving the white, male, capitalist establishment more firmly empowered than ever. None of Hirsch's critics that I have read has presented a concrete alternative view of what bare minimum of common knowledge is needed to make a pluralistic culture and vast national educational system like ours workable.

Hirsch's aims are much more modest than those many of his critics attribute to him. Although he is not entirely consistent on this point, he does not ultimately claim that either his criteria of cultural literacy or his notorious list should be the sum total of basic education; they are only projected, very tentatively, as a minimal vocabulary prerequisite to further learning—necessary but not sufficient. The list is a kind of glossary or index around which intensive curricula can be built using its contents as a common point of reference. Nor is Hirsch's position, as John Warnock claims, that "once the contents of a subject are known the means of conveying them are of little significance."[2] He only says that his ideas dictate no particular pedagogical method; they can be applied through a plurality of means that are simply outside his immediate concerns in this book.

His list was not intended as a commissarially dictated prescription, but as an empirically derived description of the vocabulary needed to understand "the information that is assumed without explanation in magazines like *The Atlantic* and general circulation books."[3] Trying to compile such a list might well have been methodologically and tactically mistaken, but would any of his critics deny that the level of literacy it is meant to delineate is a valid goal that our schools have fallen far short of in preparing students of nearly all social classes and ethnic groups?[4] On this point and others, Hirsch is not always an effective advocate of his own ideas, but in their haste to demolish him, many of his critics have failed to pursue vital issues that he raises. As a composition specialist I find two of his points immensely important. First, he effectively blows the whistle on several decades of misguided, linguistics based composition theory and instruction that emphasize form and technique at the expense of content, and syntactic concerns at the expense of semantic and rhetorical ones. Second, his chapter 2 brings research in cognitive-developmental psychology to bear on the complex question of the dialectic in learning between factual knowledge and the development of reading, writing, and reasoning skills. Some of his findings may be questionable (Robert Scholes nails him on misuse of Basil Bernstein's studies)[5], but the issues he addresses here comprise a fruitful agenda for scholars in literature, composition, and rhetoric.

For me the most important passage in *Cultural Literacy* is the following:

> It isn't facts that deaden the minds of young children, who are storing facts in their minds every day with astonishing voracity. It is incoherence—our failure to ensure that a pattern of shared, vividly taught, and socially enabling knowledge will emerge from our instruction.
>
> The polarization of educationists into facts-people versus skills-people has no basis in reason. Facts and skills are inseparable. There is no insurmountable reason why those who advocate the teaching of higher order skills and those who advocate the teaching of common traditional content should not join forces.[6]

Hirsch makes it quite clear here that he considers cultural literacy only a foundation for the development of higher order skills. His book does not spell out what those skills are, however, and pending a sequel that does, I will now spell out my own conception of them. I designate this conception *critical literacy*, with particular reference to the role of higher order skills in undergraduate and graduate curricula and as subjects for research and theory in English and other humanistic disciplines. As good a place as any to begin is with Chancellor Glenn Dumke's Executive Order 338 (1980) announcing the requirement of formal instruction in critical thinking throughout the nineteen California State University campuses. The pertinent section reads:

> Instruction in critical thinking is to be designed to achieve an understanding of the relationship of language to logic, which should lead to the ability to analyze, criticize, and advocate ideas, to reason inductively and deductively, and to reach factual or judgmental conclusions based on sound inferences drawn from unambiguous statements of knowledge or belief. The minimal competence to be expected at the successful con-

clusion of instruction in critical thinking should be the ability to distinguish fact from judgment, belief from knowledge, and skills in elementary inductive and deductive processes, including an understanding of the formal and informal fallacies of language and thought.

The study of critical thinking has merged at many points with the recent focus on literacy as the subject of advanced, interdisciplinary academic study. Out of these two movements, I and other scholars have supplemented Dumke's list with additional criteria for higher order thinking skills and psychological dispositions. My own list must be prefaced by yet another list, of the studies in diverse academic disciplines from which I have synthesized it. This list will also serve to sketch out an agenda for advanced scholarship in literacy theory that, I submit, is comparable in scope and importance for English scholars to the entire field of literary theory. It begins with the kind of research in the cognitive problems of novice college writers pioneered by Mina Shaughnessy. Shaughnessy's work, confirming my own observations in teaching both undergraduate writing and literature courses, led me to related studies in a number of areas: developmental psychology; moral education; the history and psychology of oral versus literate cultures (including studies by literary scholars like Walter J. Ong, Eric Havelock, and Ian Watt); Basil Bernstein's sociolinguistic correlations between social class and "restricted" versus "elaborated" codes; political socialization and "the culture of poverty"; Frankfurt School critical theory; the influence of television and other mass media on cognition and socialization; and Paulo Freire's approach to literacy education for political liberation. My categories of criteria for critical literacy derive from the common patterns of cognitive proficiencies and deficiencies identified by scholars from the above fields in the people they have studied. To be sure, the quality of their studies has been disputed in many cases, and English scholars need to become conversant with these disputes, but I think the criteria are useful in themselves, purely for purposes of classifying the kind of proficiencies—and all too often, the lack thereof—that teachers of both composition and literature encounter in their students. (I want to make it clear here that I find these studies most applicable to the cognitive and psychological problems encountered most often in middle class American students; the issues in teaching such students are of a very different order from Freire's pedagogy of the oppressed.)

Finally, then, here are my supplementary criteria for critical literacy. Such literacy requires these abilities:

- to unify and make connections in one's experience and academic studies;
- to sustain an extended line of thought through propositional, thematic, or symbolic development;
- to engage in mature moral reasoning and to form judgments of quality and taste;
- to reason back and forth between the concrete and abstract, the personal and impersonal, the literal and the hypothetical or figurative, and between the present, past, and future (both in one's own life and in human history);
- to be attuned to skepticism, irony, relativity of viewpoint (without lapsing into undiscriminating relativism), ambiguity, and multiplicity of meaning in linguistic or aesthetic structures;
- to form sociopolitical opinions based on open-minded and autonomous reasoning rather than on prejudice and authoritarianism, on reciprocity (Piaget's term for empathy with other individuals, social groups, and ideologies) rather than on egocentrism or ethnocentrism.

From the viewpoint of an English scholar, I must note that these criteria amount to a catalogue of precisely the cognitive traits that characterize the study of literature and literary criticism. In light of the recognition in the past decade by the public, deficiencies of young Americans in these modes of thinking, no stronger case could present itself for reaffirming the value of literary studies.

Approaching literary education and criticism from the perspective of critical thinking suggests one resolution of the recent battles over canon revision. Suppose that the selection of works to be studied were based on the case made by individual instructors or critics for which works best contribute to the development of critical thinking skills. For example, to illustrate relations between the concrete and the abstract, Plato's *Symposium* and Dante's *Paradiso* might be studied for their concepts of the ladder leading from physical to spiritual love, from the concrete language and thought of poetry to the superior abstractions of philosophy or theology. They in turn could be contrasted with Ovid's or Montaigne's skeptical reflections on the primacy of sexual over spiritual love; with Rebecca Harding Davis's protonaturalist critique, in "Life in the Iron Mills," of platonic, transcendentalist ideals in face of the brutal material conditions of nineteenth-century industrial labor; with Joseph Heller's juxtaposition in *Catch 22* of the military bureaucracy's idealistic rationalizations of war with Yossarian's discovery that "Man was matter, that was Snowden's secret"; with James Baldwin's exposure of the gap between "the Puritan-Yankee equation of virtue with well-being" and the fact that Colonial "Negroes had excellent reasons for doubting that money was made or kept by any very striking adherence to the Christian virtues"; or with Solzhenitsyn's equally corroscating exposure of the gap between marxist ideals and the realities of the Gulag Archepelago.

Incidentally, Hirsch erroneously believes the critical thinking movement is opposed to cultural literacy; he sets up a strawman advocate of critical thinking as a mechanical set of skills divorced from factual, discipline-specific knowledge. Quite the contrary is true of the mainstream of recent critical thinking scholarship. My main point of reference here is the Center for Critical Thinking and Moral Critique at Sonoma State University, north of San Francisco, and its annual International Conference on Critical Thinking and Educational Reform, which for the past ten summers has brought together teachers from a steadily widening range of disciplines (composition and literature are regularly represented) and at every level from kindergarten through graduate faculties. My colleagues on the summer faculty there have formed the National Council for Excellence in Critical Thinking Instruction, a nexus for rapidly expanding national critical thinking networks and a resource base for curriculum development and testing; we have established working relationships with the California State University and community college systems, the California State Department of Education, and College Board, and the American Federation of Teachers Educational Issues Department.[7]

The guiding principle of the center is what its director Richard Paul terms "strong-sense" critical thinking. This approach eschews formal logic in philosophy, Paul's field, and the kind of formulaic "skills" approach Hirsch also dislikes, in favor of applying to virtually every academic subject matter—as well as to moral issues and the rhetoric of public discourse—encouragement of students' attainment of autonomous thinking through skeptically questioning all inadequately substantiated claims and culturally conditioned assumptions. Strong-sense critical thinking is essentially rhetorical in its insistence that learning takes place most effectively through Socratic dialogue and debates between opposing viewpoints. Obviously, the more of Hirsch's cultural literacy students possess, the larger arsenal of information they will have for challenging claims and perceiving diverse viewpoints.

Another vital emerging force for critical literacy in American education, one that should join ranks with both critical thinking and English studies, is the incorporation of public service activism into many high school and college curricula. The California state legislature has passed a "Human Corps" bill providing academic and financial credit for service internships, and legislation is currently pending in the United States Congress proposing a similar, voluntary nationwide program as a substitute for mili-

tary service. Ralph Waldo Emerson ranked action along with nature and books as the most important sources of wisdom for the
American scholar. Especially for this generation of middle-class
youth, who have been sheltered from public conflicts far more
than the children of the sixties, service projects can provide some
exposure to people outside of their own egocentric and ethnocen-
tric circles. The most frequent form of public service in English
studies to date has been literacy corps, in which students tutor
children and adults in reading and writing. I have also found
through experiments in my composition courses that requiring
research and argumentative papers based on student service
projects—finding shelter and employment for the homeless, participating in local environmental projects, etc.—greatly en-
hances students' motivation to read academic research on the
subject and their rhetorical sophistication in evaluating and taking part in debates on it. This personal experience is also bound
to bring to life literary accounts of such subjects and can provide
fruitful material for creative writing.

My own emphasis area for critical literacy is the rhetoric of
political propaganda and ideology, particularly as mediated
through mass culture. As I put it in my introduction to a special
issue of *College English* titled "Mass Culture, Political Consciousness, and English Studies" in 1977,

> If literacy is defined, as it should be, in the larger sense of
> breadth of knowledge and capacity for reason, then it is evident
> that the greatest threats to literacy in the twentieth century
> are mass-mediated thought control and the reason-numbing ef-
> fects of mass culture, and that English, as the discipline preem-
> inently responsible for fostering literacy, must provide critical
> weapons for combatting these anti-rational forces.[8]

The political ignorance and apathy, and the resulting gullibil-
ity, of large segments of all American social classes and ethnic
groups poses a threat to the survival of democracy. This threat
demands a crash campaign for political literacy by all pertinent
academic disciplines—English foremost, through rhetorical and

semantic analysis of current events, issues, and ideologies. One of the overlooked virtues of Hirsch's *Cultural Literacy* is its emphasis on political education. I am constantly stymied in my literature and writing classes by fundamental gaps in students' political vocabulary, ignorance of the kind of terms included in Hirsch's list—which, incidentally, I find satisfactorily multi-ideological, as he claims it is. As a leftist, I can live comfortably with any list that includes *civil disobedience, civil liberties, Civil Rights Movement, class consciousness, coexistence (peaceful), Communist Manifesto, conflict of interest, cultural imperialism, Betty Friedan, general strike, Woody Guthrie, Malcolm X, My Lai Massacre, New Left, plutocracy, profit sharing, spoils system,* and *Gloria Steinem.* Conservatives should be equally satisfied by *creationism, Jerry Falwell, fellow traveler, first-strike capability, free enterprise, Milton Friedman, Lee Iacocca, invisible hand, Iron Curtain, laissez faire, risk capital (venture capital), Stalin's purge trials, states' rights,* and *supply side.*

Political illiteracy is one side of the double jeopardy facing American democracy; its dark twin is the ever more sophisticated manipulation of that illiteracy by those in power. To Orwell's characterization of political language in 1945 as "a mass of lies, evasions, folly, hatred, and schizophrenia," our age has added refinements of doublethink and Newspeak even Orwell didn't envision.[9] The era of television politics has brought about the triumph of appearance over reality, style and symbol over substance, theatrical appeal over reason—along with the daily rewriting of history and the disappearance of yesterday's lies down the memory hole. Scholarly experts are now hired by American government intelligence agencies to fabricate "disinformation," or by corporate-sponsored research institutes to conduct objective-appearing statistical studies proving that what's good for the rich is good for America.[10] As much brainpower is needed to decode all this sophisticated propaganda as to produce it; English scholars should be eminently qualified to apply their close reading skills to deciphering political texts as well as literary ones, and critical approaches like reader-response studies can be used fruitfully to analyze audience response to political rhetoric, news reports, commercial propaganda, and ideological messages in popular entertainment.

The job of those of us trying to combat doublespeak through our teaching and writing, against the current of popular opinion and professional prestige, has been made all the more difficult in recent decades by the triumph of opaque structuralist and post-structuralist discourse. The fashionable theorists dismiss as quaintly passé writers like Orwell or Camus, who insisted that "The mutual understanding and communication discovered by rebellion can survive only in the free exchange of conversation. Every ambiguity, every misunderstanding leads to death; clear language and simple words are the only salvation from this death."[11] All the current scholastical disputations over the death of the author, indeterminacy of meaning, and intertextuality are rendered fatuous, however, when confronted with the world of flesh and blood political realities, in which, today as in Orwell's time, language is "designed to make lies sound truthful and murder respectable."[12] Scholars who continue to care about such matters can find more of value in one issue of the *Quarterly Review of Doublespeak* (National Council of Teachers of English Committee on Public Doublespeak) or the more recent *Propaganda Review* (published by the nonacademic Media Alliance in San Francisco) than in several years' worth of the most prestigious current journals of literary criticism.

The study of political propaganda and ideology has been incorporated into high school and college courses less widely than the study of advertising, film and television, popular music and fiction, and other fields of mass media and popular culture. I suggest, however, that in order to form a coherent part of cultural studies or education for critical literacy, such studies need to focus on the key role these media play in the formation of political consciousness (the term *mass culture* is commonly used to designate this function, in opposition to the more eclectic view implicit in the term *popular culture* as used by those studying it).

Everyday advertising forms only part of a larger system of commercial propaganda that is as powerful a source of social and ideological control as are the government, political parties and news media. That system also includes the vast corporate industries devoted to packaging and marketing, lobbying, research, and public relations campaigns providing self-serving handouts to the media, schools, and other channels of public information. Basic consumer education may be considered by university scholars to be far too elementary a concern for them, but few of my students say they have ever had a course that addressed it. Reading books like *Diet for a Small Planet* or *Fit for Life* scares the hell out of me because I learn how naive are even we, who consider ourselves sophisticated critics, about the nutritional disinformation propagated by the food industry. Richard Ohmann's chapter "Free Messages, Messages of Freedom" in *Politics of Letters* ably deconstructs the kind of ideological "public interest" advertising put out by companies like Mobil Oil.[13] Ohmann, not incidentally, is probably our most admirable model of a literary critic and linguist devoting himself to issues of critical literacy. His latest book manages to synthesize virtually every subject whose study I have advocated in this paper, and more, within a coherent critical overview that is Marxist without being either doctrinaire or jargon-ridden.

As a final note about mass culture criticism, I am pleased to say that this is one field that has produced a wealth of useful writing by scholars in English and several other academic fields over the past decade or so.[14] Much of the best mass culture criticism has been written in comprehensible language, deriving less from continental models than from the traditions of New York intellectual journalism, the Frankfurt School's concrete studies (such as Theodor Adorno's work on television and Leo Lowenthal's on popular magazines and celebrities), recent women's, ethnic, working class, and third world cultural studies. Even some critics and journals on mass culture influenced by Althusserian Marxism, semiology, or deconstruction—journals such as *Social Text, Screen, Diacritics,* and *Camera Obscura,* recently joined by *Critical Texts* and *Cultural Critique*—are coming down to earth with concrete analyses of American mass cultural works and theoretical issues accessible to a wider range of teachers and students of literature, composition, and critical thinking. Most of these journals' politics are leftist, but conservative journals like *Commentary, New Criterion, The Chronicles of Culture,* and *American Spectator* are presenting lively counterpoints from the right on cultural politics.

In spite of all these positive developments toward a critical literacy curriculum, many obstacles still impede their full implementation. One such obstacle is the attitude common to scholars in English and other academic fields that education as a subject of scholarship is below their dignity, or at least outside their field. This attitude is compounded by the widespread disdain (sometimes warranted) toward teacher education and toward those pariahs of the academic world, education schools. The unfortunate result is that English scholars and others in the humanities have tended to be late getting the news that some of the most exciting scholarship in recent decades has been coming out of the leading graduate schools of education, and that education has become a crucial topic of critical theory with its own ranks of luminaries including Lev Vygotsky, Paulo Freire, Pierre Bourdieu, Basil Bernstein, Shirley Brice Heath, William Labov, Mina Shaughnessy, Carol Gilligan, Lawrence Kohlberg, William Perry, David Olson, Jonathan Kozol, Ira Shor, Henry Giroux, Stanley Aronowitz, Michael Apple, Sylvia Scribner, Michael Cole, Howard Gardner, Robert Coles, and Richard Paul. Another damaging attitude is the unquestioned assumption, common to most academic fields and other professional hierarchies, that those at the highest levels should be concerned with the most advanced, narrowly specialized pursuits rather than with the most basic, pressing issues of the profession and society as a whole. Intrinsic to this assumption is that the advanced pursuits be so arcane that none but the initiated can claim to understand or evaluate them, so that all criticism from outside is disarmed and mystification—sometimes outright fakery—flourishes. With the triumph of structuralist and post-structuralist theory over the past twenty years, the ante has been constantly raised in the pursuit of the most remote speculations. As the state of elementary and secondary education has worsened throughout this era of Reaganite fiscal stinginess and uncritical vocationalism, the gap has steadily grown between the lowest and highest levels of education.

If those most influential in the academic world continue to ignore the state of basic education and fail to commit themselves to fostering critical literacy at all levels of education—including advanced scholarship—they will isolate themselves ever further from a living role in American education and society. This isolation will contribute to the stifling of their students and successors and invite the enmity of public officials who will make the memory of William J. Bennett and Lynne Cheney cordial by comparison.

Notes

1. This essay incorporates studies I have conducted under a National Endowment for the Humanities Fellowship for College Teachers and a Mina Shaughnessy Scholars Program grant from the Foundation for the Improvement of Postsecondary Education—among the few national funding agencies that have provided support for these fields of study. The Shaughnessy Program was unfortunately discontinued by William J. Bennett when he became secretary of education.

2. John Warnock, "Review: *Cultural Literacy: What Every American Needs to Know,* by E. D. Hirsch, Jr." *College Composition and Communication* 38(1987):489.

3. E. D. Hirsch, Jr., *Cultural Literary. What Every American Needs to Know* (Boston: Houghton Mifflin, 1987), p. 136.

4. Robert Denham's "From the Editor: Notes on Cultural Literacy," *ADE Bulletin* 88 (Winter 1987):1–8, is the most effective critique I have seen of Hirsch's attempt to compile such a list.

5. Robert Scholes, "Three Views of Education: Nostalgia, History, and Voodoo," *College English* 50(1988):331–32.

6. Hirsch, *Cultural Literacy*, p. 133.

7. See Deborah Walsh and Richard Paul, *The Goal of Critical Thinking: from Educational Ideal to Educational Reality* (Washington: American Federation of Teachers Educational Issues Department, 1985). An equally productive center for critical thinking studies has been the institutes on writing and higher order reasoning conducted at the University of Chicago since 1982, with the collaboration of members of the Chicago English faculty like Joseph Williams and Wayne Booth, both of whom have been eloquent champions over the years of the kind of studies I am advocating here.

8. Donald Lazere, "Mass Culture, Political Consciousness, and English Studies: An Introduction," *College English* 38(1977):754.

9. George Orwell, "Politics and the English Language," in *Orwell's Nineteen Eighty-Four: Text, Sources, Criticism*, 2d ed., ed., Irving Howe (New York: Harcourt, Brace, Jovanovich, 1982), p. 256. For recent thought, see the collection of essays on post-Orwellian refinements, *Beyond 1984: Doublespeak in a Post-Orwellian Age*, ed., William A. Lutz (Urbana: National Council of Teachers of English, 1989).

10. Neil Postman, a professor of education and former member of the National Council of Teachers of English Committee on Public Doublespeak, has written some of the most powerful criticisms of the destructive effects of television on politics and education in *Teaching as a Conserving Activity* (New York: Delacorte, 1979) and *Amusing Ourselves to Death* (New York: Viking, 1985). The most fully documented case of disinformation produced by think tanks sponsored by the American government is that of the CIA-affiliated Institute of General Studies in Chile, which in the early 1970s distributed fabricated reports smearing President Allende's socialist government and otherwise colluded with the military junta that overthrew it, as confirmed by the Church Senate Committee hearings on the abuses of American intelligence agencies. For a detailed summary of this case, other instances of American-propagated disinformation, and the propaganda activities of

corporate-sponsored research institutes, see Edward Herman, and Gerry O'Sullivan. *The "Terrorism" Industry: The Experts and Institutions That Shape Our View of Terror.* New York: Pantheon Books, 1989.

11. Albert Camus, *The Rebel,* tr., (New York: Vintage Books, 1956), p. 283.

12. Orwell, "Politics and the English Language," p. 259.

13. Richard Ohmann, *Politics of Letters* (Middletown, Conn.: Wesleyan University Press, 1987). A longer version of Ohmann's chapter appeared as "Doublespeak and Ideology in Ads: A Kit for Teachers" in *Teaching About Doublespeak,* ed., Daniel Dieterich (Urbana: National Council of Teachers of English, 1976) and is reprinted in *American Media and Mass Culture: Left Perspectives,* ed., Donald Lazere (Berkeley: University of California Press, 1987). This collection is useful for teaching about doublespeak at all levels, from elementary through university.

14. For an overview and collection of recent critical perspectives on mass culture, with an orientation toward English studies, see Donald Lazere, *American Media and Mass Culture.* Also see Lawrence Grossberg, "Teaching the Popular" in *Theory in the Classroom,* ed., Cary Nelson (Urbana: University of Illinois Press, 1986), pp. 177–200.

Theories That Emphasize Skills

4 Critical Reasoning and Informal Logic

RALPH H. JOHNSON

The last few years have witnessed the rise to prominence of a battery of terms, among them *problem solving, decision making, higher order cognitive skills, lateral thinking, strategic reasoning, metacognition,* and the one which is the subject of this volume: *critical reasoning/thinking.* On any given day, one may receive a flyer, a bulletin, an announcement of a conference, a textbook that is related to this recently emergent interest in thinking. A fair question is: "What's behind all this interest in thinking and reasoning?"

I suspect that one reason stock in critical reasoning has skyrocketed is that educators at all levels and in all spheres—university, community college, technical schools—are coming to the realization that the fourth "R"—reasoning—has been neglected. If it is not quite true to say that Johnny and Janey can't reason, it is nonetheless true that they don't do it well enough. Relevant indices and data, both anecdotal and systemically gathered, are in plentiful supply. Herewith, in case anyone needs reminding, a few pieces of evidence to that effect:

> In classrooms across the country, teachers have launched
> an urgent effort to make young people think rather than just

memorize masses of facts. Many educators say nurturing of the ability to reason has been neglected in the campaign to teach basic subjects in recent years, and a catch-up is necessary to provide young people with the proper tools to prosper in an increasingly complex society.

Says Richard Paul, director of the Center for Critical Thinking and Moral Critique at Sonoma State University in California: "We need to shift the focus of learning from simply teaching students to have the right answers to teaching them the process by which educated people pursue right answers." (*U.S. News & World Report*, January 14, 1985.)

Johnny and Jenny may know a lot of facts about the Declaration of Independence, what with more emphasis being given in American classrooms to basics like history, math, and reading. But they are less able to ask significant questions about it than students were a generation ago, according to a number of educators.

Today's students are not learning as well how to identify unstated assumptions. They know less about what it means to infer, to extrapolate, to build an argument, to form and defend an opinion, to see implications. They are, in short, not learning enough about thinking critically, these educators say. (*The Christian Science Monitor*, February 28, 1986.)

Consider how effectively America's future citizens are trained not to judge for themselves about anything. From the first grade to the twelfth, from one coast to the other, instruction in America's classrooms is almost entirely dogmatic. Answers are "right" and answers are "wrong," but mostly answers are short. "At all levels, [teacher-made] tests called almost exclusively for short answers and recall of information," reports Goodlad. In more than 1,000 classrooms visited by his researchers, "only *rarely* was there evidence to suggest instruction likely to go much beyond mere possession of information to a level of understanding its implications." Goodlad goes on to note that "the intellectual terrain is laid out by the teacher. The paths for walking through it are largely pre-determined by the teacher." The give-and-take of genuine discussion is conspicuously absent. "Not even 1%" of instruc- tional time, he found, was devoted to discussions that "required some kind of open response involving reasoning or perhaps an opinion from students. . . . The extraordinary degree of student passivity stands out." (*Harper's*, June, 1986.)

My reading of such texts is that they converge around the same diagnosis: we need to teach our students how to think, how to reason. Put it another way, no matter what the missing ingredient is called, it is a process; and one important trend in higher education is to discover ways to accord proper emphasis to process without [of course] sacrificing content.

In this paper I want to discuss the contribution that informal logic can make to this new direction. In the next section I give my account of critical reasoning. Following that is my conception of informal logic, and, in the final section, I attempt to illustrate the contribution informal logic can make to critical reasoning.

What Is Critical Reasoning?

For the purpose of this paper I will assume that *critical reasoning* and *critical thinking* are synonymous.[1] This assumption is not much help because there is no consensus about the nature of critical thinking. Indeed, there are substantive disagreements between McPeck and Paul and others on such issues as whether there are general (or generalizable) thinking skills, and whether critical thinking is discipline specific.[2]

In this paper, I present a view of critical thinking that grows out of reflection on extant accounts and attempts to build on them. If I am right, critical thinking depends crucially on the capacity of the reflective agent to engage in the practice of argumentation. And since, as I shall argue, informal logic is the logic of argumentation, it then follows that there is an intimate connection between critical thinking and informal logic.

Let's begin by taking stock of the current situation as regards the nature of critical thinking. The first thing to note is that just about everyone has a definition of critical thinking these days. You can find one in every textbook, and educational policy directives (like EO #338, cited below) adopt some implicit conception of critical thinking:

> Instruction in critical thinking is to be designed to achieve an understanding of the relationship of language to logic, which should lead to the ability to analyze, criticize and advocate ideas, to reason inductively and deductively, and to reach factual or judgmental conclusions based on sound inferences drawn from unambiguous statements of knowledge or belief. The minimal competence to be expected at the successful conclusion of instruction in critical thinking should be the ability to distinguish fact from judgment, belief from knowledge, and skills in elementary deductive and inductive processes, including an understanding of the formal and informal fallacies of language and thought.[3]

To satisfy this particular definition, a thinker would have to accept the inductive/deductive distinction, be able to distinguish the two and apply the proper criteria in given instances, and would have to accept the idea that there are informal fallacies—and I am sorry to have to say that much of this is highly contentious. But that is not the issue here; rather it is that so enormous is the variety of definitions that it appears that *critical thinking* has become virtually synonymous with *righteousness of mind*.

It might be that that one way to avoid bedlam would be to limit attention to five theoretically well-developed accounts of critical thinking. They are:

- Ennis's definition of critical thinking as "reasonable, reflective thinking that is focused on deciding what to believe or do."[4]
- McPeck's definition of critical thinking as "the propensity and skill to engage in an activity with reflective skepticism."[5]
- Richard Paul's notion of strong-sense critical thinking as essentially dialogical and distinguished from weaksense.[6] More recently, Paul has offered a definition of

critical thinking in terms of a list of perfections and traits of thought: "critical thinking is disciplined, self-directed thinking which exemplifies the perfections of thinking appropriate to a particular mode or domain of thinking."[7]

- Lipman's account of critical thinking as "skillful, responsible thinking that facilitates good judgment because it (1) relies upon criteria, (2) is self-correcting and (3) is sensitive to context."[8]

- Siegel's definition of the critical thinker as the individual who is "appropriately moved by reasons."[9]

While there is some agreement among these theoreticians of critical thinking, there are also some important differences. Thus, McPeck denies while Paul affirms that there are general critical thinking skills. Almost all agree that a critical thinker cannot exist on skills alone, but what other dimensions are necessary is not a matter on which there is fundamental agreement. Is it an attitude, a set of dispositions, the critical spirit, character? Elsewhere I have argued there are problems with each of these views, but I cannot repeat that discussion here.[10] What I propose to do then is present my own account of critical thinking, one which I believe is in keeping with the spirit of these five but which has a slightly different emphasis.

To capture the identity of critical thinking, it seems to me that there are two moves to make. First, we must understand what critical thinking contrasts with. In my view, critical thinking is to be understood as contrasting, in the first instance, with uncritical or dogmatic thinking. To explain this further, consider the distinction—first brought to my attention by Richard Paul—made by C. Wright Mills about three kinds of believer: the vulgar, the sophisticated, and the critical. Paul writes:

> Vulgar believers can only operate with slogans and stereotypes within a point of view with which they egocentrically identify. . . . In contrast sophisticated Marxists are interested in reading books on capitalism or by capitalists. But they are only interested in refuting them. They might be intellectually

creative but all of their creativity is used to further one and only one point of view.

Only critical believers would, in Mill's sense, be willing to enter sympathetically into opposing points of view, for only they recognize the weaknesses in their own points of view.[11]

Mill's distinction is made with Marxists in mind; but, as Paul points out, its application to Christians, Americans, Freudians, etc., is straightforward. From this perspective, the critical thinker contrasts with both the dogmatic and the sophisticated thinker.

On the other hand, critical thinking may be contrasted with creative thinking. This is not an easy contrast to draw and some argue that the two are intimately—even analytically—related.[12] Perhaps a difference is that the creative thinker brings an intellectual product into existence, whereas the critical thinker is one who knows how to assess an intellectual product. More about this shortly.

Wary of the genetic fallacy, I nevertheless think that if we wish to grasp the nature of critical thinking, it is important to go back to the Greek root. The word *krinein*—from which we get our words *critic* and *critical*—means "to estimate the value of something." A critic then is a person who judges, appreciates, estimates the value of something. Similarly, I propose that a critical thinker is a critic of thought in much the way that a film critic is a critic of film.

Let me develop this point by considering the role of a good film critic. She applies certain standards and insights to the particular product—a film—taking into account both strengths and weaknesses in order to arrive at a judgment about its worth, and comes thereby to an overall appreciation of the film. The focus of the critical thinker's scrutiny is not a film—an aesthetic product—but rather an intellectual product, a *thought*. I take the word *thought* here in its widest sense of being an intellectual-rational product of some sort, including such items as beliefs, theories, hypotheses, news stories, and arguments, whether they are someone else's product or one's own. The task of the critical thinker is to apply the appropriate norms and standards to that product and judge its value—and to articulate that judgment.

If this is true, then critical thinking may be characterized as *thought evaluating other thought.* More specifically, critical thinking is the articulated judgment of an intellectual product arrived at on the basis of plus/minus consideration of the product based on appropriate criteria. It is in this movement that the critical thinker displays her differences from the uncritical thinker, the dogmatist who can see only the strengths in the products he likes, only the weaknesses in those he does not approve of.

An important property, or defining characteristic, of the critical thinker is the capacity to take criticism. The author of the popular *The Road Less Traveled,* M. Scott Peck, writes: "The tendency to avoid challenge is so omnipresent in human beings that it can properly be considered a characteristic of human nature."[13] The critical thinker must be wary of this tendency and to some degree have mastered it. Whether we take this to be a property or defining feature of critical thinking, it should loom large in our account.

What then does it take to become a critical thinker? The necessary ingredients referred to above are three: *information/ knowledge* [and often from more than one domain or branch of inquiry—think of the AIDs problem which involves a host of disciplines: epidemiology, demography, sociology, history, medical geography etc.]; *disposition/attitudes/character traits* [such as the passion for the truth, a capacity to take criticism, a sense of fair play etc.]; and finally *thinking skills,* among them principally the capacity to construct, interpret and criticize argumentation. More on that in the section on informal logic.

My discussion of critical thinking has thus far been quite abstract. To round it off and concretize matters, I offer this profile of the critical reasoner which will serve to put flesh and blood on these abstract bones. A critical thinker is an individual who:

> *Reasons* her way through to a position by considering the evidence available;

Knows what objections are likely to be raised to a position and knows how to examine positions by probing their assumptions and consequences;

Does not allow vivid information and anecdotal evidence to carry undue weight in his reflections;

Realizes the effect that emotions and feelings and prejudices may have on her thinking;

Is willing to revise his position in light of the reasoning of others and of contrary evidence;

Is sensitized to the demands of clarity and is able to detect objectionable vagueness in her own thinking and the thinking of others;

Remains unimpressed by the sheer force of someone's rhetoric and conviction when these masquerade as substitutes for reasoning;

Stops to think before arriving at a judgment; is able to say to himself "Hold on a minute, here. Am I being swept away by the heat of the moment?"

Thinks, judges and acts mindful of the limitations of time and information imposed by the situation.

It seems clear that to produce such an individual, the support of the whole educational system is necessary. No one course at any level can do it. And it is clear to all that a variety of cognitive skills will be necessary. Our critical thinker will have to have the capacity to draw and to appropriate inferences, clarify concepts and ideas, etc. Preeminent among the skills in the cognitive repertoire of the critical thinker is the ability to appraise arguments. In helping to achieve this ability, informal logic enters the scene.

What Is Informal Logic?

Suppose that we agree that a critical thinker must possess the capacity to appraise argumentation. How will he acquire this capacity? Some may believe that this job is already taken care of by training in formal deductive logic. But there are a number of more or less well-known difficulties with formal deductive logic [hereafter referred to as FDL] as a theory of criticism for argument evaluation. Among them is the fact that there are many arguments to which the standards of FDL [truth and validity] do not readily apply. But the main defect with FDL as a theory of criticism is that it requires the students to learn new technical concepts and procedures which probably will not survive twenty-four hours beyond the final examination; their life span on the cognitive shelf is short. In addition, the use of technical terminology cuts down on the capacity to communicate with others who don't know the theory. And finally, retention will be short if not constantly nurtured. All of these seem to me good reasons for looking elsewhere.

What's the alternative? In my view, the critical thinker will stay as close to natural language as possible because that language will stay with the student long after the end of the course. What we want is to take the critical vocabulary inherent in the English language and breathe new life into it, empower our students to use it.[14]

What is this vocabulary? Here are just a few terms in the English language that educated people should be able to deploy in critiquing intellectual products: *reason, evidence, conclusion, thesis, relevant, sufficient, inconsistent, implication, presupposition, objection.* For present purposes, not that all these terms have a natural home in the practice of argumentation. If the student is able to deploy such concepts, is able to do intellectual work with them, then that student is well on the way to becoming a critical thinker.

Next I want to indicate how informal logic can contribute to this development of critical thinking. But first we must ask: What is informal logic? Informal logic designates an alternative approach to logic and to the teaching of logic. The "informal" part of "informal logic" probably derives from Kahane's decision twenty years ago to attempt to revitalize logic using the informal fallacies as the instrument. Although Kahane does not use this term in *Logic and Contemporary Rhetoric*, his criticisms of the limitations of formal logic set the scene for what develops later:

> Today's students demand a marriage of theory and practice. That is why so many of them judge introductory courses on logic, fallacy and even rhetoric not relevant to their interests.
>
> In class a few years back, while I was going over the [to me] fascinating intricacies of the predicate logic quantifier rules, a student asked in disgust how anything he's learned all semester long had any bearing whatever on President Johnson's decision to escalate again in Vietnam. I mumbled something about bad logic on Johnson's part, and then stated that Introduction to Logic was not that kind of course. His reply was to ask what courses did take up such matters, and I had to admit that so far as I knew none did.
>
> He wanted want most students today want, a course relevant to everyday reasoning, a course relevant to the arguments they hear and read about race, pollution, poverty, sex, atomic warfare, the population explosion, and all the other problems faced by the human race in the second half of the twentieth century.[15]

In their 1988 essay, Johnson and Blair define informal logic as "the normative study of argument. It is that area of logic which seeks to develop standards, criteria and procedures for the interpretation, evaluation and construction of arguments and argumentation used in natural language."[16] Thus, informal logic is the logic of argumentation as distinguished from formal logic as the logic of implication/entailment/inference. Its identity is separate from such related enterprises as dialogue logic, problem solving, metacognition, etc. To make this identity clearer, it will be useful to distinguish between inference and argument.

Distinguishing Argument from Inference

In my view, FDL studies implication/inference,[17] as when one reasons thus: "Oh, it's raining; so we can't have the picnic today;

which means that I can just stay at home and relax." Here inferences are being drawn, but such (interior) discourse, though clearly reasoning, is not yet argumentation. Why not? Because argumentation is a practice whose chief purpose is rational persuasion. But here there is no attempt at rational persuasion; no inquiry is underway, no dialectical issue has been joined. The reasoner is simply figuring something out for herself. The performance of this inference is monolectical and occurs, I shall say, in private space.

Argumentation, on the other hand, is intersubjective. Although it doesn't take two to argue (in this sense) because a person can argue with himself, still there is a sense in which argumentation is a practice occurring in public space and requiring the support of a community. Argumentation is thus also a social practice and arguments (as products) are the issue of that practice. More specifically, an argument is an attempt to persuade someone (even oneself) on rational grounds of the "truth" of some claim or thesis or statement which, for some reason, is controversial. With arguments, then, structure follows purpose; arguments have the structure they have (premises leading to a conclusion; reasons supporting a thesis) because of the purpose they subtend.

Informal logic as the logic of argumentation (to be distinguished from inference) will be of use to the critical reasoner whenever it is necessary to appraise—or construct—argumentation. To illustrate this in more detail is the point of the next section.

Informal Logic and the Evaluation
of Argumentation

What standards (or criteria) should be applied to arguments? To appreciate the answer given by informal logic, recall that an argument is to be understood as an attempt at rational persuasion occurring in public (dialectical) space. This conception furnishes important clues about the criteria to be used in evaluating such discourse.

If I am right, an argument is a two-tiered structure, and hence will require two different sorts of criteria. To see this we need to reflect on its purpose as rational persuasion, for from this purpose its structure follows. Because we wish to persuade by reason, we recognize that the claim we are interested in must be supported by reasons. This is so because we are here supposing that the claim is not clearly and obviously true; it is precisely one that we are arguing over. I call the premise-conclusion part of an argument's structure the first tier of argumentation.

But one tier is not enough. Because as rational agents we recognize that the other reasoners will have taken different positions, or will have a variety of objections to lodge against our position, we must provide a second tier—a dialectical tier—in which this wider context is dealt with.

Thus, in evaluating an argument from the perspective of informal logic, there will be two sorts of criteria: structural and dialectical. Let me now say a few words about each sort.

The First Tier: Structural Criteria for Argument

Several informal logicians hold a theory of argument according to which the premises of an argument had to meet the criteria of relevance, sufficiency, and acceptability.[18] Though this theory is not without its difficulties, it seems serviceable here and I shall say just a few words about each of the criteria.

Relevance. It seems clear that for an argument to be a good one, the premises must satisfy the relevance requirement.

(S1)   The premises must be relevant to the conclusion.

Relevance is a fundamental concept and not easily analyzed. In *Logical Self-Defense*, we propose certain tests that one can perform to gauge whether a premise is relevant to the conclusion, but these tests and guidelines are not unproblematic. I once interpreted this criterion as an all-or-nothing affair: each premise was either relevant to the conclusion or it was not relevant. Like pregnancy, relevance did not admit of degree. I now prefer to say that the argument must satisfy the relevance criterion. How well a given premise (or premise set) meets this requirement is a matter of degree. A premise set may be highly relevant, marginally relevant, or not relevant at all.

Sufficiency. Premises may well pass the relevance test and still not provide the proper basis for rational acceptance of the conclusion. In addition to relevance, premises must pass the sufficiency requirement.

(S2)   *The premises must provide sufficient evidence for the conclusion.*

This requirement means sufficient both in quantity and in type. We need to ask not only is there enough of this type of evidence but also whether the appropriate range of evidence has been incorporated into the argument. It seems clear that the sufficiency requirement applies to the entire set of premises and also that sufficiency is a matter of degree.

Acceptability. Suppose a premise set has passed both the relevance requirement and the sufficiency requirement; then is it not thereby a good argument? No, for it is possible for a premise to be relevant and still not acceptable; and certainly the reverse is possible: a premise may well be acceptable and yet not relevant to the conclusion. Hence this additional requirement is needed.

(S3)   *The premises must be acceptable to the audience of the argument.*

If the purpose of argumentation is rational persuasion, then that goal cannot possibly be met unless the premises are ones that the intended audience will embrace.

It is clear that, whatever it means, acceptance cannot be identified with truth. The premises might be quite acceptable and yet not true; and they might well be true but not acceptable. What about truth? Don't the premises of an argument have to be true? According to FDL, truth was one of the two requirements for a good argument. Why should we abandon that old standard? Let us add this as a requirement and see what happens.

(S4)   The premises of the argument must be true.

We want our premises to be true, and yet if we insist on this as a criterion then it will probably turn out that there are very few good arguments, since it will be hard to come up with premises which are true. It was precisely such reasoning that led informal logicians to follow C. L. Hamblin's position that acceptance be the appropriate criterion to impose.[19]

On the issue of acceptance versus truth, it seems to me that some kind of compromise is eventually going to have to be reached. For it seems clear that each criterion has something to offer to our account of goodness. The premises of a good argument must stand in some healthy relationship to the outside world of facticity and evidence. Just as clearly, premises which have this relationship to the world of fact but are not accepted/ acceptable by the audience will not fulfill the purpose of rational persuasion. Thus a healthy alliance must be forged between these two criteria. Without here attempting to spell out the details of that alliance, let me say that in teaching our students to distinguish between good and bad arguments, then, I think we must ask them to look at the premises both from the point of view of their relationship to the intended audience (S3) and also to the wider world (S4). If they find problems in either direction they will have some basis for marking the argument down.

Thus far I have spoken only about the criteria that apply to the first tier. Criteria for the second tier will be more prominent in the analysis of the kind of sociopolitical discourse we want our students to be able to handle, so let me turn now to them.

The Second Tier: Dialectical Criteria for Argument

Dialectical criteria also flow from an adequate conceptualization of the nature of argumentation as an essay in rational persuasion. Implied in the notion of persuasion is that person (those persons) whom I wish to persuade, which in turn implies that they do not—at this moment—accept the conclusion which I seek to persuade them of. That the persuasion is rational means that I attempt to bring them around to my conclusion by appealing to their rationality; I must give them the evidence for my view. But that is not enough. For, given the nature of the situation, we must presume that there are other arguers urging other conclusions; that there are objections to some of my premises; and that my hearer may have heard of these dissenting views and so, if I am to speak to her as a rational agent, my argument will have to address these dialectical factors. That is, there will be others who—viewing the issue under consideration and the evidence—will come to a different conclusion. To persuade rationally in such a set of circumstances it is not possible to ignore these alternative positions. The arguer must make some attempt to deal with them, and such material will form what I call the second tier of argumentation.

Hence one dialectical criterion for argumentation is contained in the following question.

(D1)   *How well does the argument address itself to alternative positions?*

In informal logic we say that an arguer who fails to engage satisfactorily with alternative positions is guilty of the fallacy of *straw man* (if she distorts), the fallacy of *ad hominem* (if she personalizes inappropriately), or the fallacy of *red herring* (if she digresses). Hence teaching students to look for these fallacies is a way of teaching them to see whether or not (D1) is satisfied.

In any given argumentative context, there will be those who disagree with one or more of the premises. Hence the arguer is under a prima facie obligation to face up to possible objections, some of which will be housed in alternative positions, though not all need be. Hence there is a second question/criterion.

(D2)   How well does the argument deal with objections?

If the arguer fails to deal with these objections, the result will be a fallacy of insufficiency.

Further, there will be the need for the argument to face up to implications—particularly this is true of the conclusion. Thus arises a third question/criterion.

(D3)   How well does the argument handle
       consequences?

Typically, an argument that runs amok of (D3) will be guilty of the fallacy called *slippery slope.*

Perhaps this brief exposition of the second tier and its criteria make it clear why, from the point of view of informal logic, the fallacies of straw man, ad hominem, red herring, and slippery slope are particularly important in the analysis of argumentation.

To be sure, the whole subject of fallacy is fraught with difficulty; the concept of fallacy is problematic, and there are any number of important criticisms of fallacy theory.[20] Nor do I want to be interpreted as suggesting that political critique can be simply reduced to the hunt for fallacy. There is much more to the analysis of argumentation than merely the hunt for fallacy. But I do think that such a mode of critique is logically defensible, especially in connection with teaching students to think critically.

Insofar as critical thinking requires the capacity to analyze and evaluate arguments in natural language, then to that same degree informal logic—being, as it is, the logic of argumentation—has an important contribution to make to critical reasoning.

In conclusion, I want to call attention to two principles developed by informal logicians which have an important bearing on the practice of evaluating arguments.

1. The Principle of Logical Neutrality prohibits the critic from seeking to pass off substantive criticism as if it were logical criticism.[21] It is one thing to criticize someone's argument on logical grounds, saying, for example, that the premise ought to have been better defended. It is another thing to criticize that argument on substantive grounds, saying that the same premise is false.

2. The Principle of Discrimination says that in criticizing an argument, the critic should get to the heart of the matter, not get stuck on peripheral or tangential matters.[22] This principle is needed because any complex and interesting political argument will have a number of possible weaknesses. This principle requires the critic to focus on the serious flaws in the argument, to avoid nit-picking and shotgunning the argument.

Such then are some of the criteria and principles which informal logic can contribute to the task of evaluating arguments.

Conclusion: Informal Logic and Critical Thinking

Critical thinking denotes a number of things; here we have been speaking of it as a practice, an engagement of the mind. It is also an educational ideal. Informal logic, on the other hand, is a new area of logic. The argument of this paper has been that to the degree that a critical thinker must be adept at handling arguments (both in their construction and their critique), to that same degree informal logic has an important role to play in the development of critical thinkers. Of course other forms of logic and other disciplines have their contribution to make, but I leave to others the task of explaining that contribution.

Notes

1. An earlier version of the paper was delivered in March 1988 as the Thomasfest Lecture at Xavier University. The author is grateful to Professor Talaska and the Department of Philosophy for their invitations and to all those in the audience for their contributions. Given the opportunity, I would argue that there is a difference between reasoning and thinking and that it is important to make the distinction. Such is the business of that inquiry I refer to as the theory of reasoning.

2. Cf. John McPeck, *Critical Thinking and Education* (New York: St. Martin's Press), 1981, and Richard Paul, "Teaching Critical Thinking in the 'Strong Sense': A Focus on Self-Deception, World Views, and a Dialectical Mode of Analysis," *Informal Logic Newsletter* 4 (1982): 2–7. The controversy sharpens in the exchange in *Informal Logic* 7 (1985). Cf. Richard Paul, "McPeck's Mistakes," pp. 35–44, and John McPeck, "Paul's Critique," pp. 45–54.

3. This is an executive order that has been in effect throughout the California State University College System since 1980. It requires that anyone who graduates from any college in the system must have satisfied a critical thinking requirement. EO #338 has certainly sparked much interest in California in critical thinking.

4. Robert H. Ennis, "A Conception of Critical Thinking—With Some Curriculum Suggestions," *APA Newsletter on Teaching Philosophy,* Summer (1987), p. 1. Cf. also his "Critical Thinking and the Curriculum," *National Forum* 65 (1985): 28–31.

5. McPeck, *Critical Thinking,* p. 8.

6. Paul, "Teaching Critical Thinking."

7. Richard Paul, "Critical Thinking in North America: A New Theory of Knowledge, Learning and Literacy," *Argumentation* 3 (1989): 197–235.

8. Matthew Lipman, "Critical Thinking: What Can It Be?" *Educational Leadership* (September 1987): 38–43.

9. Harvey Siegel, *Educating Reason: Rationality, Critical Thinking and Education* (New York: Routledge, 1988), p. 32.

10. Cf. my paper, "The Problem of Defining Critical Thinking," in *The Generalizability of Critical Thinking*, ed. S. P. Norris (New York: The Teacher's College Press, 1991).

11. Cited by Richard Paul in "Dialogical Thinking: Critical Thought Essential to the Acquisition of Rational Knowledge and Passions," in his *Critical Thinking: What Every Person Needs to Survive in a Rapidly Changing World* (Rohnert Park, CA: Center for Critical Thinking and Moral Critique, 1990), p. 215. His reference is to C. Wright Mills's *The Marxist* (New York: Dell, 1962).

12. Cf. Sharon Bailin, *Achieving Extraordinary Ends: An Essay on Creativity* (Dordrecht, Holland: Kluwer, 1988).

13. M. Scott Peck, *The Road Less Traveled* (New York: Simon and Schuster, 1970), p. 62.

14. Both Michael Scriven and Richard Paul have made this point for many years, and I owe my awareness of it to their persistence.

15. Howard Kahane, *Logic and Contemporary Rhetoric*, 1st ed. (Belmont, CA: Wadsworth, 1970) p. vii.

16. Ralph H. Johnson and J. Anthony Blair, "The Current State of Informal Logic/Critical Thinking," *Informal Logic* 9 (1987): 148.

17. In this paper, I have not bothered with the distinction that is to be drawn between inference and implication. Cf. my "Logic Naturalized: Recovering a Tradition," in *Argumentation: Across the Lines of Discipline*, eds., Frans H. van Eemeren, Rob Grootendorst, J. Anthony Blair, and Charles Willard (Dordrecht, Holland: Foris Publications, 1987), pp. 47–56.

18. Ralph H. Johnson and J. Anthony Blair, *Logical Self-Defense*, 2nd ed. (Toronto: McGraw-Hill Ryerson, 1983).

19. C. L. Hamblin, *Fallacies* (London: Methuen, 1970). For a critique of Hamblin's doctrine and its variant, cf. my "Acceptance is Not Enough: A Critique of Hamblin," *Philosophy and Rhetoric* 23 (1990): 271–87.

20. In my view, fallacy theory represents a perfectly valid theory of criticism, and I have so argued in "The Blaze of Her Splendors; A Defense of Fallacy Theory," *Argumentation* 1 (1987): 239–52, and in "Massey on Fallacy and Informal Logic: A Reply," *Synthese* 80 (1989): 407–26.

21. For a discussion of the Principle of Neutrality, cf. Johnson and Blair, *Logical Self-Defense*, pp. 215–16. For the origin of this principle, cf. Robert J. Fogelin, "Charitable Reconstruction and Logical Neutrality," *Informal Logic Newsletter,* 4 (1981), 2–5.

22. For a discussion of the Principle of Discrimination, cf. Johnson and Blair, *Logical Self-Defense*, pp. 214–15. The origins of this principle are not clear. Scriven proposes something very much like it in his *Reasoning* (New York: McGraw-Hill, 1976) but he discusses it under the rubric of the Principle of Charity. The first to so name it as a principle (so far as I am aware) was Professor Robert Binkley of the University of Western Ontario in the *London Close Reasoner,* 1979–1980, portions of which appeared in the Examples Supplement of *Informal Logic Newsletter,* Vol. 2. (*The London Close Reasoner* was a supplement to a logic course that Binkley was teaching at that time.)

5 Education and the Fostering of Rationality[1]

HARVEY SIEGEL

In these days of educational reform—which days seem to be always upon us, either in virtue of our desire to try something new, or to return to practices and aims once rejected but now seen as tried and true—much is made of the notion of critical thinking as a target of such reform. How to understand this notion, however, and how to conceive of its place in education, is more than a little unclear. What is critical thinking? What is it to be a critical thinker? What is the role of critical thinking in education? What is its role in inquiry? Is that role constant across disciplines, or do different disciplines utilize alternative and incompatible critical techniques? If the latter, then how can critical thinking function as a general educational ideal?

In what follows I hope to shed some light on these and other questions concerning critical thinking. I shall present a conception of critical thinking according to which critical thinking is very closely linked to the notions of *reasons* and *rationality*. I shall argue that critical thinking, so conceived, is rightly regarded as an educational ideal which is general and relevant to all disciplines. While not denying that disciplines differ in their aims, criteria, principles of assessment, or techniques of inquiry,

I shall argue nevertheless that critical thinking is rightly conceived as an ideal that transcends disciplinary boundaries and that unifies and makes sense of the melange of discipline-bound activities and curricula that we know as education. After clarifying the notion of critical thinking and its place in education and as an educational ideal, I shall illustrate its impact on the disciplines by considering its role in science education. I shall conclude, finally, by suggesting that critical thinking, contrary to the familiar distinction drawn at the outset, is an ideal which is both new *and* tried and true.[2]

What Is Critical Thinking?

When we say that we want our students to be critical thinkers, or that we want our educational efforts to foster critical thinking, what exactly do we mean? Any sort of systematic answer to these questions requires that we focus on *reasons* and their role in thinking. To say of an episode of thinking that it constitutes critical thinking is to say something about its responsiveness to relevant reasons or rational considerations. Similarly, to say of a student that she is a critical thinker is to say that her thinking is generally carried out in accordance with, and adequately reflects due and proper consideration of, matters which bear relevantly on the rational resolution of whatever her thinking concerns. Critical thinking is thinking which adequately reflects relevant reasons; a critical thinker is one whose thinking is similarly reflective of reasons. We can say, in short, that a critical thinker is one who is *appropriately moved by reasons*, and that critical thinking is thinking which appropriately reflects the power and convicting force of reasons.

This conception of critical thinking—the "reasons" conception—places reasons at its center; taking critical thinking as an important educational notion places reasons at the center of our conception of the nature and purpose of education. We might even go so far as to say that critical thinking is properly regarded as a fundamental educational ideal which informs the entire range of our educational activities and aspirations. On such a view reasons are central to our educational efforts, and those efforts are conceived as having as their ultimate aim the fostering of rationality. But what is it to be "appropriately moved by reasons?" Again, but in more detail: what is it to be a critical thinker? According to the reasons conception, critical thinking involves two essential components: skills and abilities of reason assessment, and the "critical spirit."

Reason Assessment

The first component of critical thinking involves skills and abilities of *reason assessment.* For students to be critical thinkers, they must be able to evaluate the ability of considerations offered as reasons to provide warrant or justification for the conclusions, claims, and judgments for which the considerations are offered as reasons. Considerations offered as reasons sometimes constitute genuine reasons for the claims and judgments they are alleged to support; sometimes, however, putative reasons fail to afford support for those claims and judgments. Some genuine reasons offer only weak support; others offer strong or even conclusive justifications. For example, the putative reason

(1) The Bible says so

offers no support for the claim

(2) The Bible is the divine word of God

because (1) assumes what it attempts to establish: namely, that the Bible is a reliable source of information concerning its own authorship. If the Bible is not the divine word of God, then the fact that the Bible says of itself that it is the divine word of God offers no warrant at all for the claim that it is—any more than this paper, if it said of itself that it is the divine word of God, would afford any warrant for the claim that the author of this paper is not Siegel, but God. In general, self-declarations of divinity afford no warrant for the divinity of such declarations; if we seek warrant for (2) we must look elsewhere for reasons which warrant (2)—say, to circumstances surrounding the authorship of the Bible that tend to rule out human (or other nondivine) authorship. (1), then, is a putative reason for (2) which fails to provide any reason for believing (2). A critical thinker must be sufficiently adept at reason assessment to recognize the failure of (1) to count as a reason for, or genuinely warrant, (2).

This first example illustrates the case in which a putative reason fails to constitute any sort of reason at all, and fails to afford any warrant at all, for the claim it alleges to support. Many putative reasons do offer some support for judgments and claims, however; such putative reasons are genuine reasons. In such cases, the task of the critical thinker is to judge the strength of the warrant afforded by the reason for the conclusion, the degree to which the reason supports the relevant judgment or claim. For example,

(3) *Smith, a Nobel Prize winner in physics, teaches at the University of Miami;*

supports, but only weakly supports,

(4) *The University of Miami has an excellent undergraduate program in physics;*

but (3) very strongly supports

(5) *The University of Miami physics faculty includes at least one Nobel Prize winner.*[3]

(3) supports (5) very strongly, although not conclusively: it is possible, for example, that Smith teaches in the chemistry depart-

ment but that her research overlaps chemistry and physics sufficiently that she won the prize in physics; similarly, it is possible that a researcher of Smith's stature enjoys a university appointment and has no official tie to the physics department. These possibilities (and others like them) are sufficient to establish that (3) does not *guarantee* (5); it is possible for (3) to be true and (5) false. Nevertheless, (3) strongly supports (5): if Smith in fact teaches at the University of Miami and has won the Nobel Prize in physics, then it is quite likely that the University of Miami's physics faculty includes at least one Nobel Prize winner.

The relationship between (3) and (4), however, is different. (3) offers some support for (4): the fact that the University of Miami has such an eminent physicist as Smith on the faculty provides some reason to think that there are other high quality physicists at the University of Miami (if not, why would Smith stay?), and that at least some of them, perhaps Smith herself, teach undergraduates. However, it may be that the University of Miami has neglected undergraduate physics instruction for graduate and postgraduate activity; it may be that an eminent figure such as Smith does not teach at all, let alone teach undergraduates, but rather devotes her time entirely to research. We could embellish the example further if we wished, but such embellishment would be unnecessary for present purposes. The point is simply that (3) supports both (4) and (5), and is a reason for both, but supports them to different degrees. (3) strongly supports (5), but only weakly, or at least less strongly, supports (4). To recognize this, a critical thinker must be able to assess the degree to which a reason supports or warrants a claim or judgment; he must be able, that is, to evaluate the power of reasons to warrant conclusions. He must be able to tell whether a putative reason offers any justification at all for a claim or judgment, and if so, how much support it offers. A critical thinker must, that is, be able competently to assess the power and convicting force of reasons. This is what is involved in the reason assessment component of critical thinking.

What must the critical thinker master in order to be a competent evaluator of reasons? How does he know that (1) does not support (2) at all, that (3) weakly supports (4), and that (3) strongly supports (5)? The short answer is that the critical thinker must master a variety of *principles of reason assessment.* He must know, understand, and know how to apply a variety of such principles.

Principles of reason assessment come in all shapes and sizes. Consider, for example, the judgment that (1) does not support or constitute a reason for (2). (1) fails to support (2) because it begs the question: (1) supports (2) only if one thinks that the fact that the Bible says so (says of itself that it is the divine word of God) in some measure establishes the truth of what it says (that it is the divine word of God). But saying so establishes the truth of what is said only if one has some reason for thinking that its utterances are reliable, and the main reason for thinking that those utterances are reliable is exactly that the Bible is alleged to be divinely authored. If divinely authored, then the fact that the Bible says of itself that it is the divine word of God does provide reason—very strong reason indeed, given our conception of God—for thinking that what the Bible says is true, for thinking that it is in fact divinely authored. But if not divinely authored (or otherwise authoritatively authored with respect to questions concerning the divinity of authorship), then (1) fails to provide any reason for (2). (1) supports (2), then, only insofar as we assume or have reason to think that (2) is true. (1)'s status as a reason for (2) rests, then, on assuming the truth of (2). But then (1)'s status as a reason for (2) depends upon assuming exactly the point (1) is supposed to establish: (1) constitutes a genuine reason for (2) only insofar as we antecedently accept (2). This is exactly the fallacy known by logicians as begging the question: assuming in one's premises the very point at issue that one's premises are supposed to establish, or for which they are supposed to constitute reasons. Here we appeal to a principle of reason assessment to assess the ability of (1) to support (2), and we find, when doing so, that (1) fails to constitute a reason for (2). The principle in question might be stated as

(P) *Putative reasons which beg the question, which as-*
sume the very point for which they are offered as sup-
port, fail to warrant or to constitute (good) reasons for
that point.

Notice that this principle is entirely subject-neutral. It does not presuppose specialized knowledge of any discipline or field, nor is its application restricted to any selected field. Begging the question is as much a fallacy in history as it is in chemistry, in photography as much as in deciding whether to vote for Jesse Helms in the next election. Some principles of reason assessment, then, are general and subject-neutral. These are the principles studied by the field of logic—both formal and informal—and constitute one major type of principle of reason assessment.

Other principles of reason assessment are subject-specific. To know that

(6) *The battery is dead*

counts as a reason for

(7) *The car won't start,*

one must know something about cars and the workings of internal combustion engines (in particular, that they rely upon energy supplied by the battery in order to start, and that if a battery is dead it cannot supply that energy). Similarly, to know that

(8) *Her skin is yellow*

counts as a reason for

(9) *Her liver is not functioning properly,*

one must know something about human anatomy and physiology (concerning the nature of jaundice and the function of the liver).

The point here is simply that some principles of reason assessment apply only in specialized domains, and require specialized knowledge. Principles of reason assessment can be either subject-neutral or subject-specific. To the extent that a student is a critical thinker, she knows, understands, and knows how to apply both sorts of principles of reason assessment. Critical thinking, consequently, is wrongly construed as either entirely subject-neutral or entirely subject-specific. It is both. Arguments over whether it is one or the other, then, are not particularly enlightening or important.[4] Similar remarks apply to those who urge that critical thinking is thinking which is context-dependent, rather than context-independent: critical thinking is sometimes context-dependent, and sometimes not.[5]

The main point here is simply that critical thinking centrally involves reason assessment, and that a student is a critical thinker only insofar as she is a competent assessor of the power and convicting force of reasons. To be so competent, she must have an intellectual and functional mastery of a large and disparate variety of principles of reason assessment.

The Critical Spirit

Suppose that a student is able to assess reasons competently. Is he then a critical thinker? No. Competent reason assessment is a necessary, but not a sufficient, condition of critical thinking. To be a critical thinker one must not only be a competent assessor of reasons; one must also possess a *critical spirit.*

The ability to assess reasons is not sufficient for critical thinking, for it is easy to imagine people who are quite competent at reason assessment, but who fail to exercise that competence. The case of the brilliant professor who gets fooled by the used car salesperson is one stereotype of such a person; a sophist is another; a politician who uses her skills of reasoning to favor her own ends or to protect her basic principles from critical assessment is still another. In all these cases, the person in question fails to utilize her critical abilities in ways which fairly treat the subject matter at hand.

The critical thinker, in contrast, is one who not only has highly developed skills of reason assessment, but is also *disposed* to utilize them in a non–self-interested way. He has a tendency, and a willingness, to demand reasons and evidence for judgments and actions under consideration; he has a disposition to question even—perhaps especially—his own most fundamental beliefs and attitudes. He has certain habits of mind, and a certain sort of *character:* namely, one which takes as central the demand, and quest, for reasons, and which manifests a desire to conform belief, judgment, and action to the results of the fairminded evaluation of reasons. He respects reasons and lives his life accordingly; his life manifests a love of reason.

A person who does not have the dispositions, habits of mind and character traits constitutive of the critical spirit does not qualify as a critical thinker, however adept at reason assessment he might be. Similarly, a person with the critical spirit, but without the ability to assess reasons, also fails to be a critical thinker. Both components of critical thinking—the reason assessment component, and the critical spirit component—are necessary for critical thinking; they are only jointly sufficient. So understood, the ideal of critical thinking is the ideal of a certain sort of *person* as much as a certain sort of thinking.[6]

Critical Thinking as an Educational Ideal

To take critical thinking as a fundamental educational ideal is to place reasons, and rationality, at the center of our educational conceptions and endeavors. In striving to foster critical thinking, we are striving to foster both skills of reason assessment and the critical spirit, to bring about a certain sort of person, with certain sorts of dispositions and character traits, as well as a certain sort of education. This befits a philosophical characterization of a fundamental educational ideal, since education fundamentally involves the persons we strive to educate, and our best hopes for those persons. It involves, that is to say, our ideals of the educated person.[7]

But the ideal sketched thus far is not yet entirely clear. I have argued that the critical thinker is one who is appropriately moved by reasons and have divided this conception into two components: the ability to assess reasons and a critical spirit. We must ask next how each of these components relates to the characterization of critical thinking in terms of being "appropriately moved by reasons." Doing so will force the recognition of an ambiguity concerning that phrase. Treatment of this ambiguity will force the drawing of a distinction which will further clarify the reasons conception of critical thinking.

Two Dimensions of Being Appropriately Moved by Reasons

What is it to be "appropriately moved by reasons"? There are, I think, two different aspects of being so moved, which can be isolated and identified by emphasizing each of the first two words of that phrase in turn.

To be *appropriately* moved by reasons is to have one's beliefs, judgments and actions conform to the degree of support afforded them by reasons. In the context of our earlier examples, I am appropriately moved by reasons if I do not believe (2) on the basis of (1); if I judge (4) to be somewhat likely on the basis of (3); and if I confidently act consistently with (5) on the basis of (3). In each of these cases, I am *appropriately* moved because my belief, judgment and action is shaped and controlled by the power of the (putative) reasons in question to warrant the relevant beliefs, judgments and actions. In contrast, if I believe (2) on the basis of (1), and thus do not recognize that (1) begs the question (or recognize it but do not care), I would be *in*appropriately moved by reasons, in that my belief does not conform to or adequately reflect the force of the reasons offered in support of that belief.[8] The general point concerning appropriateness is this: reasons stand in certain evidential or probative relationships to the beliefs, judgments and actions for which they are reasons; reasons have *probative* or *evidential force*. To be *appropriately* moved by reasons is to believe, judge and act in accordance with the probative force possessed by one's reasons. Here the fundamental task of the critical thinker is to assess accurately the probative force of reasons. What one is assessing, when one is assessing reasons, is the probative force of those reasons. This is the role of the reason assessment component of critical thinking.

This component is not sufficient for critical thinking, however, because (as we have seen) I may realize that (1) fails to support (2) but believe it anyway; I may realize that (3) strongly supports (5), believe (3), yet fail to act as if (5) were true. In such cases my powers of reason assessment are functioning properly, but I fail to conform my belief, judgment, and action to the probative force of the reasons I have adequately assessed. Here I fail to be appropriately *moved* by reasons. To be appropriately so moved, I must *be moved* appropriately: I must not only recognize the probative force of reasons; I must also recognize the *normative impact* of reasons. That is, I must actually conform my beliefs, actions, and judgments to the strength of relevant reasons. The critical spirit can and should be seen as that component of critical thinking which sees to it that one is *affected* and *influenced* appropriately by the probative force of reasons. One recognizes and is open to the normative impact of reasons insofar as one is disposed to conform belief, judgment and action to the probative force of reasons, and insofar as one has a character such that one typically is, and seeks to be, appropriately moved by them.

There are, then, two dimensions of being "appropriately moved by reasons." One must be *appropriately* moved by reasons; and one must be appropriately *moved* by reasons. These two dimensions are captured by distinguishing between the *probative force* and the *normative impact* of reasons.[9] Reasons have both probative force and normative impact; the critical thinker is appropriately moved by reasons insofar as she recognizes, and conforms to, both aspects of reasons. Both aspects of reasons are crucial to being appropriately moved by them.

Justifying the Ideal

There is more to say about the justification of critical thinking as an educational ideal than I can say here.[10] But there are two points worth noting. First, there is a strong and obvious *pragmatic* justification for regarding critical thinking as an educational ideal. Students who are critical thinkers—as several of the contributors to this volume have argued—are in a much better position to defend themselves from the hoards of unscrupulous advertisers, ideologues, and other manipulators of their beliefs than students who are not. Students who are critical thinkers stand to gain more from their courses than students who are not. The self-sufficiency resulting from critical thinking can plausibly be expected to enhance the pursuit and enjoyment of respectable and satisfying careers (and lives). In general, there are powerful pragmatic reasons for regarding critical thinking as an educational ideal: the results of an education informed by the ideal can reasonably be thought to be quite salutary. When one takes into account the current, seemingly endless, "crisis" in education in the United States and elsewhere (on which more below), it is difficult to conceive of a redirection of education with more potential for desirable practical effects than a redirection driven by the ideal of critical thinking.

Second, there is a powerful *moral* justification for regarding critical thinking as a fundamental educational ideal. For critical thinking is the only educational ideal which takes as central the fostering of autonomy and independent judgment which are basic to treating students with respect. Insofar as treating students with respect involves respecting their independent judgment and autonomy, any educational ideal which treats students with respect will centrally involve the ideal of critical thinking. Morally acceptable educational efforts must strive to empower students to direct, ever more competently, their beliefs, actions, and lives. Critical thinking is the relevant agent of empowerment, and as such, it has important moral dimensions. Indeed, education for critical thinking is morally required, for it is the only sort of education which treats students with respect and which takes such respect as central. Critical thinking is an educational ideal which rejects indoctrination and which places education on a firm moral footing; as such, the ideal enjoys a powerful moral justification.[11]

Critical Thinking and the Language of Inquiry

Earlier we considered the generality of critical thinking; we recognized then that some principles of reason assessment are not general but are subject- or context-specific. Nevertheless, there is an important sense in which critical thinking is general and subject-neutral (in addition to the point that some principles of reason assessment are). I shall try to articulate that sense in terms of a "language of inquiry."

Inquiry is not univocal. We inquire into many different matters, in many different ways. Inquiry concerning the precise determination of the charge of an electron is conducted in quite a different way from that concerning the large-scale geometry of the universe; inquiry concerning the etiology of AIDS involves techniques (e.g., of observation) and theories (e.g., of virology) quite different from inquiry concerning the values of cultures very different from our own. Similar remarks apply to inquiry concerning the virtues of presidential candidates and the defects of cars that won't start. All of these cases are cases of inquiry; all of them utilize very different techniques. Understood in terms of *techniques* of inquiry, there is no common *method* of inquiry.[12]

Nevertheless, there are some aspects of inquiry which are constant across different types of inquiry. For example, in all the scientific examples just mentioned, observations—whether made with the naked eye, telescopes, electron microscopes, or glasses—are integral ingredients of each of the several inquiries. Moreover, these observations play similar roles in these various inquiries: for instance, we make observations to test hypotheses concerning the geometry of space-time, the structure of the HIV virus, the charge of an electron, the meaning of a foreign cultural practice, the car's failure to start, and the desirability of a political candidate. In all these cases, observations provide reasons for thinking that our hypotheses and theories are true, worthy of belief, acceptable, not worth believing, not worth further investigation, or false. Other aspects of the activity of inquiry—hypothesizing, theorizing, inferring, imagining, testing—also provide reasons for conclusions concerning the objects of inquiry. In all these sorts of inquiries, then, there is a common structure—one that defines the effort to inquire responsibly and effectively into the matter at hand—and a common language as well. The common language is just the language of critical thinking, or, more simply, the language of reasons.

The language of inquiry, I am claiming, is the language of reasons. It is the totality of our linguistic apparatus relevant to the conducting of responsible inquiry and the establishment of warrantable and warranted hypotheses. Specific linguistic conventions might be adopted by investigators in disparate areas of inquiry, just as different domains of inquiry may differ with respect to relevant principles of inquiry and assessment. For example, a physicist might say that she "sees" neutrinos in a way in which nonspecialists cannot[13]; a mathematician, a biologist, and a nonscientist might mean different things when each claims to have proved something; members of different schools of literary theory may disagree over whether an author's intentions count as evidence concerning the meaning of a work. Similarly, *empathy* may be part of the language of inquiry of the cultural anthropologist but not of the particle physicist; *intention* may be part of the language of inquiry of the historian but not of the molecular biologist; *cell* may be part of the language of inquiry of the biologist but not of the psychologist or cosmologist. With respect to these and similar considerations, we can speak of different languages (and principles) of inquiry operating in different disciplines and inquiry situations.

Nevertheless, inquiry can and should be conceived as fundamentally the same activity across contexts: namely, the activity of investigating matters relevant to responsible belief, judgment and action. Inquiry is in this basic way univocal. It involves the creation and critical examination of reasons and their power to warrant hypotheses; and it results, ideally, in belief, judgment, and action which conform to the results of such critical examination.[14] The language of inquiry is similarly univocal. Just as there can be a univocal scientific method which stands alongside and makes sense of diverse techniques of scientific investigation,[15] so too there can be a univocal language of inquiry, which stands alongside and makes sense of diverse "languages" and principles which function in diverse disciplines and areas of inquiry. The univocal language of inquiry is the language of critical thinking—the language of reasons—which empowers us to comprehend diverse disciplinary activity as inquiry in specialized disciplinary settings, to make sense of the fruits of discipline-bound inquiry, to extend the results of such inquiry beyond the bounds of its narrow disciplinary home, and to evaluate critically those results in a broader extradisciplinary context. All this is possible only because there is a language of inquiry, and a conception of inquiry which makes sense of that language, which extends far beyond the "languages" of inquiry utilized in the disparate disciplinary arenas in which specialized inquiry takes place. The task for investigators of the many "languages of inquiry" is just to relate those languages to the language of reasons.[16]

Reasons and Science Education

If the account of critical thinking offered thus far is correct, then it should tell us something about education and its proper pursuit in standard curriculum areas. I believe it does. In this section I apply the reasons conception of critical thinking to science education in order to illustrate the application to curriculum more generally.[17]

Taking critical thinking as a fundamental educational ideal has fundamental ramifications for science education and for our conception of the science curriculum. Science education, in this light, involves primarily the ability of science students to evaluate, appreciate the force of, and be moved by reasons in science. *Reasons in science* is, in this view, the key to science education.

To regard reasons as a key component of science education is to reject the view of science education that Schwab derides as a "rhetoric of conclusions"; it is also to reject the related view of science education, inspired by Kuhn, as one which aims at indoctrinating students into the reigning paradigm of the day.[18] It is rather to envision science education as trying to provide students with an understanding of the reasons we have for favoring one theory over another, for conducting this experiment rather than that, for constructing an experiment this way rather than in some other way, for interpreting results in one way rather than another, and so on. This sort of education calls for the active consideration and comparison of alternative, rival theories and hypotheses. It also calls for sustained, explicit attention to the methodology of scientific inquiry as a means of establishing the rational warrant of alternative claims and hypotheses.

A *critical* science education aims at fostering in students an understanding of the strengths and weaknesses of alternative hypotheses and methods of investigation; that is, an understanding of the reasons which ground our evaluations of those alternatives. A science student who has such understanding has an understanding of the criteria and principles which determine the character and strength of putative reasons in science. Such a student has a grasp of the way in which theoretical calculation, experimental design, and experimental result provide us with reasons for preferring one theory or hypothesis to another; she has, as well, an understanding of the principles of reason assessment utilized in science, which grounds the assessment of such reasons. In order to have this sort of understanding, she must have some understanding of the epistemology/philosophy of science, and a critical science education should include explicit and sustained attention to philosophical and methodological considerations which underlie scientific practice. Otherwise our student will have at best only a shallow understanding of why some particular experimental result strongly favors one theory, why another result only weakly favors a rival, or why another result fails to support some other rival at all. Philosophy of science consists in large part in the study of the warranting force of reasons in science. Issues concerning methodology, experimental design, confirmation, induction, falsification, the logic of science, explanation, progress, and the rationality of science all touch in more or less direct ways on the power of reasons to warrant scientific hypotheses.

A critical science education aims at empowering students to understand the rational status of scientific hypotheses and theories by providing an understanding of the principles and considerations which ground our assessment of those hypotheses and theories. An awareness of philosophical controversies concerning such considerations—for example, concerning the nature of explanation and the relevance of explanatory power to the rational evaluation of theory, or concerning the problem of induction and the confirmationist/falsificationist controversy over the ability of evidence positively to support theories—can only enhance the ability of students to understand the nature and warranting force of reasons in science. Thus the philosophy of science should be an integral part of the science curriculum, just as epistemology should be an integral part of the critical thinking curriculum more generally.[19]

A critical science education, then, rejects the Kuhnian suggestion that we should distort the history of science to hide major theoretical controversies and differences in conceptualization of scientific domains and of problems in need of investigation. It rejects the idea that the aim of science education is the production of students who believe the theories we tell them are "correct," and it rejects a science education which results in students who are blind to their own theoretical commitments. A critical science education, on the contrary, emphasizes the active consideration of alternative theories and hypotheses, the critical evaluation of those alternatives, and the philosophical considerations which underlie such evaluation. In all of this, the quest for an understanding of the nature and role of reasons in science is central.

In this respect, moreover, the language of inquiry in science is simply the language of reasons applied to various specialized scientific domains of research. For this reason, my suggestions concerning science education extend naturally to other curriculum areas. The focus on reasons in history is central to critical history education; the focus on reasons in literature is central to critical literature education; and so on. In all curriculum areas, an education which fosters critical thinking in those areas emphasizes the nature and role of reasons, the active consideration of alternative theoretical and critical perspectives, and the philosophical issues and concerns studied by the philosophy of the relevant discipline.[20] The philosophy of the relevant discipline informs our understanding of the principles governing the evaluation of reasons in that area. I hope, then, that my remarks concerning science education can be generalized to other curriculum areas. While there are surely differences between such areas—what counts as a reason in literature may well differ from what counts as a reason in biology, and the language with which such reasons are discussed and understood may differ equally as much—the language of inquiry and the quest for reasons is nevertheless central to inquiry, and to education, throughout the curriculum.

The Place of Reasons in Education

I conclude with a plea for the recognition of rationality, and its educational cognate, critical thinking, as a fundamental educational ideal; and for the recognition of the central role which philosophical theorizing concerning education should play in our conception and understanding of educational affairs.

One of the basic problems with education, and its scholarship, is the "fad" phenomenon: the rapid adoption and rejection of new, global educational panaceas. This is a phenomenon with which we are all only too familiar. A major explanation of this phenomenon is the failure of education to be informed by any enduring, underlying philosophical perspective. I should of course be delighted if the view I have argued for here came to constitute that enduring perspective. But wouldn't I be fooling myself if I thought that any philosophical view—even my own—will endure? Aren't there philosophical as well as educational fads?

Perhaps there are. Moreover, there is no question that critical thinking is in many respects a new idea, and that the contemporary critical thinking movement bears many of the marks of an educational fad. Nevertheless—to hark back to my introduction—I think that critical thinking is best regarded as an educational ideal which is both new *and* tried and true.

Critical thinking is undoubtedly in many respects a new educational idea. It is recognized and thought of as a movement— the critical thinking movement—and has been the subject of many national and international conferences, several new journals and newsletters, and a host of newly designed curricular materials. It has given rise, in turn, to an army of experts and authorities on the theory and practice of critical thinking. Grand promises for the virtues and benefits of making critical thinking central to our educational endeavors have also been made. In all this, critical thinking looks very much like another education fad and putative panacea. If it were just another fad, moreover, then I think we would have good inductive evidence concerning its power and potential for transforming and radically improving education. This evidence would not be in its favor.

However, critical thinking is not simply new. It is also an educational ideal with impressive philosophical credentials. Throughout the history of Western philosophy, major philosophers of education have articulated, endorsed and defended educational visions to which critical thinking has been central. Socrates is perhaps the clearest example of a philosopher who urged that education and society strive to imbue in all students and persons, to the greatest extent possible, the skills, dispositions and character traits constitutive of critical thinking. Plato similarly venerated critical thinking and rationality, although he was a bit less sanguine concerning the degree to which the ideal could be realized. Aristotle too championed rationality, both in theory and in practice, and uttered remarkably modern-sounding ideas concerning education's duty to develop character traits we now associate with the critical thinker. The great philosophers of the Middle Ages, no less than those of antiquity, similarly championed an education aimed at the fostering and development of rationality, believing it to be the requisite for a full realization of Christian faith. Locke, Hume, Kant, Rousseau, Mill, and other great figures of the modern and Enlightenment periods also venerated rationality and praised it as an educational aim, the realization of which would enable humans to achieve their full potential as rational beings. More recently, Bertrand Russell extolled and defended the virtues of an education in service of the ideal of critical thinking; and John Dewey developed a highly refined philosophy of education which placed rationality, reasons, and critical thinking at its center.[21] More recently still, R. S. Peters and his British associates endorsed a version of the ideal of critical thinking and placed reasons and rationality at the heart of their educational philosophy. And the preeminent contemporary philosopher of education, Israel Scheffler, conceives of critical thinking as being "of the first importance in the conception and organization of educational activities."[22] In short, from Socrates to the present day, philosophers of education have by and large championed rationality and critical thinking as fundamental educational desiderata. Again, critical thinking is an ideal which is both new *and* tried and true.

Of course, critical thinking's being tried and true among philosophers is quite different from its being tried and true for having been tested in the crucible of educational practice. It has not been so tested. This failure to ground educational practice in enduring philosophical thought is one main reason for the sorry state of contemporary education, and for the ubiquity of the fad phenomenon. Indeed, the depressingly enduring crisis in education seems to be mainly a function of education's failure to ground itself on appropriate ideals: its failure to treat students with respect; its failure to foster rationality, independent judgment, and critical thinking. Not only has education in the main failed to foster these traits, it has failed to recognize them as traits it ought to foster. This recognition is basic to education for critical thinking; it is also basic to the revitalization of contemporary education. Consequently, this failure is also a reason for being excited about the way in which critical thinking is new. Perhaps, as a faddish educational movement, critical thinking will have its chance to inform educational practice. If so, then all of us will have the chance to see what philosophers of education have seen and said for so long.

Notes

1. This paper is a modestly revised version of a paper entitled "The Role of Reasons in (Science) Education," which was presented as the

1988 Robert Jackson Memorial Lecture at the School of Education, Dalhousie University, and subsequently published in William Hare, ed., *Reason in Teaching and Education* (Halifax: Dalhousie University School of Education, 1989), pp. 5–21. I am grateful to Hare and to the Dalhousie University School of Education for permission to publish the paper here. The paper also appeared in M. Weinstein and W. Oxman-Michelli, eds., *Critical Thinking: Language and Inquiry across the Disciplines* (Upper Montclair, N.J.: Institute for Critical Thinking, Montclair State College, 1989), pp. 7–21.

2. Some of what follows draws upon my *Educating Reason: Rationality, Critical Thinking, and Education* (London: Routledge, 1988). I refer the reader to this source for a more systematic treatment of critical thinking, its relationship to rationality, its status as an educational ideal, and its ramifications for educational policy and practice and for the curriculum.

3. I am assuming here that (3) is itself justified; if it is not, then of course it fails to support either (4) or (5).

4. The main protagonists here are John McPeck (subject-specific) and Robert Ennis (subject-neutral). I discuss the debate between them in more detail in my *Educating Reason*. For a more recent treatment, see my "The Generalizability of Critical Thinking," *Educational Philosophy and Theory*, 23(1) (1990): 18–30.

5. Here I am thinking mainly of Matthew Lipman, who emphasizes in his account of critical thinking its context-dependency. See, for example, Lipman, "The Concept of Critical Thinking," *Teaching Thinking and Problem Solving* 10(3) (May-June 1988): 5–7.

6. This discussion of the critical spirit is far too brief to be adequate. For further amplification, see my *Educating Reason*.

7. Here too my discussion is unduly brief. For further consideration of critical thinking as an educational ideal, see my *Educating Reason*.

8. My belief in this case fails to be "proportional to the evidence," or, more accurately, fails to be proportional to an adequate evaluation of the evidence. The general position I am sketching is *evidentialist;* I regret that space forbids consideration of the many epistemological niceties concerning the desirability of conforming belief to the evidence and those concerning the ethics of belief. For a recent, sophisticated state-

ment of evidentialism, see Richard Feldman and Earl Conee, "Evidentialism," *Philosophical Studies* **48** (1985): 15–34.

9. I first drew this distinction in "Teaching, Reasoning, and Dostoyevsky's *The Brothers Karamazov*," in Philip Jackson and Sophie Haroutunian-Gordon, eds., *From Socrates to Software: The Teacher as Text and the Text as Teacher* (Eighty-Eighth Yearbook of the National Society for the Study of Education, 1989), pp. 115–34.

10. Once again I must beg the reader's indulgence, and refer her to my *Educating Reason*, chapter 3, for a more sustained discussion.

11. See my *Educating Reason*, chapters 3 and 5 for further discussion.

12. The distinction between methods of inquiry versus techniques of inquiry is drawn, in connection with the rationality of science, in my "What Is the Question Concerning the Rationality of Science?," *Philosophy of Science* **52** (1985): 517–37.

13. See Dudley Shapere, "The Concept of Observation in Science and Philosophy," *Philosophy of Science* **49** (1982): 485–525.

14. Thus it would be a mistake to sharply distinguish creative and critical thinking. See here Sharon Bailin's excellent *Achieving Extraordinary Ends: An Essay on Creativity* (Dordrecht, Holland: Martinus Nijhoff, 1988).

15. As I argue in "What Is the Question Concerning the Rationality of Science?."

16. And to epistemology, i.e. to the general philosophical study of the power and convicting force of reasons. Here the close relationship between critical thinking and epistemology should be apparent. I develop this theme in "Epistemology, Critical Thinking, and Critical Thinking Pedagogy," *Argumentation* **3** (1989): 127–40.

17. In this section I borrow from my *Educating Reason*, chapter 6, which discusses in detail the differences between "critical" and "uncritical" science education, and from my article "The Rationality of Science, Critical Thinking, and Science Education," *Synthese* **80** (1989): 9–41.

18. The relevant texts here are Joseph J. Schwab, *The Teaching of Science as Enquiry* (Cambridge: Harvard University Press, 1962), and Thomas S. Kuhn, *The Structure of Scientific Revolutions* (Chicago:

University of Chicago Press, 1970). For discussion of both, see my *Educating Reason*, chapter 6.

19. See my "Epistemology, Critical Thinking, and Critical Thinking Pedagogy."

20. See Israel Scheffler, "Philosophies-of and the Curriculum," in J. F. Doyle, ed., *Educational Judgments* (London: Routledge & Kegan Paul, 1973), pp. 209–18.

21. This somewhat unusual interpretation of Russell's philosophy of education is, I think, conclusively secured by William Hare. See his "Russell's Contribution to Philosophy of Education," *Russell* 7 (1987): 25–41. Dewey's understanding of these notions, and the epistemology underlying them, differs markedly from my own, however. For brief comment, see my remarks on Dewey in *Educating Reason*.

22. Scheffler, *Reason and Teaching* (London: Routledge & Kegan Paul, 1973), p. 1.

6 Creativity, Critical Reasoning, and the Problem of Content-Oriented Education

ROBERT J. STERNBERG

A conundrum in our society—and in others—concerns the relation between schooling and the development of creativity in children. By *schooling*, I refer to all levels of formal education from first grade through college. Whereas the conventional wisdom accepts that schooling fosters the development of intelligence, it seems also to accept or at least speculate that schooling may do at least as much to undermine creativity as to foster it.

It is difficult to assess the relation between schooling and creativity without a fairly well-specified theory of creativity, which is perhaps why analyses of the relation between schooling and creativity have not gone far beyond recitations of conventional wisdom. In this chapter, I will attempt to go beyond the conventional wisdom by describing a new theory of creativity and simultaneously analyzing whether modal schooling as it exists in the United States, and many other countries, fosters, impedes, or is indifferent to the development of creative thought and behavior.[1]

My theory can be characterized as a market model of creativity. The basic notion underlying the model is that in any kind of investment, one wishes to "buy low and sell high." In other

113

words, the greatest creative contributions can generally be made either within areas or with ideas that at a given time are undervalued—people in general have not yet realized their importance, and hence there is a potential for significant advance. The more in favor a paradigm—or stock—is, the less potential there is for appreciation in value, because the paradigm or ideas within the paradigm are already valued. A theory of creativity needs to account for how people can generate or recognize undervalued assets, and for who will actually pursue them rather than join the crowd. Contributions made within reigning paradigms are of some value in their own right, but they are unlikely to alter significantly existing ways of thinking about things.

We hold that there are six facets that converge toward producing creative ideation and behavior—certain aspects of intelligence, intellectual style, knowledge, personality, motivation, and environmental context. This chapter will be divided into six sections, based upon this division of the origins of creativity.

Intelligence

Two main aspects of intelligence are viewed as relevant to creativity. These aspects, based on my triarchic theory of human intelligence, are the ability to define and redefine problems, and the ability to think insightfully.[2]

Problem Definition and Redefinition

Major creative innovations often involve the seeing of an old problem in a new way. For example, Albert Einstein redefined the field of physics in proposing relativity theory, Noam Chomsky redefined the field of linguistics by distinguishing linguistic deep structures from linguistic surface structures, Jean Piaget redefined the field of cognitive development by conceiving of the child as a young scientist, Pablo Picasso redefined part of the field of art through his cubist perspective on the world, and Victor

Hugo helped redefine French literature by his novels that described the world as perceived by the lower classes. These major redefinitions of issues are rarely obvious in prospect, although they may seem apparent or even self-evident in retrospect. Often, the best problem redefinitions are the ones people feel like kicking themselves for not having seen all along when they should have been obvious.

In order to redefine a problem, one has to have the option of defining a problem in the first place. Schools only rarely give students this luxury. Tests typically pose the problems that students are to solve. Students do not pose the problems for themselves. And if the student's definition of a problem is different from the test constructor's, the student is simply marked wrong. Teachers typically structure their classes in ways that involve their setting the problems to be solved, with the students then solving these problems. Of course, textbooks work the same way: Students are presented with problems, often at the end of a chapter, and are asked to solve these problems. Even when papers or projects are assigned, the teacher will often specify the topic, and ask the student to work on this topic. Some teachers view themselves as more flexible, in that they allow students to define problems for themselves: The teachers then may proceed to mark down students whose definitions of a problem do not correspond to theirs.

In the thinking skills movement, we frequently hear of the need for schools to emphasize more heavily the teaching of problem-solving skills. Educators are then happy when students do not merely memorize facts, but rather, solve problems that use these facts. Certainly, there is much to be said for a problem-solving approach to education. But we need to recognize that creative individuals are often most renowned not for their solving of problems, but for their posing of the problems in the first place. They recognize significant and substantial problems, and choose to address these problems rather than less consequential ones. One only has to open almost any professional journal to find articles representing good problem-solving on bad, or at least fairly inconsequential, problems.

If we are to turn around schooling to emphasize creative problem definition and redefinition, we need to take some of the control from ourselves as teachers and to give it to students. We need them to take more responsibility for the problems they choose to solve, rather than taking most of this responsibility ourselves. The students will make mistakes, and generate attempts to solve inconsequential or even wrongly posed problems. But they will only learn from their mistakes, and if we do not give them the opportunity to make mistakes, then they will have no mistakes to learn from. Instead of giving children the problems, we need to let them find the problems that they are to solve. We need to help them develop their problem-definition and redefinition skills, not just their problem-solving skills.

Insight Skills

Insight skills are involved when people perceive a solution, usually to an ill-structured problem, where the solution is nonobvious and is high in quality. We have proposed a theory of insight whereby insights are of three kinds.[3]

The first kind involves seeing things in a stream of inputs that most people would not see. In other words, the individual is able to zero in on particularly relevant information for her purposes that is embedded in a stream of information, most of which is irrelevant. For example, the insightful detective (and possibly scientific or medical detective) sees clues to the solution of a mystery that most people would ignore. Sherlock Holmes, of course, is the prototypical example of an expert in this kind of insight.

The second kind of insight involves seeing how to combine disparate pieces of information whose connection is nonobvious and usually elusive. For example, the insightful detective is able to fit together the clues at the scene of a crime in a way that points toward one particular culprit as opposed to other, apparently plausible suspects. Similarly, a doctor needs to figure out how to put together information about a set of symptoms in order to diagnose a disease.

The third kind of insight involves seeing the nonobvious relevance of old information for a new problem. Creative analogies and metaphors are representative of this kind of insight. For example, the detective might remember a case he solved some years back where the pattern of events resembled that in a present case. A scientist might recall a similar problem from the past that lent itself to a certain methodology in pursuit of a solution.

Problems requiring insightful solution are almost always ill-structured, meaning that there is no one right path, or even several readily available paths, to solution. Rather, much of the difficulty in problem solution is figuring out what the steps to solution might be. Problems used in schools, however, are usually well structured, meaning that there is a path (or there are several clear paths) that guarantee a prompt and expedient solution. For example, in standardized tests, there is always a path that guarantees a "correct" solution: The examinee's problem is, in large part, to find that guaranteed path. Similarly, textbook problems are often posed so that there can be an answer key for the teacher that gives the "correct" answers. Problems such as these are unlikely to require insightful thinking, and hence to encourage creative thinking. One ends up trying to "psych out" the thought processes of the person who formulated the problem, rather than to generate one's own insightful thought processes.

Of course, creative innovations are not limited exclusively to well-structured problems. However, sometimes even problems that seem on their surface to be well structured are not, and it is their latent lack of structure that poses difficulty for those seeking to solve the problems. For example, many mathematicians have sought to prove Fermat's Last Theorem, all without success. On the surface, the problem may seem well structured: After all, all mathematicians know what the problem is. What they do not know, however, is how to pose the problem in a way that renders it solvable. Similarly, when Watson and Crick sought to find the structure of DNA, the nature of the problem was clear, but the way in which to solve it was not clear at all. Creative innovations tend to address ill-structured problems, not the well-structured ones we typically use in school settings. If we want students to think insightfully, we need to give them the opportunities to do so by increasing our use of ill-structured problems.

Intellectual Styles

Intellectual styles refer to how people choose to use, or exploit, their intelligence. Thus, styles concern not abilities, but how these abilities are utilized in day-to-day confrontations with the environment.

I have proposed elsewhere a theory of intellectual styles based upon a notion of "mental self-government."[4] The basic idea is that people need to govern themselves mentally, and that styles provide them with a way to do so. The ways in which people govern themselves are mirrors, at an internal level, of the kinds of government we see in the external world. Only that part of the theory of mental self-government that is relevant to creativity will be considered here.

The Legislative Style

One aspect of mental self-government is the set of functions government can serve. These can be classified as legislative, executive, and judicial. The legislative function is concerned with the creation of laws and regulations, the executive, with their implementation, and the judicial, with their evaluation.

Individuals have styles that correspond to these basic functions. A legislative individual is someone who enjoys formulating problems for herself, and creating new rule systems and ways of seeing things. An executive individual likes implementing the systems, rules, and tasks of others. And a judicial individual enjoys evaluating people, things, and rules. People do not have just a single style that they always use, regardless of task constraints. Rather, they have one or more preferred styles, which they seek to use whenever possible. For example, legislative people will seek out tasks and situations where they can structure what they are doing, rather than having it structured for them. And even in tasks and situations where the structure is given, they are likely to try to change what is given.

Creative people are likely to be those with a legislative proclivity. The reason, quite simply, is that creativity requires a person to see things in new ways, and people are more likely to see things in new ways if they want to do so. Others may have the ability to do so but not exploit it. On any number of occasions, for example, I have had students with the abilities to be highly creative, but without the legislative proclivity. As a result, they can be creative should they choose, but they don't choose.

Schooling rarely encourages the legislative proclivity. To the contrary, the executive style is much more heavily encouraged and rewarded. Students do well in school if they do as they are told, and work within the structures that are given to them. Standardized tests are the example par excellence of the rewarding of the executive style: Examinees are given a problem structure, and to succeed on the test, they need to work within that structure. If they depart from the structure, they are likely to be in trouble. Similarly, teachers rarely encourage students to depart from the framework, and even the views, the teachers themselves have. Because styles are at least somewhat flexible, people respond to the reward structure of the school, and are likely to shift in the direction of an executive style, even if it is not their natural proclivity.

The Global Style

Another aspect of intellectual style is the level at which one applies one's intellect. In government, one can deal with either global or local levels of government. For example, the federal level of government would be more global, and the civic level of government would be more local. Similarly, people have preferred levels for dealing with problems. Some like to deal with more local problems, others with more global ones.

Creative contributions are possible at both global and local levels. Moreover, almost any task requires some going back and forth between global and local levels. However, major creative contributions are likely to involve more global than local processing, if only because such contributions deal with big problems. Someone who does not wish to recognize the forest among the trees is unlikely to make major creative contributions. The person may be creative, but not in a way that changes the shape of a field or a problem.

Knowledge

In order to make a creative contribution to a field of knowledge, it is necessary to have knowledge about that field. Without such knowledge, one risks rediscovering what is already known. And without knowledge of the field, it is difficult for the individual to assess what the problems in the field are, and which are the important ones. Indeed, an important emphasis in cognitive psychology during the past ten years or so has been on the importance of knowledge to expertise.

Schools can scarcely be faulted for not making efforts to impart knowledge. Indeed, that seems to be their main function. Yet, I have reservations about the extent to which the knowledge they impart is likely to lead to creativity. My reservation has two bases.

First, there is a difference between knowledge and usable knowledge. Knowledge can be learned in a way that renders it inert: The knowledge is stored in the brain, but the individual is unable to use it. For example, almost every college undergraduate who majors in psychology takes a course in statistics as a part of that major. Yet, very few of the undergraduates who have taken statistics are able to use what they have learned in the design and analysis of scientific experiments. They are fine just so long as they are given highly structured problems in which it is obvious which statistical technique applies. But they have trouble when they have to figure out which technique to apply, and when. The context of knowledge acquisition is so different from the context of knowledge use that the knowledge is simply unavailable for use.

My experience with knowledge learned in statistics courses is, I believe, the rule rather than the exception. Students do not generally learn knowledge in a way that renders it useful to them. To the contrary, they are likely to forget much of what they learn soon after they are tested on it. We have all had the experience of studying for an exam, and then quickly forgetting what we studied. The information was learned to be useful in the context of a structured exam, and once the exam is finished, so is the use of the knowledge.

A second problem is that students are not taught in a way that makes clear to them why the information they are learning is important. Students do much better in learning if they believe that they can use what they learn. Study of a foreign language provides a good example. People who need to use it learn it. Those who don't need it rarely retain much of it. Unless we show students why what they are learning should matter to them, we cannot expect them to retain what they are taught. And often, I believe, we don't really know ourselves of what use what we are teaching to students will be to them.

Another concern we need to have about knowledge regards the trade-off that can develop between knowledge and flexibility. We have suggested that increased expertise in terms of knowledge in a given domain can often come at the expense of flexibility in that domain.[5] We can become so proceduralized with respect to a certain way of doing things that we forget that other ways are even possible. We can become entrenched, and have trouble going beyond a perspective on things that we have come to find to be very comfortable. Because creativity requires one to view things flexibly, there is a danger that with increasing knowledge, one will lose creativity by losing the ability to think flexibly about the domain in which one works. As someone who has worked with countless teachers in hundreds of schools, I have run into many teachers who are so self-satisfied and happy with the way they are doing things that they are closed to new ways of doing these things, or even to considering doing things that differ from what they are already doing.

On the one hand, I do not wish to underemphasize the importance of knowledge to creativity. On the other hand, I do want to emphasize the importance of the knowledge being usable, and of its being learned and used in a way that does not undermine one's flexibility. Often, we need to adopt the maintenance of flexibility as a goal self-consciously to be achieved. We might go to in-services, read new kinds of books, learn about a new domain of knowledge, seek to learn from our students, or whatever. If we want students to be creative, we have to model creativity, and we won't do it if we seek to turn students' minds into safe-deposit boxes in which we store our assorted and often undigested bits of knowledge.

Personality

Creative people seem to share certain personality attributes. Although one can probably be creative in the short term without these attributes, long-term creativity requires most of them. The attributes are tolerance of ambiguity, willingness to surmount obstacles and persevere, willingness to grow, willingness to take risks, and courage of one's convictions.

Tolerance of Ambiguity

In most creative endeavors, there is a period of time during which the individual is groping—trying to figure out what the pieces of the puzzle are, or how to put them together, or how to relate them to what she already knows. During this time period, the individual is likely to feel some anxiety, and possibly even alarm, because the pieces are not forming themselves into a creative solution to the problem being confronted. The creative individual needs to be able to tolerate this ambiguity, and to wait for the pieces to be balanced.

In many schools, most of the assignments students are given are due either the next day, or within a very short period of time. Individuals do not develop a tolerance of ambiguity, because they cannot afford to allot the time for a situation to be ambiguous. If an assignment is due in a day or two, ambiguities need quickly to be resolved. A good way to help students develop tolerance of ambiguity is to give them more long-term assignments, and then to encourage them to start thinking about the assignments early so that they are able to mull over whatever problems they face.

Willingness to Surmount Obstacles and Persevere

Almost every major creative thinker has surmounted obstacles at one time or another, and his willingness not to be derailed is a crucial element of his success. Confrontation of obstacles is almost a certainty in creative endeavor, because most creative endeavors threaten some kind of established and entrenched interest, and hence those representing such interests are likely to be threatened by what one is doing. Unless one can learn to face adversity, and to conquer it, one is unlikely to contribute creatively to the field in which one is working.

We need to learn to think of obstacles and the need to surmount them as part of the game, rather than as outside it. We should not think of obstacles as something we uniquely have, but as something that every creative person has. What differs is not whether creative people face obstacles, but how they face them.

I believe that schools provide fairly good proving grounds for learning to surmount obstacles, because so many of them seem to befall us while we are in school. But it is perhaps unfortunate that what schools teach us best, with respect to creativity, is how society is likely to get in the way of creativity, rather than to support it.

Willingness to Grow

When one has a creative idea, and is even able to get it accepted, one may find oneself highly rewarded for that idea. It then becomes difficult to move on. For one thing, the rewards for staying with the first idea are great. For another thing, one often has a deep-seated fear that one's next idea won't be as good as one's first one. Indeed, the phenomenon of regression toward the mean would suggest that subsequent ideas actually will not be as good—will regress toward the mean. In short, there is a fair amount of pressure to stay with what one has and knows. But creativity exhibited over prolonged periods of time requires one to go beyond that first creative idea, and even to see problems with what at one time may have seemed like a superb idea. I believe that schools often encourage growth, but usually not the kind of growth that will matter to creativity. The reason for this is that they do not encourage growth that requires students to take risks.

Willingness to Take Risks

A general principle of investment is that, on the average, greater return entails greater risk. For the most part, schools are not environments that are conducive to risk-taking. To the contrary, students are as often, or possibly more often than not, punished for risk-taking. Taking a course that is in a new area, or that is in an area of weakness, is likely to lead to a low grade, which in turn may dim one's future prospects. Risky responses on exams or in response to paper assignments are likely to be undertaken only with great trepidation, because of the fear that a low or failing grade may ruin one's chances of a good grade in the course. And there is usually some safe response to the situation that is at least good enough to generate the grade for which one is hoping. Many teachers are not themselves risk-takers—teaching is not a profession that is likely to attract the biggest risk-takers—and hence they may feel threatened by students who take large risks, especially if the teacher perceives them to be at his expense. The child who draws a purple tree, or who writes an essay on the psychology of thinking that explores how present-day schooling is inadequate, is taking a big risk, and few students are willing to take such risks. Unfortunately, their unwillingness to take risks has developed as a result of their socialization in the schools, which are environments that encourage conformity and often stereotypy of thinking.

Courage of One's Convictions and Belief
in Oneself

There are times in the lives of almost all creative people when they begin to doubt their ideas, and themselves as well. Their work may not be achieving the recognition it once achieved, or they may not yet have succeeded in getting recognition in the first place. At these times, it is difficult to maintain belief in one's ideas, and most of all, in oneself. It is natural for people to go through peaks and valleys in their creative output, and there are times when creative people worry that their most recent good idea will end up being their final good idea. At such times, one needs to draw upon deep-seated personal resources and to believe in oneself, even at times when others may not.

Schools teach some students to believe in themselves—namely, those who consistently receive high grades. Ironically, receiving high grades not only does not guarantee creative performance, but may actually work against it: The skills one needs to get high grades are often quite different from those one needs to be creative. Thus, those who go out and set their own course may receive little encouragement, whereas those who play the game and get good grades may develop a confidence in themselves that may be justified, but not necessarily in terms of their past or even future potential creative contribution. Those who most need to believe in themselves may be given every reason not to.

Motivation

There is now good evidence to suggest that motivation plays an important part in creative endeavors. Two kinds of motivation are particularly important: intrinsic motivation and the motivation to excel.

Intrinsic Motivation

Amabile has conducted and reviewed a number of studies suggesting the importance of intrinsic motivation to creativity.[6] People are much more likely to respond creatively to a task that they enjoy for its own sake than to one they work at exclusively or even primarily for extrinsic motivators, of which grades and similar rewards would be examples. Indeed, there is even research to suggest that extrinsic rewards undermine intrinsic motivation.[7]

There is little doubt as to the way in which most schools today motivate students: through grades. Grades are the ultimate criterion of one's success in school, and if one's grades are not good, love of one's work is unlikely to be viewed as much of a compensation. Students in schools rewarding performance find a system of study that is just sufficient to get them an A. If they put too much into a course, they risk jeopardizing their performance in the other courses they are taking. Whatever intrinsic motivation the children may have had at the start is likely to be drummed out of them by a system that rewards extrinsically, not intrinsically.

Motivation to Excel

White identified a desire to achieve competence in one or more of a person's endeavors as effectance motivation.[8] In order to be creative in a field, one generally will need to be motivated not only to be competent, but to excel.

Schools vary in the extent to which they encourage students to excel. Some schools I have visited seem to want nothing more than for all their students to be at some "golden mean." Many schools, however, encourage excellence. Unfortunately, it is rare in my experience for the kind of excellence that is encouraged to be creative excellence. It may be excellence in grades, which generally does not require great creativity to attain, or excellence in sports or extracurricular activities, or whatever. There is nothing wrong with these kinds of excellence. Indeed, they are undoubtedly important in today's world. But they do not facilitate, and may even interfere with creativity. When a student is simultaneously taking five or six courses, there is not much of an opportunity to spend the time, or to expend the effort, to be creative in any of them.

Environmental Context

Creativity cannot be viewed outside an environmental context. What would be viewed as creative in one environmental context might be viewed as trivial in another. The role of context is relevant to the creative enterprise in at least three different ways— in sparking creative ideas, in encouraging follow-up of these ideas, and in rewarding the ideas and their fruits.

Sparking Creative Ideas

The first way in which environmental context is relevant to creativity is in the degree to which context sparks ideas. Some environments provide the bases for lots of creative sparks, whereas other environments may provide the bases for none at all.

Do schools provide environments for sparking creative ideas? Obviously, the answer to this question is necessarily subjective.

But given the discussion in the preceding sections of the chapter, I would have difficulty saying that they do. Rather, they provide environments that encourage learning and dealing with existing, rather than new, concepts. There is a lot of emphasis on memorization, some emphasis on analysis, but little emphasis on creative synthesis. Indeed, it is difficult for me to remember more than a handful of tests I ever took in school that encouraged creative thinking. To the contrary, the tests we give students tend to reward students for spitting back what they have learned, or at best, analyzing it in a fairly noncreative way.

Encouraging Follow-up of Creative Ideas

Suppose a student has a genuinely creative idea, and would like to pursue it within the academic setting. The question is whether there is any vehicle for such follow-up. Occasionally, students will be allowed to pursue projects that encourage them to develop their creative thinking. But again, spending a great deal of time on such projects puts them at risk in their other courses and academic work. It is quite rare that any allowance is made whereby students can be excused from normal requirements in order to pursue a special interest of theirs. Of course, such opportunities are occasionally found. Yale had a Scholars of the House program for seniors, for example, that enabled seniors in the college to pursue some project of interest to them over the course of an entire academic year. The program was discontinued. Other institutions may have other vehicles, but such vehicles are few and far between.

Evaluating Creative Ideas

Most teachers, in grading papers, would be adamant in their belief that they reward creativity. But if the experience of other teachers is similar to that of the teachers with whom I have worked, they don't find a whole lot of creativity to reward. And I sometimes worry whether they would recognize creativity in student work were it to confront them. I do not except myself from this problem: I have more than once failed to see the value of a student's idea at a point in time, only to see it later on—after the student has decided to pursue some other idea, partly at my urging. I don't doubt that teachers genuinely believe they reward creativity. But the rewards are few and far between.

Look at any school report card, and assess the skills that the report card values. One will probably find creativity nowhere on the list. I actually analyzed the report cards given to children in several elementary schools. A number of skills were assessed. In none of the report cards was one of those skills creativity in any field whatsoever. The creative child might indeed be valued by the teacher, but it would not show up in the pattern of check marks on the report card.

Conclusion

Those who invest are taught that most obvious of strategies: buy low and sell high. Yet, few people manage to do so. They don't know when a given security is really low, nor when it is really high. I believe we do not have much better success with creativity. We often don't recognize creativity when we see it. And although most of us believe we encourage it, the analysis in this chapter suggests that schools are probably more likely to work against the development of creativity than in its favor. The conventional wisdom is largely correct: Schools probably do at least as much to undermine creativity as to support it.

Schools could change. They could let students define problems, rather than almost always doing it for the students. They could put more emphasis on ill-structured rather than well-structured problems. They could encourage a legislative rather than, or in addition to an executive style, by providing assignments that encourage students to see things in new ways. They could teach knowledge for use, rather than for exams, and could emphasize flexibility in using knowledge rather than mere recall of that knowledge. They could encourage risk-taking and the other personality attributes associated with creativity, and they could put more emphasis on motivating children intrinsically rather than through grades. Finally, they could reward creativity in all its forms, rather than ignoring or even punishing it. But for schools to do these things, it would take a rather fundamental re-valuation of what schooling is about. I, at least, would like to see that revaluation start now. Let's do all that we can to value and encourage creativity of students in our schools, rather than put-ting obstacles in their paths, even if we do so inadvertently.

Clearly, creative thinking is not the only kind of thinking that is of importance, in school or outside it. Critical thinking, involving analysis and evaluation of ideas, including one's own, is important too. Indeed, creative and critical thinking are com-plementary, in that a good thinker needs to analyze and evaluate his or her own creative ideas in order to determine which are the better ones and which the worse ones. Ideally, schools would help students develop both their critical and their creative thinking, and help them learn how to use these two kinds of thinking in a coordinate fashion in order to optimize students' use of their minds in the great variety of situations they will face in their ev-eryday lives.

Notes

1. Robert J. Sternberg, "A Three-Facet Model of Creativity," in Rob-ert J. Sternberg, ed., *The Nature of Creativity* (New York: Cambridge University Press, 1988), 125–47; and Robert J. Sternberg and Todd I. Lubart, "An Investment Theory of Creativity and Its Development," *Human Development* 34 (1991):1–31.

2. Robert J. Sternberg, *Beyond IQ: A Triarchic Theory of Human In-telligence* (New York: Cambridge University Press, 1985), and Robert J.

Sternberg, *The Triarchic Mind: A New Theory of Human Intelligence* (New York: Viking Press, 1988).

3. Janet E. Davidson and Robert J. Sternberg, "The Role of Insight in Intellectual Giftedness," in *Gifted Child Quarterly* 28 (1984): 58–64; and Robert J. Sternberg and Janet E. Davidson, "The Mind of the Puzzler," in *Psychology Today*, 16 (June, 1982): 37–44.

4. Robert J. Sternberg, "Mental Self-Government: A Theory of Intellectual Styles and Their Development," *Human Development* 31 (1988): 197–224.

5. Robert J. Sternberg and Peter Frensch, "A Balance-Level Theory of Intelligent Thinking," *Zeitschrift für Pädagogische Psychologie* (Journal for Educational Psychology) 3 (1989): 79–96.

6. Theresa Amabile, *The Social Psychology of Creativity* (New York: Springer-Verlag, 1983).

7. Mark R. Lepper, David Greene, and Richard Nisbett, "Undermining Children's Intrinsic Interest with Extrinsic Rewards: A Test of the 'Overjustification' Hypothesis," *Journal of Personality and Social Psychology* 28 (1973): 129–37.

8. Robert W. White, "Motivation Reconsidered: The Concept of Competence," *Psychological Review* 66 (1959): 297–333.

**||▌ Beyond Skills
and Content**

7 Teaching Critical Reasoning in the Strong Sense: Getting Behind Worldviews

RICHARD W. PAUL

No abstract or analytic point exists out of all connection with historical, personal thought: . . . every thought belongs, not just somewhere, but to someone, and is at home in a context of other thoughts, a context which is not purely formally prescribed. Thoughts . . . are something to be known and understood in these concrete terms.

Isaiah Berlin, *Concepts and Categories*

The Weak Sense: Dangers and Pitfalls

To teach a critical thinking course is to make important and often frustrating decisions about what to include and exclude, what to conceive as one's primary goals and what secondary, and how to tie all of what one includes into a coherent relationship to one's goals. These decisions are necessarily occasioned by the realization that no one course in critical thinking can possibly change in a significant fashion habits of thought in the making for twenty years or more. Nevertheless, the intellectual needs that instruction in critical thinking is intended to fulfill are so central to education that they must be given serious attention and central focus in at least one foundational course. There have been considerable and important debates on the value of a "symbolic" versus a "nonsymbolic" approach, the appropriate definition and classification of fallacies, appropriate analysis of extended and nonextended arguments, and so forth. There has been little discussion, and, as far as I know, virtually no debate on how to avoid the fundamental dangers in teaching such a course: that of sophistry on the one hand (inadvertently teaching students to use critical concepts and techniques to maintain their most deep-seated prejudices and irrational habits of thought by making them appear more rational and putting their opponents on the defensive), and that of dismissal (the student rejects the subject either as sophistry or in favor of some supposed alternative—feeling, intuition, faith, higher consciousness, etc.).

Students, much as we might sometimes wish it, do not come to us as "blank slates" upon which we can inscribe the inference-drawing patterns, analytic skills, and truth-facing motivations we value. Students studying critical thinking at the university level have highly developed belief systems buttressed by deep-seated uncritical, egocentric, and sociocentric habits of thought by which they interpret and process their experiences, whether academic or not, and place them into some larger perspective. Consequently, most students find it easy to question simply, and *only*, those beliefs, assumptions, and inferences they have already rejected, and very difficult, often traumatic, to question those in which they have a personal, egocentric investment.

I know of no way to teach critical thinking so that the student who learns to recognize questionable assumptions and inferences only in egocentrically neutral cases *automatically* transfers those skills to the egocentric and socioeconomic ones. Indeed, I think the opposite more commonly occurs. Those students who already have sets of biased assumptions, stereotypes, egocentric and sociocentric beliefs, taught to recognize bad reasoning in neutral cases (or in the case of the opposition) become *more* sophistic rather than less so, more skilled in rationalizing and intellectualizing their biases. They are then *less* rather than *more* likely to abandon them if they later meet someone who questions them. Like the religious believer who studies apologetics, they now have a variety of critical moves to use in defense of their a priori egocentric belief systems.

This is not the effect, of course, we wish our teaching to have. Virtually all teachers of critical thinking want their teaching to have a global Socratic effect, making major inroads into the everyday reasoning of the student, enhancing to some degree that healthy, practical, and skilled skepticism one naturally and rightly associates with the *rational* person. Therefore, students need experience in seriously questioning previously held beliefs and assumptions and in identifying contradictions and inconsistencies in personal and social life. When we think along these lines and get glimpses into the everyday lives and habits of our students, most of us probably experience moments of frustration and cynicism.

I don't think the situation is hopeless, but I do believe the time has come to raise serious questions about how we now teach critical thinking. Current methods, as I conceive them, often inadvertently encourage critical thinking in a weak sense. The most fundamental and questionable assumption of these approaches (whether formal or informal) is that critical thinking can be successfully taught as a battery of technical skills that can be mastered more or less one by one without giving serious attention to self-deception, background logic, and multicategorical ethical issues.

The usual scenario runs something like this. The teacher begins with a general pep talk on the importance of critical thinking in personal and social life. In this pep-talk she reminds students of the large-scale social problems created by prejudice, irrationality, and sophistic manipulation. Then she launches into a discussion of the difference between arguments and nonarguments and students are led to believe that, without any further knowledge of contextual or background considerations, they can learn to analyze and evaluate the arguments by parsing them into, and examining the relation between, premises and conclusions. (The nonarguments presumably do not need critical appraisal.) To examine that relationship, students look for formal or informal fallacies, conceived as atomically determinable and correctable "mistakes." Irrationality is implied thereby to be reducible to complex combinations of atomic mistakes. One roots it out, presumably, by rooting out the atomic mistakes, one by one.

Models of this kind do not effectively teach critical thought, though they may do some good if the basic intellectual skills they foster are followed up in subsequent courses. However, most college and university professors are not fundamentally focused upon the need of students to think for themselves. Professors do not, in general, spend much time considering how students' fledgling reasoning skills, initially stimulated in a general education course, might be reinforced or built upon in the courses they teach. Rather, most are focused on designing and delivering courses that cover a large body of content in their specialized field and which test students with difficult, content-centered questions. The result is that students do not feel that they have the time—even when on rare occasions they have the motivation—to follow up their basic critical thinking courses with more practice in reasoning. Consider this excerpt from a letter by an undergraduate:

> It has been something of a struggle to hold everything down, probably because of my waning excitement for school. I am excited about learning but quite exhausted with the process of school. Perhaps I have myself to blame for not understanding more quickly, but it seems that my courses plunge ahead, incessantly trying to get to the next reading. . . . It doesn't matter to the professor how deeply we understand. But thisis frustrating when the ideas are interesting. I feel that I have learned nothing after a quick reading, so I end up spending hours that I don't have going back while class goes ahead.

Or this one from a graduate student:

> School is going fine, so I think I'll make it through another quarter. The other new graduate students are quickly disappearing. Some don't like the orientation of the department and others simply don't like the general lack of encouragement. I am a bit more cynical I guess. I don't expect to be encouraged or inspired. I expect to play the game and get through the program. If I were dedicated to truth and wisdom, I'd pack my bags too, but I want my degree and a chance to teach. I'm too busy cramming con-

tent into my skull to think about what I read, let alone to develop an intelligent view. When do I get to think for myself? Am I condemned to be a memory bank of meaningless words? How am I supposed to be able to reason well in a dissertation if I never practice reasoning prior to then?

The most common situation, then, is this: Where critical thinking courses exist, they are designed in a questionable way, focused upon what I am calling here an "atomistic," "weak-sense" approach. Furthermore, whatever good they do tends to be lost because they are not followed up. Neither critical thinking instructors nor those focused on traditional courses seem willing to come to terms with the fact that students get through most of their courses doing very little independent, self-directed thinking. What we need, then, is twofold. We need a new theory of critical thinking instruction that will shift the emphasis in critical thinking courses from a weak-sense to a strong-sense approach, and we need a college-wide or university-wide shift in emphasis from a didactic to a critical teaching model. Table 7.1 contrasts some assumptions concerning knowledge, learning, and literacy, which are used by the two opposing models of instruction. We need to keep these assumptions in mind in designing instruction that emphasizes critical thinking across the curriculum.

I will concentrate here on the theory of critical thinking. How should instruction in critical thinking be reconceived? How should we understand the major pitfalls of most present critical thinking instruction? The atomistic weak-sense approach and the questionable assumptions underlying it should be contrasted with an alternative approach specifically designed to avoid its pitfalls.

The alternative view rejects the idea that critical thinking can be taught as a battery of atomic technical skills independent of egocentric beliefs and commitments. Instead of "atomic arguments" (a set of premises and a conclusion) it emphasizes argument *networks* (worldviews); instead of evaluating atomic arguments it emphasizes a more dialectical and dialogical

Table 7.1: Assumptions underlying didactic and critical theories of teaching.

Topic	Didactic Theory	Critical Theory
The fundamental needs of students:	Students need to be taught more or less *what* to think, not *how* to think; they will learn the how if they learn the what.	Students need to be taught *how* not *what* to think; they should learn significant content by considering live issues that stimulate them to gather, analyze, and assess that content.
The nature of knowledge:	Knowledge is independent of the thinking that generates, organizes, and applies it.	All knowledge of "content" is generated, organized, applied, analyzed, synthesized, and assessed by thinking; one must *think* to truly gain knowledge.
Model of the educated person:	An educated, literate person is fundamentally analogous to an encyclopedia or a data bank, directly comparing situations in the world with facts that he or she has absorbed.	An educated, literate person is fundamentally a repository of strategies, principles, concepts, and insights embedded in processes of thought rather than in atomic facts.
The nature of knowledge:	Knowledge, truth, and understanding can be transmitted from one person to another by verbal statements in the form of lectures or didactic teaching.	Knowledge and truth can rarely, and insight never, be transmitted from one person to another by the transmitter's verbal statements alone.
The nature of listening:	Students do not need to be taught skills of listening to learn to pay attention. This is fundamentally a matter of self-discipline and will power.	Students need to be taught how to listen critically. This is an active and skilled process that can be learned by degrees with various levels of proficiency.
The relationship of basic skills to thinking skills:	The basic skills of reading and writing can be taught without emphasis on higher order critical thinking.	The basic skills of reading and writing are inferential and require critical thinking; critical reading and writing involve raising and answering probing, critical questions.

Table 7.1: Continued

Topic	Didactic Theory	Critical Theory
The status of questioning:	Students who have no questions typically are learning well, while students with a lot of questions are experiencing difficulty in learning; doubt and questioning weaken belief.	Students who have no questions typically are not learning; having pointed and specific questions is a significant sign of learning. Doubt and questioning, by deepening understanding, strengthen belief by putting it on more solid ground.
The desirable classroom environment:	Quiet classes with little student talk are typically reflective of students learning while classes with a lot of student talk are typically disadvantaged in learning.	Quiet classes with little student talk are typically classes with little learning while classes with much student talk focused on live issues is a sign of learning.
The view of knowledge (atomistic vs. holistic):	Knowledge and truth can typically be learned best by being broken down into elements, and the elements into subelements, each taught sequentially and atomically. Knowledge is additive.	Knowledge and truth are heavily systemic and holistic and can be learned only by many acts of synthesis, moving from wholes to parts.
The place of values:	People can gain significant knowledge without seeking or valuing it, and hence education can take place without significant transformation of values for the learner.	People gain only the knowledge they seek and value. All other learning is superficial and transitory. All genuine education transforms the basic values of the person educated.
The importance of being aware of one's own learning processes:	Understanding the mind and how it functions, its epistemological health and pathology, are not important or necessary parts of learning.	Understanding the mind and how it functions, its health and pathology, are important and necessary parts of learning.

approach. Arguments need to be appraised in relation to counter-arguments. One can make moves that are very difficult to defend or ones that strengthen one's position. An atomic argument is merely a limited set of moves within a more complex set of moves reflecting a variety of logically significant engagements in the world. Argument exchanges are means by which contesting points of view are brought into rational conflict. A line of reasoning can rarely be refuted by an individual charge of fallacy, however well supported. The charge of fallacy is a move; however it is rarely logically compelling; it virtually never refutes a point of view. This approach more accurately reflects our own and the student's experience of argument exchanges.

By immediately introducing students to these more global problems in the analysis and evaluation of reasoning, we help them more clearly see the relationship between worldviews, forms of life, human engagements and interests, what is at stake (versus what is at issue), how the question of what is at issue is often itself at issue, how the unexpressed as well as the expressed may be significant, the difficulties of judging credibility, and the ethical dimension in most important and complex human problems.

Some Basic Theory: Worldviews, Forms of Life

Here are some basic theoretical underpinnings for a strong-sense approach:

- As humans we are—first, last, and always—engaged in interrelated life projects which, taken as a whole, define our personal "form of life" in relation to broader social forms. Because each of us is engaged in some projects rather than others, each organizes or conceptualizes the world and her place in it in somewhat different terms than others do. Each of us has somewhat different *interests*, somewhat different *stakes*, and somewhat different *perceptions* of the world. Each makes somewhat different assumptions and reasons somewhat differently from others.

- Each of us also expresses to himself and others a more articulated view of how he sees things, a view only partially consistent at best with the view presupposed by and reflected in our behavior. We have, then, *two* world-views overlapping each other, one implicit in our activity and engagements, another implicit in how we describe our behavior. One must recognize contradictions between these conflicting views to develop as a critical thinker and as a person in good faith with one's self. Both traits are measured by the degree to which we can articulate what we live and live what we articulate.

- Reasoning is an essential and defining operation presupposed by all human acts. To reason is to use elements in a logical system to generate conclusions. Conclusions may be explicit in words or implicit in behavior. Sometimes reasoning is explicitly cast into the form of an argument, sometimes not. However, since reasoning presupposes a system or systems of which it is a manifestation, the full implications of reasoning are rarely (if ever) exhausted or displayed in arguments in which they are cast. Arguments presuppose questions at issue. Questions at issue presuppose a point of view and interests at stake. Different points of view frequently differ, not simply in answers to questions, but in the appropriate formulations of questions themselves.

- When we, including those of us who are logicians, analyze and evaluate arguments important to us (this includes all arguments which, if accepted, would strengthen or weaken beliefs to which we have committed ourselves in word or deed), we do so in relationship to prior belief commitments. The best we can do to move toward increased objectivity is to bring to the surface the set of beliefs, assumptions, and inferences from the perspective of which our analysis proceeds, and to see explicitly the dialectical nature of our task, the critical moves we might make at various points, and the various possible countermoves to them.

- Skill in analyzing and evaluating reasoning is skill in reciprocity, the ability to reason within more than one point of view, understanding strengths and weaknesses through comprehending the objections that could be raised at various points in the arguments by alternative points of view.

- Laying out elements of reasoning in deductive form is useful, not principally to see whether a "mistake" has been made, but to see critical moves one might make to determine the strengths and weaknesses of the reasoning in relation to alternatives.

- Since vested interest typically influences perception, assumptions, reasoning in general, and specific conclusions, we must become aware of the nature of our own and others' engagements to recognize strengths and weaknesses in reasoning. Only when we recognize that a given argument reflects or, if justified, would serve a given interest can we, by imaginatively entertaining a competing interest, construct an opposing point of view and so an opposing argument or set of arguments. By developing both arguments dialectically, we can see their strengths and weaknesses.

- Arguments are not things in themselves but constructions by specific people who must further interpret and develop them, for example, to answer objections. By recognizing the interests typically correlated with given arguments, we can often challenge the credibility of others' premises by alluding to discrepancies between what they say and what they do. In doing so we force them to critique their own behavior in line with the implications of their arguments, or to abandon the line of argument. There are a variety of critical moves they may make upon being so challenged.

- By reflecting on interests as implicit in behavior, one can often much more effectively construct the assumptions most favorable to those interests. Once formulated, one can begin to formulate alternative competing assumptions. Both can then be more effectively questioned and arguments for and against them can be entertained.

- The total set of factual claims that buttress a worldview, and hence the various arguments generated by it, is usually indefinitely large and often involves shifting conceptual problems and implicit judgments of value (especially shifts in how to formulate the "facts"). The credibility of an individual claim often depends on the credibility of many other claims; very often the claims themselves are very difficult to verify directly and atomically. Very often, then, to analyze an argument, we must judge relative credibility. These judgments are more plausible if they take into account the vested interests and the track records of the sources.

- The terms in which an argument is cast often reflect the biased interest of the person who formulated it. Calling into question the very concepts used or the use to which they are put is an important critical move. To become adept at this, we must practice recognizing how social groups systematically and selectively move back and forth between usage in keeping with the logic of ordinary language and that which accords with the ideological commitments of the group (and so conflicts with ordinary usage). Consider the ways many people use key terms in current international debate—for example, *freedom fighter, liberator, revolutionary, guerrilla, terrorist*—and reflect on: (1) what is implied by the *logic* of the terms apart from the usage of any particular social group; (2) what is implied by the usage of a particular group with vested interests (say, U.S. citizens, Germans, Israelis, Soviets); and (3) the various historical examples that suggest inconsistency in the use of these by that group, and how this inconsistency depends on fundamental, typically unexpressed, assumptions. Through such disciplined reflection, one can identify predictable, self-serving inconsistencies.

Multi-Dimensional Ethical Issues

Teaching critical thinking in the strong sense helps students develop reasoning skills precisely in those areas where they are most likely to have egocentric and sociocentric biases. Such biases exist most profoundly in areas of their identities and vested interests. Their identities and interests are linked in turn to their unarticulated worldviews. One's unarticulated worldview represents who one *is* (the view implicit in the principles which guide one's actions). One's articulated view represents the person that one *thinks* one is (the view implicit in the principles used to *justify* one's actions). Excepting honest mistakes, the contradictions or inconsistencies between these two represent the degree to which one reasons and acts in bad faith or self-deceptively.

Multi-dimensional issues involving proposed ethical justifications for behavior are ideal for teaching critical thinking. Most political, social, and personal issues which most concern us and students are of this type—abortion, nuclear energy, nuclear arms, the nature of national security, poverty, social injustices of various kinds, revolution and intervention, socialized medicine, government regulation, sexism, racism, problems of love and friendship, jealousy, rights to private property, rights to world resources, faith and intuition versus reason, and so forth. Obviously one can cover only a few such issues, and I believe that the advantages lie in covering fewer of them deeply and intensively. I am certainly unsympathetic to inundating the student with an array of truncated arguments set up to illustrate atomic fallacies.

Since I teach in the United States, and since the media here as everywhere else in the world reflect, and most students have internalized, a profoundly nationalistic bias, I focus one segment of my course on identifying national bias in the news. In doing this, students must face issues that, to be approached dialectically, require them to discover that mainstream American reasoning and the mainstream American point of view on world issues are not the only dialectical possibility. I identify as mainstream American views any which have significant support with the Democratic and the Republican parties. This segment of the course is valuable for several reasons:

- Though most students have internalized much media propaganda, so that their egos are partly identified with it, they are neither totally taken in by that propaganda nor incapable of beginning to question it systematically.

- The students become more adept at constructing—and more empathetic toward—alternative lines of reasoning as the *sociocentric assumptions* of mainstream media coverage come more and more to the surface. Here are some examples of these assumptions: (1) The U.S. government, compared to other governments, is more committed to ideals; (2) U.S. citizens have more energy, more practical know-how, and more common sense than others; (3) the world as a whole would be better off (freer, safer, more just) if the U.S. had *more* power; (4) U.S. citizens are less greedy and self-deceived than other peoples; U.S. lives are more important than the lives of other peoples.

- Explicitly addressing and constructing dialectical alternatives to political and national as well as professional and religious party lines and exploring the contradictions in these positions enables students to draw parallels to their personal and their peer groups' party lines and the myriad contradictions in their talk and behavior. Such discoveries explicitly and dramatically forge the beginnings of a commitment to developing the critical spirit, the foundation for strong-sense skills and insights.

A Sample Assignment and Results

To indicate how my concerns and objectives can be translated into assignments, I've included a sample. In a course I taught, the following was assigned as a take-home midterm examination, approximately six weeks into the semester. The students were allowed three weeks to complete it.

> The objective of this midterm is to determine the extent to which you understand and can effectively use the basic concepts of the course: worldview, assumptions, concepts (personal, social, implicit in language, technical), evidence (empirical claims), implications, consistency, conclusions, premises, questions at issue.
>
> You are to view and critically and sympathetically analyze two films: *Attack on the Americas* (a right-wing think-tank film alleging Communist control of Central American revolutionaries) and *Revolution or Death* (a World Council of Churches film defending the rebels in El Salvador). Two incompatible worldviews are presented in those films. After analyzing the films and consulting whatever background material you deem necessary to understand the two worldviews, construct a dialogue between two of the most intelligent defenders of each perspective. They should each demonstrate skills in explicating the basic assumptions, the questionable claims, ideas, inferences, values, and conclusions of the other side. Both should be able to make some concessions to the other point of view with-

out conceding their basic positions. Each should be able to summarize some of the inferences of the other side and raise questions about those inferences (e.g., "You appear to me to be arguing in the following way. You assume that. . . . You ignore that. . . . And then you conclude that . . .").

In the second part of your paper, write a third-person commentary on the debate, indicating which point of view is in the strongest position logically in your view. Argue for your position; do not simply assert it. Give good reasons for rejecting or accepting whatever aspects of the two worldviews you reject or accept. Make clear to the reader how your position reflects your worldview. The dialogue should have at least fourteen exchanges (twenty-eight entries) and the commentary should be at least four typewritten pages.

A variety of background materials were made available, including the U.S. State Department *White Paper,* an open letter from the late Archbishop of San Salvador, a copy of the platform of the El Salvador rebels, and numerous current newspaper and magazine articles and editorials on the issue. The students were encouraged to discuss and debate the issue outside of class (which they did). The students were expected to document how the major newspapers were covering the story, noticing, for example, that accounts favorable to the State Department position tended to be given front page coverage while accounts critical of that position, say from Amnesty International, were buried within the front section. There was also discussion of internal inconsistencies within the accounts.

Many of the students came to see one or more of the following points:

- In a conflict such as this the two sides disagree not only on conclusions but even about how the issue ought to be put. One side will put the issue, for example, in terms of the dangers of a communist takeover, the other in terms of the need for people to overthrow a repressive regime. One will see the fundamental problem as caused by Cuban and Soviet intervention, the other side by U.S. intervention. Each side will see the other as begging the essential question.

- A debate on how to word the issue will often become a debate on a series of factual questions. This debate will be extended into a series of historical questions. Each side will typically see the other as suppressing evidence. Those favorable to the Duarte regime, for example, will see the other side as suppressing evidence of the extent of communist involvement in El Salvador. Those favorable to the rebels will see the other side as suppressing evidence of government complicity in right-wing terrorism. There will be disagreement about which side is committing most of the violent acts.

- These factual disagreements will at some point or another give way to *conceptual disagreements:* which acts should be called "terrorist" and "revolutionary," and which "acts of liberation." This debate will at some point become a debate about *values,* about which acts are reprehensible or justified. Very often the acts which from one perspective seem required by circumstances will be morally condemned by the other.

- At various points in the discussion the debate will become philosophical or anthropological, involving broad issues concerning the nature of humanity and the nature of human society. The side supporting the government tends to take a philosophical position that plays down the capacity of the masses to make rational and appropriate judgments in their own behalf, at least when under the influence of outside agitators and subversives. The other side tends to be more favorable to the masses and suspicious of the government's capacity or right to make what appear to them to be decisions that should be left to the people. Each side thinks the other begs important questions, suppresses evidence, stereotypes, uses unjustified analogies, uses faulty causal reasoning, misuses concepts, and so forth.

Such assignments help students appreciate the kinds of moves that typically occur in everyday argument, put them into perspective, and construct alternative arguments, precisely because they more clearly see how arguments develop in relation to each other and so in relation to a broader perspective. They give students more practical insight into the motivated nature of argument "flaws" than the traditional approach does. Students are therefore better able to anticipate these flaws and more sensitive to the special probing moves that need to be made. Finally, as a result of such assignments, students are much more sensitive (than I believe they would be under most weak-sense approaches) to the profound ethical consequences of ego-serving reasoning, and to the ease with which we can fall prey to it. If we can indeed accomplish something like these results, then there is much to be said for further work and development of strong-sense approaches. What I have described here is, I hope, the beginning of such work.

Postscript

In the years since I wrote this paper, I have become increasingly convinced that if students are to learn to think critically in a strong sense, they must be exposed to critical thinking over an extended period of time, over years, not months. To think critically in a strong sense is to become a critical person. It is to develop particular values and traits of mind in addition to particular skills and abilities. If we are committed to critical thinking in a strong sense, we must then be committed to major reform of education, for most schooling is didactic in nature and discourages rather than encourages critical thinking and the values and dispositions essential to it. If we wait until students are in college—and of course only a small minority of people ever attend college—we will not significantly transform their thinking, even with the ideal critical thinking course.

A commitment to critical thinking is a commitment to fostering the traits of mind essential to strong sense critical thinking. Consider the following brief characterizations:

Independence of Mind – the disposition and commitment to autonomous thinking, thinking for oneself. Unfortunately, the human mind does not instinctively value autonomy of thought. Many of our beliefs are acquired at an early age, when we have a strong tendency to form beliefs merely because we want to believe or because we are rewarded for believing. To develop independence of thought, students must learn to question what is presented to them as true. They must learn to analyze issues for themselves, reject unjustified authorities at the same time that they recognize the contributions of justified authorities. They must thoughtfully form their own principles of thought and action, determine for themselves when information is relevant, when to apply a concept, and even when to make use of a skill. They must learn how to resist intellectual manipulation.

Intellectual Curiosity – the disposition to wonder about the world. Unfortunately most people tend to lose their curiosity at an early age. Critical thinkers need to be curious about their environment. They need to seek explanations of apparent discrepancies and speculate about possible causes of these discrepancies. They need to develop an interest in how they came to be the persons they are. They need to wonder about the nature and direction of their lives. They need to appreciate the mystery of much of human life, of how we have come to be such a paradoxical species, of how we can be capable simultaneously of both such high thought and such low action. They need to be curious about language, about how it works, about how we live in and through it. They need to be perplexed about how we can deceive ourselves so much, how we can know so much about ourselves at the same time that we fail to grasp our contradictions and inconsistencies.

Intellectual Courage – having a consciousness of the need to face and fairly address ideas, beliefs, or viewpoints toward which we have strong negative emotions and to which we have not given a serious hearing. Intellectual courage is connected with the recognition that ideas commonly considered dangerous or absurd are sometimes rationally justified (in whole or in part) and that conclusions and beliefs inculcated in us are sometimes false or misleading. To determine for ourselves which is which, we must not passively and uncritically accept what we have learned or been taught. Intellectual courage comes into play here because inevitably we will come to see some truth in some ideas considered dangerous and absurd, and distortion or falsity in some ideas strongly held in our social group. We need courage to be true to our own thinking in such circumstances. The pressure to conform can be great. The penalties for nonconformity can be severe.

Intellectual Humility – awareness of the limits of one's knowledge. This includes sensitivity to circumstances in which one's native egocentrism is likely to function self-deceptively; sensitivity to bias and prejudice in, and limitations of, one's viewpoint. Intellectual humility is based on the recognition that one should not claim more than one actually knows. It does not imply spinelessness or submissiveness. It implies the lack of intellectual pretentiousness, arrogance, or conceit. It implies insight into the foundations of one's beliefs: knowing what evidence one has, how one has come to believe, what further evidence one might need to examine or seek out.

Intellectual Empathy – having a consciousness of the need to imaginatively put oneself in the place of others in order to genuinely understand them. This requires explicit consciousness of our egocentric tendency to identify truth with our immediate perceptions of long-standing thought or belief. This trait correlates with the ability to reconstruct accurately the viewpoints and reasoning of others and to reason from premises, assumptions, and ideas other than our own. This trait also correlates with the willingness to remember occasions when we were wrong in the past despite an intense conviction that we were right, and, therefore, with the ability to imagine ourselves similarly deceived in the case at hand.

Intellectual Integrity – recognition of the need to be true to the intellectual and moral standards implicit in our judgments of the behavior or views of others. We need to be consistent in the intellectual standards we apply; to hold ourselves to the same rigorous standards of evidence and proof to which we hold our antagonists; to practice what we advocate for others; and to honestly admit discrepancies and inconsistencies in our own thoughts and actions.

Intellectual Perseverance – willingness and consciousness of the need to pursue intellectual insights and truths in spite of difficulties, obstacles, and frustrations. This requires firm adherence to rational principles despite the irrational opposition of others; a sense of the need to struggle with confusion and unsettled questions over an extended period of time to achieve deeper understanding or insight.

Faith in Reason – confidence that, in the long run, one's own higher interests and those of humankind at large will be best served by giving the freest play to reason. This includes encouraging people to come to their own conclusions through the development of their own rational faculties. It is faith that, with proper encouragement and cultivation, people can learn to think for themselves, to form rational viewpoints, draw reasonable conclusions, think coherently and logically, and persuade each other by reason, and become reasonable persons despite the deep-seated obstacles in the native character of the human mind and in society as we know it.

Fairmindedness – Willingness and consciousness of the need to treat all viewpoints alike. This is the ability to reason without reference to one's own feelings or vested interests, or the feelings or vested interests of one's friends, community, or nation. Fairmindedness implies adherence to intellectual standards without reference to one's own advantage or the advantage of one's group.

Because of the need to approach education for critical thinking in a global way, laying the intellectual foundations in the earliest school years, I have written four books for teachers (grades K–3, 4–6, 6–9, and high school) on how to foster critical thinking.[1] These books integrate the teaching of intellectual traits of mind into traditional subject-matter instruction. However, just as no ideal critical thinking course will transform students into critical thinkers, so no set of books will instantly transform teachers. This is the reason why it is crucial that the field of critical thinking expand into every discipline and that commitment to it grow progressively over many years. Only through such evolution will the results become socially significant.

If critical thinking is to be encouraged in every discipline, every discipline must reconceptualize the manner in which students acquire its knowledge. Knowledge and thought must be understood to exist in a reciprocal relation. Science instruction must focus on scientific thinking, history instruction on historical thinking, mathematics instruction on mathematical thinking, and so on for every discipline. The content covered must represent nothing more than an occasion for thinking, not an end in itself, not stuff to be committed—as now it typically is—to short-term memory. The traits of mind essential to critical thinking must be fostered in every subject area or domain, not just in selected assignments, and to achieve this it must become common knowledge within every field how to teach for this end. Education and scholarship are merely at the beginnings of this understanding; subject matter specialists are just now beginning to explore this reorientation. Perhaps in ten to fifteen years we will see a significant shift and the foundations laid for the emergence of critical societies, societies in which fairminded critical thinking is a prominent social value. I take it as axiomatic that no such society has yet existed.[2]

Notes

1. Richard Paul, A. J. A. Binker, and Daniel Weil, *Critical Thinking Handbook: K–3; A Guide for Remodelling Lesson Plans in Language Arts, Social Studies, and Science* (Rohnert Park, Cal.: Foundation for Critical Thinking, Sonoma State University, 1990); Richard Paul, A. J. A. Binker, K. Jensen, and H. Kreklau, *Critical Thinking Handbook: 4th– 6th Grades: A Guide for Remodelling Lesson Plans in Language Arts, Social Studies, and Science* (Rohnert Park, Cal.: Foundation for Critical Thinking, Sonoma State University, 1990); Richard Paul, A. J. A. Binker, D. Martin, C. Vetrano, and H. Kreklau. *Critical Thinking Handbook: 6th–9th Grades: A Guide for Remodelling Lesson Plans in Language Arts, Social Studies, and Science* (Rohnert Park, Cal.: Center for Critical Thinking, Sonoma State University, 1989); Richard Paul, A. J. A. Binker, D. Martin, C. Vetrano, and H. Kreklau. *Critical Thinking Handbook: High School: A Guide for Redesigning Instruction* (Rohnert Park, Cal.: Center for Critical Thinking, Sonoma State University, 1989).

2. For further reading, see Richard Paul, *Critical Thinking: What Every Person Needs to Survive in a Rapidly Changing World* (Rohnert Park, Cal.: Center for Critical Thinking, Sonoma State University, 1990).

8 The Interpretive Focus: A Prerequisite for Critical Reasoning

LENORE LANGSDORF

On the first day of each new critical thinking course, I tell the assembled group that this is not a course in logic. I give students the time and location of the introductory courses for that semester, and assure them that if they would like to leave right then in order to change from this course to that one, I'll not be offended. Usually, nobody leaves at that point. Sometimes, somebody says: "I don't know whether logic or critical thinking is what I want, since I don't know what they are or what the difference is." If nobody does say that, I suggest that people may be thinking it. For I need to say right then—for the first, but not last time—just what is to be taught in this particular classroom, under the title of "critical thinking."

The same requirement is present in contributing to a volume of reflections and suggestions on the place of critical reasoning in contemporary culture. For I want to propose that there is a crucial prerequisite to the varieties of critical thinking discussed in this volume. As the first step in doing that, I begin by locating my own teaching practice within the spectrum of five models which predominate in the field. Then I discuss the importance of a radical shift in attitude—away from direct concern with the text,

157

and toward an interpretive focus—for my own practice, which is an adaption of "strong-sense critical thinking."

This approach to teaching reasoning skill (not skills) seems to me most appropriate as a way of presenting the content of those texts we like to teach in humanities courses.[1] In saying "like to teach," I mean "try to teach." For I find that there is a widespread pedagogical problem behind much of the current interest in teaching reasoning as part of the humanities curriculum: we open the Great Books (or perhaps, a version of the extended canon) and we offer them to our students. Often we do so with a profound sense of the extent to which what we are offering has formed our culture as well as our lives as individuals. But we end class sessions, whole days, and entire semesters with the sense that the great ideas have not connected with our students' lives; have not transferred from the page to the person in any but the most superficial manner. I've learned, from friends who teach in the grade and high schools and from conversations with teachers at conferences and workshops, that teachers' lounges are filled with despair over that sense of nontransfer. College teachers are somewhat protected from that form of despair, I suspect, by two institutional factors: we don't have teachers' lounges, and we do have a tradition of nonconcern with pedagogy as a mark of the successful professor. It seems to me that both factors, but especially the antipedagogical tradition, are unfortunate.

To some degree, readers of these pages already have questioned the wisdom of that tradition. It's especially in relation to teaching at the university level that I want to present two claims to those readers. First: reflective and interpretive skill is basic if we, and our students, are to understand, evaluate, and use the great ideas of our various traditions in ways that speak to contemporary goals, values, and needs. In other words: we need to *interpret* what's said or read, if our goal is to present—sympathetically, accurately, and imaginatively—the clearest, fairest, and strongest versions of both our own and others' ideas as to what human goals, values, and needs have been, are, and might be. The second claim is that an approach to humanities texts that stresses interpretive skill as part of (more precisely, as prerequisite for) strong-sense critical thinking can be more successful in achieving connection with the great ideas than approaches which presume or downplay interpretation skill in favor of immersion (critical or otherwise) in the content—in the text themselves.

In order to make a case for those claims, I need to differentiate strong-sense critical thinking and my interpretive adaption of it from four other models for developing reasoning skill: introductory logic, informal logic, argument construction, and evaluative reasoning. I find that these models (and their variations and combinations) are suited to different emphases within the broad goal of improving reasoning skill. The fact that all of these models are used confirms my belief that there is no consensus as to just what we want to encourage when we set out to improve reasoning skill through classroom instruction. After describing the models, then, I'll turn to my own adaption of strong-sense critical thinking for teaching humanities texts.[2]

The "introductory logic" model focuses on basic concepts and techniques of formal logic (e.g., deduction and procedures for syllogistic and propositional logic). These are taught in relative or complete abstraction from social contexts and literary or journalistic texts; that is, either in symbolic form or through decontextualized examples devised to illustrate a particular method or form. Although some consideration of topics in informal logic often is included, this usually is limited to a small group of fallacies, which are identified primarily or solely by their Latin names. An implicit theme here is that good argument fits those formal patterns, or can be reformulated without loss of essential meaning so as to fit Aristotelian or Fregean patterns. Correlatively, poor arguments are those that can't be restated in a standard form, as well as those which rely on fallacies. Perhaps the best known textbook following this model is Irving M. Copi's

Introduction to Logic, which has gone through many editions. A recent text that continues in this tradition is J. Hintikka and F. Bachman, *What If . . . Toward Excellence in Reasoning.*

The "informal logic" model emphasizes developing skills in the service of "clear thinking." Usually this means a stress on identifying fallacies in real or realistic examples. Also, attention to real-life situations often involves analysis of semi-argumentive texts, such as those in advertisements. Attention is given to whether any reasons (and even "good reasons") are offered for the claims found there, as well as to whether fallacies are present. Another major interest in this tradition is reconstructing "incomplete" arguments—that is, those that would fit standard (inductive or deductive) forms if implicit claims ("missing premises") were supplied. Ralph Johnson and J. Anthony Blair's *Logical Self-Defense* and Robert Fogelin's *Understanding Arguments: An Introduction to Informal Logic* exemplify this model.

The "argument construction" model is more concerned with producing good arguments than with identifying poor ones. In this context, *good* means, primarily, "persuasive" rather than "valid." This model derives from the rhetorical tradition, and thus (in a sense) is the oldest. Most current textbooks that exemplify it are written by authors whose academic backgrounds are in rhetoric or composition theory, and who are especially interested in writing that uses good reasoning "across the curriculum" (although that phrase often is shunned). Examples would be Vivian Rosenberg's *Reading, Writing, and Thinking: Critical Connections,* and Barbara Warnick and Edward S. Inch's *Critical Thinking and Communication: The Use of Reason in Argument.*

The "evaluative reasoning" model focuses on the assessment of argumentation and emphasizes interaction (dialogue) in actual argumentive situations, whether oral or written. Attention is given to a reflective and even investigative attitude toward language. Features of both the "argument construction" and strong-sense models are discernable in this model, which encourages developing sophistication and creativity in responding to communication that isn't direct or transparent. Rather than evaluating arguments as given, or as reformulated to fit one or another "standard form," this approach looks for implicit as well as explicit assumptions and reasons, and gives more attention than the other models to discourse that doesn't provide recognizable arguments. Michael Scriven's *Reasoning* surely is the purest example of this model, although *An Introduction to Reasoning*, by Stephen Toulmin, Richard Rieke, and Alan Janik, achieves much the same effect through somewhat different means.

The strong-sense critical thinking model stresses comparison of the positions taken in an argument as reflecting a context of interests, attitudes, and worldviews that are themselves to be the focus of criticism. In effect, this means that ideas, rather than arguments, are the focus of analysis. Reflective comparison of these ideas, preferably in dialogue which considers the strongest versions of divergent positions, takes precedence over concern with logical techniques of any sort. Identifying and criticizing these contextual elements means working with themes and procedures more often associated with epistemology, metaphysics, rhetoric, political science, and psychology than with logic. Since this approach stresses the reformulation of existing teaching materials so as to encourage a somewhat skeptical reflective attitude, it does not lend itself to the writing of textbooks. The phrase "strong sense" itself, as well as the program it designates, is associated closely with Richard Paul. His article, "Teaching Critical Thinking in the 'Strong Sense': A Focus on Self-Deception, World-Views, and a Dialectical Mode of Analysis" is the best introduction to the model. (A recently revised version is included in this volume.) John Chaffee's *Thinking Critically* is a textbook that reflects the thrust of this model.

Given this variety of models—and of course, a spectrum of possibilities for combining and modifying them—the question to be addressed by anyone who is or wants to be teaching critical thinking is: just what is *my* goal, and my institution's goal, in teaching this course? In going on from posing that general question to describing a particular problem that I encountered, and then to consideration of my own goal in teaching critically and to the adaption of strong-sense critical thinking that I made in response to that goal, I do not mean to suggest that my goals and methods are preferable to those of others. Rather, I describe my own purpose and procedures for critical teaching as a starting point from which others can reflect on their own goals and on which model or combination of models might best serve those goals. I do suspect that the problem I encountered is widespread, although my analysis and response may well differ from those of other teachers who encounter it. Accordingly, I'll begin by describing the teaching situation in which the problem arose, and then go on to portray my diagnosis and response.

As a member of a small philosophy department in a large state university, I taught a large number of undergraduate students who were not particularly interested in the humanities. Most of these students were business or engineering majors who appeared in the liberal arts college at all only because of required courses in English and history, and a less precise stipulation that they take a few additional hours chosen from among electives in the college. The particular pedagogical difficulties which brought me to investigate critical thinking, and to adopt and adapt strong-sense critical thinking, arose in teaching these students. But since the particular teaching goal I had contributed to that difficulty, I should discuss that goal before going on to describe the situation and my response.

My own goal in teaching is to enable students to understand and evaluate the ideas presented in whatever texts demand their attention. By *text* I mean both verbal and visual means of communicating ideas; that is, textbooks, newspapers, novels, song lyrics, and television programs. Understanding and assessment of the ideas in these texts requires a good deal of what I call "interpretive thinking" of the sort promoted in strong-sense critical thinking. It places far more emphasis on understanding claims—including the social, political, and biographical contexts from which they come—than on assessing the strength or validity of arguments that may be formed from those claims. This is not to say that interpretation replaces logical evaluation in this form of thinking critically. But it is to assert that there are prerequisite dispositions, skills, and attitudes which comprise what I like to call (by analogy to the teaching of reading) "evaluation readiness."

One further point is relevant to spelling out my goal. I don't see learning to understand texts as an end in itself. Rather, my ultimate purpose is to enable students to appropriate the meaning of texts; that is, to use, as they see fit, the ideas, issues, and possibilities that are offered in those texts. In an important sense that's often overlooked by those who fear that thinking critically will mean the destruction of values, this ability to appropriate the meaning of text is a profoundly conservative force. For students are more apt to be impressed by the values inherent in the texts of our cultural tradition—if indeed, there are impressive values there—when they can accept them on the basis of their own considered understanding and skeptical affirmation, rather than as dogma imposed upon them or as unexamined presuppositions. This is to say that my own goal in teaching critically incorporates an understanding of critical thinking as a means for empowerment; for coming to understand ideas, issues, and possibilities so that we can choose what to do, how to decide, or which to believe—rather than be governed by force, chance, custom, or ignorance.[3]

The interpretive aspect of thinking critically has been neglected, I believe, for at least two reasons. First, as suggested in my sketch of the five models, a good deal of what's taught as critical thinking relies on examples devised to illustrate a particular point, and (in contrast to real-life events and texts) the need for interpreting those examples is, by design, minimal. Also, we haven't given sufficient attention to the crucial differences between the everyday, conventional use of language for conversation that's familiar to our students, and the use of language in the written texts that we assign. It was recognizing that crucial difference between *oral discourse* and *written text* that brought me to believe that a reflective and interpretive attitude is crucial for thinking critically in those models of critical thinking that use real or realistic texts, rather than devised examples. Accordingly, the interpretive thinking adaption of strong-sense critical thinking that I use stresses an interpretive method that emphasizes two themes: reflection and criticism. Reflecting on what's been said, and especially on what's been written, requires us to take into consideration our distance from the writing (or saying). Criticism refers to translating the ideas in a text so that the reader can overcome this distance. Critical thus means interrogating the texts analogously to the way we question a dialogue partner, in oral discourse. It does not mean fault-finding.

I can now describe the difficulty I encountered in some detail, against the background of this brief summary of the situation and goal of my own teaching. In teaching those students who happened into introductory philosophy courses in order to fulfill the humanities requirement, I found a widespread—indeed, almost universal—inability to understand and evaluate the viewpoints, positions, and ideas presented in the traditional texts of our cultural, and especially philosophical, heritage. Correlatively, students would give, at most, the conclusion of a chain of reasoning when they were asked to identify, paraphrase, and evaluate an argument in an extended text. Examples of the texts that presented this problem are Socrates' argument for granting him a pension in the *Apology*, or Luther's defense of free will in *Treatise on Christian Liberty*, or Descartes' methodological proposals in *Discourse on Method*. When queried as to *why* the authors state those convictions (which had been elucidated as the conclusions of arguments), the almost universal response was something about it being the author's feeling or opinion. In other words: students did not distinguish between the *text's position* and the *author's opinion*. Any attempt to criticize a position was taken as criticism of the author. Furthermore, when criticism was directed toward a student's own work (that is, when the student was the author) defensiveness along the lines of "everybody's entitled to his or her own opinion, and this is mine" resulted.

As I came to identify this problem in my introductory philosophy courses and discussed it with colleagues in other departments and institutions, I discovered that they had similar experiences. Then I found the same pattern in teaching critical thinking from the evaluative reasoning model. Here it appeared in connection with the sections in two different textbooks that deal with the distinction between "cause" and "reason." These were very difficult for students to comprehend. In reflecting upon these and other teachers' experiences, I formulated this hypothesis: associating *conclusions* with *reasons*—that is, understanding a passage and even an entire essay, article, or story as a series of descriptions and assertions, some of which are offered as evidence, support, backing, or reason for others—is an ability (perhaps, even a disposition) that's generally found among teachers, but rarely present among students. To state this thesis a bit differently: at most, students typically *explain* a conclusion as the effect of a psychological motivation that functions (more or less) like a physical cause. (I say "at most" and "typically" because some students are also poor at causal reasoning, while others excel at both causal reasoning and the activity of joining parts of a story into a whole, which I call "interpretive reasoning.") But what's almost always absent is the ability, disposition, or skill that enables *understanding* a conclusion on the basis of *reasons* for it—in contrast to *explaining* the *author* in cause-and-effect terms.[4] The difference here is between focusing upon the opinions and standpoint intrinsic to an author, in contrast to the positions and viewpoint portrayed in a text. Explanation of an author's opinions uses a variation of causal reasoning. Understanding a text's positions uses interpretive reasoning.

Immediately upon naming these two sorts of reasoning, I want to stress that this is not a matter of good versus bad reasoning. Rather, it's a matter of choosing appropriate reasoning patterns. In some contexts, we need to use causal reasoning; in others, we need to use interpretive reasoning. Harvey Siegel's characterization of critical thinking as being "appropriately moved by reasons" provides a way of emphasizing the importance of this point.[5] For there are times—such as in following or constructing an argument—when being moved by reasons is appropriate. And there are other times—such as in deciding whether light or heavy clothing is appropriate on a particular day—when it's appropriate to be moved by causes. Recognizing which sort of situation is present (or, since most situations are not as clear-cut as these examples, recognizing to what extent either or both situations are present) is the first step toward choosing an appropriate pattern of reasoning. The second step, then, is developing skill in both patterns.

Yet, in itself, identifying these two patterns and realizing that most students were unaware of their different characteristics and so could not begin to choose the appropriate pattern of reasoning, was of no help in trying to respond to students' difficulties in understanding and evaluating the ideas presented by the texts in our classes. I had only a theoretical hypothesis, and no sense of how to transform that into a helpful classroom practice. Two remarks by students provided clues as to how I could introduce interpretive reasoning in a way that would give students a foothold toward recognizing appropriate occasions for employing that alternative to their more usual (causal) pattern of reasoning.

The first remark was volunteered by a student majoring in business who characterized himself as "good in math" and doing well in classes for his major, but "afraid" of both his English literature and philosophy classes. Both of these, he said, involved a lot of "abstract reasoning" that was very different from the "concrete problems" involved in his business courses. The second remark was, more precisely, a question and implicit complaint. It's one that colleagues who teach literature have heard even more than I have: "Why do they take so long to get to the point, and use such fancy language to do it, instead of just telling you what's happening?" As I reflected on these questions, it occurred to me that what seems long-winded and abstract is whatever goes beyond the plot. For example Socrates' *Apology* can be summarized, quite easily, in a few brief sentences that tell what happened: Socrates was put on trial for corrupting the youth and being an atheist. He said that he was doing the state a favor by encouraging people to ask searching questions, and so should be given a pension. But the court didn't appreciate the favor and sentenced him to death.

What's left out of this plot summary, of course, is all of the "abstract reasoning" that's given—both explicitly and implicitly—in the text of this Platonic dialogue. Yet that sort of content is precisely what teachers usually want students to understand and evaluate when we teach history, literature, and philosophy. Another way to focus on that orientation toward evaluation of ideas is by noticing the difference between the texts we study in these courses and mystery novels. The latter are similar to those "concrete problems" which were familiar and comfortable territory to the business major: the mystery story gives, in narrative form, at least most of the parts as well as the whole that puts them together. For instance: we're given a lot of events and the murder that ties them together. We need only figure out just *how* they fit together: how the given means connect with the given end. Causal or semicausal reasoning (that is, treating psychological motivations as causes) plays the major role in solving such problems.

This is the sort of reasoning that Richard Paul calls "intra-system thinking": "It functions well when confronted with questions and issues that fall clearly within its system, but is at its worst when facing issues that cross systems, require revising a system, or presuppose explicit critique of the system used."[6] The mystery novel, in giving us a series of events, presents just such a system. It sets the task of figuring out how some (but usually not all) of the given parts connect to the whole; that is, which events serve as clues to the solution of the mystery. Or, in Paul's terms: it requires the sort of thinking that decides which elements fit together in just which ways to make up the system. But the mystery novel rarely encourages or requires us to think beyond the system itself. In other words, it does not encourage us to revise or critique the system itself.

A very different sort of reasoning is present in the classroom texts that present our students with the difficulties I've been discussing. In the *Apology, The Federalist Papers, Hamlet, A Tale of Two Cities, Death of a Salesman, Letter from a Birmingham Jail,* and *Under Six Flags: A History of Texas,* we are confronted with ideas and viewpoints, rather than with means to ends. These are portrayed at some length, and often in what students see as "fancy language" that simply doesn't get to the point in any direct way. The ways in which these ideas are connected are *argued,* rather than presented. In other words, these texts raise questions as to what systems *could* be formed, rather than simply depict the system they *do* form. Thus, issues are raised that encourage us to cross systems and even embark upon revising a system. The possibility of explicit critique develops as we interpret the system in relation to other possibilities—which is to say, as we interpret the system so as to discern how it could be otherwise. If that ability has not developed, even students who characterize themselves as good readers will report that they get to the bottom of a page in Thoreau, John Stuart Mill, or Marx, for example, without knowing what it is they've read.

Thus far, I've discussed two problems that arose in my own teaching experience, although conversation with colleagues confirms the generality of the problems I've identified here. I need now to discuss another aspect of this difficulty in teaching the great ideas embedded in the traditional literary canon, and still present in revised versions. This aspect has to do with differences between varieties of the spoken, in contrast to the written, word. Although the connection between this theme—differences between oral discourse (and especially conversation) and printed text—and the earlier themes (differences between reasons and causes, as well as between intrasystemic and critical thinking) is a close one, I can't draw it until after discussing the differences between discourse and text.

In conversation, we're automatically *present* in the *context* that's producing the ideas at issue in the conversation. Without overlooking the fact that hidden purposes and even deception may be present, at least some of the purpose of a conversation is apt to be evident to the participants, and implicit meaning (missing premises) often can be filled in by simply interrupting the flow of dialogue and asking just what was meant by the other speaker. Conversation analysts report that we have many habitual techniques for clarifying ambiguity, establishing continuity, and explaining terms through modes of paraphrase, as well as for repairing lack of comprehension and for responding to even subtle clues that we've lost our audience. To some degree, we also use these techniques in the classroom. Also, some of them are retained in the forms of discourse our students are most likely to experience outside of the classroom: television and radio news, talk shows, rap music, and sermons. By retaining vestiges of conversational strategies, these forms of discourse retain something of a conversational sense—which is to say that the *actual* distance between speaker and hearer, which discourages conversational interchange, is minimized.

Also, discourse enables communication to occur in nonverbal ways that demand our physical, in addition to mental, presence. Body language engages sight far more easily than do marks on a page; our hearing is exercised in noting changes in pitch, stress, and pace; our senses of touch and smell often are activated. Indeed, we're more alert by virtue of movement itself, for we almost never stand or sit as still when talking, or even when just listening, as we typically do when reading. Although television discourse rules out engaging the senses of smell and touch, it requires strong involvement of vision—indeed, most programming makes far more demands on seeing than on listening.[7] As a result of all of these factors, we (human beings who are both minds and bodies) are very present in conversational situations. Also, most of the nonconversational discourse that we hear minimizes the actual distance between speaker and hearer. Correlatively, the content of discourse is minimally distant: outside of the classroom, we rarely—and our students almost never—find ourselves talking about something we don't know anything about and in which we may not have any interest.

In contrast to the event which is discourse and the very present event which is conversation, any text is a distant object. This is especially true of texts which are written in literary and philosophical styles. A text is an *object*, rather than an *event*, in that we typically perceive it as an already finished product, available in much the same way as are other things like trees, spoons, and dogs. Discourse, in contrast, happens when we make it: conversation requires active participation. Even monologue presumes that somebody's listening—since, outside of very special situations, we frown on people talking to themselves. Furthermore, there's a basic difference in the temporal nature of the two: discourse is fleeting, but text endures.[8] The implicitly known fact that what we're hearing is new—even novel—and will not be available after the present moment, may serve to command our attention. Correlatively, the indefinitely available written text, in a sense, is always already old, and can always be consulted at some other time. One way to summarize this difference is to characterize discourse as real in that it can be identified as present at a *particular* time and place. In contrast, a written text is ideal in that it is *indefinitely* available to anyone who can read, without regard for time or place.

It is precisely this universal accessibility of ideal objects that makes written texts *distant* objects. We aren't automatically present in their contexts, as we are present in the contexts of conversations and (to some extent) in all discourse. A written text is available in a wide variety of places and times; but it originated at some time and space other than the here and now. This is especially obvious in relation to those texts of our cultural tradition which give students so much more difficulty than mystery novels and newspapers. The ideas presumed and proposed by their authors, and the very subject matter discussed, are often (figuratively if not literally) foreign. We aren't part of the context in which those written texts were created, and their authors aren't available to supplement them—as are conversation partners or even platform speakers who respond to questions in a semiconversational manner at the close of their presentations.

Clearly, even this brief reflection on various types of speaking and writing reveals a spectrum of accessibility, rather than an all-or-nothing situation: A congenial conversation between two people who know one another well probably would be on one end of the spectrum, reading Kant's *Critique of Pure Reason* probably would be on the other, and the typical sermon probably would be in the middle. But the overall dramatic differences which distinguish these two ways of using language are clear. The meaning of discourse—the ideas proposed and the subject matter to which they refer—is comparatively accessible. The meaning of written text—again, the ideas proposed and the subject matter to which they refer—is comparatively inaccessible, since the context of its composition and the context of its reading are different. Discourse is personal, but text is anonymous. Discourse is present, but text is distant. Discourse is an event, but text is an object.

We can now connect these reflections upon the differences between discourse and text to the earlier descriptions of problems students have with distinguishing between the opinions of an author and the positions of a text, as well as in following "abstract" reasoning—especially when there's no narrative form in which the whole and parts (the system and its elements) are already configured. The foothold for connecting these three themes is critical thinking in the strong sense. For what is needed in order to understand (and even appropriate) these texts is skill in connecting with and reflecting upon the context for the text's positions, together with ability to interpret the text as a configuration of parts that could be otherwise—that is, as implicitly presenting possibilities and explicitly presenting actualities.

Some elaboration on the sketch of strong-sense critical thinking given earlier may be helpful at this point in order to show its applicability to this need for multiple interpretations. The general characteristics of this model which are most relevant to that need is its focus on "multilogical" rather than "monological" thinking, together with its stress on "the ability, and presumably the disposition also" to engage in reflexive criticism of a "holistic" sort that includes our own "most fundamental categories of thought and analysis."[9] Richard Paul gives this list of the "basic drives and abilities" involved in that endeavor:

> (a) an ability to question deeply one's own framework of thought, (b) an ability to reconstruct sympathetically and imaginatively the strongest versions of points of view and frameworks of thought opposed to one's own, and (c) an ability to reason dialectically (multilogically) to determine when one's own point of view is weakest and when an opposing point of view is strongest.[10]

Paul notes that these abilities are needed when "we attempt to suspend our egocentric tendency to confuse the framework of our own thinking with 'reality.' "[11] This suspension is the first step in thinking critically in the strong sense. It is a change in attitude that prepares us to take our leave from the actual situation in which we live when we begin to read.

What is called for in order to accomplish this leave taking is not a denial of our own situation, but a joining of it to the situation of the text—which results in the creation of a new context. In order words: we need to accomplish a re-situation that enables us to (in Paul's phrase) "reason dialectically (multilogically)" in what is, figuratively speaking, a world that does not exist in either my, or the author's *actual* situation; a *possible* "world of the text."[12] Willingness to suspend the actual and re-situate within the possible is basic for the interpretive thinking that enables us to understand and appropriate the ideas in humanities texts. We now need to reconsider the difficulties I identified earlier (differentiating between author's standpoint and text's position, and between causal and interpretive reasoning) in relation to this movement from a monological presumption of congruence between a person's actual framework for thinking to a multilogical resituation within possible positions.

The connection I see between these themes is this: the student who cannot distinguish between *understanding* the *reasons* for a *position* and *explaining* the *causes* for an author's *opinions*, is a person who has not been able to suspend the everyday habit of causal reasoning which we usually employ in conversation. For when we talk with one another, and to varying degrees when we only listen to discourse, we habitually and quite appropriately respond as an individual, to another individual who's speaking. In other words: within the encompassing reality of discourse, we take what's said to be a display of a person's thinking, and we quite naturally and unreflectively fail to distinguish between the speaker and what's spoken. Thus we naturally, habitually, and unreflectively explain what's said by referring to what we know or can guess about the speaker.

We need now to remember that face-to-face conversation is the communicative event most familiar to our students, and that speakers and hearers who make conversation must be focused on the personal, *present* character of that event. I say "must" for two reasons. First, the very character of the conversational situation is one in which (as I noted earlier) our senses are actively engaged in the unique construction of this particular and ongoing *event*. Also, our cultural practices require us to focus on the person. "Making good conversation" means taking turns in speaking and watching for pauses, rather than talking at the same time or leaving gaps in the flowing exchange of views. Yet the taking of turns must be accomplished without giving it so much attention that we lose track of what's being said. In my own experience as a teacher and parent, I've noticed that children and adolescents learn this cultural pattern slowly. Once we learn it, however, it has the status of being natural.

When we reconsider these characteristics of conversation (and discourse in general) in the framework of Richard Paul's terminology, we recognize that conversation is itself a multilogical problem which we often approach monologically or single-mindedly. The more socially acceptable single-minded focus is on the other person who's talking. But we sometimes have the experience of trying to talk with people who appear to be focusing primarily or solely on themselves. Depending on the circumstances, and on how charitable we are, we speak of them as people who can't get outside of their own heads, or as poor conversationalists, or as egocentric. In some cases, at least, "absent-minded" would be a more accurate characterization. This sort of behavior is relevant to our present interest when it is due to focusing on the *content* of the conversation—the ideas or subject matter which are distinct and even conceptually distant from the actual circumstances of the conversation. The distance can be so great as to render that content anonymous—which is to say, unconnected with any speaker at all, including those present. In such cases, personal contact with the present *event* of the conversation is lost.

There is an alternative and more positive way to characterize this behavior: the absent-minded person is in fact present to the *content* of the conversation, rather than to the *event* of conversing. Although it's culturally inappropriate to function in this way, it is just this attitude that we are attempting to cultivate in the classroom, when we ask students to understand and evaluate the ideas in a text. We are demanding that they suspend some (only recently and slowly learned) cultural patterns for communication. I would borrow a phrase from my own favorite teacher to characterize this demand: we want our students to perform an unnatural act. Rather than continuing with the patterns, attitudes, and dispositions appropriate to the personal, present, and real *event* of conversational discourse, we're asking for patterns, attitudes, and dispositions appropriate to those anonymous, distant, ideal *objects* called texts. To look at this requirement in a slightly different way: we're requiring students to suspend their customary causal reasoning, which they habitually use to *explain events* (including discourse), in favor of interpretive reasoning, which is appropriate in order to *understand objects* (including texts). Furthermore, we make this demand implicitly, without any explicit introduction of what's involved in the alternative attitude, and without any explicit practice in doing the unnatural. If we compare our teaching practices in this area with the ways we teach other subjects and skills, for example, arithmetic, tennis, foreign languages, or woodworking, we may cease to be surprised that our students do so poorly when they encounter the great ideas in textual form.

Given this description of what may well add up to an enormous, and even unreasonable, demand, we need to distance ourselves from the portrayal in order to recognize how we can use strong-sense critical thinking abilities to formulate an alternative approach. For we need to consider our usual pedagogical practices not as an event (as something we're doing), since doing so is apt to mean that criticizing it involves criticizing ourselves. Rather, I would consider this portrayal as a text: as a series of descriptions and assertions, some of which are offered as evidence, support, or reason for others, and which can be considered in abstraction from events and from ourselves as the actors (agents) in those events. The ability to consider textual passages in this way, I noted earlier, is one that's generally found among teachers, but is rarely present among students. However, that we can do it doesn't mean that it's always easy to do. In my experience, it's most difficult when we need to do it in regard to portrayals of ourselves—which is just to say that it's both literally and metaphorically difficult to gain any distance from ourselves, so that we can see our own behavior as clearly as we can see the behavior of others. And this is just why developing our ability to understand texts is valuable both for that immediate purpose, and for thinking critically about events (including discourse).

This may seem to be a paradoxical assertion, since I have been stressing that we habitually use causal reasoning in explaining what occurs in discourse. In effect, I'm now asking not only that we learn to perform that unnatural act which we demand of our students in their encounters with texts, but that we extend it to discourse. I can offer some justification, which begins by reconsidering the connections I stated earlier: the student who cannot distinguish between understanding the reasons for a position and explaining the causes of an author's opinions is a person who has not been able to suspend ordinary habits of causal reasoning. These habits develop as we learn to engage in conversation.

What happens when I (so to speak) distance myself from conversational experience is that I turn from my habitual involvement in events, to a reflective involvement in their constitutive features. My attitude changes from one of straightforward *participation* in an event to reflective *criticism* of an object. In other words: I must *suspend interaction* in discourse if I want to *institute reflection* on that discourse. I do this by shifting my focus from my discourse partner to the content of what's said. Since I'm no longer focused on what a person is doing (saying), I no longer need to use psychological (semicausal) explanation of the causal interaction displayed in that behavior. This change in attitude and focus frees me for describing and interpreting the features and connections that are intrinsic reasons for that object; the basis for the content that's been said. I can refocus attention from explaining the person who speaks to understanding what's been said.

It's this change of focus (from one that is straightforwardly productive, participatory, and causal, to one that's critically reflective, distanciated, and interpretive) that gives our students such great difficulty. My response to that difficulty begins in recognizing that it's easier to accomplish this change in attitude with a text that's already a distant object, than with discourse, such as conversation, that is so obviously a present event. In other words, shifting into an interpretive attitude toward a text is easier than making that shift in focus in regard to a discourse event. Once this is recognized, two rules of our everyday, natural experience become relevant. First, as teachers we know that we teach the less difficult before the more difficult: simple division before long division; sewing aprons before dresses; serving and returning the ball before strategies for winning the game. Likewise, we do well to learn interpretation by reflective criticism of texts before we do so in conversation, much less, in argument. The second rule is one that we already practice when we recognize that physicians should avoid treating members of their own families, and that spouses who are in conflict, or out of communication, should go to a family counselor rather than to one of their mothers. The critical spirit that's sought in the physician or counselor is one that has enough distance from a situation—while still at home in its context—to successfully practice reflective interpretation and accomplish understanding of the ideas motivating the situation.

The last requirement for an interpretive focus has been suggested in my reference to the combination of distance and shared context. I have been extolling the advantages of distanciation for interpretation, and now must speak to its disadvantages. We can only appropriate the text's world of ideas if they are not so distanciated from our situation as to lack a shared context. If that context is not evident, we must be translators before we can be interpreters. Just as preachers learn to retell the ideas of scripture in contemporary terms, we need to portray the ideas in humanities texts in terms that are comprehensible to readers who do not naturally share the place and time at which the text became an object. I have focused here on a major prerequisite to thinking critically about the ideas in a text; namely, appreciating the distanciated text as an object available for an endless variety of appropriative events. But that is not to say that other prerequisites—and specifically, translation—are easy tasks. Rather, my limited focus reflects the fact that translation is part of *how* we interpret, and this discussion is focused primarily on *why* we need to interpret as well as evaluate.

We now know something about both the "why" and the "what" of what needs doing if we are to develop the ability to reason multilogically. More specifically, we have located, in the everyday phenomenon of absent-mindedness, some clues that can help to cultivate skill in identifying contexts that require interpretive rather than (or, in addition to) causal reasoning. This reflective analysis, which has thematized that ability or skill, also provides an example of interpretive reasoning that looks for reasons within a situation. In other words: This essay uses a hermeneutic phenomenological method in order to analyze certain pedagogical events and propose a response to certain "why" and "what" questions that arise in teaching. A specification of that same method can respond to the "how" question that my analysis has, thus far, avoided. Before doing so, it may be helpful to summarize the method.

There are five stages, each of which consists in applying a particular hermeneutical rule. The method begins (so to speak) prior to itself. For prior to this telling, I made certain *observations* while participating in particular teaching situations. While reflecting upon those experiences—which is to say, after distancing myself from the place and time in which they occurred—I prepared the *description* which forms the center of this essay. In order to accomplish that, I relied upon *categorization* in order to reduce the wealth of experiential data to a coherent portrayal of recognizable events (student difficulties, conversational practices, etc.) that seem to capture the basic or essential features of the experience. Then I proposed an *interpretation* of the events, while keeping in mind that this was but one possible interpretation—and one that, inevitably, relied upon the particular categories and observations that I had made as participant-analyst. Any particular analytic experience ends with *communication* of the analyzed experience. In a sense, the method does not end with completion of this (or any) analysis, since the telling of what has been discovered is in fact another mode of participation. But at this (second) stage of participation, the communicative circle includes not only the original participants, but anyone with sufficient linguistic skill and interest to read these words.

Although I've developed this method as a variation upon phenomenological description and the "hermeneutic circle," the result is more a spiral than a circle. It begins and ends in participation (in lived experience), but the second stage of participation is augmented by the reflective process. Perhaps this can be stated more clearly by stating this "hermeneutic phenomenological spiral" method in skeleton form: participation/ observation, description/articulation, reduction/categorization, interpretation/analysis, communication/participation. . . . The analytic portrayal which results is an extended argument as to the nature of the situation at issue, rather than an apodictically certain description.

This same method, adapted to the particularities of the written text, provides a procedural response to "how" questions:

1. read the text in a natural, straightforward mode of encountering a verbal lived experience;

2. shift to an attitude of reflective description that includes refocusing on the text as distant from the personal interests and causal connections that are intrinsic to human behavior, but not to textual objects;

3. identify the ideas and connections that are present to this reflection, and consider whether other ideas and connections might, plausibly, be embedded within the text;

4. develop coherent evident and alternate portrayals of the text in a variety of configurations;

5. communicate the results of reading the text in this interpreted (reflected upon and articulated) form.

This may seem like a great deal to do, under the heading of "interpretation," before even thinking of evaluating the claims that can be located within the text. The encouragement I would offer is that the process becomes easier with practice. Also, since it's a nonsubject-specific procedure, there are a lot of opportunities to practice. Furthermore, since that practice is on a variety of texts, rather than with any sort of standard form (or texts which need reformulation to approximate such a form) the issue of transfer from particular standardized or constructed exercises to actual texts does not arise.[13]

We need, at last, to consider two very different ways that teachers can go about introducing interpretive reasoning. We can impose it from on high (so to speak) in much the same way that logical analysis often is introduced. I don't recommend that, since it places teachers in the untenable position of saying: "If you want to be a critical thinker, do just as I say." Instead, both ethics and effectiveness speak for introducing the change in attitude needed for interpretive reasoning by showing that it utilizes strategies we already possess, although we aren't usually aware of them as useful for thinking critically. Sports provide helpful analogies here: we all know how to run, jump, and hit a ball, but we all recognize the advantages of working with a coach and reflectively focusing on those abilities as configurations that can be improved.

The absent-minded conversationalist I mentioned earlier is a good place to begin that process. This is a person, I suggested, who can be so focused on the content of the discourse that he or she lacks personal contact with the present event of conversation. By *content*, I mean the ideas and connections which are relatively anonymous—even when spoken by an actual conversation partner. We are all, at one time or another, absent-minded. Furthermore, we know that at least some of the time, we choose to be: that is, we are already able to shift our attention from the speaker to what is being said; from the discourse event to the content communicated to us in and by that event.

What we need to do as critical thinkers is increase the distance (between speaker and what's said) that's already present when we're absent-minded. In other words, we need to be absent from the personal and present character of the real event, in order to be reflectively and critically present to the ideas which can be focused on by means of that event, and thus brought into the foreground of our thinking as an ideal object. The way to begin teaching interpretive reasoning, then, is by encouraging our students to be absent-minded. Or, more precisely, we should begin by encouraging our students to focus on just what's involved in their absent-minded moments. Coming to understand that change of attitude and focus as evidence of skill in reasoning is the first step in cultivating critical thinking as an ability that is already present and so available for improvement.

Notes

1. As an explication of "the humanities," these remarks by Ralph Barton Perry seem timelessly accurate:

> I define "the humanities," then, to embrace whatever influences conduce to freedom. "The humanities" is not to be employed as a mere class name for certain divisions of knowledge or parts of a scholastic curriculum, or for certain human institutions, activities, or relationships, but to signify a certain condition of freedom which these may serve to create. . . . By freedom I mean enlightened choice. I mean the action in which habit, reflex or suggestion are superseded by an individual's fundamental judgments of good and evil; the action whose premises are explicit; the action which proceeds from personal reflection and integration. . . . The extent to which a man is free, that is, exercises enlightened choice, depends in the first place upon the extent to which he is aware of the possibilities. . . . Freedom is proportional to the range of options. The first condition of freedom, then, is "learning."

These reflections are taken from Perry's "A Definition of the Humanities" in Theodore Green, ed., *The Meaning of the Humanities* (Princeton: Princeton University Press, 1938), pp. 4–6.

2. In developing these models I've drawn on several sources: J. Anthony Blair and Ralph H. Johnson, "The Current State of Informal Logic," *Informal Logic* 9 (1987): 147–51; Ralph Johnson and J. Anthony Blair, "Recent Developments in Informal Logic," in *Informal Logic: The First International Symposium* (Inverness Cal.: Edgepress, 1980); Trudy Govier, "Five Different Ways of Approaching the Teaching of Reasoning Skills," (unpublished); Richard W. Paul, "The Critical Thinking Movement: A Historical Perspective," in *National Forum* 65 (1985): 2–3, 32, reprinted in Richard W. Paul, *Critical Thinking* (Rohnert Park, Cal.: Center for Critical Thinking, Sonoma State University, 1990), pp. 1–6; Michael Scriven, "Critical Thinking and the Concept of Literacy," *Informal Logic* 9 (1987): 94–110; Perry Weddle, "On Theory in Informal Logic," *Informal Logic* 7 (1985): 119–26.

3. This is not to say that we *always* have the opportunity to choose. Rather, teaching critical thinking is worthwhile because we *sometimes* have that opportunity, and want to be prepared to choose reasonably when we can choose at all.

4. For a broader discussion of this difference as one of skill in instrumental reasoning in contrast to judgment, and some causal reasoning of my own as to why students are disposed toward the former rather than the latter, see my "Is Critical Thinking a Technique, or a Means of Enlightenment," *Informal Logic* 8 (1986): 1–17, "Dialogue, Distanciation, and Engagement: Toward a Logic of Televisual Communication," *Informal Logic* 10 (1988): 151–68, and "The Emperor Has Only Clothes: Toward a Hermeneutic of the Video Text," in Alan Olson, Christopher Parr, and Debra Parr, eds., *Video Icons and Values* (Albany: State University of New York Press, 1990), pp. 45–62.

5. See "Educating Reason: Critical Thinking, Informal Logic, and the Philosophy of Education, Part One: A Critique of McPeck and a Sketch of an Alternate View," *APA Newsletter on Teaching Philosophy* (Spring-Summer 1985): 10–13. A revised version of this article is incorporated in his *Educating Reason: Rationality, Critical Thinking, and Education* (New York: Routledge, 1988).

6. "The Contribution of Philosophy to Critical Thinking," in *Critical Thinking*, p. 458. This "intra-system thinking" shares central characteristics with what I call "instrumental reason" (see note 4). The contrast is with judgment: an attitude that looks beyond the parameters of any present (given) system in order to reflect upon the system itself, as

a whole that is but one among an unknown number of possible systems and as a configuration of parts that could be connected otherwise. In speaking of such a system, I follow phenomenological practice in always including within the reflection the person who reflects. In other words, reflection is also reflexion. I often characterize strong-sense critical thinking as "thinking critically in the broad sense," in order to suggest this encompassing character. Correlatively, Paul's "intra-system thinking," or my "judgment," are "thinking critically in a delimited sense."

7. I discuss these differences in detail in *Reasoning across the Media: Verbal, Visual, and Televisual Literacies* (Upper Montclair, N.J.: Montclair State College: Institute for Critical Thinking, 1989).

8. Video and tape recording, of course, blur these distinctions. Then again, I've observed that people will go to hear a lecture but not a sound recording of it. We're more accepting of videotape, I suspect, because it engages sight and thus is closer to the actual discourse event. What it lacks, however, is the shared context which allows supplementation through conversation with the author, and so the recorded event takes on much of the distant-object character of written text. Correlatively, some people prefer recorded music to attending concerts. Here, I suggest, the same phenomenon may be present in reverse: putting sight, touch, and smell out of play enables greater exercise of hearing. Also, since attending a concert doesn't usually involve conversation with the composer, conductor, or musicians, the dialogical exchange that characterizes a verbal event is absent. (There are, however, many other relevant differences between verbal and musical events.)

9. Richard Paul, "Critical Thinking and the Critical Person," in *Critical Thinking*, p. 109.

10. Ibid., p. 110.

11. Ibid., p. 109.

12. The phrase is Paul Ricoeur's; see, for example, his *Interpretation Theory: Discourse and the Surplus of Meaning* (Fort Worth: Texas Christian University Press, 1976). The re-situation process I describe here is taken quite directly from the extensive developments of hermeneutic by Hans-George Gadamer (his *Truth and Method*, New York: Seabury, 1975, is one example) and by Ricoeur.

13. After some amount of practice, gaining a more theoretical understanding by means of some introductory readings on phenomenology and hermeneutics may be attractive. Two appropriate books are *The Way*

of Phenomenology by Richard M. Zaner (New York: Pegasus Press, 1970) and *Experimental Phenomenology* by Don Ihde (New York: Putnam, 1977). For a more advanced theoretical introduction, see Don Ihde, *Hermeneutic Phenomenology* (Evanston: Northwestern University Press, 1971).

Part II: PROBLEMS FOR
          THEORY OF
          CRITICAL REASONING

|||█ The Problem
of Methodology

9 Taking Cover in Coverage: Critical Reasoning and the Conflict of Theories

GERALD GRAFF

No discussion of critical reasoning as an educational goal would be complete today without a consideration of the sudden and spectacular growth of theory across the cultural disciplines of the university. In departments of literature in particular, debates over how to increase the critical reasoning capacities of undergraduates and graduates alike inevitably become embroiled in the larger debate, often highly polarized and acrimonious, over the place of literary theories such as feminism, Marxism, poststructuralism, and the new historicism and their corresponding methodologies of reading. This debate over theory is closely related to other well-publicized debates such as the one over the humanistic canon and the claims of the traditional Western classics over against those of minority and multicultural traditions and popular media.

The argument of this essay (aspects of which I have been developing elsewhere) is that for furthering the cause of critical reasoning, the most effective step educational institutions can take in the face of this conflict over theory and its implications is to make the conflict itself a central object of study. Instead of viewing the conflicts over theories, canons, traditions and

189

countertraditions as an unfortunate disruption of the unity and coherence of the curriculum, educators should look for ways to structure these conflicts into the curriculum, using them to give the curriculum a new kind of coherence. The point has application to other fields besides literary studies or even the humanities. Educational institutions need to begin making productive use of ideological, methodological, and philosophical differences rather than treating those differences as a symptom of malaise.

Any such effort to make productive use of theory conflict in the curriculum, however, comes up against a traditional organizing structure that has systematically discouraged academic institutions from acknowledging their internal conflicts, much less exploiting them as objects of study. In my argument, this structural fact about the organization of various forms of teaching and research in modern universities—which I call the field-coverage model—more crucially determines the educational experience of students than do the form and content of individual courses and teaching practices. In my view, the goal of helping students to increase their critical reasoning abilities is best furthered not by trying to change what teachers teach or the way they teach it (an effort doomed to futility), but by organizing the necessarily diverse existing teaching practices in a way that enables central conflicts and differences to be clarified within the curriculum itself rather than being hidden from students behind the scenes.

In the cultural disciplines, as I noted, the debate over critical reasoning has become embroiled in the larger debate over the status of theory, which is usually counterposed against traditional literary studies. Here a certain confusion must be addressed, for though most of what passes for theory aims to subvert traditional notions of cultural and political hierarchy, there is nothing intrinsically leftist about it. That is, it is perfectly possible to defend the infusion of theory into the curriculum on traditional grounds, namely, that students need theoretical frameworks in order to conceptualize and talk about literature. Until recently, in fact, it was traditionalists who called for more theory, in opposition to the disconnected empiricism of positivist literary history and formalist explication, where the faith seemed to be, as the literary scholar Norman Foerster caustically observed in 1941, that "the facts, once in, would of themselves mean something." Most scholars, Foerster went on to complain, "have left virtually un-inspected the theory upon which their practice rests," or they have proceeded "as if that theory were an absolute good for all time."[1] While a great deal of current literary theory does radically attack the premises and values of traditional literary humanism, that attack revives many of the questions about literature and its cultural functions that have always concerned traditional humanistic critics.

The real enemy of tradition has been the established form of literary study, which has neglected traditional theoretical ques-tions about the ends and social functions of literature and criti-cism. There is something strange about the belief that we are being traditional when we isolate literary works from their con-texts and explicate them in a vacuum or with a smattering of background information. A humanist like Matthew Arnold would have recognized little that was traditional or humanistic in these established forms of pedagogy. I am not saying that re-cent literary theory is nothing more than the application of tra-ditional Arnoldian culture by other means. What I am saying is that recent theory has reawakened some of the large questions that traditional humanists like Arnold raised, even while reject-ing the Arnoldian answers as no longer sufficient.

In fact, it was the breakdown of agreement of the Arnoldian answers that inspired the current popularity of theory and that ensures, I think, that this interest will not be a passing fad. By one definition that seems to me valid, literary theory is simply the kind of discourse that is generated when presuppositions that were once tacitly shared about literature, criticism, and culture become open to debate. Theory is what breaks out when agree-ment about such terms as *text, reading, history, interpretation, tradition,* and *literature* can no longer be taken for granted, so their meanings have to be formulated and debated. Admittedly, this is to use the term *theory* in a very broad sense, denoting an examination of legitimating presuppositions, beliefs, and ideologies. By this definition, even those who attack the more abstract form of theory (as Arnold and F. R. Leavis did and as many literature teachers today do) qualify as theorists, insofar as they, too, theorize about the premises of literature and culture and the place of literature and culture in modern societies. In this sense, all teachers of literature operate on theories whether they choose to examine these theories or not, which is another way of saying we are all teachers of critical thinking.

Clearly, we need to reserve another sense of *theory* to denote the technical, abstruse, and systematic speculation typical of recent continental thought. But here is another misconception—that theory is necessarily obscure, technical, and abstruse, and therefore too advanced or esoteric for the average college or high school student. This belief fails to recognize that all teaching involves popularization, and that even the most difficult current theories are not intrinsically more resistant to popularization than the so-called New Criticism that dominated the teaching of literature until recently, and that had its own abstruse conceptual origins in Kant, Coleridge, and Croce.

It is the average-to-poor student who suffers most from the established curriculum's poverty of theory, for such a student lacks command of the conceptual contexts that make it possible to integrate perceptions and generalize from them. This point is missed by teachers who boast that they have no truck with theory and "just teach the books." All the close concentration in the world on the particularities of literary texts will not help a student make sense of these particularities unless the student has a group of categories that give them meaning. For this reason, those who oppose the pedagogical spread of theory in the humanities seem to me to have things exactly backward when they contrast theory with tradition and with close literary analysis and demand that we minister to the ills of literary studies by desisting from theoretical chatter and getting back to teaching literature itself. It was precisely the isolation of "literature itself" in a conceptual vacuum that stranded students without a context for *talking about* literature, and that still forces many of them to resort to *Cliff Notes* and other such cribs. It is easy to disdain such cribs, but marketing pressures have actually forced their producers to think through the problems facing the average literature student more realistically than have many department curricular planners. *Cliffs Notes* supply students with the generalized things to say about literary works that the literature program too often takes it for granted they will somehow get on their own. The irony of the current cry of "back to literature itself" is that it was the exclusive concentration on literature itself that helped create a situation in which the *Cliffs Notes* on a given work of literature is often more readily available in campus bookstores than the work itself.

My purpose here, however, is not to make a case for theory in the literature program, but to point up some difficulties that arise once we have decided that teaching theory furthers the goals of critical thinking. In addressing the pedagogical uses of recent literary theory, we tend to treat the issue as if it were primarily a matter of figuring out how to integrate this theory into individual classrooms. We form conference workshops, which concentrate on technical questions like how to use reader-response criticism to teach *Hamlet,* or poststructuralist theory to teach the romantic lyric, or feminist critiques of the established canon to restructure the nineteenth-century-novel course. Such innovations at the level of individual teaching practice can be useful and necessary, but if we do not go beyond them we will limit theory to its instrumental uses, making it into nothing more than a means of sprucing up ritualized procedures of literary explication. We will apply theory within the existing structure but will fail to make a theoretical examination of the structure itself. The same point can can be made about critical thinking, which can easily degenerate into yet another panacea if we treat it simply as a set of contents to be taught rather than a result of changes in institutional structure.

I want to suggest that one of the first things we need to do with literary theory is to train it on the literature department itself, particularly on the way the department, other departments, and the university are organized. Insofar as a literature department represents a certain organization of literature, it is itself a kind of theory, though it has been largely an incoherent theory, and this incoherence has reinforced the impression that the department has no theory.

In deciding to call ourselves departments of English, French, and German—rather than of literature, cultural studies, or something else—and in subdividing these national units into periods and genres, we have already made significant theoretical choices. But we do not see these choices as choices, much less as theoretical ones, because the categories that mark them—English, eighteenth century, poetry, novel—take on the appearance of neutral administrative conveniences and thus as facts of nature that we take for granted. We need to recognize that the way we organize and departmentalize literature, or any subject, is not only a crucial theoretical choice, but one that largely determines our professional activity and the way students and lay people understand or fail to understand it.

To say this is not to agree with those who think that the departmentalization of literature itself was a kind of original sin and look back nostalgically to the days before the creative imagination was bureaucratized. Anyone seriously committed to the idea of democratic mass education has to acknowledge the obvious necessity for some form of bureaucratic departmental organization and the specialized division of labor that this entails. But the form this organization takes is neither self-evident nor inevitable, and it will have a lot to do with considerations of theory.

I use the term *field-coverage* as a convenient description of the model of organization that has governed literature departments since the dawn of the modern university in the last two decades of the nineteenth century. According to the field-coverage model, a department considers itself adequately staffed when it has acquired the personnel to "cover" an adequate number of designated literary fields, and it assumes that the core of the curriculum will consist of the student's coverage of some portion of those fields. The field coverage model arose as an adaptation to the modern university's ideal of research specialization: dividing the territory of literature into fields supervised by specialists imitated the organizational form that had made the sciences efficient in producing advanced research. But the field-coverage model had a humanistic justification as well, the argument being that a student who covered the fields represented by a department would get a reasonably balanced exposure to the humanistic tradition.

It was its administrative advantages, however, that made the field-coverage model irresistible, especially in a newly expanding university where short-term expediencies rarely afforded leisure for discussion of first principles, and where first principles in any case were increasingly open to dispute. One of the most conspicuous operational advantages was the way field-coverage made the department virtually self-regulating. By assigning instructors roles predetermined by their literary fields, the model created a system in which the job of instruction could proceed as if on automatic pilot, with no need for instructors to confer with their peers or superiors. Assuming that individual instructors had been competently trained—and by about 1900 the American system of graduate study had sufficiently matured to see to that—instructors could be left on their own to carry out their teaching and research jobs without elaborate supervision and management.

A second advantage of the field-coverage model was that it made the department immensely open to innovation. By making individuals functionally independent of one another in carrying out their tasks, the model enabled the department to assimilate new subjects, ideas, and methodologies without having to face the conflicts that would otherwise have had to be debated and worked through. It thus allowed the modern university to overcome the chronic stagnation that had beset the old nineteenth-century college, where new ideas that challenged the established Christian orthodoxy were usually excluded or suppressed. The coverage model solved the problem of how to make the university open to innovation and cultural diversity without incurring paralyzing conflicts.

Unfortunately, these advantages came at a high price that we have been paying ever since. The same arrangements that allowed instructors to do their jobs efficiently and independently also relieved them of the need to discuss and reflect on the values and implications of their practices. The field-coverage form of organization left literature departments without any need to discuss matters of fundamental direction either with their own members or with members of other departments, and it is a rule of bureaucratic organizations that whatever these organizations are not structurally required to do they will tend not to do. Moral exhortation unaccompanied by structural change will be largely wasted. The modern university department was open to innovation as the college had not been before, but in circumstances that were almost as effective in muffling the confrontations provoked by innovation as the old system of repressive control had been. Previously there had been little open debate over first principles because dissenters had been excluded. Now dissenters were invited in, but the departmental structure kept them too isolated from their colleagues for open debate to take place.

Not that vigorous controversy did not arise and spread. But it went on usually only behind the scenes of education, in specialized journals, departmental meetings, or private gossip—all places where students derived little benefit from it, usually knew nothing of its existence, and certainly did not participate in it. Instructors were freer than they had previously been from administrative tyranny, but at the expense of important possibilities of intellectual community.

To put it another way, the field-coverage model "solved" the problem of theory. Departmental organization took the place of theory, for the presence of an ordered array of fields, fully staffed, made it unnecessary for anyone to have a theory about what the department should do in order for the work of teaching and research to go on. The theoretical choices had already been taken care of in the grid of periods, genres, and other catalogue rubrics, which embodied a clear and seemingly uncontroversial conceptualization of what the department was about. With literature courses ranged in periods and genres, instructors did not need to ask what *period* or *genre* meant or what principles justified the established demarcations. The connections and contrasts between periods and genres, so important for understanding these categories, fell between the cracks. So did other large issues such as the relation between the sciences and the humanities, which was the responsibility of neither the sciences nor the humanities.

Latent conflicts of method and ideology that had divided the faculty from the outset and the larger cultural conflicts that these academic disputes often exemplified did not have to be confronted and taught. Fundamental disagreements over the study of literature were embodied, for example, in the conflict between the research scholar, who adhered to a positivistic methodology, and the generalist man or woman of letters, who was impatient with facts in themselves when their broader meanings were neglected. Later, this became a conflict between both these types and the analytical New Critic. But while the department *enacted* these conflicts, it did not put them explicitly in the foreground and engage them. As long as scholars, generalists, and critics covered their separate turf within self-enclosed classrooms, the average student could not become aware of their clashes of principle, much less use them to stimulate his own critical thinking.

This accounts for the otherwise inexplicable persistence of the fiction of shared humanistic purposes during a period when conflicts in method and ideology were becoming progressively more frequent and antagonistic. Since the official premise that humanistic values governed the department did not have to be theorized or subjected to regular review and discussion, there was no particular reason to notice that the premise was wearing increasingly thin. Not only did the structure provide no necessary occasion for questioning the content of that humanism which, according to the catalogue, theoretically held the diverse and conflicting viewpoints of departments together, but the illusion could be maintained that nobody even had a theory.

And of course it was true that the department did not have *a* theory, for it harbored many theories without any clear way to integrate them. Here we arrive at the central problem: How does a department institutionalize theory when there is no agreement on what the theory is to be? The question leads to a stalemate, however, only if it assumed that a department must achieve theoretical consensus before it can achieve theoretical coherence.

The perennial assumption seems to have been that professional and cultural conflicts have to be resolved before they can be presented to the students: students, apparently, must be exposed only to the results of the conflicts dividing their teachers, not to the process of conflict itself, which presumably would confuse or demoralize them. Surely one reason why we tend, as I noted earlier, to reduce pedagogical questions to questions about teaching strategies in individual courses is that we doubt the possibility of agreement on larger collective goals. Our doubts are well founded in experience, but why need we assume that we have to agree in order to integrate our activities? Must we have consensus to have coherence?

The unfortunate thing is not that faculty conflicts of method and ideology have often proved unresolvable, but that we have been able to exploit so little of the potential educational value of our unresolved conflicts. Part of the reason for this loss of opportunity in literary studies stems from the literary mind's temperamental resistance to airing differences; the old-fashioned version of this attitude held that open debate is unseemly, while the more up-to-date version holds that there are no privileged metalanguages, no fact-of-the-matter outside interpretations, no "decidable" answers to questions, which leaves nothing to argue about anyway. But even if these sources of resistance to debate were to disappear, there would remain a problem of structure. The coverage model prevents exemplary differences of method, ideology, and value from emerging into view even when we want them to.

The humanities curriculum mirrors and reproduces the evasion of conflict characteristic of the departmental structure. Hypothetically, the curriculum expresses a unified humanistic tradition, yet anyone who looks at it can see that in every era down to the present it has expressed not a consensus on humanistic values but a set of political trade-offs and compromises among competing professional factions. We need not enter into the now disputed question of whether the curriculum can or should be determined by any more lofty principle than political trade-offs, for again this is precisely the type of theoretical and cultural question that does not have to be resolved in order to play an effective part in education. If the curriculum is probably going to continue to express political trade-offs, as it seems likely to do unless one faction in the current disciplinary conflict can wholly liquidate its opposition, then why not bring students in on whatever may be instructive in the conflict of political principles involved?

Instead of confronting such conflicts and building them into the curriculum, however, the department (and the university at large) has always responded to pressures by *adding* new subjects and keeping them safely sealed off from one another. This practice can be justified educationally only on the increasingly hollowpretense that exposure to an aggregate of teachers, periods, genres, methods, and points of view somehow comes together in the student's mind as a coherent humanistic experience. The tacit faith is that students will make sense of the aggregate even if their instructors cannot. It is surprising how many students manage to do just that, but most do not. Recognition of this failure stimulates further curricular innovation, which in turn, however, is assimilated into the cycle of accretion and marginalization.

Over the hundred-year span of our institutional history, language and literature departments have had a succession of methodological models, each with a corresponding pedagogy, from linguistic philology to positivist literary history to New Critical explication, all of which now remain as strata overlaid by the new theories and methodologies. Each of these revisions has marked a paradigm shift in which the conception of what counts as literature, scholarship, and criticism altered radically. Yet, as I attempt to show in *Professing Literature*, an institutional history of academic literary studies in the United States, the one constant through all this change has been the field-coverage model.[2] The contents have been radically reshuffled, but the envelope has remained the same, and with it the method of assimilating innovation. The changes undoubtedly represent progress in critical sophistication and cultural range, but the benefits for the average student have been less than they might have been.

Nor is it just the students who have paid a price under the field-coverage system; the faculty have paid as well. Since the principle of selection for recruiting a literature faculty has systematically screened out intellectual commonality, the result is a kind of programmed professional loneliness. Consider the consequence of the mighty effort departments make to achieve a balanced spread of interests. If the interests of candidate X overlap those of faculty member Y, their shared ground is an argument for not hiring X—"We already have Y who does that." The calculus of need that determines hiring priorities thus tends to preselect exactly those instructors who have the least basis for talking to one another. In compensation, the department builds a salutary diversity, but the potential benefits of diversity are blocked. Nor is the problem just hypothetical: the recent proliferation of humanities conferences and symposia suggests that these gatherings have become substitutes for the kind of general discussion that does not take place at home.

The moral is that if the introduction of literary theory is to make a real difference in encouraging critical thinking in the average literature student, we must find some way to modify the field-coverage model. Otherwise, theory (and perhaps critical thinking itself) will be institutionalized as yet another field, equivalent to literary periods and genres—which is to say, it will become one more option that can safely be ignored. We will lose theory's potential for drawing the disconnected parts of the literature curriculum into relation and providing students with the context needed to develop their critical reasoning capacities. So, I would argue, the real threat that theory faces today comes not from its outright opponents, some of whom are at least willing to argue with it, but from those who are perfectly willing to grant theory an honored place in the scheme of departmental coverage so that they can then forget about it.

This pattern seems to be establishing itself now, as literature departments clamor to hire literary theorists to get the new field covered, after which they assume that the relation of theory to the interests of the rest of the department will take care of itself. In practice, this policy passes the buck to the students, leaving them to figure out how theory courses correlate with others. And of course as long as theory is conceived as a special field, the rest of the department can go on thinking that its work has no connection with theory.

Then, too, offering students doses of theory in individual courses without helping them make the requisite connections with other courses often confuses students, a fact which anti-theorists can then cite as proof that theory is inherently over the students' heads. For the average student to profit from recent theory, the courses that incorporate it must be not only linked with other courses in literature and beyond, but also enabled to operate as a central means of correlation and contextualization.

In other words, literature departments should stop kidding themselves. They should stop pretending that, as long as individual courses are reasonably well conceived and well taught, the aggregate can be counted on to take care of itself. If they are serious about incorporating theory, they should not let it remain an option but should make it central to all their activities—not, however, by putting theory specialists in charge, but by recognizing that *all* their members are theorists and that students need to participate in the conflict of interpretations and theories in order to develop their critical reasoning potential.

To put it another way, introducing more theory will only compound our problems unless we rethink the assumption that the essential unit of all teaching has to be the single, self-sufficient course that students correlate with other courses on their own. Literature programs can fail just as badly teaching a new canon in a theoretical way as they have failed in teaching an old canon in a nontheoretical way. Unless the disparate discourses of literary studies and other disciplines begin to form more connections, it seems likely that even the most radical theories and canon revisions will have less impact than they might on the way most students take in what is put before them.

To close, then, I offer a few schematic suggestions:

- In relation to other courses in the department, theory courses should be central, not peripheral; their function should be to contextualize and pull together the student's work in other courses (outside as well as inside the literature department). Wherever possible, therefore, they should be required courses rather than electives.

- In taking stock of its strengths, a department should evaluate not just how well it is covering standard fields and approaches, but also what potential conflicts of ideological and methodological perspectives it harbors; it should then ask itself what curricular arrangements might exploit these conflicts for students. There need be no single way of doing this—but one idea (suggested by Brook Thomas) is to couple courses to bring out conceptual relations and contrasts—between, say, views of literature in earlier and modern literary periods, or between competing and complementary methodologies of interpretation.

- Another way to use conflicts and differences to connect subjects rather than simply covering them would be to thematize the academic term. There is no bureaucratic reason why any given semester or quarter cannot have a theme in order to give focus to points of convergence and divergence across already existing courses or across several departments. Instructors could assign several common texts and agree to arrange some joint symposia, along the lines of an academic conference, that would organize the separate discourses represented by the courses into a common discussion. Thus a theme like "The Canon Conflict," for example, or "The Crisis of the Traditional Humanities," or "Social Constructionism and its Discontents" (a debate taking place in many different disciplines), could be used to turn the curriculum in a given term into a vital intellectual forum instead of just a scattering of more or less good courses which have no way of speaking to one another even when their concerns converge. Since, however, the theme would change from term to term, there would be no need for the kinds of unresolvable conflicts that invariably ensue from attempts to formulate a common core of subjects.

- In line with this principle of organizing and teaching the conflicts rather than merely covering subjects, the conflict over theory itself (again, one that is going on across disciplines and departments and could be therefore used to connect them) should be emphasized in the curriculum, with due allowance, of course, for the level at which it is introduced to students of varying experience and abilities. Thus a literature department harboring a conflict between theorists and antitheorists should look for ways to build this conflict into its courses, so that students can situate themselves in relation to the controversy and take an active role in it. The department should also look for ways such disputes can be used to complicate and challenge period and genre distinctions, without necessarily eliminating them.

- A literature department should consider the unit of teaching to be the issue or context, not the isolated text; texts to be taught should be chosen not only for their intrinsic value but for their usefulness in illustrating exemplary problems, issues, and debates.

- As a means of accomplishing the previous goal on a structural scale, the university should eventually subsume literary studies under cultural studies and cultural history, conceived not as a privileged approach with a single political bias but as a framework for ideological dialectic. Several institutions have already moved in this direction.

The point is that theory is not only a field to be covered, though it is that at one level. It is something that all teachers of literature and all readers practice and that all have a stake in. The worst thing we can do is to institutionalize theory in a compartmentalized way that keeps partisans of opposing theories from having to hear what they are saying about each other—and keeps students from observing and joining in the battle.

I should make clear that the villain in the foregoing account is not the idea of field-coverage itself, but the lack of any principle that encourages the fields covered in the university to engage their central differences and conflicts. What stifles critical reasoning, according to this analysis, is not that the curriculum asks students to cover a variety of fields, but that it fails to give them more than an intermittent glimpse of the differences and conflicts inside and across those fields. As long as students experience each course and each professorial discourse in separation from the other courses and discourses, it will be difficult for many of them to perceive the conversation in which these courses and discourses are implicitly engaged, much less enter into it as equal participants.

In this analysis, then, educators who want to improve students' ability to reason more critically will act more productively not by seeking directly to change the way teachers teach or what they teach, but to change the way diverse teachers are organized (a change which will in turn affect individual practices). Advising teachers to teach one way rather than another is always a tactic of limited value, if only because factors of talent and training make it difficult for most teachers to behave differently from the way they are used to behaving. Individual teaching practices are the least promising place to start in improving the quality of education, for such practices are the aspect of the educational system that is most subject to idiosyncrasy and least susceptible to programmatic control. It is true that the occasional charismatic teacher will transcend the system in which she works. But students' experiences are shaped not by individual teachers in a vacuum, but by the total system that organizes individual teachers and limits what they can accomplish.

Encouraging students to do more critical reasoning, then, should not be primarily a matter of *teaching* critical reasoning. Still less should it be a matter of teaching certain formalized techniques of thought predefined as specifically critical, as in some pedagogical approaches that invoke the term *critical thinking* today. Such approaches have always proved futile, partly because of the impossibility of getting more than a small minority of faculty to conform to the same model, but also because principles of thinking are of little value when abstracted from the social contexts in which thinking takes place.

Critical thinking cannot be taught as an isolated technique or body of principles. Just as the best way to learn a foreign language is to live in the country in which the language is spoken, the best way to learn critical thinking is to be part of an intellectual community in which such thinking is being practiced (where there will probably be debate over which forms of thinking count as critical, or even as thinking, and which do not). Even the best-taught course in principles of critical thinking will fail for most students unless it is part of a larger experience of membership in an intellectual community. But it is difficult for any course to create the larger experience of intellectual community as long as the curriculum continues to be structured as a disconnected series of courses ordered only by the coverage principle. So, given the average spread of academic subjects and modes of thought in the standard curriculum today, whether the curriculum can be made more critical or not should be seen as a problem of reorganizing what is taught rather than of modifying its content (though, again, a change in organization would inevitably change the content).

For me, then, increasing the critical capacities of students depends not on formalizing and teaching certain critical modes of thinking, but rather on providing students with a more satisfactory exposure to the intellectual community that is now represented only fragmentarily and confusingly by the coverage model. Given the increasingly contested and embattled condition of today's academic intellectual community, this will inevitably mean an exposure to cultural and ideological conflicts. In short, increasing students' critical thinking means helping them to better understand, appreciate, and participate in the intellectual and cultural conflicts that rage around them, outside as well as inside education.

Notes

1. Norman Foerster, "The Study of Letters," in Foerster et al., eds., *Literary Scholarship: Its Aims and Methods* (Chapel Hill: University of North Carolina Press, 1941), pp. 11–12.

2. Gerald Graff, *Professing Literature: An Institutional History* (Chicago: University of Chicago Press, 1987).

10 Whose Reason?
Which Canon?
Critical Reasoning
and Conflicting Ideas
of Rationality

R. W. SLEEPER

*We are all convinced by inductive arguments, and our
conviction is reasonable because the world is so constituted that inductive arguments lead on the whole
to true opinions.*[1]

When Frank Ramsey wrote these words in 1926 he was addressing the contentions of the mainstream philosophers of science
and logic in his own day. Since Hume had shown that hypothetical inference could not be brought under the canons of formal
deduction, nor justified by them, induction was widely regarded
as a "scandal to philosophy."[2] Quoting his words in the present
context alludes to the fact that our mainstream philosophies of
science and logic have changed but slightly between his day and
ours: *events* in the practices of both science and human reason
have a way of running ahead of the philosophical mainstream.

It is not just that our practices in science, as in our everyday
reasoning, continue to provide the warrant for induction that our
theories have lacked. Nor is it just that human events—such as
those occurring in Eastern Europe, to the shocked surprise of
"Superpower" theorists of both East and West—have continued
to defy the accepted canons of "rational" prediction and control.
More importantly, it is that what has so long been regarded as a
"scandal to philosophy" must now be recognized as central to our
theories of rationality itself.

It will scarcely have escaped notice in this context that the title chosen for my essay is as allusive as the epigraph. Whether by design or happenstance, Alasdair MacIntyre's latest contribution to the rising tide of interest in "virtue ethics" asks just the right questions: *Whose Justice? Which Rationality?*[3] If liberty is taken in altering those questions to the shape that they take at the head of this essay, it should be seen as both compliment and complement. *Compliment* in the sense that both justice and rationality are plainly central to the problems that are, or at least ought to be, the substance of our canon of cultural literacy, and *complement* in that both of MacIntyre's queries, as well as the answers that he gives, are subsumed under the questions "Whose reason? Which canon?"

MacIntyre leaves us in no doubt at all as to whose conception of rationality he favors and would make canonical for all of us if he could find a way. We have, he tells us, been blinded by the Enlightenment conception of rationality and its pluralistic offshoots to the only conception of rationality that can save us. What we need to recover is

> [a] conception of rational enquiry as embodied in a tradition; a
> conception according to which the standards of rational justifi-
> cation themselves emerge from and are part of a history in
> which they are vindicated by the way in which they transcend
> the limitations of and provide remedies for the defects of their
> predecessors within the history of that same tradition.[4]

Given this description it is no surprise at all that MacIntyre's paradigm of preference is the post-Augustinian canon of rationality embodied in the Scholastic tradition.

It is not that he would have us stop with the great synthesis of Greek and Augustinian conceptions of rationality worked out by St. Thomas Aquinas, nor with the brilliant defense of classical metaphysical realism constructed by Duns Scotus. It is just that what we need to recover is the sense of continuity with such achievements; the sense of security which, he tells us, we have lost in the uncertain rationalities of the post-Enlightenment breakup of the tradition. What MacIntyre misses in modernism is the sense of an authoritative tradition of agreed-upon canons of rationality that can be counted upon to be of use in resolving new problems and controversies as they arise in the ever changing circumstances of this postmodern world.

We have a sense that MacIntyre is standing up for philosophical "foundationalism" (though he doesn't use the word) in a philosophical world that has largely turned "antifoundationalist." But MacIntyre is far too astute a critic of postmodern culture to hold out any hope for the recovery of philosophy by building it anew on the eroded foundations of antiquity. Nor would he, despite his evident nostalgia for it, return us to the holistic culture of the Middle Ages, as some of his critics have suggested. MacIntyre is too good a scholar of history, both ancient and modern, to hold out for such an antihistoricist ideal. It is just that he sees the need to recover a tradition in which philosophy is not, as its postmodern critics have proclaimed, "over."

What MacIntyre wants is what Richard Rorty refers to as "solidarity," a united front against the characteristic products of Enlightenment rationalities which, according to both philosophers, has turned out to sanction a universal acceptance of moral relativism, the most damaging result of which (according to Rorty) is our habit of cruelty against humankind. But MacIntyre does not think that this solidarity can be had on Rorty's own prescription of "ungrounded social hope." As his words quoted above make clear, MacIntyre would ground hope for human solidarity in an emergent, self-corrective, and authoritative tradition of rationality if he could find one. Since he thinks that there *is* no such tradition that fits this description, other than post-Augustinian Scholasticism, it is not surprising that MacIntyre's critics have charged him with trying to take us back to the Middle Ages. But we would also expect to find at least some critics offering their own preferred canons of rationality as authoritative traditions in the mold that MacIntyre describes, but varying widely in content.

It would seem natural, for example, for those who have been proclaiming the "renascence of American philosophy" to respond to MacIntyre that there is indeed just such a tradition of authoritative rationality available if he would but open his eyes to it. It could be pointed out that, from Emerson through Peirce, James, and Dewey, there has emerged a tradition of rationality that continually insists upon justifying its practices by reference to its principles and its principles by reference to its practices. It is, they could argue, a tradition that meets MacIntyre's criterion of "a conception according to which the standards of rational justification themselves emerge from and are part of a history in which they are vindicated. . . ."

Moreover, pointing perhaps to the enormous impact of pragmatism upon American democratic political and pedagogical practices, they could show that this tradition has the distinct virtue of having the capacity to "transcend the limitations of and provide remedies for the defects of their predecessors within the history of that same tradition." They might dwell on how thoroughly Charles Sanders Peirce reconstructed not merely the early Cartesian conception of Enlightenment rationality but, through his allegiance to the metaphysics of "Scotistic reals," absorbed the best of the ancient metaphysical conception of reason bequeathed to us by Plato, Aristotle, and the Stoics. And they might point to the respective transformations of pragmatism by James and Royce, who, even more than Peirce, wanted to accommodate the romantic and transcendentalist conceptions of reason worked out by Thoreau and Emerson.

Despite the cogency of such suggestions, however, it would be open to MacIntyre to object to these proposals on the grounds that American philosophy, with few notable exceptions, has been radically naturalistic all the way. Though changing, sometimes almost imperceptibly, from Emerson's great essay on "Nature" to Dewey's *Common Faith*, American philosophy has found in the experience of nature (and the nature of experience) all the authority for rationality that it needed. Moreover, despite its openness to what James called the varieties of religious experience—an openness characteristic of even John Dewey, clearly the most anti-supernaturalist of them all—American philosophy has been closed to the authoritarianism of the tradition (and canon) that MacIntyre finds paradigmatic. It is significant that the words with which Emerson prefaced the essay on nature could be taken as prolegomena to the whole anti-authoritarian, even antitraditionalist, sweep of classical American philosophical thought:

> Our age is retrospective. It builds sepulchres of the fathers. It writes biographies, histories, and criticism. The foregoing generations beheld God and nature face to face; we, through their eyes. Why should we not also enjoy an original relation to the universe? Why should not we have a poetry and philosophy of insight and not of tradition, and a religion of revelation to us, and not the history of theirs?[5]

If nothing could be more plain than Emerson's rejection of an authoritative, MacIntyre-style canon designed to save us, it is just as plain that MacIntyre's complaint evidences the contemporary appeal of the "sepulchres of the fathers." If our age is not yet retrospective in the sense that Emerson deplored, it may yet become so if *some* of the participants in the canon wars have their way. It is for that reason that the questions "Whose reason? Which canon?" make sense. But it is for that same reason that the canon of classical American philosophy, insofar as it *is* a canon, remains problematic.

Emerson's response to the canon wars that raged in his own day—torn as he was between the empirical rationality of Hume and the transcendental rationality of Kant—was a question: "Why should we not also enjoy an original relation to the universe?" Dewey put his own response differently in 1930, but it asks essentially the same question. He cast it in the form of a critique of the ways in which we habitually construct our canons of criticism. In an address on "Construction and Criticism" he put it this way:

> We are given to associating creative mind with persons regarded as rare and unique, like geniuses. But every individual is in his

own way unique. Each one experiences life from a different angle than anybody else, and consequently has something distinctive to give to others if he can turn his experiences into ideas and pass them on to others. Each individual that comes into the world is a new beginning; the universe itself is, as it were, taking a fresh start in him and trying to do something, even if on a small scale, that it has never done before.[6]

Dewey was not, in these words, addressing the "problem" of relativism as put before us by the contemporary canonists of either the cultural literacy movement or the critical thinking advocates.

Rather than seeing relativism as a problem to be done away with, Dewey saw it as a condition from which all of us emerge as children. And he saw our cultures in much the same way, as well. As with every child, every culture is a "new beginning" that has something to contribute to the universe if a way can be found to turn the vast variety of cultural experience into ideas that can be passed on to others. It was in this sheer variety, Dewey saw, that we find the springs of creativity.

It hardly needs to be pointed out these days, as Dewey felt the need to do in his, that the relativism that stimulates creativity is all too often stifled by the sort of canonical authority that MacIntyre envisages as liberating us for lives of virtue. For Dewey, the absolutism of the real, the authoritarianism of the traditional doctrine of fixed essences, of a priori principles and ideals, of unchanging natural law, was one such authoritative canon. Another, no less authoritative was the canonical reason descended from Plato and Descartes through Frege, in which, as Frege put it in his best known aphorism on logic: "Its laws are not laws of nature, but laws of the laws of nature."[7] Wondering at this canonization of formal mathematical rationality (for which we may read "logicism") and at how it could be squared with empirical and experimental science, Dewey questioned the very idea of laws of nature as well as the a priori grounds of the logical canon itself.[8]

The architects of natural law morality from Aristotle and Aquinas to its present day defenders have, like MacIntyre, appealed to an order of reality which transcends the empirical world of change and accident. In like fashion, designers of the canonical logics have appealed to a priori principles and self-evident truths as the foundational elements from which they have drawn their conceptions of rationality. Dewey understood that the identification of natural law morality with the canonical rules of the *ecclesia* had not occurred by accident, and that the authority of the supernatural origins of such morality had not been casually invoked. Nor was he blinded to the similar appeal to authority implicit in the canonical logics from Aristotle to Frege, Russell, and Carnap, or to its often disguised foundational appeal to the residue of transcendent Platonic ideas and ideals. But what bothered Dewey most about such appeals was the implicit assumption that we *know* the truths of these doctrines to correspond to what is really out there in the real world of "being itself" or, to put the same matter as Bernard Williams has recently done, "what is there *anyway*," independently of inquiry.[9] Convinced that both traditions—the natural law foundation of morality, as well as the a priori foundations of formalist logic— were the long-standing results of mistaken theories of knowledge, Dewey criticized them both as products of what he called "*the* philosophic fallacy."

Dewey thought of this fallacy as resulting, "as so many philosophic errors have sprung, from a substantiation of eventual functions. The fallacy," he said, "converts the consequences of interaction of events into causes of the occurrences of these consequences."[10] And in a text explicitly aimed at mainstream epistemology which, for Dewey, encompassed both the "moral sciences" that had come under the authority of natural law, as well as the "logical sciences" that had fallen under the spell of logicism, Dewey put the matter this way:

> Wondering at how something in experience could be asserted to correspond to something by definition outside experience, which it is, upon the basis of epistemological doctrine, the sole means of "knowing," is what originally made me suspicious of the whole epistemological industry.[11]

When he wrote these words in response to some "friendly" criticisms of his 1938 *Logic: The Theory of Inquiry*, Dewey had already rejected the products of the "epistemological industry" of the time which were, he contended, simply diverting the attention of philosophers from the genuine problems at hand. He was writing in 1941, only a few short months before the attack on Pearl Harbor.

It is Dewey's pejorative allusion to the "epistemological industry" that prompts the citation here. For what the present essay will suggest is that we philosophers are again in danger of being diverted from the real problems that face us—current estimates of the level of *functional* illiteracy are running from twenty-five percent of our population and upwards—by the peculiar forms in which the "epistemological industry" manifests itself in our own day.

Already one wing of that industry, mutated but slightly from Dewey's day, has produced bestselling jeremiads designed to persuade us that we are wallowing in a swamp of cultural illiteracy and moral relativism owing to our disregard of the historical canons of the arts, the sciences and the humanities. For want of a better term than their own, I'll refer to this wing of the industry as the *conservative right* although I mean to include many who would disown the label in its current political usage and connotation.[12]

Concurrently, another wing of the industry (changed but little from its heyday in the form of logicism) is positioning itself to solve the very problems of cultural degeneracy so popularly exploited by the conservative right. These problems, they contend, are scarcely such as to be resolved by reviving the canonical texts, or the forms of rationality that they contain. What is required is just more of what has been available all along but rarely *made* available in the practices of our schools and colleges. What is required is the critical logic of analysis, the canons of which have simply been buried in the texts of formal logic and often restricted to applications in the mathematical and physical sciences. Liberated from these confines, unleashed to work on practical problems, critical reasoning will answer to the variety of our human needs in our morals as in our sciences. If a term of art is needed to designate this wing of the industry, why not call it the "conservative left"? As before, the political connotations of "left" and "right" are risked, but not ignored. And, in any case, the industry is itself conservative by nature.[13]

It is at this point that more direct aim can be taken at the questions "Whose reason? Which canon?" by a critical (albeit cursory) look at the alternatives. I commence with the conception of reason (or rationality, in deference to MacIntyre's usage) that descended from Frege and Russell, the mainstream logic ensconced in myriad textbooks of formal and informal logic in general use throughout most of the present century. The single trait which best characterizes the canonical logic of this tradition is its intolerance of conceptual vagueness, a trait that is at least associated with, if not the primary cause of, its conversion of the argument forms of natural language into symbolic (or mathematical) form. As Michael Dummett put it as recently as 1981, the inevitable presence of vagueness is "an unmitigated defect of natural language."[14]

Frege's famous rejection of conceptually vague predicates, provided the rationale for the dismissal of whole regions of philosophy as meaningless exercises, as beyond the boundaries of rational inquiry. "Meaningless" concepts, Frege wrote,

> [are] such as have vague boundaries. It must be determinate for every object whether it falls under a concept or not; a concept-word which does not meet this requirement on its meaning is meaningless.[15]

The justification for this wholesale rejection of the vagueness characteristic not only of natural language, but of theological and metaphysical predicates, and those of the moral sciences as well, is made clear by Frege. It is a matter of the failure of such predicates to measure up to the standards required for expression in terms of logic itself:

> [A] concept that is not sharply defined is wrongly termed a con-
> cept. Such quasi-conceptual constructions cannot be recognized
> as concepts by logic; it is impossible to lay down precise laws for
> them. The law of the excluded middle is really just another form
> of the requirement that the concept should have a precise
> boundary.[16]

Given such boundaries it is not at all surprising that the traditional concepts of theology and metaphysics were discarded by
mainstream philosophy as meaningless, or that induction should
be seen as a "scandal to philosophy."

Moreover, natural law morality, its foundations destroyed by
the Fregean dictum, was quickly replaced by noncognitivism in
ethics and positivism in the philosophy of law. The irony of this
history is that the Fregean quest for the "laws of the laws of nature" did more to destroy the credibility of natural law morality
than the combined attacks of the Kantians and utilitarians; nor
did either the *Gesinnungsethik* or the *Erfolgsethik* survive in the
aftermath. The new canon of rationality embraced by mainstream logic and its epistemology left only the ethics of emotivism (with its implicit moral relativism) as the sole remaining
option. Dewey sums up the result succinctly: "We take out of our
logical package what we have put into it, and then convert what
we draw out to be a literal description of the actual world."[17] Excluded from the mainstream "logical package," cognitive ethics
(moral objectivity) could not then be drawn out of it, any more
than could a proof of induction.

Of course it oversimplifies matters to put the blame for the
erosion of moral objectivity on Frege's enthusiasm for the "laws
of the laws of nature" to be found in logistic. For, as Stephen Toulmin points out, Frege was merely following the tradition of "theory centered" philosophy that had been in vogue since the early
seventeenth century.[18] That style of philosophical argument, set
in motion by Descartes and followed by the epistemological industry from Leibniz to Russell and Carnap, sets aside all discourse involving the rough-and-ready concepts of natural

language in use in the inductive inferences of the everyday world. The "vagueness" of such language precludes it from arguments involving criteria of rational validity and formal standards of proof. Rationality, it is held, demands arguments cast as chains of written propositions, and the tests of argumentational soundness rely upon canons of the formal relations among the propositions. Inductive arguments, unfortunately, commit the formal fallacy of affirming the consequent and so must be uniformly rejected.

Toulmin cites Pascal's attack on the casuistry of the Jesuits as a turning point in ethics, away from practical moral concerns to abstract theory as in Kant and, even, in Hume and the utilitarians. Moreover, as a recent study of G. E. Moore's early ethical writings has shown, even Moore's determined effort to return ethics to practical matters was stymied by the way in which the canons of accepted rationality required the elimination of value propositions from canonical cognitivity. Facts—according to the way the "naturalistic fallacy" argument soon became interpreted, though that was not Moore's intention at all—cannot be validly used in support of value judgments. What commenced as an attempt at a theory of rational and practical ethics ended up as a defense of ethical emotivism and noncognitivism in the hands of Frankena and Stevenson. The ontological dichotomy of facts and values had become an integral part of the canon of analytic philosophy almost without anyone noticing it.[19]

As MacIntyre himself points out, even those analytical philosophers to whom emotivism always seemed implausible "because it is evident that moral reasoning *does* take place," continued to maintain the mythical ideal of value-free inquiry across the board. What eventually became the moral realism movement was careful to distinguish between inquiries rationally designed to establish the scientific fact of the matter and those rationally designed to demonstrate the authority and objectivity of the moral rules. The equivocation on the term *rationally* even being celebrated, in some quarters, by the discovery of the "bicameral mind."[20]

It is the canonical dichotomy of fact and value, and the consequent division of rationality into split-screen applications, which still bedevils the theoretical foundations of our programs of critical thinking and informal logic. In attempting to establish some theoretical guidelines for determining appropriate contexts in which "CT" (as its advocates often refer to critical thinking programs) should be introduced into the school curriculum, for example, it has been suggested that the place to begin is with the identification of "communities of discussion." Here is what one writer offers as specific illustrations of them:

> Examples of such groups come readily to mind. Scientists seek to learn what is the case about the physical world so that they might explain, predict, and even sometimes control events. In seeking to serve these purposes, scientists now look for mathematical expressions or interpretations of experienced patterns of events. Christian theologians, on the other hand, seek to learn from revealed scripture about the nature of human spirituality so that they might help people pursue their salvation after physical death. Ethicists seek to learn what is justifiable morally and otherwise so that they might provide guides to living an ethically proper life. Here they may study any of a variety of things from the scriptures to the causes of human pleasure. Legislators (ideally) seek to study humans in society so as to devise a set of laws and a group of procedures for the application and enforcement of those laws. They strive for civil order and the just production and distribution of necessities and luxuries. Those in the community of teachers seek to acquire a body of knowledge (both process and product knowledge), as well as techniques or art for conveying this knowledge to others so that they might teach and (perhaps) in this teaching nurture the autonomy of their students. And so it goes.[21]

The limitless fragmentation of rationality implied in the subject-matter divisions and distinctive "uses of reason" thus listed is evidence that the goals of each "discussion community" are simply accepted as *givens;* since they represent value judgments they are not to be *subject* to the process of critical thinking which is to take place internally within the given context. It is not that the writer fails to acknowledge that there *are* contexts of wider parameters, it is just that there seems to be no "discussion community" available for exploring such external questions.[22]

Paul Tillich, whose attempt at rational theology impressed even the most dogmatic of his opponents, customarily referred to the concept of multifaceted rationality implicit in "internalist" criticism as "heteronomous reason" and deplored it. In similar fashion Dewey criticized such fragmented conceptions of rationality as misconstruals of the unity of fact and value, of ends and means, and of the natural *continuity* of instrumental reason:

> Reasonableness or rationality is, according to the position here taken, as well as in ordinary usage, an affair of the relation of means and consequences. In framing ends-in-view, it is unreasonable to set up those which have no connection with available means and without reference to the obstacles standing in the way of attaining the end. It is reasonable to search for and select the means that will, with the maximum probability, yield the consequences which are intended. It is highly unreasonable to employ as means, materials and processes which would be found, if they were examined, to be such that they produce consequences which are different from the intended end; so different that they preclude its attainment.[23]

Rationality, whether for Tillich or Dewey, is not one thing in theology and another in physics; it is not heteronomous, *nor is it autonomous either.*

Most of the advocates of critical thinking programs recognize this, acknowledging that rationality—like virtue and individual autonomy—is something to be taught and nurtured. But what they so often miss is that rationality *cannot* be taught and nurtured by means of any preselected canonical method whatsoever; it is *not* an end in itself. Like logic, rationality has its own history; it develops (and can only be developed) as a *consequence* of inquiry, and not as its canonical "end in view."

To underscore exactly this point, Dewey closed his 1938 *Logic* with these words:

> Failure to institute a logic based inclusively and exclusively upon the operations of inquiry has enormous cultural consequences. It encourages obscurantism; it promotes acceptance of beliefs formed before methods of inquiry had reached their present estate; and it tends to relegate scientific (that is, competent) methods of inquiry to a specialized technical field. Since scientific methods simply exhibit free intelligence operating in the best manner available at a given time, the cultural waste, confusion and distortion that results from the failure to use these methods, in all fields in connection with all problems, is incalculable. These considerations reinforce the claim of logical theory, as the theory of inquiry, to assume and to hold a position of primary human importance.[24]

It has often been pointed out (though not often enough) that Dewey's reconstruction and reformulation of canonical logic in terms of "free intelligence operating in the best manner available at a given time" offers a philosophy of inductive science that is continuous not only with a critical account of moral values and valuations but also with social and economic policies that allow him to offer an empirical (both rational and inductive) defense of the kind of pluralist and democratic social practices that he is well known to have favored.[25]

But that sort of social democracy is clearly not what is favored by either MacIntyre or the canonists of the cultural literacy movement from Allan Bloom and E. D. Hirsch, Jr., to William Bennett and Lynn Cheney. (They take pluralist practices as "divisive" of the social fabric, as evidence of the disastrous consequences of moral relativism.) In the curious logic embraced by Bloom, the "closed minds" that he encounters among his students at the University of Chicago, are not so much those of a *mis*educated elite, as one that has *already* been thoroughly schooled in the relativism of a culture which both he and MacIntyre deplore. In order to trace the path of critical thinking that Bloom employs, we have to see that Bloom's students are—

as the reviewer of Bloom's paperback edition of *The Closing of the American Mind* puts it—"so open-minded that their brains have fallen out." Bloom shares, with William Bennett in *To Reclaim a Legacy*, the vision that Matthew Arnold shared with Samuel Taylor Coleridge: a vision of an elite "clerisy" empowered to promote for the rest of us "a common culture rooted in civilization's lasting vision, its highest shared ideals and aspirations, and its heritage."[26]

Hirsch also shares this vision of just such a "common culture" but rejects the elitist means that Bloom, Bennett, and Chaney would employ to achieve it if they could find a way. Like MacIntyre and the advocates of critical thinking programs, Hirsch's strategy in countering the gathering gloom of cultural illiteracy is more democratic but no less conservative. (It is tempting to use the word *reactionary*, here, but *conservative* will do.) But, unlike MacIntyre, Hirsch shares with the CT proponents the conviction that he *has* found a way to bring it off. It is not, of course, that he shares their program or their canonical convictions as to the nature of rationality. It is just that Hirsch has plans of his own for reform of the school curriculum, a matter concerning which Bloom has little to say of constructive intent.

Where Bloom shows no more tolerance than Rousseau or Hobbes for the kind of moral relativism that is inherent in the going concerns of *actual* democratic cultures, Hirsch recognizes the need to make our students more literate in the very culture that Bloom condemns. Where Bloom's catalog of cultural complaints fastens upon such *consequences* of relativism as rock music (p. 69), sexual permissiveness (p. 97), antismoking campaigns (p. 121) and the sixties rebellion (p. 131), Hirsch conducts a serious search for the *causes* of the cultural illiteracy that they both deplore.

The trouble is that Hirsch's search is conducted with a preconceived result that guides his investigations all the way. What Hirsch "discovers" is that the central and overriding cause of cultural illiteracy in America is the control of the school curriculum exercised by the National Education Association. Beginning with a report commissioned by that organization and issued by the federal government in 1918 as a document entitled *Cardinal Principles of Secondary Education*, it has been all downhill for cultural literacy ever since, according to Hirsch.[27]

In its own way, Hirsch's line of reasoning is as curious as Bloom's, though it more perfectly illustrates what Dewey baptized as "*the* philosophic fallacy" in its conversion of the consequences of events into their antecedent causes. The way the NEA commissioned report caused the long slide from cultural literacy, according to Hirsch, is by means of its federally sanctioned curriculum recommendations that transformed the schools of America into "child-centered" incubators of subject-matter ignorance. Hirsch has no doubt at all concerning who was responsible for the ideas that caused this "fragmentation" of the curriculum. Oddly enough it turns out to be one of Bloom's heroes. The "child-centered curriculum" that has done all the damage, Hirsch argues, stems from a misguided application of ideas that he traces to Jean-Jacques Rousseau:

> From the perspective of intellectual history, the conception of natural human growth has been the most decisive influence on American educational theory over the past decades. Although schools of education have clothed this romantic idea in the language of developmental psychology, their basic assumptions owe more to Rousseau than to Piaget. As the originator of these ideas, John Dewey is usually given too much credit (or blame), and Jean [sic] Rousseau too little. In basic educational assumptions Dewey was a disciple of Rousseau.[28]

Although the unwitting deconstruction of intellectual history apparent here has not gone unremarked (or unrefuted) by educational historians and Dewey scholarship, it is not this feature of the cultural literacy industry commenced by Hirsch that rankles scholars most.[29] It is the casual way in which Hirsch and his collaborators have compiled their canon of "What Literate Americans Know."

We are left to wonder, for example, as to what we are supposed to "know" when the list gives us the name of Job and the follow-up phrase, several pages later, "patience of Job." Are we to know that *Job* names a biblical book or its central character? the most elusive gentile in the Hebrew canon or the allusive hero of countless plays and poetry? God's victim or Satan's toy? Are we to know that the "patience of Job" is a phrase from the Epistle of James in the King James Version, that it is absent from the same Epistle in the Revised Standard Version, and that it appears to be almost totally unrelated to the Old Testament character of Job in either version?[30]

It is doubtless with questions like these in mind that critical thinking programmers offer their wares, proposing that more refined contexts are needed in the form of "discussion communities" before such items in the list of "What Literate Americans Know" can even begin to be approached. And yet, by dividing their constituency up in the ways that they do, they predetermine the very relativistic results that Hirsch and his collaborators have sought to remedy by the offer of their canonical list in the first place. The fact of the matter (if, indeed, there is one) appears to be that if the goal of cultural literacy is conceived *either* as knowledge of items representing cultural content compiled in a canonical list, *or* as a goal to be achieved by a canonical code of critical thinking, cultural literacy in any coherent sense that could transcend the alleged evils of moral, cognitive, and cultural relativism will continue to elude us.

And it should. For both canonical programs are guilty of converting their "ends in view" into the means of achieving them. And to do so, wittingly or not, is not merely to commit "*the* philosophic fallacy," but to sin against the very ideals of the culture to which they are committed and which they would save.

The word *ideals* is used here cautiously, and with the assumption that all sides in the controversies that we have been contemplating concede the cultural objectives that we are in the habit of referring to as those of "liberal social democracy." And, if that is the case, all sides must concede that respect for individual persons requires that they have the right to choose for themselves the moral standards that they follow, constrained merely by such minimal restrictions as may be required for their own protection, and that of minorities, against the power and authority of a consensual majority. Moreover, it is an essential element of this respect that no government has a right to impose upon its people either a state religion or its moral counterpart in a canonical body of moral doctrine. But because that is so, it is equally the case that no government, or any other body, has a right to dictate the forms that inquiry shall take, or what shall count as its legitimate product. Far from precluding objective knowledge, freedom of inquiry—including the forms and methods that inquiry takes—is required for its achievement. Indeed, as Hilary Putnam has remarked, "If there were no such thing as [objective] moral wrong, then it would not be *wrong* for government to impose moral choices." And he continues the thought with these words:

> The fact that many people fear that if they concede any sort of moral objectivity out loud then they will find some government shoving *its* notion of moral objectivity down their throats is without question one of the reasons why so many people subscribe to a moral subjectivism to which they give no real assent.[31]

Perhaps the resistance we feel to the canonical offerings of Bloom and Hirsch on the one hand, and of the CT programmers on the other, stems from a similar and not unreasonable fear.

How, then, are we to answer the questions with which we began? Frank Ramsey's response to the question "Whose reason?" makes at least as much sense as any that we have considered:

> We all agree that a man who did not make inductions would be unreasonable: the question is only what this means. In my view it does not mean that the man would sin in any way against formal logic or formal probability; but that he had not got a very useful habit, without which he would be very much worse off, in the sense of being much less likely to have true opinions.

This is a kind of pragmatism; we judge mental habits by whether they work, i.e. whether the opinions they lead to are for the most part true, or more often true than those to which alternative habits would lead.

Induction is such a useful habit, and so to adopt it is reasonable.[32]

And his answer to "Which canon?" is like in kind:

The different scientific methods that can be used are in the last resort judged by induction by simple enumeration; we choose the simplest law that fits the facts, but unless we found that laws so obtained also fitted facts other than those they were made to fit, we should discard this procedure for some other.[33]

Perhaps it was because of answers like these that Professor D. H. Mellor called Frank Ramsey "The greatest of all Cambridge philosophers" in his inaugural lecture in the University of Cambridge on January 21, 1988.[34]

Notes

1. Frank Plumpton Ramsey, "Truth and Probability," in Richard B. Braithwaite, ed., *The Foundations of Mathematics*, (New York: Humanities Press, 1950), 197.

2. Ian Hacking changes Ramsey's phrase, given here, to "scandal of philosophy" in an essay which gives a brief sketch of the matter in "The Theory of Probable Inference: Neyman, Peirce and Braithwaite" in D. H. Mellor, ed., *Science, Belief and Behaviour*, (Cambridge: Cambridge University Press, 1980), 142–44.

3. Alasdair MacIntyre, *Whose Justice? Which Rationality?* (Notre Dame, Indiana: Notre Dame University Press, 1989).

4. Quoted from a review in *The American Scholar* 58, no. 4 (1989), 608.

5. Ralph Waldo Emerson, "Nature, 1836," in *Emerson: Five Essays on Man and Nature*, Robert E. Spiller, ed., (New York: Appleton-Century-Crofts, 1954), 1.

6. John Dewey, *Later Works*, vol. 5, Jo Ann Boydston, ed., (Carbondale: Southern Illinois University Press, 1984), 127.

7. Quoted from William Kneale and Martha Kneale, *The Development of Logic* (Oxford: Clarendon Press, 1984), 739.

8. Dewey, *Later Works*, vol. 12, 440.

9. Bernard Williams, *Descartes: The Project of Pure Inquiry* (Harmondsworth: Penguin, 1978), 64.

10. Dewey, *Later Works*, vol. 1, 200.

11. Dewey, *Later Works*, vol. 14, 179.

12. See the review of the literature in *Qualitative Studies in Education* 2 (1) (1989):81–86. This treats both Bloom and Hirsch more extensively than is possible here.

13. The conservative nature of mainstream logic is treated more extensively in R. W. Sleeper, *The Necessity of Pragmatism* (New Haven: Yale University Press, 1986), passim, and in Kneale, *Development of Logic*.

14. Michael A. E. Dummett, *The Interpretation of Frege's Philosophy* (London: Duckworth, 1981), 316.

15. Gottlob Frege, *Posthumous Writings* (Oxford: Blackwell, 1979), 122.

16. Gottlob Frege, *Translations from the Philosophical Writings of Gottlob Frege*, P. Geach and M. Black, eds. (Oxford: Blackwell, 1970), 159. I am indebted to Christopher Hookway's essay "Vagueness, Logic and Interpretation" (forthcoming) for this and the foregoing references to Frege's writings.

17. Dewey, *Later Works*, vol. 4, 197.

18. Stephen Toulmin, "The Recovery of Practical Philosophy," *The American Scholar* 57 (3) (1988).

19. Robert Peter Sylvester, *The Moral Philosophy of G. E. Moore*, Ray Perkins, Jr., and R. W. Sleeper, eds. (Philadelphia: Temple University Press, 1990).

20. See Joseph Margolis, *Texts Without Referents* (Oxford: Blackwell, 1989), 3–11, for a fascinating discussion of the theory of Julian Jaynes and other dualist views.

21. Charles V. Blatz, "Contextualism and Critical Thinking: Programmatic Investigations," *Educational Theory* 39 (2) (1989), 109. This essay discusses the conceptual differences between the views of John E. McPeck and Robert Ennis (both authors included in the present volume),

and offers his own suggestions as to how they might be reconciled. It is not clear that either McPeck or Ennis would favor his approach.

22. What is objectionable about Blatz's construal of CT is his assumption that "pragmatic procedures . . . are not ones of discovering the truth" (Ibid, 112). It is perhaps this assumption that leads him to react to the issue of relativism by restricting CT to the examination of "internal questions." In any case, such a reaction is evidence of an aversion to accepting the continuity of facts and values, and the willing acceptance of this disjunction as a background feature that is a given.

23. Dewey, *Later Works*, vol. 12, 17. Dewey acknowledges his debt to Charles Sanders Peirce in a note on this page; Peirce's theory of the continuity of inquiry precludes the fact-value dichotomy, as well as the "internal-external" distinction.

24. Ibid., 527.

25. See Hilary and Ruth Anna Putnam, "Epistemology as Hypothesis," an essay on Dewey's theory of inquiry (forthcoming) in *Transactions of the Charles S. Peirce Society*.

26. Matthew Arnold, *Culture and Anarchy*, cited from the edition edited by J. D. Wilson (Cambridge: Cambridge University Press, 1935); William Bennett, *To Reclaim a Legacy* (Washington: National Endowment for the Humanities, 1984), 1–2; Samuel Taylor Coleridge, *On the Constitution of Church and State*, 4th ed. (London: Edward Moxon, 1852).

27. National Education Association, Commission on the Reorganization of Secondary Education, *Cardinal Principles of Secondary Education*, Bulletin no. 35 (Washington: G.P.O., 1918).

28. E. D. Hirsch, Jr., *Cultural Literacy: What Every American Needs to Know*, with an appendix, "What Literate Americans Know," by E. D. Hirsch, Jr., Joseph Kett, and James Trefil (Boston: Houghton Mifflin, 1987), 119.

29. See note 12.

30. See the discussion of these alternatives in *The Book of Job*, translated and with an introduction by Stephen Mitchell (San Francisco: North Point Press, 1987).

31. Hilary Putnam, *Reason, Truth and History* (Cambridge: Cambridge University Press, 1981), 149.

32. Frank Plumpton Ramsey, "Truth and Probability," 197–98.

33. Ibid., 198.

34. D. H. Mellor, The Warrant of Induction: An Inaugural Lecture (Cambridge: Cambridge University Press, 1988), 1.

||| The Problem
of History

11 Postmodernism and the Possibility of Critical Reasoning

STANLEY ROSEN

The expression *critical thinking* is charged with a heavy burden of historical baggage. It was not so long ago that modernists were referring to theirs as an age of criticism, thus striking, perhaps unconsciously, a note of decayed Kantianism. The role of the critic, as is evident from the etymology of the term, is to discriminate between better and worse. The etymology is Greek, but there is a modern pedigree as well, going back to Milton, who says in the *Areopagitica* that "reason is but choosing." For the ancient as well as for the early modern, choice is rational if one chooses well. The tangled history of modernity has unfortunately tended to result in a suppression of the judgment of better and worse from the act of judgment, which culminates in our ostensibly postmodern age in the mere expression of difference. Even further, it is now not the reader but the text that acts as critic, which is accordingly transformed into ontological excitation. Criticism is no longer rational choice but what might be called uncritical crisis. How did we arrive at this hyperbolical and antirationalist stage? In the following paragraphs, I offer a few suggestions.

The contemporary version of the postmodernist phenomenon has its origins in the doctrines of Nietzsche. One of the most striking manifestations of that phenomenon is the current debate about the end of philosophy. More sharply stated, the debate takes its bearings by the widespread agreement that the age of metaphysics (philosophy in the traditional sense) is over. According to this understanding of the term *metaphysics*, the classical doctrine of two worlds, or of eternity and temporality, as represented by the orthodox interpretation of Platonism on the one hand and the Judeo-Christian tradition on the other, has been overcome, or less melodramatically, has withered away. Modernity is consequently understood as the historical process of that overcoming or withering away. It follows, however, that if the process is complete, then modernity has itself withered away, or suppressed itself. We therefore presumably stand, at the very least, upon the threshold of the postmodern epoch, or, to paraphrase Nietzsche, with one foot beyond the world of modernity. If this account of things is correct, two further conclusions may be drawn. The first is that our transitional situation allows us to understand the recently concluded modern epoch from outside, or beyond, and hence, presumably, more accurately than was previously the case. The second is that, poised as we are at the threshold of some new epoch, with, so to speak, one foot in the air, we are still free to decide the direction in which to move.

This little sketch of the present moment raises a number of questions. The first is whether the expression *postmodernist* has any discernible cognitive content. This in turn depends upon our understanding of modernity itself. For it is entirely possible that the experience (or rhetoric) of postmodernism is itself a characteristic phenomenon of modernity. The second question turns upon the sense of the expression *metaphysics*. This notoriously ambiguous word has its philological origins in Aristotle, or rather in his editors, and may be nothing more than a librarian's term of classification ("the writings coming after, or placed next to, the writings on physics"). Even if this explanation is false or inadequate, the fact remains that modern critics of metaphysics, or speakers for its demise, improperly derive the sense of the term from Plato, and it is an open question whether they are entitled to do so. What is normally referred to by scholars as "Plato's theory of ideas," the ostensible basis for the two-worlds doctrine, is not to be found in the Platonic dialogues. What we find instead is a variety of extremely ambiguous and inconsistent conversations, in the form of questions and answers, about the relation between forms and their instances, in more than one sense of the term *form*. Postmetaphysicians pride themselves upon their hermeneutical subtlety, and their capacity to hear the unspoken and deeper dimension underneath the spoken or superficial stratum of the written text. Yet they are singularly unable to exercise this hermeneutical skill in the case of the Platonic dialogues. Their interpretation of the two-worlds doctrine is as superficial and hence philosophically inaccurate as that of the most unimaginative philologist. A third question might be raised concerning the accuracy of Nietzsche's interpretation of Christianity, an interpretation which, as I have suggested, is today extremely influential among postmodernists. Is Christianity intelligible as a taking of vengeance against, and hence a devaluing of, the created world? Do we do justice to the Christian doctrine of love by understanding it as the will to power? Fourth: If metaphysics has not been overcome until the end of the nineteenth or the beginning of the twentieth century, what is the difference between antiquity and modernity as conventionally defined? Fifth: If we do indeed stand outside the modern epoch, perhaps, as so detached (or partially detached), we understand modernity *less well*, rather than better, than its surpassed residents. Finally, is it not true that those who stand with one foot in the air run a grave risk of falling on their faces?

No doubt this list of questions could be extended, but it is a fair representation of the difficulties raised by contemporary discussions of postmodernity. The avid postmodernist might perhaps object that my questions are themselves outmoded consequences of modernity, or even of metaphysics, or of the former, scientifically articulated, will to power which valued clarity, rationality, and common sense. I believe that there is a very simple reply to objections of this sort. The advocates of postmodernism themselves distinguish in their practice between criticism and refutation of metaphysics and modernity on the one hand, and the articulation (if that is the right word) of postmodernist texts on the other. When attempting to persuade us that philosophy is at an end, the postmodernists talk, or attempt to talk, *our* language. Only after we are persuaded do we ourselves begin to chant postmodernism. In this essay, I am concerned with one question: is the thesis of the end of philosophy, and so of modernity, sound? I shall have no interest at all in the ostensible ontological profundities of the Marquis de Sade, the presumed superiority of difference to sameness, or other preferred topics of the postmodern school(s). In other words, I shall accept the thesis, for the purpose of discussion, that we are at the threshold of a new age, and that, with one foot beyond modernity, we can discuss intelligently what is to be done. I shall not, however, accept without argument the thesis that the new age we attend is postmodern. On the contrary, it is my view, and the view which I shall here defend, that there is no valid distinction between the modern and the postmodern, but that the actual distinction lies between the ancient and the modern.

A crucial preliminary point needs to be made. I am not a spokesman for antiquity or an advocate of a return to the past. This form of inverted historicism holds no appeal for me. A criticism of this or that aspect of modernity is not equivalent to a rejection of modernity. The decisive consideration is this: the rejection of modernity is a typically modern phenomenon. The ancients did not comment on the merits or defects of the moderns. It is modern man who dwells perpetually within epochal contrasts, whether in the form of longing for the past or dreaming of the future, flitting from one historical period to another on the wings of imagination. The apparent exception to this remark is, in my opinion, a sign of its soundness. I am thinking here of doctrines of commitment, resolve, and genuineness as manifested in a project. These doctrines advocate a termination of nostalgia or dreaming, and a settling down within the fundamental circumstances of one's own time. But they, too, grant the transience of commitments and projects, or their epochal, historical nature. On the one hand, commitment to a project is a simulacrum of eternity, or an admission that man cannot exist as a radically historical being. On the other hand, it is a self-conscious attempt to *forget* the truth about radical finitude, an attempt which can be undertaken only by someone who recognizes, or believes himself to recognize, that the truth of historicity is nihilism.

Modernity arises as a project, namely, as the conscious rejection (by a few remarkable individuals) on antiquity. The subsequent rejection of modernity is then simply a reenactment of the institution of modernity. To say this is not in itself to condemn the spirit of modernity. Perhaps human beings are so constituted that starting afresh is necessary and salutary for them. Whether or not this is so, I want to suggest that there are two, and exactly two, fundamental human situations, represented only from the modern perspective by the quarrel between the ancients and moderns. Once we leave the ancient or classical epoch, there is no return, except by a forgetfulness induced by something like the eternal return of the same. We cannot induce forgetfulness of this sort by an existential resolve. Let me illustrate this by a brief consideration of the thesis, associated with Heidegger, that technology is the current manifestation of the will to power. What possibilities are available to us with respect to technology? First, we may use it, consciously or inadvertently, to destroy ourselves. Self-destruction will lead to an escape from modernity, but it is not an entrance into the post or premodern epoch. Second, we may continue in our attempts to master nature or, in the Heideggerean jargon, to cover over Being by the dominance of beings. By definition, this will produce an extension of modernity. Third, we may change our attitude toward technology, not so as to reject it (which would not be a "genuine" response to the concrete historical situation), but rather to shift from the modality of domination (and hence covering over of Being) to that of letting be, namely, to assisting in the process by which Being reveals itself, if only in the disguise of the ontic articulation of a new epoch. But what precisely does this mean?

Since technology is human activity, designed explicitly to modify nature in terms of human desire, how can we reorient ourselves toward technology in a postmodern, postmetaphysical, nondominant sense? We are not here searching for a Marxist, or quasi-Marxist transformation of human society in such a way that human beings will no longer exploit one another with the assistance of technological artifacts. Such a transformation, assuming it to be desirable and possible, would not be a surpassing, but rather a fulfillment, of modernity, or at least of one centrally important aspect of the dream of modernity. What sense does it make to speak of the fulfillment of modernity as a surpassing of modernity, or an entrance into the postmodern? None at all, I submit. The essence of modernity is to remove restrictions to the human will. A shift from one restriction to another is not a suppression of modernity. And restrictions will not be entirely suppressed with the withering away of the state. To state only the melodramatic instance, men will still face the restriction of morality itself, or of death.

It is not a social resolution, then, for which we search, but rather an ontological one. Now I must confess that I am unable to attach any positive significance to the thesis that such an ontological resolution is possible. Either art completes nature or it reconstitutes, that is, creates, nature. The first alternative is the thesis of the ancients; the second is the thesis of modernity. There is no postmodern attitude toward technology, because (as is admitted by the view under attack) technology is itself, or is the expression of, the essence of modernity. One way in which to understand the current fuss about the postmodern is as panic induced by the recognition of the enigmatic and deeply unsatisfying nature, as well as the inescapability (by any route short of self-destruction) of modernity. The contemporary attitude toward technology may serve as the paradigm of this panic. I disregard, of course, those for whom technology presents no problem, since for such persons the entire problem of the modern and postmodern is invisible. As for the rest of us, we may be divided into two main camps. The first is made up of those who fear technology, more or less explicitly, whether because of its effects on the soul or because of its dangers to the body. The second includes all those who have sublimated their panic into an aggressive optimism, articulated by the rhetoric of existential commitment, and solaced by science fiction. For both camps, the present is either intolerable or deeply menacing. Since the only way to return to the past is by projecting it into the future, the result is a diversified yet essentially homogeneous obsession with the "next" historical epoch.

Obsession with history is a necessary consequence of the will to recreate and thereby master nature. It is also a version of metaphysics, if by that term we mean a doctrine of two worlds, or of a radical distinction between eternity and temporality, between essence and appearance. The doctrine of radical historicity assures us that eternity is unthinkable or inaccessible. It thereby transforms historicity itself, whether understood as Being or as the filter through which Being "drips" into eternity and essence. Each finite historical epoch is an appearance of the essence of Being; the structure of meaning secreted by a radical existential commitment is a simulacrum of eternity. If we put to one side such exotic flora as Plato's so-called theory of ideas or Aristotle's divine intellect, one can say that the ancients were as unmetaphysical a people as ever lived. A genuine overcoming of metaphysics would return us to the world of the Greek gods and the polis. But no such overcoming is possible. As an amusing sign of this, I point to the effort by the positivist movement of the 20s to abolish metaphysics. If the reader will permit an unorthodox comparison, I would liken, say, Rudolph Carnap to Descartes, with the radical difference that Carnap was not faced with the need to institute a revolution against theology, and consequently never developed an interesting rhetoric. However this may be, the fruits of positivism, as we now know, are the essentialist metaphysics of modal logic, a Proustian emphasis upon the "ways of world-making," and a two-worlds doctrine of logical satisfaction as distinguished from the cognitively inaccessible domain of meaning. To make the same point in a slightly different way, the current popularity of surrealism and dadaism in the philosophy of science, which is derived from the writings of the later Wittgenstein, has its deeper cause in the bankruptcy of the effort to banish self-consciousness or reflection from a rational analysis of modern science.

Whatever one's objections to Cartesian dualism, understood in the superficial sense as the radical distinction between mind and body, there is, in my opinion, no escape from the dualism of will and formal structure. When my hard-headed contemporaries object to the assertion that science is metaphysics, or the will to power, they silence these slogans by force of their will, as, for example, by the brute (or subtle) exercise of academic power, and not by argument. Voltaire "refuted" Christianity by laughing at it. Positivists and their progeny attempted to refute metaphysics by laughing at it. Now the laugh is on them. Laughter is no doubt refreshing for the soul, and it has important political consequences. The same can be said of spiritual fatigue and boredom. In the academy, the current split between the hardheaded professors and those who dance to softer muses is a metaphysical battle between two versions of the damage done to the human soul by its inescapable impetus toward freedom from restrictions. This impetus leads both to exhilaration and fatigue, sometimes within the same breast, and often in the most subtle of blends. We acquire immunity from these ultimately debilitating moods not through the freedom of infinite progress *or* of radical finitude but through the loss of self-consciousness, and hence of freedom in any meaningful sense.

In this necessarily circumscribed format, I have now indicated how I would respond to three of the six questions directed toward advocates of postmodernism or the end of metaphysics. To summarize the answer to the first question concerning whether the expression *postmodernist* has any discernible cognitive content: the difference between the ancients and the moderns is that, for the ancients, art completes nature, whereas for the moderns, art creates nature. There is no valid or sound cognitive content to the notion of postmodernism, which is itself a typically modern slogan. And metaphysics cannot be refuted by exposing the logical flaws or existential inconveniences of the doctrine of two worlds, because man is, by his self-conscious nature, a two-worlds being. I have also implied an answer to the fourth question about the difference between antiquity and modernity. Since we are all always either standing with one foot in the air or falling on our faces, dragging ourselves erect to some slightly different location, and raising our feet, there is not much difference between freedom and stumbling about in the dark. The answer to a fifth question (about whether or not we understand modernity better than the surpassed residents of modernity understood it) follows trivially from my previous answers. Since none of us is "outside" modernity, the question is misleadingly posed. But if some of us could extricate ourselves from modernity, we would promptly lose consciousness and hence fail to understand anything at all. The one question which I have not attempted to answer concerns the nature of Christianity. I would prefer to leave this question to those who are far more competent than I to deal with it. Nevertheless, I will venture the opinion that Nietzsche's interpretation of Christianity is initially tempting but finally wrong and inadequate. This interpretation is tempting, of course, not to Christians, but to those who have not been touched by that religion, to those who have broken away from it, and to the hard headed who suppose that religious faith can be refuted, whether by argument or sociological observation, by psychological analysis or mockery.

There is, then, no end to metaphysics and certainly no end to philosophy. Man is by his nature the philosophical animal, and never more so than when he attempts to overcome himself. In this sense, I agree with Nietzsche's observation in *Thus Spoke*

Zarathustra, that man is an unfinished animal. This observation was certainly intended as a rejection of ancient philosophy, understood by Nietzsche as a doctrine of finished ends (or "values") and natural essences. To take Nietzsche's paradigmatic example, the distinction within the Platonic dialogues between the ideas, or pure forms, on the one hand, and the world of genesis on the other, both set an artificial limit to man's development and devalued the historical world. I cannot enter here into the extremely difficult question of the true sense of the doctrine of ideas. I do want, however, to make a remark about the distinction between the ideas and genesis that is appropriate to the present discussion, in which our emphasis is upon politics in the broadest sense of the term.

The political sense of the doctrine of ideas is that it serves to define the revolutionary nature of philosophy. The point is entirely obvious in Plato's *Republic*, and especially in the famous allegory of the cave. However, the fundamental difference between classical, or Platonic, and modern, or Cartesian, revolution is that the first is theoretical whereas the second is practical. Most obviously, Socrates rebels against Greek tradition and universal common sense in his verbal founding of the ostensibly just city, which is, however, not an open society in the modern sense but an incarnation of the difference between the few and the many, or the philosophers and the nonphilosophers. The revolution, so to speak, is stopped in its tracks even as it occurs. In the Cartesian revolution, on the other hand, a great show is made of the compatibility between the new science and the old theology. The revolution is ostensibly technical or methodological; but this in itself is a practical revolution, and one which leads inevitably to an open society of progressive science and technology. To state this as concisely as possible, the technician is the mediator between the theoretician and the nontheoretician. Granting that the shift from Platonic to Cartesian science is theoretical, it gives rise to a practical revolution that is entirely non-Platonic.

The split between the philosophers and the nonphilosophers is overcome in principle. And this is the basis for modern doctrines of egalitarianism, to be brought about not merely by the withering away of the state, but by genetic engineering and, in general, by science.

The theoretical nature of the Platonic revolution does not, however, amount to a rejection of the Nietzschean thesis that man is an unfinished animal. In the first place, that revolution takes place in speech, not in deed. Socrates makes it all but explicit that the city he describes is virtually impossible. He leaves it to our judgment whether it is, in fact, as he claims, the city that all just men wish for. Wishing is the symbol for unfinished business. Let me try to restate this point in a slightly different manner. The nonphilosophers must be restricted by education and force, not because they are finished, but because they can *never* be finished. They are radically incomplete. On this point, I see no difference at all between Plato and Nietzsche. Plato, however, infers from the radical incompleteness of the nonphilosopher, the political destructiveness of what we now call historical progress. Nietzsche aside, the difference between Plato and the typical contemporary thinker is, from Plato's standpoint, that between liberty and libertinism. Turning now to the philosophers, it must be said that they, too, are incomplete, if in a different sense from the nonphilosophers. Socrates makes it explicit in the dialogue that wisdom is impossible for human beings. The highest stage accessible to man is philosophy, or the love, which is also a lack, of wisdom. Passing over the paradoxical aspects of this thesis (properly noted by Hegel), its relevance for us is plain. Philosophers know that they are incomplete and attempt to rectify this deficiency while taking prudent steps to limit the dangerous consequences of the attempt to become complete. Nietzsche, on the contrary, shouts out from the rooftops human incompleteness, and transforms into the highest nobility the impetus to accomplish in and *upon* the public (or the body politic) the

uncompletable and hence extraordinarily dangerous revolution—
and this despite his regular, exaggeratedly Platonic denunciation
of the many.

This brief comparison between Plato and Nietzsche was intended, among other things, to illustrate the following principle.
No one believes more strongly than I that an accurate knowledge
of a philosophical teaching depends upon a minute and comprehensive analysis of the body of relevant texts. Nevertheless, from
time to time it is necessary for us to raise our heads from the
texts and to attempt to grasp in the broadest possible terms the
nature of the teaching to which we address ourselves. (I am well
aware that the picture I am painting consists of very broad
strokes, however, I contend that it is accurate in the sense that it
conforms to the standards appropriate to pictures painted in
broad strokes.) One cannot understand the specific technical
points of a philosophical teaching if one has no idea of the role
they play within the overall conception of the philosopher in
question. For our present purposes, then, one cannot understand
the difference between antiquity and modernity unless one is
able to distinguish between specific methodologies, arguments,
and technical terminologies on the one hand, and the fundamental intentions of the philosopher on the other.

This same principle applies in the case of attempts to distinguish between one modern philosophical doctrine and another.
The reader may well have been asking himself, as he has considered the preceding paragraphs, whether there is not a difference
between this or that modern school, even if I am right in denying
the sense of distinction between the modern and the postmodern. There are such differences. It is also true that any effort to
enforce a precise distinction between ancient and modern teach-
ings on a basis of chronology will fail. To give only one example
among many, the political teaching of Rousseau contains crucial
elements of Platonism. Nevertheless, it is impossible not to see
the difference between Rousseau and Plato. One could also say
that my previous comparison between Descartes and Carnap,

even at the broadest level, is marred by the presence of Scholastic or for that matter Platonic elements in the Cartesian teaching. I would reply simply that the distance from Duns Scotus (to say nothing of Plato) to Descartes is infinitely great, while the distance from Descartes to Carnap is finite. The most pedestrian reading of Descartes and Carnap will not fail to observe that, however important their technical and theoretical differences, they are united in their attempt to mathematize the world. Again at the level of the pedestrian, suppose it is objected that God plays a crucial role in Cartesian metaphysics but is entirely absent from Carnapian metaphysics. I do not need to reply with a complex argument that denies any but a rhetorical importance to the Cartesian God. Let us assume that Descartes was a devout Catholic, and sincerely believed that God guarantees clear and distinct ideas, and so, too, the entire edifice of mathematical physics. This belief is philosophically and historically irrelevant, when we raise up our heads to look at the broad picture. Within the broad picture, the "project" of mathematicizing the world is an act of the human will which makes God, sooner or later, and sooner rather than later, a *superfluous hypothesis.* As soon as the Cartesian revolution occurs, God is effectively dead, whether or not all members of that revolution are believers.

To turn to another example, we are today living through a quarrel, not between the ancients and the moderns, but between two modern schools who for purposes of convenience (and in keeping with their own slogans) may be characterized as the analysts and the continentalists. I have no doubt that this distinction is an absurd one. In the first place, philosophical analysis originated not at Oxford or Harvard but on the European continent. In the second place, phenomenologists, existentialists, and the rest who are classified under the rubric of "continental thinkers" engage in just as much analysis as do the self-styled analysts. Third and more important, both camps are at heart closely united by a fundamental historicism; both are in a process of continuous decay, with the result that the quarrel is turning, at an ever increasing rate, into a mixture and even in some cases a marriage (if only of convenience). Yet who would wish to deny that there are many differences of intention, method, and terminology between the analysts and the continentalists? I myself would go a step further. Disregarding the differences among them, if Quine, Davidson, Kripke, Rawls, and Searle, let us say, were to determine the future development of academic philosophy (for this is the extent of their power), the results would be quite different from those which might follow from the dominance of Habermas, Derrida, Deleuze, and (to name an American neocontinentalist) Rorty. I grant all of this. Nevertheless, it is all irrelevant from the standpoint of the present discussion. It may be true that, explicitly or implicitly, the analysts as a group place greater emphasis upon logic, mathematics, and natural science than do the continentalists as a group. But the continentalists are not advocating the abolition of science or a return to the classical view that art completes nature. What they are instead doing is placing a greater emphasis than the analysts upon the role of the will in the modern project. The logical analysis of the language of intentionality, whatever its technical interest, is a radical misunderstanding of the philosophical significance of the will, which is better addressed by Nietzsche's doctrine of the will to power, however vague and even illogical that doctrine may be.

Speaking in very general but widely admitted terms, analytical philosophy is itself divided into two camps, originating, more or less, in the writings of the early and the later Wittgenstein. Early analysis is a continuation of the positivist tradition, which in turn descends to us from the mathematical side of the Cartesian revolution. Later analysis rejects positivism in favor of a broader conception of human language, a conception which descends to us from the Cartesian doctrine of the priority of the will to the intellect. If this last point is not as immediately clear as the former, let the reader compare the Cartesian thesis on eternal truths with the later Wittgenstein's philosophy of mathematics, or, more generally, with his doctrine of rules. The bridge between the two apparently disparate dimensions of Descartes' teaching, and the corresponding two schools of contemporary analytical philosophy, is Kant. Kant attempts to reconcile the doctrine of the autonomy of the human will and the mathematical, or rule-governed, paradigm of rationality. Without going into the details, it is plain that his reconciliation depends upon two crucial theses. The first is the distinction between the phenomenal and the noumenal (let us say crudely between the knowable and the unknowable), and the second is the eternal validity of classical mathematics and physics. The retention of the first thesis in the temporalized form of historicism or linguistic relativism, and the rejection of the second thesis, under the impetus of non-Euclidean geometries, relativity physics, and deviate logics, reduces the theoretical differences between the two major contemporary schools of analytical philosophy to a point of rhetoric or ideology. The penchant of one camp for formalisms, and of the other for epigrams and charming literary interpretations, is theoretically insignificant. Analytical philosophy is moving steadily toward surrender to continentalism, regardless of temporary local deviations due to academic custom or power politics. This is of course *not* to say that interest in formalism will disappear, but rather that such interest is *already* understood by the majority in terms of the dominance of the will, or, as it is sometimes called today, of human creativity. If then we are capable of lifting our noses up from our logic texts or our treatises on the new hermeneutics for a long enough time to survey the comprehensive situation, I submit that the view is clear. Contemporary fashions are variations on the central theme of modernity, which was well stated by Fichte: freedom is higher than being. These words might well serve as the motto of the later Wittgenstein, as well as of the contemporary successors of Carnap and Russell.

Nothing I have said thus far is intended as a denial of the obvious fact that we are living in an age of rapid transition. The most I would claim is that the rapidity of the transition is a typical sign of Modernism. Another way to put the point is in terms of technology. We are currently obsessed with technique and its correlative, methodology, whether we count ourselves as disciples of the hard or the soft muses. For reasons which would have to be considered with great care, we are now undergoing a technical explosion, and one which is, to put it mildly, not always marked by theoretical reflection. As a central example, I cite the case of mathematical logic, set theory, and closely related branches of mathematics. When one reads the masters in this series of disciplines, Cantor, Frege, Russell, Brouwer, Hilbert, Skolem, and Gödel, to note some of the most important names, one sees at once that they are philosophers and not merely technicians. Mathematical analysis is in the service of deep philosophical investigation, touching upon the most comprehensive problems of thinking, intelligibility, and human nature. One of the most important questions of our generation, a question which is not raised by the most fashionable descendants of the aforementioned masters, is why the production of technical artifacts has replaced philosophical speculation in the philosophy of mathematics.

This rage for technical innovation has also engulfed the humanists among us, as is patent in the current popularity of hermeneutics with its often preposterous emphasis upon methods, technical terms, and a dehumanized textualism. It is interesting to note that technicist hermeneutics is no longer the center of attention in Paris, where much of the most extreme work of this sort originated. The center of hermeneutics is now the United States, the land par excellence of technology. What used to be called "literary criticism" has at last reached the exalted status of mathematically oriented economics, in which imaginary technical artifacts (models in the one case, texts in the other) replace commonsense observation of what is actually happening, or what has actually been written. If one takes a sufficiently broad view, there is a deep relationship between, say, the efforts of Robert MacNamara and his associates to run the American government, and specifically the war in Vietnam, by computers, and the efforts by structuralists, poststructuralists, and deconstructivists to detach works of art from their creators and consequently from their readers. To say that the text has a life of its own, independent of the intentionality of the author or the reader, is to identify life with abstract structures and, in this sense, is like treating the mathematical model of reality apart from the reality. In order to be more than provocative, this analogy would have to be spelled out at much greater length than I have space for. I must therefore rest content with the possibility that the reader will be provoked into a consideration of the analogy between rule-governed thinking, or the technologizing of reason, and the suppression of common sense from the art of reading a book or interpreting a work of art.

On all fronts, then, the whirling dervishes of methodology have produced intense currents of change. They have also provoked countermovements, from neoconservatism and the moral majority to a perceptible recognition among academicians that technical progress without moral sensibility, and indeed moral responsibility, is inadequate and destructive. One could perhaps wish that these quarrels were conducted at a deeper level of theoretical understanding. But whatever genius has been invested in this quarrel is technical, and hence not postmodern. Modernity is the age of *technē*. There is no technical exit, no exit at all other than death or total self-destructiveness. But this means that we cannot return to antiquity. What is required, if I am not mistaken, is the same as in any epoch, whatever name we give to the epoch itself: we must first understand who we are before we do something about whom we should like to be.

The reader may protest that I am taking refuge in a platitude. Let me close this essay with the attempt to defend myself against such a charge. As more fully developed, the charge runs something like this: The modern period, from Montaigne to Kant, is defined by a central concern with the question, "Who am I?"

Post-Kantian idealism may accordingly be understood as the transformation of the empirical "I" into the absolute ego. The deconstruction of the ego by Nietzsche and Freud simply continues the work of idealism, except that the absolute ego is now understood as the subconscious self, or id. Nietzsche and Freud thus represent the transition from the modern to the postmodern period, in which latter the absolute is no longer divine but subhuman. From this standpoint, the development of postmodernism during the past seventy-five years has been the process by which the subhuman (i.e., will to power, instinct, libido) is generalized into the nonhuman (formal structure of cybernetics on the one hand, poststructural deconstructivism on the other). The net result is the suppression of psychologism, subjectivity, and, in general, anthropocentrism.

The first thing to be said in reply to this charge is that the question "Who am I?" is also central to antiquity, and hence to Platonism. The view under inspection is thus an alternate version of the thesis that the modern epoch is an extension of Platonism. Metaphysics is then presumably essentially related to, if not identical with, subjectivism, anthropocentrism, and what Nietzsche calls perspectivism. It follows easily that an obsession with the ego deteriorates into egomania and consequently into the will to power. But the will to power, as is plain from the examples of Nietzsche and Freud, is also the suppression of the ego. The net result is that the tripartition of ancient/modern/ postmodern disappears; or rather it is itself transformed from a rigid articulation of history into a dialectical process *continuous* with history. The surface structure of history is then rigid and illusory, the deep structure is dialectical: *all* European history, or at least European history from Socrates onward, is then postmodern! However, if we accept the radical distinction, insisted upon by Nietzsche and Heidegger, between the pre-Socratics and Socrates, then it becomes more coherent, even by dialectical standards, to reestablish the distinction between the ancient and the modern epoch, with the essential proviso that Socrates is the first modern man. It is not dialectical, but nonsensical, to describe *all* of European history as postmodern. And the characteristic doctrines of the adherents of postmodernism dissolve the conventional distinction between antiquity and modernity in such a way as to establish an essential, if dialectical, continuity between the result of that dissolution and themselves.

Let me repeat the main point here. The will to power, ostensibly the essential feature of the modern (i.e., ancient plus modern) epoch is also, as the deconstruction of the ego, the essential feature of the postmodern epoch. For once the ego is entirely suppressed, so too is history, whether in the sense of "story" or historicity. Whatever the source of the structure of their intentionality, the protagonists in a story are self-conscious egos. It is hardly by accident that postmodern fiction frowns on the story, or the view that works of art are extensions of human experience. If there is such a phenomenon as postmodernism, then it is the abyss beyond the end of history. Let us call it the day of judgment, even if one upon which there are no more judges and no one to be judged. Whether in speculative philosophy or the mathematical sciences, an excess of ontologizing leads to the dissolution, not to the saving, of the phenomena. To say this, however, is not to be committed to a return of the conventional rigidities of the distinction between the ancients and the moderns. From the deepest standpoint, which coincides with the surface of things, it is of no ultimate importance whether Socrates or Montaigne is to count as the first modern man. What counts is man (the counting animal), and hence the question "Who am I?" As Heidegger himself points out, this is the proper formulation of the question "What is man?"

Whether in a conventional or in an orthodox sense, we need to reestablish what should never have been overlooked, what can be disregarded but never suppressed apart from self-destruction. The ostensible deconstruction of the ego is in fact an answer to the question: "Who am I?" The answer may vary in its specific words, but in one way or another it repeats the Odyssean reply:

"no one." In the *Odyssey,* however, this reply is a conscious concealment, one which represents in miniature Homer's concealed representation of the fundamental truth about man in the persona of *Odysseus.* If there is a postmodern epoch, its assertion of "no one" is not a conscious concealment, but rather the conscious assertion of nihilism. Postmodernism, even on this account, is then the attempt to assert Nietzsche's doctrine of noble nihilism while suppressing nobility. Once again, it stands identified as a defective version of modernism.

12 Critical Reasoning and History

RICHARD A. TALASKA

The Apparent Conflict Between Critical Reasoning and Foundational Opinion

Nomos as Foundational Opinion

There is something irremediably basic about opinion. The Greeks (and who doubts their extraordinary insight into such fundamentals?) attributed to Pindar a sentence that elegantly and succinctly manifests its power: "*Nomos ho pantōn basileus*," meaning "Law [is] the lord of all."[1] One must understand that by *nomos*, or *nomoi* in the plural, the Greeks meant those shared ruling opinions of a political society or culture that, whether written into the laws themselves or unwritten, constitute foundational traditions, customs, or beliefs, especially about what is right and what is wrong. Such ruling opinions of a political society or culture are so basic that they are, as it were, no longer themselves seen, but that through which everything else is seen. So foundational in the character or mores of a people are these, that not only are they not questioned, but they act as a kind of lens through which all other phenomena are brought into perspective.

Plato explicitly connects law and opinion and describes their foundational nature in the *Republic*. In books 2–4, in his search for the perfectly good city on the basis of which to determine the definition of justice, he proposes a system of education to mold the guardians of that regime into perfectly morally good citizens. Education is presented as a way of instilling into citizens morally correct opinions. The laws determine what those opinions will be and thus determine what will and will not be acceptable to teach the young. Plato compares the process of educating the young to have "the right and lawful opinion" to the process of colorfast dying, so that those who have received "the proper nature and rearing" would preserve those opinions "through everything."[2] The philosophical founders of the perfect regime discover, by reasoning, the truth about what is good for human beings, and on the basis of that truth make particular laws, including the ones to regulate education. In the founders (and later, the philosopher-kings who are not founders but rulers), there is knowledge of the basic principles of good and bad. In them, such knowledge replaces foundational opinions or beliefs (*nomoi*) as the source of morality. The laws made by the philosophers about education are intended to bring about and maintain in the non-philosophical citizens the correct foundational opinions and beliefs about good and bad that thereafter determine their thinking, feelings, and actions. These foundational opinions and beliefs reflect the knowledge possessed by the philosophers.

But if Plato's intention, as Cicero says, is not to present a regime to be hoped for but rather to show the nature of moral and political things, then we can draw from Plato's account certain basic moral and political distinctions.[3] First, there is, apart from the distinction between knowledge and opinion, a distinction between *nomoi* understood in the primary sense as the foundational opinions and beliefs of a political society or culture (e.g., in our society, the belief in the priority of the individual), and *nomoi* understood in the secondary sense as the individual laws of a society that reflect, confirm, and maintain the more foundational beliefs (e.g., laws concerning education, affirmative action, etc). In every imperfect regime, that is, every regime not founded upon reason (which, for Plato, means every existing regime), there is no strictly critical knowledge of ultimate moral principles. There are only opinions about what is right and just. The foundational values of a culture or society are not determined by reasoning but are merely handed down from some time in the distant past and assumed to be the correct ones. The origins of such values, and the values themselves, remain unquestioned. Secondary or minor laws are made on the basis of the foundational values already established in the culture. The secondary laws, in turn, serve to confirm and maintain the more basic cultural *nomoi*. By providing the basis for such distinctions in the *Republic*, Plato manifests the operative nature of foundational opinion as a kind of communal prereflective lens through which the members of a political society or culture bring their surroundings into perspective. This theme of the prereflective or nonreflective character of the *nomoi* is especially clear when he says that the person "properly reared," "due to his having the right kind of dislikes, . . . would praise the fine things . . . taking pleasure in them" and "would blame and hate the ugly in the right way while he's still young, before he's able to grasp reasonable speech."[4] The *nomoi* operate at the most basic, nonreflective, emotional level. Such prereflective *nomoi* or foundational opinions are not themselves scrutinized for their validity but all else is scrutinized through them. So basic are the *nomoi* that it is rare, even in a society of many highly educated individuals, for such opinions to be questioned.

Individualism as a Contemporary Nomos

A contemporary example of such a foundational opinion of the order of the *nomoi* described by Plato is modern individualism, or the belief in the right of self-subsistent particularity, the right of the individual to be satisfied (Hegel).[5] That this opinion operates in the West, particularly in the United States (as opposed, for example, to Latin American countries), prereflectively as a kind of traditional or historical lens through which other phenomena are focused is seen in the way any movement toward individualism in the East is characterized in the West as a form of enlightenment. Individualism is assumed to be the true doctrine. It is not impossible that this foundational opinion may in fact be true, but insofar as it constitutes an element in our shared historical beliefs, it operates as a kind of prereflective regulatory principle of the way we in the liberal West—and the best educated are not exempt from this—order our reasoning about certain social and political phenomena. It forms a necessary component in our understanding of things. This is not to say that, when we have achieved the ability "to grasp reasonable speech," some of us do not reflect upon the fact that we believe in (rather than know the truth of) individualism. Nor is it to say that it would be impossible for us to discover arguments for our belief or for us to achieve a standpoint from which to appreciate political societies that do not share this belief. But even if we were to acquire the ability to see things from a non-Western point of view, such an understanding would never be possible from the inside, as it were, would not be acquired in the way that it is acquired by a non-Western person. Rather, it would be acquired only through gradual insight gained by starting from the *nomos* of individualism and seeing it contrasted to opposing examples. Thus, the Greek idea that the *nomos* or foundational societal opinion rules all turns out to be true in the most radical epistemological sense. The *nomos* rules even the way we approach the phenomena and begin to reason about them.

*Critical Reasoning, The Historical Structure of
Understanding, and the* Nomoi

In spite of the hegemony of the *nomos*, Greek philosophers considered the highest use of mind the ability to escape opinion, which is always of the particular, the changing, and the arbitrary, and to search for and contemplate what is universal, what does not change, and what is necessary.[6] This use of mind might be called, using more recent vocabulary, and indeed ignoring many traditional distinctions about the various uses of mind, "critical reasoning." This search for the universal truth, untainted by the untested assumptions characteristic of opinion, became for the Greeks the end or *telos* and thus the highest purpose of the human mind, the highest activity or *energeia* possible for human beings.[7] But Plato especially recognized that the search after truth starts from an analysis of the *nomoi*. This accounts for the procedure of the *Republic*, where the entire first book consists of an analysis of opinions about what is right.

Gadamer's analysis of the historical structure of understanding[8] shows that it is a necessary condition for our understanding of things that we approach them from the point of view of our own mental history.[9] That history includes, first and foremost, the foundational shared *nomoi* of our social and cultural tradition. It is impossible to separate ourselves completely from our own history, of which the *nomoi* are essential components, in the manner of finding some completely neutral Archimedean point from which to understand things with absolutely no presuppositions guiding our thought. But if this is true, would not the Greek scientific ideal of reasoning freed from the particularities of opinion appear to be vain? All experience and conceptualization, as Husserl has shown, develop from the communal system of meanings imbibed from the world of ordinary life.[10] Husserl calls this ultimate communal system of meanings the "lifeworld."[11] On the basis of the lifeworld arise the foundational meanings, expressed in language, with which we think and on the basis of which all new meanings, including the scientific ones, become possible for us.[12] It is, therefore, part of the way we understand things to do so from a perspective, the most foundational of which is the communal system of meanings drawn from our history, that is, from our culture, political society, tradition.[13]

This is simply a fact of human consciousness. Far from being a mere prejudice to be overcome, foundational opinion is the necessary basis for thinking to be possible at all, and thus the necessary avenue to the understanding of opposing beliefs.[14] But the highest use of mind, or reasoning in the highest sense, has always, since the Greeks, been characterized by the contrast between knowledge and opinion. The former, unlike the latter, is understood as not based upon mere assumptions but rather as bringing all assumptions forward for examination.[15] How can the traditional philosophical or scientific demand for critical reasoning and objective certainty be reconciled with the fact, only more recently isolated and understood, of the historical structure of the understanding?

The Question of Critical Reasoning

In the light of the apparent contradiction between the traditional scientific demand for critical reasoning as the highest achievement of reason, and the more recently acquired idea of the historical structure of understanding, the question about reasoning in the highest sense (critical reasoning), and its conditions needs to be asked again for contemporary culture. What is critical reasoning, and what are the conditions, particularly educational conditions, necessary to achieve it? What is the relationship between critical reasoning and the content of our lifeworld experience, which for us includes the history of Western cultural achievements?

This way of stating the problem gets at the heart of an educational battle that has for the most part heretofore been waged by educators at the practical level of experiments with the curriculum. On the one side are those who have criticized the information-oriented curriculum of the past, claiming that it is overly concerned that students assimilate content and thus leaves their critical reasoning abilities underdeveloped. On the other side are those who have criticized experiments in the direction of critical thinking and away from content on the grounds that students simply become incompetent when content is neglected. But once we connect the idea of the historical nature of understanding with the traditional idea of critical reasoning as reasoning freed from opinion, it becomes clear that neither of these approaches on its own reflects the way reason develops. Reason necessarily starts from the whole tradition of cultural *nomoi* imbibed from childhood, yet it is precisely on that basis that experience and critical thought develop. Critical thought becomes possible when our *nomoi* are seen to be contradicted, thus requiring us to question the *nomoi* and, perhaps, change our thinking. Thus, all advances in experience and reasoning can occur only on the basis of the lifeworld, which itself, in contemporary culture, encompasses the history of literate culture. The question about critical reasoning now becomes the much more subtle question of the relationship between the content of contemporary literate culture and the ability to free oneself from the domination of that content.

History and the Idea of Critical Reasoning

As a way of further clarifying the kinds of issues at stake in considering critical reasoning in contemporary culture, we may profitably start from the history of ideas about critical reasoning itself. These reflections on the history of ideas of critical reasoning will themselves serve to show how the study of history is a necessary condition for critical reasoning to be possible.

The Classical Tradition and Critical Reasoning

For the Greeks, the *telos* of the human understanding is universal, unchanging, and necessary knowledge, knowledge about *physis* or nature, or the natures of things. The search for such knowledge starts with questioning the *nomoi*, noticing their particular, changing, and arbitrary character, and wondering whether there are any more ultimate answers to the most important questions—the ones traditionally answered by the *nomoi*.[16] The search for knowledge proceeds by a methodical search for answers that transcend time, place, and culture, and for which evidence, of the type that all can share, can be provided.[17] The *pros hen* or ideal referent of such knowledge, for the Greeks, is the kind achieved in what Aristotle described as the theoretical sciences, wherein, according to the particular subject matter, a knowledge of certain particular kinds of essences, or more broadly construed, a knowledge of the natures of things, is achieved.[18] The kind of knowledge, the degree of precision to be achieved, and the appropriate method to achieve these are considered by the Greeks and the tradition following them to be parasitic upon and proportionate to the subject matter under discussion.[19] The tradition also assumed that the sciences reflect the way things are: *Ens et verum convertuntur* ("Being and what is true are convertible").[20] But these high achievements of reasoning begin by questioning the *nomoi*, and there is no better example of this than the example of Socrates.[21] Socrates is the critical reasoner par excellence.

Early Modernity and Critical Reasoning

Early modernity is characterized not by its reflection upon and questioning of ordinary *nomoi*, but rather by its reflection upon and questioning of the philosophic thought of the classical philosophical tradition. But the claim of early modernity was that the entire tradition of classical science was nothing more than pseudoscience. That is: the tradition had become nothing more than opinion, since the practitioners of classical science merely accepted uncritically the authority of their predecessors, whose basic premises the moderns judged to be false.[22] Early modernity criticized Aristotelianism, meaning Scholasticism, for a lack of certainty due to erroneous basic principles about the subject matter of philosophy, the lack of a single productive method, the lack of any practical results, and the lack of systematic unity among the sciences.[23] These criticisms actually reduce to two: lack of certainty and lack of practical results. Unity of method and subject matter as well as systematic connection among the sciences were perceived as means to the more basic two desiderata, certainty and practical results. Since Descartes, reasoning in the highest sense has been characterized as having its completion, its *telos*, in a kind of absolute certainty imitative of mathematics. This presupposes, above all, that the beginning of reasoning in the highest sense must be characterized by a lack of the kinds of prejudices that could vitiate our understanding of things. The standpoint of reason must be one completely freed from opinion.[24] Early modernity saw itself as attempting to achieve, and actually achieving, the Socratic demand for certainty to a degree that Socrates never dreamed of.[25] It considered itself to have achieved such a standpoint by connecting the idea of certainty and presuppositionless beginnings with the idea of universal method and subject matter and the idea of the systematic construction of an edifice of knowledge generated by such a single unified method.

The consequences of the modern demand for a presuppositionless beginning and for the gradual buildup of an edifice of knowledge are well known. It meant the universal application of the mathematical-experimental method not only to physics but to all disciplines, including those that study human nature, and even those hitherto considered recalcitrant to the precision and formal abstraction proper to mathematics, namely, ethics and politics.[26] But the result for these disciplines was that what had formerly been considered possible knowledge—knowledge of the good and happiness for human beings, including knowledge of the virtues that constitute such happiness—was now rejected as mere opinion.[27] By reducing the study of human nature to what could be subsumed under the new method and rejecting as unknowable those higher things formerly considered knowable, the moderns traded what they considered to be a shaky knowledge of what is highest, and thus no knowledge at all, for a certain knowledge of what is lowest but at least solid.[28] Politics deals no longer with the highest goal—happiness or the good life for human beings—but only with the necessary conditions for survival and comfort, a goal the ancients considered lowest even if most urgent.[29]

Considerations Preparatory to an Historical
Understanding of Critical Reasoning

Since, according to Greek philosophers, critical reasoning begins by reflecting upon and questioning the *nomoi*, that is, reflecting upon the parochial and changeable character of the various *nomoi* of the various cities, and proceeds by searching for universal and eternal knowledge, it is clear by implication that the Classical tradition understood in at least a fundamental way the historical character of opinion. But that tradition was never led to reflect upon how knowledge is itself historical, how scientific paradigms themselves become higher-order systems of opinions, which, after becoming entrenched, operate normatively upon all further particular scientific achievements,[30] and thus themselves lose the original self-evidence present to their creators.[31] Nor did the tradition reflect upon how scientific achievements are themselves affected by and even based upon unquestioned lifeworld experience.[32] Such reflections could only have occurred once certain historical conditions had been met that simply could not have been met in the Greek experience. What the Greek experience lacked was the experience of scientific revolution, and thus of a diversity of scientific paradigms or worldviews, as well as the experience of technology and the popularization of science.

The Greeks began philosophy by reflecting upon their prephilosophic background, which consisted in their religious and cultural *nomoi*. When modern philosophy rejected Classical thought and substituted an entirely new paradigm within which to conceive the natures of things, it did so by reflecting upon its own prephilosophic background, which included Classical philosophy. This background was "prephilosophic," insofar as the early moderns considered themselves to be doing philosophy for the first time. This new relationship between philosophy and what it questions represents a fundamental change. The relationship is now no longer that of philosophy to the *nomoi*, but rather that of philosophy conceived anew to traditional philosophy. Furthermore, the Classical tradition in philosophy never affected ordinary life, with its entirely nonscientific *nomoi*, in such a way as to infect it with vulgarized scientific opinions. The latter infection of nonphilosophical life occurred only with modernity, which consciously sought what Classical thought never conceived possible: an alliance of the philosophers and the many, of science and political society. Once modern philosophy conceived its project of the mastery of nature, it began to attempt to convince the public of its need for philosophy and of philosophy's need for public financial support if science were to be able to serve the public.[33] Part of the rhetoric necessary to convince the public of its need for science was to flatter the public by claiming that it, too, was capable of philosophic enlightenment, because reason is by nature equal in all.[34] Once the public became convinced of its own competence and its need for philosophy, the conditions were set for the vulgarization of philosophic thought into ordinary society. By our own time, the background of our own philosophizing includes philosophic thought as vulgarized or popularized in society at large. The belief in the priority of the individual is an example of vulgarized philosophy.

Hence our perspective is decidedly different from that of the Greeks, and even that of the early moderns. For the Greeks began philosophy by questioning their prephilosophic world, which included only nonphilosophic religious and cultural *nomoi*, and the early moderns began philosophizing by questioning philosophy itself as done up to their time. But we can begin philosophizing only by questioning a world that includes philosophic thought proper as well as vulgarized philosophic thought, philosophic thought already having become popular opinion. Such a situation, in which it becomes clear how scientific thought itself becomes popularized and thus operates as another level of *nomoi* in addition to the other beliefs of culture, could only have been achieved after modernity altered the traditional conception of philosophy (which rejected the idea of popularization), substituted a new conception (which demanded popularization), and then influenced ordinary life by its ideas. The reflections about the historical nature of understanding, with its roots in the lifeworld, and about how even science becomes part of the lifeworld through popularization, could only have occurred once the history of thought had progressed in precisely the right direction and to the right point for such insights to be possible.

But the fact that vulgarized or popularized philosophy or science has become part of our lifeworld has consequences for critical reasoning in contemporary culture. We tend to focus on things through the lenses of certain ideas that owe their origin to the modern philosophic project. Thus we assume, but do not examine, for example the truth of the doctrine of modern individualism. We assume, but do not examine, the superiority of the modern scientific method. But to assume these doctrines without examining them is to have them operate as *nomoi* and thus to be unable to reject them even if they may in fact be problematic. Critical reasoning requires the examination of *nomoi* and thus the possibility of rejecting them. To examine the above-mentioned *nomoi* would require the study of the texts that were their sources, as well as the texts those sources were rejecting. But those texts are all philosophical, scientific, and political texts out of the past—they are historical texts. Thus, to be a critical reasoner requires the study of history. Let us examine this more closely.

Early modernity considered itself to have achieved the highest possible critical standpoint by restricting itself to what could be tested by the new scientific method. When Descartes laid out his project for the New Science in the *Discourse on the Method*, he started by assuming a humanistic premise defended in another context by Machiavelli. The humanistic premise is that man is first and foremost always regulated by selfish passions.[35] Descartes had to add to this premise the further premise that science, to be worthwhile—to be science at all—must exist to satisfy those passions. He made it clear that the certainty of science was itself subordinate to the practical goal, that science should create the technology to satisfy the passions. Only science with a practical goal would hereafter count as science.[36] That goal is not itself the product of that alone which is intended to produce certainty, namely the method, but in fact guides and determines method and its results.[37] Thus the *telos* itself (the benefit of mankind) guiding all of science and determining what counts as science turns out to lack the certainty of the means to it, namely the new mathematical method. The only science which turns out to be able to achieve this *telos* is the one that sufficiently lowers the goal of philosophy so as to be able to achieve certainty and reduces the subject matter of philosophy to what can be physically manipulated with the help of mathematics and method, that is, to matter. The history of later modernity is so affected by the early modern turn from the concerns of antiquity that, in spite of differences among later moderns, Western thought would never fully recover from the basic reorientation effected by early modernity.[38] There is apparently no return in the West to either Classical natural science with its idea of a diversity of methods or Classical natural right with its rejection of the absolute priority of the right of the individual. But this means that the modern scientific paradigm rules by default, since its origins are no longer critically examined but merely accepted, and operate as a kind of higher order opinion within which particular scientific achievements continue to be brought about. The practical successes of modern natural science and modern liberal politics are apparently sufficient in the eyes of their practitioners to preclude any waste of time in the reexamination of origins. But the above brief examination of origins reveals certain difficulties with the foundational early modern arguments. Only historical investigations uncover the prejudices and problems inherent in the modern point of view. Thus, critical reasoning requires the study of history.

Critical Reasoning as Making Historical Presuppositions Thematic

With investigations such as those of Husserl and others into the history of philosophy and science, a new reflection on the meaning of critical reasoning comes about. It is based upon the insight that not only our moral and political *nomoi* but also our scientifically achieved concepts, in both natural science and in morality and politics, themselves constitute a *"Welt"* or *"Umwelt"*, a "world." They do so in the same way that the *nomoi* constitute a world—not an objective one, but a subjective system of concepts through which everything else is focused and understood.[39] Even the world of modern natural science has become a system of concepts within which we think but which we take for granted. We have forgotten the origins of these concepts in early modernity because of the tremendous sediment of intervening achievements and continuing progress that have obscured those origins. By a study of history, the full implications of Vico's alteration of the Classical proposition, *"Ens et verum convertuntur"* ("Being and what is true are convertible") to the proposition *"Factum et verum convertuntur"* ("What is made and what is true are convertible"), become clear. This is a movement from the classical idea that the human mind discovers nature to the modern idea that the human mind constructs it.[40] Scientific paradigms or systems of concepts are constructed by human beings in order to "salve the phenomena," in order to put order and reason to our experience. Scientific truth is not simply the *adaequatio rei et intellectus* ("correspondence of the thing and the intellect"),[41] but a construction of the intellect to understand things.

Once we humans make a new hegemonic scientific theory, or paradigm, our successors no longer spend time thinking through in evidence the original thoughts that brought such theory about, but rather merely assume them and go on. This process of the replacement of evidence by rules and procedures can be exemplified in geometry.[42] Although proofs of later propositions presuppose proofs of earlier ones, the proofs of the earlier ones no longer remain consciously before our minds. They continue to operate, not in direct evidence, but rather as rules replacing direct evidence. We use the earlier propositions as rules for generating new ones without having to keep the evidence of earlier proofs present to our minds. Because of this process, the origins become obscured or sedimented over by later achievements. This process itself is an expression of the historical character of consciousness.

The problem Husserl saw with the late modern scientific situation was that the origins of modern scientific or philosophic thinking had become sedimented over by the later results of modern thought. Unless the sediment could be removed, modern thought would not be able to recover from the problems to which its origins had logically led it.[43] Such problems have their source in the origins which have been forgotten but which continue to operate by default, as it were, in modern thought. One of those problems is the very common belief that the specifically human things, such as morality, are fundamentally incapable of scientific treatment and thus are merely a matter of opinion, or of religious revelation, or of special insight on the part of a chosen few. Such a claim is a form of irrationalism, or at least, of anti-intellectualism. Husserl's claim was that, because the origins of early modernity had fallen into obscurity, later modern man, still under the spell of the victory of modern natural science, could in no way conceive of a science of man that dealt with the specifically spiritual in man—the specifically human—but assumed all real treatment of man and his situation to be ultimately explicable only by reducing all explanation to physical causes.[44] But since the sciences were so unsuccessful in dealing with man in this way, and since this so-called scientific approach to human things seemed even to worsen rather than ameliorate the human condition, this approach opened the door to the above-mentioned irrational reaction against any claim to rational or scientific knowledge of man. The mistaken claim that the specifically human is incapable of treatment by science stems from a *nomos*, taken over from and built upon since early modernity, that construes science as fundamentally physicalistic.

Thus the problem of this form of irrationalism is not the result of any problems inherent in the power of reason itself. Rather, irrationalism stems from reducing the idea of critical, scientific reasoning to the idea of reasoning as understood by physicalistic positivism, and failing to see the inherent difficulties with that approach because of a lack of examination of its problematic origins. The study of those origins manifests positivism's now-hidden assumptions. Husserl's historical studies led him to discover those assumptions, but even more importantly, to understand how such assumptions can become obscured and cause one falsely to think one has achieved a viewpoint free of prejudices when one has not done so. Husserl saw that what seemed to Descartes and the early moderns to be an absolutely presuppositionless starting point was not so,[45] and that, as a result of early modern claims, even science has become a kind of higher-level system of *nomoi* that, now entrenched, obscures original evidence and works as a set of mere assumptions. What seems to be critical, scientific reasoning turns out to have conditions that prevent it from being critical in the purest sense. But this insight can only occur after a study of history.[46] Thus critical reasoning in contemporary culture presupposes a study of history.

The above excursus on philosophy and its self-conception over time and in particular, its conception of that in which critical reasoning consists, points towards how that conception itself is affected by history: to understand the idea of critical reasoning today presupposes an understanding of the history of the meanings of critical reasoning. The study of the history of critical reasoning, when carried through to Husserl's insight into the problems of the lifeworld and of sedimentation, sets the stage for the appearance of the apparent conflict between the search for a *nomos*-free starting point and the historical nature of the understanding. In the same way that we are affected by a vulgarized but nevertheless widely accepted notion of science before we even begin to study science rigorously, so also are we affected by ideas of what it is to be a critical thinker long before any of us takes up the task of seriously examining the meaning of critical reasoning. The contemporary common nonphilosophical ideas about science and critical reasoning, one way or another, have, imbedded in them, the history of thinking about science and critical reasoning—perhaps most especially the most problematic part of that history, namely, the modern period with its positivistic and physicalistic assumptions. But the apparent conflict between a starting point freed from assumptions and the historical nature of the understanding has a resolution. By studying history (in this case, the history of ideas of science and critical reasoning), we make such assumptions thematic and thereby free our discussion from unspecified presuppositions.

If critical reasoning is more than the mere knowledge and application of rules of logic, if, indeed, by the very doctrines of traditional logic, the grasping of true first principles freed from prejudice is more important even than the application of the rules of logic (which we tend to use correctly even without formal training in logic) to discourse, then the highest point of critical reasoning is its starting point in the questioning of, freeing ourselves from, and getting beyond the prejudices of our own history. But this important starting point cannot be initiated except from the point of view of already established opinions, or history. History can be both implicit and explicit. If it is merely implicit, it operates without our knowing it, and thus operates as a system of unexplicit presuppositions: it operates as the *nomoi* operate. Making history explicit is an attempt to make thematic our presuppositions, and thus to achieve a kind of presuppositionless beginning. But this can only occur through a study of what makes up our cultural history. In the history of thought, that means texts. Critical Reasoning in contemporary culture, therefore, requires that we make our historical presuppositions thematic, and to do so requires the study of foundational texts.

An Example of the Connection between Critical Reasoning and the Study of History

The above discussion has done two things. First, based upon a study of the history of the meanings of critical reasoning, it has established an idea of critical reasoning in contemporary culture, namely, the idea that critical reasoning consists in making historical presuppositions thematic. Second, it has provided an example of how a study of history is necessary for critical reasoning to be possible by taking the very idea of critical reasoning itself and showing that we cannot be completely critical with respect to *it*, without a study of *its* history.

Let us now provide a more straightforward example of how the study of our own cultural history is necessary for us to escape its influence upon us as unexamined tradition. One of the best examples of this is the one mentioned at the beginning of this essay: the way in which the belief in individualism operates as a higher-order *nomos* in the liberal West, causing those who believe in it to perceive political phenomena in a particular way. For the doctrine of individualism to cease to operate as a prejudice, we must reconstitute the origins of individualism and evaluate the philosophical arguments that gave rise to its eventually being accepted and then handed down as an unquestioned assumption. Such examination of origins requires a study of the foundational texts in which such arguments occurred. These are early modern texts such as those of Hobbes. It also requires a study of the texts representing the opposing arguments against which the early moderns directed their attack. The opposing arguments are contained in various texts of the Classical tradition. The following is intended to show how a study of history helps one achieve a critical standpoint with respect to the *nomos* of individualism by uncovering the forgotten origins of the doctrine and thereby subjecting it to rational analysis. Of course, critical reasoning is not achieved by studying interpretations such as those presented here but by reading the texts themselves upon which such interpretations are based.

The Classical Understanding of Natural Right and the Rejection of Individualism

The subtitle of the *Republic, peri dikaiou* ("on what is right," or, "on what is just"), indicates its theme.[47] The book is the first to answer the question about what is right in terms of *physis* ("nature") rather than *nomos*. It is thus the first and greatest work of political philosophy, the start of the classical natural right/law tradition, and the model for philosophical nonarbitrary investigation into the nature of right.

Dikaion/dikaiosunē bear two senses: "the right/rightness" in the sense of "what is right" and "the just/justice" in the sense of "fairness."[48] Aristotle explains the two uses in *Nicomachean Ethics* 5.1 and 5.7. In 5.7, he divides *dikaion politikon* ("political right") into *physikon* ("natural") and *nomikon* ("conventional"), which he distinguishes by explaining that natural right is universal, whereas conventional right is arbitrary and depends on the decisions of particular cultures.[49] Aquinas, citing Cicero, confirms that *justum naturale* ("what is just by nature") means *jus naturale* ("natural right").[50] Therefore, Plato's *dikaion* and *dikaiosunē*, Aristotle's *dikaion physikon*, Cicero's and Aquinas's *justum naturale*, bear a common partial meaning: "What is [morally] right" as determined by nature as a standard.

Jus naturale ("natural right") and *lex naturalis* ("natural law") are two aspects of one thing, and the terms are often used synonymously. According to Aquinas, right is to particular acts of justice as the idea that preexists in the mind of the craftsman is to his particular productions. Right performs the function of a standard.[51] Written law is the concretization into discourse of natural right[52]; natural law is the rational creature's participation by speech and thought in the eternal law.[53] Thus, in the tradition, *lex* and *jus* merge, *jus* being related to *jungere* ("to bind"): both indicate obligation. From Plato onwards, natural right means a moral state of health that comes from living *kata physin* ("according to nature"),[54] doing that "for which [one's] nature [makes] him naturally most fit,"[55] or "the having and doing of one's own and what belongs to one."[56] This is "minding one's own business,"[57] acting in accordance with one's own nature. Aristotle refuses to put a definition to natural right other than to say by contrast with the right by convention that it has the same force everywhere and stands as the universal to the particular.[58] Aquinas defines it as what by its nature is appropriate or commensurate to another.[59] By this he means both a duty to act in accordance with nature and an appropriateness of receiving what is in accordance with nature. What is right is what is in accordance with human nature, and our actions, to be in accordance with nature, must conform to the demands of human nature, both in ourselves and in our relations with others.[60] Grotius, still within this Classical tradition, defines *jus naturale* as "a dictate of right reason which points out that an act, according as it is or is not in conformity with rational nature, has in it a quality of moral baseness or moral necessity; and that, in consequence, such an act is either forbidden or enjoined by the author of nature, God."[61] In sum, in the Classical tradition, the common meaning of right is primarily that it is a moral necessity to act in a certain way, a duty to fashion our lives in accordance with human nature at its best. All political philosophy looks back to Plato as the originator of natural right, and Classical natural right stems from Plato's isolation of it in the *Republic* as a duty to act *kata physin* ("according to nature").

This Classical idea of natural right as duty rather than entitlement is connected with the Classical idea that human beings are primarily social and political beings.[62] That we are primarily social or political results from the character of the human soul. Apart from those necessities imposed upon us by our physical nature, all the other parts of human nature (the moral sentiments, all habits, reason itself) owe their origin to political society and education.[63] We could not even speak, much less acquire the right personal habits to enable us to act correctly or to reason critically—to do philosophy—if not for the nurturing influence of political society. Everything we are comes from the community.[64] Therefore, human beings are primarily social and political beings, and natural right has the character of something owed back to political society rather than the character of entitlement. Even the obligations we have to ourselves to acquire personal virtues for the sake of happiness have a social *telos*. This is the import of Plato's suggestion that the virtues and happiness of the city as a whole stem from individuals doing what is right by nature.[65] In summary, Classical natural right stems from a decidedly social view of human nature that is quite consciously opposed, by Classical philosophy, to individualism. The opposition is conscious because the argument on behalf of individualism is given by Glaucon in the beginning of book 2 of the *Republic*. The astute political theorist David Hume recognized this as the classical expression of the Hobbesian argument for individualism.[66] The positive argument of the rest of the *Republic* is, of course, Plato's rejection of this view.

The Modern Understanding of Natural Right and the Liberal Tradition of Individualism

The liberal tradition beginning with Hobbes changes the meaning of right from what is essentially a duty to entitlement: "rights." Hobbes explicitly distinguishes between *jus* ("right") and *lex* ("law") and criticizes the tradition for not keeping these notions apart. *Right* he defines as bare liberty, and *law* as what limits bare liberty. But, contrary to the tradition, Hobbes makes right, not law, the fundamental natural moral idea.[67] He does so by a rather long argument that has as its premises the entirety of his mechanical version of modern natural science, his treatment of the universe, or nature, as a whole. The argument, in its most brutal and basic form, attempts to show that, as the universe or nature as a whole is a material mechanism, determined in all its parts, so also is human nature. There is, therefore, no free will in the traditional sense. Human beings are natural mechanisms with two basic mechanical motions going on inside their bodies. These are vital motion, or the motions of life, such as the motion of the blood, heart, etc., and animal motion or voluntary motion, which is the motion, initiated by desire, whereby we seek to satisfy ourselves. Animal motion exists to preserve vital motion. Another way of saying the latter is merely to say that human beings are creatures of passion; all of our actions and thoughts are directed to the satisfaction of the passions. We necessarily seek the satisfaction of the passions. In the state of nature, each of us would necessarily seek the satisfaction of our individual passions, even at the expense of others, should we come into conflict with them. Thus, human beings are not by nature social, but are atomistic, self-seeking individuals. Due to the private nature of our bodies as physical mechanisms, portions of matter separate from all others, we have our own private passions, which we will necessarily seek to satisfy in isolation from others. Since we cannot control the passions, our attempt to satisfy them ought not be considered wrong, or, positively stated, we have a right, or the liberty, without any restrictions by nature, to satisfy our passions.[68] This right, for Hobbes, is the basis of all morality and the starting point for the derivation of the natural or moral law, which is nothing other than a series of prudential imperatives aimed at the satisfaction of the passions.[69] The state is in turn generated as a means of ensuring mutual adherence to those prudential imperatives, all for the purpose of preserving the right to self-preservation and to a commodious life.[70] On this view, modern natural right stems from a decidedly individualistic view of human nature that is quite consciously opposed, by modern philosophy, to the Classical view.

On the above characterization of the Classical tradition and the beginning of the modern tradition on the idea of natural right, the Classical tradition comes to light as defending the idea that what is right by nature is primarily a series of moral imperatives for action. Modernity in morality begins with the idea that what is right by nature is primarily liberty for self-satisfaction. These views are connected with corresponding views of the human nature, which are in turn connected with corresponding views of nature as a whole. On the Classical view, human beings are primarily social beings and achieve their highest actualization in association with others. Even theoretical reason depends for its material conditions upon the state and its nurturing education. On the modern view, human nature is primarily individualistic and human beings achieve their highest actualization in the isolated satisfaction of their personal passions. The state is only a concession intended to relieve the incommodities that necessarily attend our natural isolation. Even within the state, the primary good is our personal satisfaction.

Modern Individualism as a Nomos *of*
Contemporary Western Culture

Without a study of history and a clear understanding of the differences between the classical and modern perspectives on the issue of right, our own understanding of things tends to be skewed by presuppositions which have not been made thematic. Earlier I referred to the common tendency among those in the liberal West to interpret any form of movement toward Western ideas on the part of the East as a form of enlightenment. Such interpretations are laden with presuppositions going all the way back to Hobbes and the early modern rejection of Classical thought. The assumption that individualism is the true doctrine represents the employment of a moral and political doctrine whose original self-evidence has become sedimented over by the whole system of later moral and political accretions based upon it. Thus its original self-evidence is no longer actively present. Rather, individualism operates now as earlier geometrical propositions operate much later in the development of a geometry: as rules substituting for direct evidence. Individualism, once a scientific proposition supported by proofs such as those of Hobbes, has become a *nomos*. Only if the evidential origins of this *nomos* are sufficiently reconstituted can we claim, in this particular area of morality and politics, to have achieved the critical standpoint, or the standpoint of reasoning in the highest sense. Such reconstitution requires a study not only of the arguments of the early modern originators of individualism, but also of those they rejected, those of the Classical tradition. Without that, individualism continues to operate as a *nomos*. One of the proofs of this is the fact that only when we dig into texts, such as those of Machiavelli, Hobbes, and Locke, in relation to the texts of classical antiquity against which they directed their arguments, do the problematic origins of modern individualism become evident. Only then is it possible for us to take a stance critical of individualism, and thus achieve the standpoint of critical reasoning with respect to our own *nomoi*.

Once origins become evident, the door is open for problems to become evident. For example, after study, the following kinds of considerations, all stated with an eye to questioning *our nomoi*, might occur to us. The doctrine of individualism is based on the doctrine that man is only a creature of passion. That idea itself is of Machiavellian origin. But Machiavelli's proof is only a probable proof, based upon his own experience of men and study of the actions of men past. Yet is not this doctrine that human beings are creatures of passion precisely the one Descartes used to stipulate that science, to be science, must satisfy human passions? Hobbes saw this difficulty and claimed to have proven, from modern natural science, that we are only creatures of passion, and thereby to have proven the doctrine of modern individualism. But is not Hobbes' own doctrine vitiated by his inability to prove the fundamental premise of his natural philosophy upon which the doctrine of individualism is based, namely that the universe is only a material thing? And is not his attempt to defend that doctrine dependent upon his already having decided that the Aristotelian doctrine of separated essences, as he understood that doctrine, was false? But it is probable that he misinterpreted the true Aristotelian meaning of that doctrine.[71] If so, does this not make the whole doctrine of individualism of questionable origin, and thus of questionable validity? Someone might object that its questionable origins do not necessarily falsify it. There may be newer, better arguments available. The reply is that, unless we study the origins, we will not be able to disentangle the questionable old arguments from any possible new argument on behalf of individualism, since, as we saw earlier, concepts carry with them a history that influences us unwittingly if that history is not made explicit. For we often construct such new arguments on the basis of the *nomos* created by the old arguments, and even more, we often construct the new arguments on the basis of our having already accepted the old doctrine and understood it in the old way—precisely with an eye to proving that which we already accept. This is nothing but apologetics. For critical reasoning to occur, the old *nomos* needs to be made patent once again with all the old arguments that rendered it so powerful as to make it a permanent part of our consciousness. But in reconstituting those arguments by the study of the original texts in which they first appeared, we need to reconstitute also the worldview that those arguments were intended to demolish, and to appreciate *its* reasonableness. And while creating new arguments on behalf of our *nomos*, we need to consider possible new arguments on behalf of the view our *nomos* replaced. The very fact that questions such as the above can be raised only after a study of history, and that only by asking such questions do we free ourselves at least to some degrèe from individualism in its character as *nomos*, shows that the critical standpoint cannot be achieved without investigations into the origins of our own conceptual history. Only then is it possible to achieve the standpoint whereby individualism as a doctrine becomes doubtful or questionable, and thus open to renewed investigation in hopes of finding better evidence in its support. Only then is the Socratic standpoint, that of questioning our own *nomoi*, achieved. Only then are we reasoning critically.

Education and the Problem of Achieving the Critical Standpoint

The Apparent Conflict Between Critical Reasoning and the Historical Nature of Understanding

In our earlier résumé of how reasoning in the highest sense has been characterized in the history of Western philosophy, what constitutes the common element in that history that allows us to refer to all periods as *philosophy*, as critical reasoning? Is there still a common thread to the various conceptions of critical reasoning? One might suggest, with Heidegger, that what is greatest about philosophy is its origin. This origin affects all that follows, and thus the idea of reasoning in the highest sense as characterized by the Greeks continues to operate in all three as the common partial sense.[72] Thus the idea of critical reasoning has its ideal, or *pros hen*, referent, in the questioning of Socrates: the attempt to use rational, logical arguments to unmask presuppositions and search for evidence as a foundation for new answers to questions hitherto answered by the *nomoi*. Neither early modernity nor more recent philosophy fails to follow Socrates in this basic requirement. The Socratic ideal remains the *telos* of philosophy, or thinking in the highest sense. Education into the highest form of reasoning always means education into critical reasoning, howsoever the differences between the various disciplines, their methods, and their content, are conceived. Education retains the Socratic ideal that the highest form of knowing requires some sort of freedom from mere opinion. But we are still led to wonder whether the discovery of the lifeworld and the problem of sedimentation, which has led ultimately to a recognition of the apparent conflict between the Socratic demand for objective certainty and the doctrine of the historical structure of understanding, has brought an end to the traditional understanding of critical reasoning. Although Husserl himself always sought to achieve the standpoint of philosophy as a rigorous science, and thus opposed historicism, did not his isolation of the lifeworld ultimately prove the truth of historicism?[73] If critical reasoning requires freedom from opinion, what could that freedom mean if we cannot completely eliminate the influence of history?

This latter question can now be asked in a way more clearly related to the educational theme of the present volume. What is the relationship between the disposition of critical reasoning as reasoning without prejudices and the actual content of what we take as the accumulated knowledge of our time, our communal intellectual history, our culture? Let us again take as an example philosophy, understood broadly in its older sense as universal knowledge, the parts of which would then include the natural and humanistic sciences. We are not at the beginning of philosophy or universal science, but well along the way. The content of our historical consciousness—our world—includes philosophy and its history, the sciences, the arts, literature, sociopolitical history, and all of the human achievements that fall under the so-called disciplines and professions. That is to say: our world includes all the disciplines and human achievements that constitute the literate culture of our age. Most of the latter content, although constantly operative in society as a whole in the way intended in Husserl's idea of lifeworld and in our example of individualism, becomes most specifically and actively operative in the individual by being learned in and confirmed by the education process. How does learning that content affect the achievement of the critical Socratic standpoint, traditionally conceived?

The Progress of Modernity and the Problem of
Indoctrination versus Critical Reasoning

By the seventeenth century, before modern natural science supplanted Aristotelian science, the Aristotelian curriculum with its huge Scholastic apparatus accumulated over a period of nearly two millennia was loaded with content. Students were required to learn that content.[74] Questioning was indeed encouraged in one of the very forms in which education took place—the disputation—but not questioning the general Aristotelian paradigm itself. Twentieth-century philosophy of science has shown that, once a scientific paradigm becomes entrenched, the scientific investigators who use its concepts to explain things tend to use the paradigm to answer local questions, but do not tend to question the paradigm itself. They presuppose and use the larger paradigm with its more basic concepts in the manner in which geometricians presuppose earlier proofs without constantly having them in actual evidence before their minds. Such basic concepts are used but not questioned. Radical questioning with corresponding insights into possible new paradigms seems to be reserved for the ingenious few great creative teachers of the human race. This is why certain early modern documents in natural science, such as Galileo's *Dialogue Concerning Two Chief World Systems*, or Descartes' *Discourse on the Method of Conducting One's Reason and Seeking Truth in the Sciences*, or in morality and politics, Machiavelli's *The Prince*, or Hobbes's *Leviathan* are such extraordinary examples of a different kind of questioning that is more foundational. For instead of using the preestablished system of concepts to answer particular questions in a new way, these authors questioned the whole system itself. They had enough creative insight to sketch a completely new way of explaining things.[75] However, once modern natural science gained the victory by its great achievement of the mastery of nature, and once the Aristotelian system disintegrated—at least in natural science—a new positivistic Scholasticism took its place.[76] But it could not, as had its predecessor, be criticized for lack of results or for useless distinctions, since the victory of modern natural science lay, in large part, in its achievement of the mastery of nature. In spite of all the criticisms of modern natural science, especially those of recent European philosophy, the Anglo-American world by and large remains under the spell of the early modern optimism about its project.[77]

By the late twentieth century, teachers of any one of the sciences—natural, moral, or political—struggle to pass on the heavy load of information alone that has accumulated since Galileo, Descartes, Hobbes, and others razed Scholasticism and laid the foundations for the new edifice. But the foundations themselves—the mathematical view of nature and mathematical/experimental method as well as the moral and political theory of individualism connected with these by Hobbes—have not been questioned in as radical a way as the Aristotelian paradigm was questioned by early modernity. To the extent that such original and monumental achievements of modern natural science continue to be part of the unquestioned framework within which science is achieved, the achievers of science are to that extent technologists who work with established procedures to further knowledge as defined within the current paradigm of science. This kind of achievement lacks the cognitive status of the Socratic achievement which requires that everything be in evidence.[78] This is why Socrates, and even Plato, put such priority upon questions and conversation, for in the active engagement of a conversation, the things themselves are always in front of the participant in the talk: one cannot really converse without making sure that one understands his or her interlocutor. But the progress of science could not be achieved as quickly if the

Socratic requirement were always met. In the teaching of the huge body of basic preliminary information that must be known before one can move forward in science, what progress would be made if everything—especially origins—had always to be made evident? The paradigm itself, along with its method, must be learned and used and not continually questioned if progress is to be made. But is not such learning indoctrination?

No good teacher would claim merely to indoctrinate students into the content of the various disciplines. Every good teacher thinks he or she teaches students to be critical reasoners. But the question must be raised about the relationship between content and critical thinking. Baldly put, can overemphasis upon content destroy the possibility of radical critical reasoning because the very act of passing on content presupposes uncritically the very system of concepts within which such content takes on meaning?

One might suggest that there is a crucial relationship between content and critique such that the latter cannot exist without the former. For criticism is parasitic upon the content it criticizes, and cannot, in any case, be totally separated from the mental contents already present in the questioner (i.e., his or her history). But if the latter is the case, there is a need for a judicious answer to the question about just how much and what kind of content is necessary to provide a serious foundation for critical thinking without undermining it. This is especially so in an age when the current disciplines have accumulated so much content that a lack of knowledge of that content constitutes incompetency and much time and effort must be spent in the mere transmission of information.

Content and Critical Reasoning

If one accepts the idea of the necessarily historical nature of the understanding, then the question about critical reasoning does not reduce to the simple opposition between skills and content and the question of which is prior. The skills/content dichotomy is an oversimplification of the problem of understanding and reasoning. For we do not acquire one first, and then the other, but both simultaneously, in ever greater degrees of complexity. The issue is rather how experience, understanding, and critical reasoning are made possible, given the historical nature of our understanding and the complex development of thinking in the individual. Thus the question of critical reasoning really turns on the relationship between the content of our cultural history and the critique of that content. Critical reasoning is achieved in the interplay between the continually acquired content of our cultural history, and the continual serious attempt to reach standpoints from which to focus upon and criticize our historically acquired prejudices. That serious, indispensable attempt is the careful study of foundational historical texts.

Thus there is no contradiction between the historical nature of human understanding and the ideal of critical reasoning as freedom from historical prejudices. Rather, making explicit the tension between these two poles points in the direction of how to overcome it. It is overcome by the study of our intellectual history in foundational texts. This study makes thematic our historical prejudices and thereby frees us in some measure from them. But we are always freed only "in some measure" since we can never, due precisely to our historical nature, achieve a view of the Whole *sub specie aeternitatis*. Philosophy is irremediably anticipatory.[79] This is perhaps the meaning of Socrates' refusal to give up his customary questioning even in the afterlife.

Notes

1. Fragment 169, in *The Odes of Pindar Including the Principal Fragments*, ed. and trans., John Sandys, *The Loeb Classical Library* (Cambridge: Harvard University Press, 1937), pp. 604–5.

2. *Republic* 429d–430c, trans., Allan Bloom (New York: Basic Books, 1968). For the Greek, see the Oxford critical text of John Burnet (Oxford: Clarendon, 1902), which Bloom follows with minor changes.

3. Cicero, *De re publica* 1.52: "[*Plato*] *requisivit civitatem optandam magis quam sperandam, quam minimam potuit, non quae posset esse, sed in qua ratio rerum civilium perspici posset, effecit"* ("Plato sought for the city that should be chosen rather than one that should be hoped for; [he created one] as minimal as possible: not one that could be, but one in which the nature of civil things could be perceived." For the text, see Cicero, *De re publica; De legibus,* ed. and trans., Clinton Walker Keyes, *The Loeb Classical Library* (New York: G. P. Putnam's Sons, 1928), pp. 160–63. The translation is mine.

4. *Republic* 401d–402a. cf. 522a.

5. "The right of the subject's particularity, his right to be satisfied, or in other words the right of subjective freedom, is the pivot and centre of the difference between antiquity and modern times," Hegel, *Philosophy of Right,* §124, translated with notes by T.M. Knox (Oxford: Oxford University Press, 1952); G. W. F. Hegel, *Grundlienien der Philosophie des Rechts* (Stuttgart-Bad Cannstatt: F. Frommann, 1964), p. 182. Cf. §§ 185, 206, 260. Cf. the second to last sentence of Leo Strauss's *Natural Right and History* (Chicago: University of Chicago, 1950, 1953), which reads: "The quarrel between the ancients and the moderns concerns eventually, and perhaps even from the beginning, the status of 'individuality'," and Richard H. Kennington, "Strauss's *Natural Right and History,*" *Review of Metaphysics* 35 (1981): 60.

6. Cf. Plato, *Republic,* 479a, 474d–e, 527a–b, and in general 502c–541b; Aristotle, *Metaphysics,* 982a1–983a10; 993b19–30; *Posterior Analytics* 71b8–72a8; 73a21–73b1; 73b25–32; 75b21–27. For a nice passage on the difference between knowledge and opinion, see *Posterior Analytics* 88b30–89b9. See Edmund Husserl, "Philosophy and the Crisis of European Humanity," appendix 1 in David Carr's translation of Husserl's *The Crisis of European Sciences and Transcendental Phenomenology* (Evanston: Northwestern University, 1970): "Scientific acquisitions . . . are imperishable; repeated production creates not something similar, at best equally useful; it produces in any number of acts of production by one person or any number of persons something identically the same, identical in sense and validity . . . . In a word, what is acquired through scientific activity is not something real but something ideal" (pp. 277–78). "In science the ideality of the individual products of work, the truths, does not merely denote repeatability . . . . It wants to be uncondi-

tioned truth. This involves an infinity which gives to each factual confirmation and truth the character of being merely relative....
Correlatively, this infinity lies also in what 'actually is' in the scientific
sense, as well as, again in 'universal' validity, validity for 'everyone' "
(p. 278). This lecture by Husserl appears in the "Abhandlungen,"
pp. 314–48, of Walter Biemel's edition of *Die Krisis der Europäischen
Wissenschaften und die Transzendentale Phänomenologie*, vol. 6 of
Husserliana (The Hague: M. Nijhoff, 1954). I owe much to Thomas
Prufer for my understanding of these and many other essentials in this
chapter.

7. "What is most essential to the theoretical attitude of philosophical man is the peculiar universality of his critical stance, his resolve not
to accept unquestioningly any pregiven opinion or tradition so that he
can inquire, in respect to the whole traditionally pregiven universe, after
what is true in itself, an ideality," Husserl, "Philosophy and the Crisis of
European Humanity," in Carr, tr., *Crisis of European Sciences* p. 286
(*Husserliana*, vol. 6, p. 333). On the idea of philosophy as the spiritual
telos and entelechy of European humanity, see the same essay, p. 275
(*Husserliana*, vol. 6, pp. 320–21) and what follows, as well as in the *Crisis* itself, §6. Martin Heidegger says that "The Greeks struggled precisely
to conceive and to enact this contemplative questioning as one, indeed
as the highest mode of *energeia*, of man's 'being-at-work'." This quote
appears in "The Self-Assertion of the German University: Address, Delivered on the Solemn Assumption of the Rectorate of the University of
Freiburg," and "The Rectorat 1933/34: Facts and Thoughts," translated
by Karsten Harries, *The Review of Metaphysics* 38 (1985): 472–73. The
original text appears in Martin Heidegger, *Die Selbstbehauptung der
Deutschen Universität: Rede, gehalten bei der feierlichen Übernahme
des Rektorats der Universität Freiburg i. Br. am 27.5.1933*, and *Das Rek-
torat 1933/34: Tatsachen und Gedanken* (Frankfurt A.M.: V. Kloster-
mann, 1983), p. 12.

8. Gadamer acknowledges his debt to Husserl, and especially to
Heidegger, in this. See Hans-Georg Gadamer, *Truth and Method* (New
York: Crossroad, 1986; first published, Sheed and Ward, 1976), pp. 229–
34; original German: *Wahrheit und Methode*, 4th ed. (Tübingen: J. C. B.
Mohr [Paul Siebeck], 1975), 244–50, especially the last sentence of
the section.

9. "A person trying to understand a text is prepared for it to tell him something. That is why a hermeneutically trained mind must be, from the start, sensitive to the text's quality of newness. But this kind of sensitivity involves neither 'neutrality' in the matter of the object nor the extinction of one's self, but the conscious assimilation of one's own fore-meanings and prejudices. The important thing is to be aware of one's own bias, so that the text may present itself in all its newness and thus be able to assert its own truth against one's own fore-meanings," Gadamer, *Truth and Method*, p. 238; *Wahrheit und Methode*, pp. 252–53. In general, see the whole section entitled: "(B) Prejudices as Conditions of Understanding," pp. 245–74; *Wahrheit und Methode*, pp. 261–90.

10. *Crisis*, §28, second to last paragraph (in Carr, tr., pp. 110–11; *Husserliana*, vol. 6, pp. 112–13).

11. See, for example, the introductory sections (§§28–33) to part IIIA of the *Crisis*. See §44 of the *Crisis*, in which Husserl briefly presents the formal object of his study, viz., the lifeworld, the study of which begins in §45. Husserl says that the study of the lifeworld is the study of "the disparaged *doxa*" (in Carr, tr., p. 155; *Husserliana*, vol. 6, p. 158). In his "Philosophy and the Crisis of European humanity," Husserl describes "world" (*Umwelt*) as a subjective structure: " 'Surrounding world' is a concept that has its place exclusively in the spiritual sphere. That we live in our particular surrounding world, which is the locus of all our cares and endeavors—this refers to a fact that occurs purely within the spiritual realm. Our surrounding world is a spiritual structure in us and in our historical life," (in Carr, tr., p. 272; *Husserliana*, vol. 6, p. 317). See, e.g., *Crisis*, §§45–50, in which Husserl gives a kind of preliminary view of the kinds of things to be analyzed in studying the lifeworld.

12. On the primordial character of the lifeworld, as constituting even the foundation for the meanings of science, see *Crisis*, §9h, especially par. 3 (in Carr, tr., pp. 48–53; *Husserliana*, vol. 6, pp. 48–54); §28, the last three paragraphs (in Carr, tr., pp. 110–11; *Husserliana*, vol. 6, pp. 112–13); §34b–f (in Carr, tr., pp. 125–29; *Husserliana*, vol. 6, pp. 128–32).

13. Recent phenomenological and hermeneutical studies have made this issue of the historical character of understanding clear. But the recognition that understanding is parasitic upon the opinions one holds from one's own historical tradition or culture is seen even in Plato, who starts from the opinions of his interlocutors in attempting to beget un-

derstanding in them. This is seen also in Aristotle and the Greek commentators when they explain even the title of the *Metaphysics* as that part of philosophy to be learned after the study of the physical treatises in accordance with the fundamental Aristotelian distinction between what is first to us and what is first in itself. On the order of learning in the Aristotelian tradition, see my "Aristotelian 'Order' and 'Form' According to Hobbes," *Rivista di storia della filosofia* 43 (1988): 10–22.

14. See Gadamer, *Truth and Method*, pp. 245–341; *Wahrheit und Methode*, pp. 261–360.

15. See Husserl's nice formulation of this in "Philosophy and the Crisis of European Humanity" (in Carr, tr., *Crisis of European Sciences* p. 285; *Husserliana*, vol. 6, p. 331–32).

16. "The distinction between nature and convention, between *physis* and *nomos*, is therefore coeval with the discovery of nature and hence with philosophy," Leo Strauss, *Natural Right and History*, p. 90.

17. On this, again, see Strauss's nice formulations in *Natural Right and History*, pp. 81–95.

18. See Aristotle, *Metaphysics* E (6).1 (1025b1–1026a33). Cf. also A (1).2 (982b11–21); Lambda (12).9 (1075a1–3); α (2).1 (993b19–30); K (11).7 (1064a10–b14).

19. Cf. Aristotle, *Metaphysics* α (2).3 (994b30–995a20); *Nicomachean Ethics* 1.3 (1094b11–27); 2.2 (1103b26–1104a11); *Physics* 2.8 (199b15–27); 2.9 (199b35–200b10).

20. Thomas Aquinas, *On Interpretation*, trans., Jean T. Oesterle (Milwaukee: Marquette University, 1962), book I, lesson 1, no. 5; for the Latin, see S. Thomae Aquinatis, *In Aristotelis libros Peri Hermeneias et Posteriorum Analyticorum Expositio*, ed., Raymund M. Spiazzi (Turin: Marietti, 1955).

21. Cf. Heidegger, *"Selbsbehauptung"* ("Self-Assertion"), German, p. 13, English, p. 474: "What was in the beginning the awed perseverance of the Greeks in the face of what is, transforms itself then into the completely unguarded exposure to the . . . questionable. Questioning is then no longer a preliminary step, to give way to the answer and thus to knowledge, but questioning becomes itself the highest form of knowing. . . . Questioning then forces our vision into the most simple focus on the inescapable."

22. See Descartes, *Discourse on the Method*, part 6, par. 6, and part 1, par. 13, and Hobbes's scathing critique of Scholasticism and Aristotle in ch. 46 of *Leviathan*, where, among many other things, he says: "And since the Authority of Aristotle is onely current there [in the universities], that study is not properly Philosophy, (the nature whereof dependeth not on Authors,) but Aristotelity" (par. 13). In the following, for Descartes' *Discourse*, see the Donald A. Cress translation (Indianapolis: Hackett, 1980), and for Hobbes, the C. B. Macpherson edition (Baltimore: Penguin, 1968). In both, texts will be referred to by major section and paragraph number. For Descartes, paragraphing in Cress is the same as that in Adam-Tannery, eds., *Oevres Complètes* (Paris: Vrin, 1965).

23. On the idea of the predominance of Aristotle in the universities, Hobbes said of his own time that Aristotle's "opinions are at this day, and in these parts of greater authority than any human writing," *The Elements of Law* 1.17.1, ed., Ferdinand Tönnies, 2nd ed., 1928 (London: F. Cass, 1969), p. 88. Joseph Glanville noted that the Aristotelian philosophy had predominated even to his own time, until the New Science began to replace it (*The Vanity of Dogmatizing*, 1st ed., London: E. Cotes, 1661, p. 146). See also Descartes' careful comparison between the edifice of the Scholastic sciences and houses torn down by their owners to be rebuilt. He prudently suggests that it is reasonable to raze the latter but not the former. On the uncertain foundations of Scholastic doctrine, see previous note and reference to Hobbes and Descartes. On the criticism of Scholastic method, see Hobbes, *Leviathan*, ch. 46, par. 11, and Descartes, *Discourse on the Method*, part 2, par. 5, and part 6, par. 5. On the idea of a unified method imitative of mathematics, see Hobbes, *De corpore*, ch. 6, and Descartes' entire *Discourse*, part 2, as well as his *Regulae ad directionem ingenii*. On the idea of method to produce practical results in all the sciences, compare Descartes' statements in the last paragraph of *Discourse*, part 2, with the first two paragraphs of part 6. Finally, on the idea of modern system, see my "The Emergence of the Early Modern Concept of System," *Philosophy Research Archives* 11 (1985), microfiche supplement, pp. 1–83.

24. One need merely compare Descartes' first rule for method in *Discourse*, part 2, with the first four of the *Regulae*.

25. Although not a quotation, I owe this instructive formulation to a conversation with Richard H. Kennington. Note Hobbes's wonderful

comments in the Epistle Dedicatory to his *De corpore*: "Galileus in our time . . . was the first that opened to us the gate of natural philosophy universal . . . . Lastly, the science of *man's body*, the most profitable part of natural science . . . was first discovered with admirable sagacity by our countryman Doctor Harvey . . . . Natural Philosophy is therefore but young; but Civil Philosophy yet much younger, as being no older . . . than my own book *De cive*" (*The English Works of Thomas Hobbes*, ed., William Molesworth, vol. 1, London: J. Bohn, 1839; reprint Aalen: Scientia, 1966, pp. viii–ix).

26. Compare with Aristotle's claims about the limits of ethics and politics (*Nicomachean Ethics* 1.3 [1094b11–27]; 2.2 [1104a1–11]), Hobbes's extravagant claims to have demonstrated all moral and political doctrines (with the exception of his preference for monarchy as the most commodious form of government) and to have solved the problem of internal civil disorder (*De cive*, The Preface to the Reader, ed., Howard Warrender, *De Cive: The English Version*, Oxford: Clarendon, 1983, Warrender par. 22; *Leviathan*, ch. 30, par. 5; ch. 31, par. 41).

27. Hobbes, *Leviathan*, ch. 6, par. 6–7; ch. 11, par. 1–2; ch. 46, par. 32.

28. "Positivism, in a manner of speaking, decapitates philosophy," Husserl, *Crisis*, §3, par. 6 (in Carr, tr., p. 9; *Husserliana*, vol. 6, p. 7). Thus Hobbes could hold that while the claim to know the *summum bonum* was spurious and indeed dangerous, because liable to be used for the profit of the few to the detriment of the state (*Leviathan* 46.18), the claim to know that all men seek to preserve themselves amidst the commodities of a comfortable life was not only undeniable from ordinary experience (*Leviathan* ch. 13, passim, and especially par. 10) but derivative from the most certain principles of modern natural science. By the premises of the New Science, man operates according to the same mechanical laws as does nature, and can be known with the same precision as can nature. That all men would, in the state of nature, seek to preserve themselves even at the expense of others, is simply a necessary consequence of the mechanism of man's body that impels him to seek his own preservation and comfort. The science of politics, then, becomes merely the science of how to create a state mechanism to channel the individual passions in such a way as to profit all by bringing about security and the conditions of a comfortable life. On the problem of Hobbes's systematic

connection of ethics and politics to natural science, see my "Sacksteder and Talaska on System in Hobbes," *Journal of the History of Philosophy* 26 (1988): 648–53.

29. A distinction Strauss "never tired of stressing," says Thomas L. Pangle in his introduction to *The Rebirth of Classical Political Rationalism* (Chicago: University of Chicago Press, 1989), p. xxvi. Strauss himself says, in discussing what is right by nature in Plato and Aristotle: "There is a universally valid hierarchy of ends, but there are no universally valid rules of action . . . . When deciding what ought to be done, i.e., what ought to be done by this individual (or this individual group) here and now, one has to consider not only which of the various competing objectives is higher in rank but also which is most urgent in the circumstances. What is most urgent is legitimately preferred to what is less urgent, and the most urgent is in many cases lower in rank than the less urgent" (*Natural Right and History*, p. 162). The difference between the ancients and the moderns can be seen most clearly in Strauss's next sentence: "But one cannot make a universal rule that urgency is a higher consideration than rank." For the moderns, urgency is always a higher consideration, for in fact, no ranking of ends can be known, since the only common end is the satisfaction of the passions, the first of which, the passion for self-preservation, is the only true common end, the others differing according to individual. Compare references to Hobbes in note 27 with the absolutely clear statement by Hobbes that the common end is preservation and contentment (*Leviathan* 17.1). The former passages, together with *Leviathan* 6.5–7, show that happiness is contentment, but that it differs in different individuals and in the same individual at different times. The state is intended, then, only to provide the most urgent conditions necessary for individuals to have security enough to pursue the satisfaction of their private passions, the first condition being life itself.

30. On how science becomes art or technology, see Husserl, *Crisis*, §56 (in Carr, tr., pp. 194–95; *Husserliana*, vol. 6, pp. 197–98). See Heidegger's characterization of science which has become technique as "conscientious adherence to or eager tinkering with established procedures," *Selbsbehauptung* ("Self-Assertion"), German, p. 17, English, p. 478.

31. Husserl, "Origin of Geometry," in Carr, tr. *Crisis of European Sciences*, pp. 365–69; *Husserliana*, vol. 6, pp. 375–78.

32. See above, n. 12.

33. Cf. Francis Bacon, *The New Organon*, book I, aphorism 129, trans., James Spedding et al., ed., Fulton H. Anderson (New York: Macmillan, 1985), pp. 117–19; James Spedding et al., eds., *The Works of Francis Bacon*, vol. 1 (Cambridge: Riverside Press, 1863); Descartes, *Discourse*, especially part 6, but also his optimism about the universal application and usefulness of method in part 2, and in the opening sections of the *Regulae*; Hobbes, *Leviathan*, ch. 46, par. 1. On the seeking of state funding for scientific research, see Descartes, *Discourse*, part 6, par. 7, second to last sentence, and the commentary on this line by Étienne Gilson in his famous edition of the *Discours de la Méthode* (Paris: Vrin, 1976), p. 466.

34. See the famous fallacy in the opening lines of Descartes' *Discourse*, and their almost verbatim repetition in Hobbes's *Leviathan*, ch. 13, par. 2. See also Kant's little essay, "What Is Enlightenment," in Lewis White Beck, ed., *Kant: Selections* (New York: Macmillan, 1988), pp. 462–67; *Kant's Werke*, in the edition of the Preussischen Akademie der Wissenschaften, vol. 8 (Berlin: W. de Gruyter, 1923), pp. 35–42.

35. Machiavelli, like Descartes, has elicited a variety of interpretations due to the complexity of his thought and the manner of his presentation. But few would deny that Machiavelli viewed man as a creature regulated by selfish passions. See *The Prince*, (trans., Harvey Mansfield, Chicago: University of Chicago Press, 1985, ch. 3, par. 12, pp. 14–15), where Machiavelli says that man has a natural desire to acquire, and that the only blame comes from not being successful; ch. 15, par. 1, p. 61, where he states that to act virtuously among so many who are not good will only bring about one's ruin; ch. 18, par. 3, p. 69, where he says that "if all men were good, this teaching [that one need not keep faith with them] would not be good; but because they are wicked and do not observe faith with you, you also do not have to observe it with them"; and ch. 18, par. 6, p. 71, where he says that "in the world there is no one but the vulgar." For the Italian see Niccolò Machiavelli, *Il Principe e le opere politiche* (Milan: Garzanti, 1976). These premises confirm his claim in chapter 15 to establish a new kind of realistic political philosophy based upon the premise that men do not act virtuously and upon the idea that the most urgent goal, one's preservation, is the only goal of politics. Machiavelli is founder of modern political philosophy because he is the first to reject the classical idea of the *summum bonum* and the

ordered hierarchy of ends. For a controversial but brilliant treatment of the complexity of interpreting Machiavelli, see Leo Strauss, *Thoughts on Machiavelli* (Chicago: University of Chicago, 1958).

36. "But as soon as I had acquired some general notions in the area of physics, and . . . had noticed just how far they can lead . . . I believed I could not keep them hidden away without greatly sinning against the law that obliges us to procure as best we can the common good of all men. For these general notions show me that it is possible to arrive at knowledge that is very useful in life and that in place of the speculative philosophy taught in the Schools, one can find a practical one . . . and thus make ourselves, as it were, masters and possessors of nature. This is desirable not only for the invention of an infinity of devices that would enable us to enjoy without pain the fruits of the earth . . . but also principally for the maintenance of health, which unquestionably is the first good and the foundation of all the other goods in this life," *Discourse*, part 6, par. 2.

37. For an overall picture of the complexity of interpreting Descartes, see Richard H. Kennington, "Rene Descartes," in Leo Strauss and Joseph Cropsey, eds., *History of Political Philosophy*, 2d ed. (Chicago: University of Chicago Press, 1973), pp. 395–412.

38. "Physical objectivism of the modern sort, with its physicalistic tendency and its psychophysical dualism, does not die out; that is, many feel quite comfortable here in their 'dogmatic slumbers'. . . . As for the momentum of objectivistic philosophy, in a certain way it sustained itself as the momentum in the development of the positive sciences," Husserl, *Crisis*, §56 (in Carr, tr., pp. 193–94; *Husserliana*, vol. 6, p. 196–97). Of course, the momentum of objectivism as modern natural science is connected with its success: "The result of the consistent development of the exact sciences in the modern period was a true revolution in the technical control of nature" ("Philosophy and the Crisis of European Humanity," in Carr, tr., *Crisis of European Sciences*, Husserliana, vol. 6, pp. 315–16).

39. Compare Husserl's ideas on this subject with those of Thomas S. Kuhn on scientific paradigms in *The Structure of Scientific Revolutions* (Chicago: University of Chicago Press, 1962). For an excellent short treatment of the idea of the modern reformation of the conceptual tools to explain nature, see Alexandre Koyré, "Galileo and Plato," *Journal of the History of Ideas* 4 (1943): 400–428.

40. For expressions of Vico's *factum/verum* theory, see *On the Ancient Wisdom of the Italians* 1.1, 1.4, the first *New Science*, §40, and the third *New Science*, §331. These references can be found in Vico, *Selected Writings*, ed. and trans., Leon Pompa (Cambridge: Cambridge University Press, 1982). See Pompa's introduction, pp. 5–10. Vico has been compared to Hobbes on this idea of knowing as knowing what we ourselves make. See Arthur Child, "Making and Knowing in Hobbes, Vico, and Dewey," *University of California Publications in Philosophy* 16 (1953): 271–310. See Hobbes, *De homine* 10.5, (in Moleworth, ed., *Latin Works*, vol. 2 (London: J. Bohn, 1839; reprint Aalen: Scientia, 1966), pp. 93–94. It was through Thomas Prufer that I first gained an appreciation of the importance of these contrasting formulations.

41. Thomas Aquinas, *Summa theologiae*, Prima Pars, q. 16, art. 1. See S. Thomae de Aquino, *Summa theologiae*, vol. 1 (Ottowa: Impensis Studii Generalis O.Pr., 1941).

42. Although Husserl's "Origin of Geometry" speaks in terms of the broader sense in which, e.g., modern geometry depends ultimately upon achievements made by earlier generations of geometricians, the same principle can be seen in the way in which, within a particular geometry, much later propositions depend upon and use earlier ones, without each time bringing the earlier ones to direct evidence by recalling their proofs.

43. In "Philosophy and the Crisis of Europena Humanity," Husserl locates the crisis in the *"apparent failure of rationalism* [emphasis original]," i.e., in the failure of rationalism understood as objectivism, of which modern natural science is the fruit (in Carr, tr., *Crisis of European Sciences*, p. 299; *Husserliana*, vol. 6, p. 347). The failure of this rationalism to solve human problems (*Crisis* §2, pp. 5–7; *Husserliana*, pp. 3–5), as opposed to controlling physical nature, leads to an anti-intellectualism that concludes that science cannot make men wise (in Carr, tr., pp. 289–90; *Husserliana*, vol. 6, pp. 336–37), i.e., that the moral realm, the specifically human, cannot be treated by reason. This conclusion stems from equating scientific reason with positivism, and failing to see the inherent problems with positivism because of lack of examination of its origins, which would manifest the now-hidden errors. "There are only two escapes from the crisis of European existence: the downfall of Europe in its estrangement from its own rational sense of life, its fall into hostility toward the spirit and into barbarity; or the rebirth of Europe from the spirit of philosophy through a heroism of

reason that overcomes naturalism once and for all" (in Carr, tr., p. 299; *Husserliana*, vol. 6, pp. 347–48). For a similar sentiment, see Heidegger, *Selbstbehauptung* ("Self-Assertion") German, p. 19, English, pp. 479–80.

44. See "Philosophy and the Crisis of European Humanity," paragraphs 1–5, for the view of modern natural science, and paragraph 6 for Husserl's criticism of the latter as the source of the crisis, since it rests on "portentous prejudices" (in Carr, tr., *Crisis of European Sciences*, pp. 271–72; *Husserliana*, vol. 6, pp. 314–17). Also, see the whole first part of the *Crisis* for Husserl's criticism of the reductionism of modern philosophy, with its refusal to treat the "metaphysical" themes that Classical philosophy thought one of the proper subject matters of philosophy. See especially §3.

45. *Crisis* §57, par. 1 (in Carr, tr., *Crisis of European Sciences*, p. 198–201; *Husserliana*, vol. 6, pp. 201–4).

46. According to Gadamer, however, Husserl did not complete the task of laying bare the meaning of history. This was only brought to fulfillment by Heidegger, who isolated and explained the historical nature of human being, and thus of the understanding. See *Truth and Method*, p. 214 (*Wahrheit und Methode*, p. 229): "The first man to bring to general awareness the radical challenge to historical being and knowledge presented by the inadequacy of the concept of substance was Heidegger."

47. See Burnet's footnote to the title of the dialogue and Bloom's second footnote to book 1.

48. This is the import of Socrates' statement at *Republic* 442d–e, where he suggests testing his definition of justice in the light of vulgar standards. The examples given (primarily stealing and lying) show that by vulgar justice, Socrates intends justice as understood by Cephalus and Polemarchus, viz., justice as fairness. Socrates' own definition of justice (see 335c–d, 433a, 434a, 443d–e, 444d–e, 445c) is a broader one meaning natural right, which includes vulgar justice as a part.

49. For text and translation, see Aristotle, *The Nicomachean Ethics*, ed. and trans., H. Rackham, *The Loeb Classical Library* (Cambridge: Harvard University Press, 1926).

50. S. Thomae Aquinatis, in *decem libros Ethicorum Aristotelis Expositio* 5, lect. 3, n. 992; lect. 12, nn. 1016, 1019, 1023. This can be found in the edition of A. M. Pirotta (Turin: Marietti, 1934).

51. *Summa theologiae*, 2-2, q. 57, art. 1, reply to 2d obj. This is in volume 3 of the Latin edition.

52. Ibid.

53. *Summa theologiae*, 1-2, q. 91, art. 2. See vol. 3. Latin edition.

54. *Republic*, 444d.

55. Ibid., 433a.

56. Ibid., 434a.

57. Ibid., 433a.

58. *Nicomachean Ethics*, 5.7.

59. *Summa Theologiae*, 2-2, q. 57, art. 3: "Ius sive iustum naturale est quod ex sui natura est adaequatum vel commensuratum alteri."

60. *Summa theologiae*, q. 57, art. 1; q. 58, art. 1.

61. *De jure belli ac pacis*, 1.1.10: "*Ius naturale est dictatum rectae rationis indicans, actui alicui, ex ejus convenientia aut disconvenientia cum ipsa natura rationali, inesse moralem turpitudinem aut necessitatem moralem, ac consequenter ab auctore naturae Deo talem actum aut vetari aut praecipi.*" The original and the translation can be found as follows: Hugonis Grotii, *De jure belli ac pacis libri tres*, vol. 1: *Reproduction of the Edition of 1646* (Washington, DC: Carnegie Institution, 1913); Hugo Grotius, *De jure belli ac pacis libri tres: The Translation*, vol. 2, trans., Francis W. Kelsey (Oxford: Clarendon, 1925).

62. *Nicomachean Ethics* 1.7 (1097b7–11).

63. See *Nicomachean Ethics* 1.12 (passim); 2.1 (1103a14–b7); *Republic* 2–4 (376c–427c). Compare especially the almost identical statements by Plato and Aristotle about rearing: *Republic* 449d and *Nicomachean Ethics* 2.1 (1103b21–25).

64. *Crito* 50a–53a.

65. *Republic* 420b–421c; 433a–c; 435e–436b.

66. See *An Enquiry Concerning the Principles of Morals*, sect. 3, part 1, par. 15, n. 1. This can be found in *Enquiries Concerning Human Understanding and the Principles of Morals*, ed., P. H. Nidditch, 3d ed. (Oxford: Clarendon, 1975), p. 189.

67. See *Leviathan*, ch. 14.

68. See the conclusion to this argument as stated in *Leviathan* in ch. 14, par. 4. The argument itself is developed in the preceding chapters.

69. *Leviathan*, ch. 15, last paragraph.

70. *Leviathan*, ch. 17, paragraphs 1–2.

71. See my article, "Aristotelian 'Order' and 'Form' According to Hobbes," pp. 5–43.

72. Cf. Heidegger, *Selbstbehauptung*, ("Self-Assertion"), German pp. 12–13, English, p. 473.

73. Herbert Spiegelberg calls Husserl's 1911 "programmatic essay" on "Philosophy as Rigorous Science" a "devastating attack on historicism," *The Phenomenological Movement: A Historical Introduction*, 3rd revised and enlarged edition (The Hague: Martinus Nijhoff Publishers, 1984) p. 110. By 1936 when he wrote "The Origin of Geometry," even with its major theme of the need for historical studies, Husserl was still able to say quite emphatically in the third to last paragraph "that historicism . . . is mistaken in principle" (in Carr, tr., *Crisis of European Sciences*, p. 378, *Husserliana* vol. 6, pp. 385–86).

74. This is, of course, clear from the scathing criticisms by early moderns of Scholasticism in the universities. See, e.g., Descartes, *Discourse*, all of part 1, part 2, paragraphs 1–3 on reformation; part 6, paragraphs 6 and 11; Hobbes, *Leviathan*, ch. 46, passim; ch. 3, par. 12; ch. 4, par. 1; and his description of the Aristotelianism he learned at Oxford in his verse autobiography, *T. Hobbes Malmesburiensis vita*, in William Molesworth, ed., *Thomae Hobbes Malmesburiensis Opera philosophica quae latine scripsit omnia*, vol. 1 (London: J. Bohn, 1839; reprint Aalen: Scientia, 1966), pp. lxxxvi–vii. For a traditional treatment, see Richard Foster Jones, *Ancients and Moderns: A Study of the Rise of the Scientific Movement in Seventeenth-Century England* (New York: Dover, 1961), pp. 119–47. Recent historical studies of the seventeenth-century Oxford curriculum reveal that the influence of humanism there was restricted to the return from Scholastic commentaries to the study of the actual ancient texts, but that the content of the curriculum was still Aristotelian. Cambridge also remained under the influence of Aristotelianism, if less so than Oxford. See such works as W. T. Costello, *The Scholastic Curriculum at Early Seventeenth-Century Cambridge* (Cambridge: Harvard University Press, 1958); L. Jardine, "Humanism and Dialectic in Sixteenth-Century Cambridge," in R. R. Bolgar, ed., *Classical Influences on European Culture* A.D. *1500–1700* (Cambridge: Cambridge University Press, 1976); C. B. Schmitt, "Philosophy and Science in Sixteenth-

Century Universities: Some Preliminary Comments," in J. E. Murdoch and E. D. Sylla, eds., *The Cultural Context of Medieval Learning* (Dordrecht: Reidel, 1975); J. M. Fletcher, "The Faculty of Arts," ch. 4.1, in *The History of the University of Oxford*, ed. T. H. Aston, vol. 3: *The Collegiate University (Oxford: Clarendon, 1986)*.

75. This is not to limit the great teachers of humanity to early moderns, but to illustrate the point in question, viz., that those are the creative geniuses who create completely new directions of thought for the rest of us. On the distinction between the merely great philosopher and the one who "contributes a motif which gives unity to a historical sequence," see Husserl, *Crisis*, §56 (in Carr, tr., pp. 191–92; *Husserliana*, vol. 6, p. 194).

76. "A great deal of effort is involved . . . to free ourselves from the constant misconstructions which mislead us all because of the scholastic dominance of objective-scientific ways of thinking," Husserl, *Crisis*, §34 (in Carr, tr., p. 128; *Husserliana*, vol. 6, p. 132).

77. In commenting on Husserl, Spiegelberg says: "In order to understand fully Husserl's attitude toward science, it is important to take account of a development which has not struck the American consciousness as forcibly as it has the European: the so-called 'crisis of science.' The New World, especially as regards the spectators and cheerleaders of science, still displays a naive faith in science as the panacea for all the ills and problems of our time, apparently unaware of the fact that this faith is no longer shared by many of the front-line scientists, who have to grapple with the mounting perplexities and moral problems posed by their astonishing findings," *The Phenomenological Movement*, p. 73.

78. See Husserl, *Crisis* §56 (in Carr, tr., pp. 194–95; *Husserlian*, vol. 6, pp. 197–98).

79. An expression of Thomas Prufer.

||█ The Problem
of the Unity of
Source for
Critical Reasoning

13 Critical Reasoning and the Second Power of Questions: Toward First Questions and First Philosophy

EVA T. H. BRANN

Critical reasoning I take to consist in making just discriminations and in discerning rightly, particularly in the realm of the mind and the spirit. It seems to me to require (1) learning and (2) insight.

1. Learning, by which I mean good knowledge of the central texts of our whole cultural tradition and a decent acquaintance with on-going work, is necessary for stimulation and for perspective. It allows us to appropriate ideas beyond our own capacity to discover, and it saves us from reinventing primitive versions of the wheel. The following essay relies very much on the textual canon of our tradition as well as on recent work.

2. The insight of critical reasoning (as distinct from intuition or constructive thought) seems to me to show itself almost entirely in the putting of pertinent questions. The Greek word for answer, *apokrisis*, displays this point beautifully. It is visibly related to the word *critical* and means, accordingly, a separation, a

299

setting apart. To give an answer is to make a distinction. But, of course, the discerning answer is solicited and, I shall claim, shaped by the question. Consequently, as the Greek word implies, critical reasoning begins with question-asking—and, I infer, thinking about critical reasoning had best begin with thinking about questions. Accordingly, this essay attempts a synoptic inquiry into the kinds, the forms, the uses, the hierarchies, and also the contemporary fate of questions.

I. Questioning Questions

By "the second power of questions" I mean that realm of inquiry which arises when questions are raised about questions—when the questioning function is applied to itself and raised, as it were, to the second degree. This reflective activity seems to proceed on three levels: the scattered pursuit of particular workaday problems concerning questions; the pointed effort to determine the essential nature of questions in general; and the questionable venture of determining a question of questions, a First Question.

The center of the inquiry would seem to lie in the middle level where the question "What is a question?" is raised. It is, therefore, no wonder that the most pertinent objections to taking questions to the second power are also raised on that level. The first level, that of research with definite results, can, of course, always be faulted for not reaching to the depth of a unifying principle. The third level is, on the other hand, so deeply enmeshed in philosophical perplexities that it is readily ignored. Hence it is in the middle level of inquiry that the examination of questions as such is subject to explicit attack.

One such line of attack is at once silly and theoretically unanswerable. The questioning of questions, it has been objected, invites an indefinite recursion. In my terms, one could raise the questioning function to a third, fourth, and fifth degree. Here is a blanket obstruction which would stop *any* reflective enterprise at the start. It has only a pragmatic answer: Sufficient unto the day are the projects thereof—let us worry about raising reflections about questions one power at a time. We do, of course, submit questions to the third degree, questioning the questioning of questions—as I am doing right here—but everyone senses that in this enterprise, exponential progress is madness, though at some time, it might be worth inquiring why that is.

There is, however, another, less free-swinging objection which is much more trenchant, the one mounted by Wittgenstein[1]: He lists a number of "language-games," such as commanding, describing, stating, and asking. He then warns us that if we do not keep this multiplicity of activities in view, we will perhaps be inclined to ask a question like "What is a question?" And then we will be tempted to answer by papering over the difference in the various games; we will attempt, for example, to transform questions into statements. Thus "What is a question?" becomes "I want to know what a question is." Or we might try to satisfy ourselves by the dodge of ascribing to each game its peculiar frame of mind, for instance to questions, uncertainty. Wittgenstein is prescient here: These *are* among the attempted answers recently given to the question "What is a question?" Yet, however serious his objections may be, the reply must again be pragmatic. Perhaps we do not want to be relieved of our confusions as Wittgenstein offers to relieve us. Perhaps a risky plunge gives us more than does a pure abstemiousness.

Besides, one can indeed learn quite a lot about what a question is before going in boldly to define its essence. It is possible to give illuminating classifications of questions in anticipation of their definition because questions are so readily recognized empirically (see section III).[2] There happen to be at least four question indicators, which are used in all sorts of combinations: (1) the syntactic indicator of a question is the inverted word order; the statement "You asked a question" yields "Did you ask a question?" (2) inflection, the raising of the pitch of speech at the end of the utterance, audibly indicates a question; (3) the typographic sign, such as "?" in English texts, "¿ . . . ?" in Spanish texts, and ";" in Greek texts, is a visible question mark; (4) and finally, there is a gestural indicator, the questioning look—eyebrows raised, head cocked. Moreover, we normally have no trouble differentiating among different sorts of questioning activities and confidently use numerous different question terms, such as Anglo-Norman *question, quest, query, inquest, inquiry, request, requisition,* and Latinate *interrogation, interrogatory, rogation,* and good old English *asking.* Consequently we can classify questions quite well without exactly knowing their nature.

What, finally, moves the quest concerning questions? It is, of course, the same sort of impulse that persistently makes us think about thinking even in the face of the fact that it is a bootstrapping operation which ought to be, as such, impossible—we do it nevertheless. However, those who think about questions in particular also have particular agendas.

First off, some people have a bread-and-butter reason for interesting themselves in questions: They can tell a fruitful subject full of promising applications when they see it, and they do much of the useful spade work (see section VI). At the other end of the spectrum of productivity are the friends of flux and flexibility, the lovers of the quest over the quarry, who dwell on questions to keep themselves off balance and in their element of suspended belief.

There are yet others who are enticed by the priority of questions over statements, by what one might call their dialectical or their conversational firstness: In some straightforward way questions precede answers, and, in preceding them, select them, somewhat as dredges are meant to rake up oysters, pots to trap crabs, and hooks to catch fish.

But the greatest incitement for thinking about questions, which lurks somewhere in most people who are studying the subject, is the sense that a human being in the questioning mode is somehow related to the world in a quintessentially human way. Here are deep waters to be sure, in which not everyone wants to fish.

II. Studying Questions

It is a notorious quandary of inquiry that studying a subject earnestly and reflecting on its questions seriously are fairly incompatible activities. The former consists of advancing in detailed knowledge not only of the subject but of expert opinions about it, in gaining competence. The latter means regressing to the elements, forgetting learned views and calling the very foundations of knowledge into question.

In the inquiry concerning questions this quandary must be doubly acute because questions are the arsis, the upbeat, of learning. That fact makes it so much the harder to keep the actuality of questioning in view as the weight of accumulated fact, analysis, and reflection settles down over the primary experience, the human event of being seized by a question. And it is indeed an enormous weight, the result of both a very ancient tradition and a very recent burgeoning. For two and a half millennia, the main line of reflection about questions has been philosophical, but in the last three decades literature concerning questions has developed in many special fields as well. Not only have questions been made newly thematic in philosophy, especially in phenomenology and hermeneutics (see the section entitled "Ordering Questions"), but in the mid-fifties a new logic was formulated and named: "erotetic" (from the Greek verb "to ask"). Meanwhile, in linguistics, such matters as the transformation of declaratives into interrogatives were studied,[3] while in pragmatics, which is a fairly new field dealing with the intention and competence of an utterance insofar as it is meant to communicate, questions were analyzed as "performative" linguistic events. In cognitive psychology question-asking and comprehension were studied by means of quantitative experiment and procedural models.[4] But the largest—and most disparate—literature dealt with practical applications, with information-gathering, with questionnairing, with counseling techniques, and above all with educational uses, where the measurable efficacy of pedagogic question-asking has been under review (see the section entitled "Using Questions").

It might seem that the old theoretical study of questions has developed a practical side only recently. Not so: its roots too go back to antiquity. Witness the often-cited and ill-considered term *Socratic method*, as practiced, for example, by that television Torquemeda of law school, Professor Kingsfield of the "Paper Chase." Although his prosecutorial grilling is a travesty of Socratic teaching, which is precisely not a method, it does, in a debased way, hold on to one aspect of Socratic questioning: It is a pedagogical practice rather than an erotetic theory.

This subtle distinction is brought out in the one Platonic dialogue where question-asking is the explicit theme, the *Meno.* Meno himself, known from elsewhere as a scoundrel, is here shown as the exemplification of the Socratic claim that the great human vice is an unwillingness to learn. At an embarrassing point in the conversation, Meno, who is a smart man, tries to extract himself with a brilliant blanket paradox, such as will stop all questions at once:

> By what method, Socrates, will you inquire into something whose nature you don't know at all? What sort of thing among the ones you don't know will you put forward to inquire about? Or if you do indeed happen upon it, how will you know that it is the one you do not know?[5]

Meno has indeed discovered—though he has not taken in— the paradoxical essence of a question: that it is a sort of directed ignorance (see item 3c in the list on pages 316–18).

For present purposes, the point is that Socrates does not answer the question about questions—he resolves it practically. He tells the famous "myth of recollection." Its thesis is that we have it somehow in us—in the terms of the myth, by learning acquired in a previous lifetime—to ask and to answer. He does not mean, as do the moderns, that we create or construct answers, but that we can *find* them within, so that with minimal preparation we can answer yes or no to alternatives we propose to ourselves. "So," Socrates concludes, "we must not listen to the quibbling argument, for it would make us lethargic, while the other makes us active and ready for inquiry." The questioning of questions should not be allowed to clog the springs of inquiry—by this eminently practical approach Socrates recognizes something irreducibly "pragmatic" about questions, an issue which will come up again more than once (see sections IV and VII).

For Aristotle, on the other hand, the prereflection which Socrates evades is a patent necessity. "For," he says, "it is absurd to inquire after knowledge and the method of knowledge at the same time." Consequently he practically paraphrases Meno's point:

> Those who inquire without having reviewed the perplexities are like people who do not know where they need to go; moreover they do not even know whether the thing inquired after has been found or not.[6]

For Aristotle, the review of method which precedes knowledge is not, to be sure, intended to establish what a question is but rather what the questions are. What precedes inquiry is a fixing of "the perplexities," the set of philosophical quandaries to be resolved. This pre-fixing of the problems is a beginning wedge driven between the spontaneous questioning, which for Socrates is itself a moral-practical activity, and the focussed theory, distinct from practice or application, which philosophical science is to become (see section VI).

In this vein it is not surprising that Aristotle produced the first four elements of an erotetic theory, all of which are still the stand-bys of contemporary treatments. The first is the logical analysis of trick questions such as "double questions," which will be taken up later (see section V).[7] The theoretically most weighty is the basic classification of all questions into two kinds.

First in force for Aristotle is the "dialectical," that is, the argumentative question type, which requires a yes-or-no answer. The other, less direct kind is the "What is . . ." question, which requires something more than a choice between contraries. (The semantic and syntactic relations between these two questions will become an erotetic issue in section III). Aristotle indicates a preference for the dialectic question insofar as it gives the answerer a definite line of reply.[8] Such questions do, in fact, make up the bulk of Socrates' kind of dialectic, those long interrogatory passages in the Platonic dialogues where the lucky victim is forced into incriminating his own opinions. What seems to govern both Aristotle's theory and Plato's practice is an enormous respect for the indwelling power of mere judgment, of saying yes or no when confronted with a proposition. Of course, it is well known that Socrates is the premier practitioner of the "What is . . ." question as well, and I shall argue finally that this is the truest question, or rather, that it is most truly a question (see section VII). But the dialectical question is without doubt somehow more pointedly addressed to the conversational partner's judgment.

And here Aristotle's third contribution comes in: He is acutely aware of what is now called the "pragmatic" aspect of questions, or their "illocutionary force."[9] Aristotle brings out the communicative intention of the dialectical question by defining it as a "request for an answer": a question is, before anything else, a demand on the other person. Some of the pragmatic background, for example of the question "What is a question?" can, in fact, be included explicitly within it. This is done by transforming it into an indirect-question form: "I want you to tell me what a question is." But there is much more to be considered within the pragmatic frame. For example, is the asker asking candidly or hypocritically? Is the question addressed to one, all, or none? The pragmatic pole will be further taken up in sections VI and VII.

Finally, and to my mind least edifyingly, Aristotle offers practical lessons in asking captious questions and in evading them.[10]

The point in this section was to recall that the student of questions in our time may profit from and must contend with, a long and live tradition, a tradition top-heavy with enormous amounts of research. If ever learning posed a seductive threat to thinking, it does so in the questioning of questions.

III. Classifying Questions

With this caveat in mind, I cautiously take a very convenient way to sort out my thoughts: survey all the ways questions have been grouped. There may, moreover, be hope here of discovering some indices to their essence.

To distinguish a question as a question has, as was pointed out in section I, usually been the least of problems. Even in non-linguistic media, such as music, recognizable questions can be posed, like Charles Ives's "Unanswered Question." Even perfectly contentless questions, like the mere mark ? that witty graffitists like to scrawl on walls, carry significance. Even linguistic questions posed without the characteristic inversion are recognizable, as are the curious oscillations between question and statement by which modest persons mask their assertions and dogmatic persons spoil their questions. Thus the heavy-treading young heroine of Charlotte Yonge's *The Clever Woman in the Family*, suddenly noticing the decoration worn by a young officer (later her husband, I am glad to report) whom she has been lecturing on gallantry, says to him: "That is not the Victoria Cross?"

If recognition of questions is no problem, sorting out their kinds is. The most obvious classification of classifications appears to be this: One type is derived from the point of view of the answer implied, and another takes its departure from the attitude of the asker.[11] Classifications from the resultant answer are the more frequent, because, as will come out especially in the attempt to formalize questions (see section V), the firmest handle on them is by way of the bundle of replies they pick out. In the following paragraphs are set out classifications of questions made according to the answers they receive.

1. Among the most servicable is the classification by categories. Ten categories were explicitly established by Aristotle (listed

in his work by that name).[12] A recent list, composed specifically to enumerate questions, contains thirteen. The Greek root of the word *category* ordinarily means a charge or accusation. A category is, thus, a way of holding the world responsible, of making it answerable. Aristotle's categories are accordingly named from interrogative pronouns and adverbs: "the 'what is'," "the 'where'," "the 'when'," "the 'how'." If questions about the world are classified in terms of categories, questions about what underlies the world are classified by Aristotle in terms of "causes."[13] Again, the word means "responsibility," that is to say, it designates in things that which answers when we ask "according to what (form)?" "out of what (stuff)?" "for what (purpose)?" "by what (agency)?" Thus the answering categories and causes classify the main questions—though one might argue that this sorting of questions is really accomplished by a mere linguistic tabulation, that Aristotle simply surveys the available interrogative pronouns and adverbs. In any case, the causal classification of questions has been carried into our century, for example by Piaget.[14] His protocols show that children's questions develop over stages, in which conflations and confusions occur, into the same classes as are used by adults: mechanical cause, final purpose, psychological motive, and logical justification.

2. The second, widely paraphrased, basic classification is the one already mentioned, Aristotle's two types: the dialectic and the "What is it?" questions. Lonergan calls the former type questions of reflection since they require consideration of a proposal, and the latter type questions of intelligence since they require insight.[15] In line with a long dialectical tradition, he classes the more determinate dialectic question as the higher, presumably because it is a link in a systematic demonstrative chain, such as yields philosophical "science." In grammar, Jesperson terms these two kinds "nexus-questions" and "x-questions" respectively; "nexus" because dialectic questions call for the combination or disassociation of a subject with a proposed predicate ("Did he ask a question *or not?*"), "x" because "what" questions ask

about an unknown ("*What* is a question?").[16] The latter questions employ the interrogative pronouns such as who, what, when, and where, and they demand categorical answers, that is, answers determinate and within the required region: "When did he kiss you?" should not be answered by "Under the mistletoe," but by "At 2:30 P.M." In erotetic logic, too, these two types are taken to exhaust the elementary questions.[17] Even those who argue that the various *wh*-pronoun questions are syntactically transformable into dialectical "whether" questions (as is shown in the parallelism of the respective indirect question: "I ask whether . . . ," "I ask who . . . ," "what," "when," etc.) admit that they are semantically distinct.[18] It has, however, been argued that the "whether" questions do not actually require simple alternative yes-or-no answers but may have a whole continuum of responses: "Can you answer my question?" "Well, I can try." Consequently Belnap and Steel propose that questions be classified not by the number of possible responses (*i.e.*, two for "whether" questions, an indeterminate number for *wh*-pronoun questions), but by the manner of the response: The former should make explicit the number of responses to be tolerated, the latter rather furnishes a categorical matrix, a framework within which a sensible answer must be sought. For example, "When was America discovered?" finds its answer by reference to the matrix of dates: . . . 1184 B.C. . . . A.D. 1491, 1492 . . . 1776.[19]

3. Of deepest philosophical interest is a classification according to the reflexive effect the answer has on the inquiry (see section VII). Thus there are proddings that are brought to a halt by repartee, rejoinder, or reply. Dilemma questions invite resolution. Problems require solution. All the foregoing belong to a type of question which calls for the answer to do away with the question. In contrast there are mystery questions which are posed as impregnable and which eventually lapse. The distinction is caught perfectly by a fourth-grader, as reported in *Thinking, The Journal of Philosophy for Children:* "If I were to find myself on the moon, it'd be a mystery how I got there and it'd be a problem

how to get back."[20] Of course some mysteries never lapse: the so-called big questions. So there are, third, what I want to denominate the "true" questions. These are never resolved nor do they lapse, but they collect about themselves an ever-live complex of reflective results.

4. Questions by and large can be classified as requiring either a linguistic response or an active one, as does the problem above of the child in the moon. Active responses may be showings, deeds, or inciting words.[21]

5. Questions can be classified according to the temporal mode of the knowledge they are after.[22] They may root out the forgotten, elicit the presently known, or pursue the putatively or provedly unknowable. It is a present-day article of faith that the big questions mentioned above are of the latter sort. But so are certain very technical questions, such as "What line squares the circle?"

6. It may be that there are questions so different in rank-order that they belong to an entirely different class (see section VII). Thus Heidegger claims that the philosophical question is abruptly different from the scientific question.[23] For, whereas the scientific question arises in a continuous transition from ordinary life, the philosophical question steps out of this order and is "deranged," at once marvellous and mad.

The following paragraphs give the classifications from the side of asking.

1. Questions can be distinguished by addressee: the second person (that is, "you"), oneself, the wide world or a discriminated subject-province within it. The latter type, the *quaestio* of medieval dialectic, which is addressed to no person but to an issue, will be discussed in section VII.

2. Questions are very commonly classified according to the pragmatic disposition of the questioner, which means classification with respect to the asking activity. The asker may merely crave to know, may be cloaking a command, or may be preempt-

ing the answer, as in a rhetorical question. Questions may be asked idly or avidly, as in the two great kinds of gossip; anxiously as in adolescent jags of identity crisis; detachedly as in the (somewhat mythical) scientific mode; and passionately as in "why me?" questions. These intentions can, of course, be articulated in indirect questions: "I ask you truly . . . ," "Just asking . . . ," "I am troubled by. . . ." It is an interesting pragmatic fact that the truth value of the simple question is not formally subject to questioning—it is self-verifying. If I ask: "Are you stupid?" then the indirect question-statement "I am asking whether you are stupid" is ipso facto true. Nonetheless, it is humanly as false as a lie is: I am not asking. Pedagogues know all about question-lies (see item 4 in the list in section VI).

3. Husserl distinguishes two kinds of questions by a progression in pragmatic intent.[24] There are primary "plain" questions and there are secondary "justificatory" or "truth" questions. The first kind results from an immediate condition of doubt. The second kind supervenes when the answer already obtained is to be certified and full assertoric truth is to be reached.

4. Finally, questions divide around their illocutionary force, the intention which the asker has toward the answerer: Questions can be promises to listen, invitations to consider together, kindly probings, questionings of motives, invasive bullyings. The following passage from *Jane Eyre* is a prime example of the last of these. The awful Reverend Brocklehurst is catechizing candid little Jane:

"And the psalms? I hope you like them?
"No, sir."
"No? Oh, shocking!"

IV. Defining Questions

Once the spade work of distinction is done, it is time to begin looking for that answer to the question "What is a question?"

which will most adequately take account of the multiplicity of kinds of question. Again, in the face of so long a history of reflection, a review of the main definitions so far given is in order. Of course, these definitions both overlap and run aslant of each other, just as do the classifications. By a definition I naturally mean here not a circular lexical reference but an attempt, even groping and murky, to catch the essential character. The many attempts ready at hand again quite naturally fall into those which fix on the answering proposition and those which begin with the asking activity. I will say right now that the first are more useful in formalization (see section V), but the second are more stimulating to reflection. That probably accounts for the fact that there are more of the latter.

Nevertheless, there is something quite natural—linguistically natural—about answers as the starting point. For questions are so clearly inversions, perturbations of prior propositions, which are then recovered in, and posited by, the answer to the question. For example: "Are questions statements?" "Yes, questions are inverted statements." So, too, the rising inflection awaits the answering fall; what goes up must come down. The speech-melody confirms that the question was nothing but an answer held up for consideration—hereby hangs the whole erotetic tale (see section VII). So, in the following paragraphs are set out definitions of questions taking their bearings by answers.

1. The baldest such definition says that the denotation of a question is the set of its possible answers.[25] Thus the question "Is a question a proposition?" denotes the answer "Yes, it is" and "No, it isn't," and they may be fairly said to be the meaning of the question, for: "Knowing what counts as an answer is equivalent to knowing the question."[26] Though it may seem to put the cart before the horse, this definition really makes good sense. Ask yourself what is essential to an ordinary, serviceable question, what gives it "erotetic efficiency." It is having a discernible set of answers. Of course, Heideggerian "deranged" questions precisely lack such answer criteria, but as he himself says, there *is* a fairly

smooth road from ordinary questions to scientific ones, and by extension to a formal erotetic. The point will be made clearer in section V.

2. A rather dry version of the answer approach is that taken by Cohen: The question is neither a psychological provocation nor an ambiguous assertion, but is rather itself already a sort of proposition.[27] A "what" question is a propositional function such as $x = 3 + 5$, with a variable calling for replacement by a value. He intimates that the most sensible questions are those which are turned into identities by an algorithm. A "whether" question belongs to that subclass of propositional functions which have as yet undetermined truth values. That is to say, it is temporarily undetermined whether or not the predication within the proposition holds. Valid questions have one and only one answer set, that is, they have neither none nor indefinitely many answers. If they do, they are invalid (see section V).

Clearly Cohen has reduced questions to mathematical problems, to logical forms in which the solution is implicit.[28] Thus he rigorously excludes those humanly unavoidable questions for which there may be no answers or indeterminately many answer attempts.

This logicistic approach is explicitly reversed by Collingwood who says bluntly that "a logic in which the answers are attended to and the question is neglected is a false logic."[29] For questions and answers are correlatives: One cannot tell what an answer means unless one knows the question it is meant to answer. Collingwood did not accomplish the replacement of a proposition-based logic by a question-based logic which he had projected, but his flawed attempt has prompted several efforts, such as those of Gadamer and Harris, to give priority to the question in inquiry.[30] As Gadamer shows, the recovery of the problem behind an action or of the question behind a text is a much more delicate business than Collingwood admits, since the erotetic reconstructions attempted by the historian and the interpreter, which are recovered ex post facto from records and texts, may be quite different from the originating personal intentions of the actor or the writer. Nevertheless questions must be given "hermeneutic preeminence," that is to say, they must be given priority in attempts to interpret the world or texts. Obviously, such a nonformal approach will not give concise, explicit, criteria-furnishing definitions but, instead, descriptive intimations, approaches to the intrinsic character of a question. Here then, in the following paragraphs, are given the definitions from the asking side.

1. The most hard-headed understanding from this perspective is that questions are essentially commands, grammatically but not pragmatically differentiable from imperatives. In questioning, the addressee is subordinated to the questioner.[31] The interrogative form may give the command a softer, more civil, suggestive tinge: "Won't you come into my parlor?" said the spider to the fly. However, some interpreters in fact understand the position of subordination to be quite the reverse. Here is a definition by Bolinger: A question is "an utterance that 'craves' a verbal or other semiotic response and a speaker subordinating himself to his hearer."[32] The social structure of erotetic super- and subordination clearly offers rich opportunities for sociological research.[33]

The formulation which best holds on to the demand character of a question without losing its knowledge-seeking function calls it an "epistemic request."[34] Most questions are quite naturally transformable into "indirect questions," the analogues of indirect statements. In these the illocutionary pole, the request, is made manifest, as in "I want you to tell me . . ." To answer this by saying "Yes, you do" shows ignorance of the fact that, like a good child in the drawing room, the illocutionary prelude of a proposition may be seen but should not be heard, in the sense of being given the honor of a response. In other words, the request function of a question may be peripherally acknowledged, but the direct response is to the epistemic aspect. This circumstance has a deep implication: There may be questions—as I think, the most absorbing ones—which have no illocutionary force at all (see section VII).

2. Another "hard" definition of questions comes from information theory.[35] In this discipline mental activity is understood in terms of a switchboard whose configuration defines states of readiness to act. In that context a question is an invitation to intervene, an offer of access to the asker's "switches," while a command is a claim of access to the receiver's "switches." Thus the main function of a question is to bring about, by remote control, a change in the questioner's own state of readiness. (This readiness consists of a certain setting of switches which, when activated, will result in corresponding activity.) In the language of information theory the asker is "trying to get some of his switches set for him." The interrogative meaning of a question so defined is that it identifies to the receiver the switches of the asker that need setting. If it fails to do that it is meaningless. The answer is, then, a setting of the switches.

Contrary to the impression given by the electronic language, this definition is actually quite tolerant. For example, it admits theological questions like "Is there a God?" as meaningful because it recognizes that readiness to act is often at stake in them.

3. Under this third paragraph come all the understandings in terms of consciousness, understandings that try to capture the essence of the human questioning activity.

  a. Harris, following Collingwood's lead concerning the situational priority of the question, defines it as the consequence of a conflict in the attempt to organize our experiential schemata.[36] Thus a question indicates a disequilibrium in our explanatory structures. Harris is thinking primarily of questions in progressive science; hence his definition is in terms of prior knowledge structures.

  b. A similar, earlier, understanding by Husserl does without these terms.[37] He speaks of "modalized certainty," certainty in a vulnerable mode. Questions are the striving to get back from uncertainty to a firm decision or judgment. *"Questioning is thus a practical attitude having reference to judgments.*" Indeed, Husserl comments, all rationality is practical. "Practical" is here intended in the old Kantian sense; it is a desire, a will, to make a judgment. As a question is an uneasiness, so an answer is a settling. It fulfills the sense of striving. Husserl prefers the dialectic question, the one which calls for settling judgment. I might anticipate here a deep distinction: If the dialectic question is driven by perplexity, the "what" question is drawn by wonder (see section VII).

c. This wonder is the mark of a third cluster of understandings. Certain questions of the sort usually called philosophical, particularly "what" and "why" questions, are understood as the expression of a sudden defamiliarization of the world, an estrangement from it.[38] It is an estrangement not anxious but rather absorbedly detached—just that wonder which, for Socrates and Aristotle, was the beginning of philosophy. It is, incidentally, intriguing that this same defamiliarizing function is explicitly assigned by the poets, by Shelley and Stevens, to the imagination. Novelists, too, claim such a mission: In his *Book of Laughter and Forgetting* Milan Kundera says, "The wisdom of the novel comes from having a question for everything. . . . The novelist teaches the reader to comprehend the world as question." Who would deny that the imagination can cast on the world a questionable light? Yet I would distinguish questions of the imagination from those of the intellect somewhat as positive evil is distinguished from negative evil in theology: The former are marked by the presence of the thing questioned, the latter by the absence of the thing sought.

The aboriginal questioning disposition of the intellect is most explicitly articulated by Gadamer.[39] "The essence of the question is the laying-open and holding-open of possibilities." Gadamer proposes to work out the logical structure of this openness and to characterize the questioning consciousness. He discovers the following main features, which I paraphrase here. Intrinsic to question-asking is a kind of negativity: things are *not* as we thought. There is, moreover, a second, more radical—one might say, a reflective—negativity: in asking we *know* that we do not know. As Socrates puts it: "I know myself as not knowing." Furthermore, the openness of asking is focused; it has a directional sense. Yet it does not predetermine the answer but keeps itself in suspension: one might say that it is a species of directed desire.[40] Still, it does determine a horizon within which the question seeks its answer—to that extent it is positive. Consequently a question may be logically valid but functionally false, for it may obstruct the answer by false presuppositions; it may contract the horizon and misplace its center, so to speak. If openness directed to possibilities is the essence of a question, the corresponding answer must reach all the possibilities. It must not only make its affirmations reasonably, but it must also justify its denials knowledgeably.

Behind Gadamer's exposition stands a passage from Heidegger.[41] He discerns three immediate elements of a question: (1) that which the question is after (*das Gefragte*), (2) that which is being questioned (*das Befragte*), and (3) that which is intended in the question (*das Erfragte*). It can be argued that these three elements must be understood as identical.[42] Only when what we set out to learn, when what we look to for a response and what we finally come away with are seen to be the same, do we understand what sort of problem Meno's paradox, that unbreakable "circle of inquiry," poses (see section II) and how Socrates, in effect, breaks it. For what Socrates suggests is that a question is a sort of directed ignorance or a guided openness (see items 1–6 of the list in section VII) and that we can look within ourselves to find that we already know what we are yet searching for.

V. Formalizing Questions

I now pass from the most reflective to the most formal treatment of questions. The reason for this abrupt regression is that the answer-based definitions of the previous section are largely justified by the formalizations they permit—which are also of interest in themselves.

A question logic, an erotetic logic, was bound to be attempted in time, along with all the other nonstandard logics. Aside from the intellectual challenge, there were many incentives, minor ones like exposing trick questions, and urgent ones, like making computers answer and even ask questions. There is no getting around the fact the assertoric logic has the historical, logical and even the pragmatic priority over erotetic logic. For while questions may be first in the elevatedly human state of pursuing truth, in the ordinary human condition of having opinions, assertoric entrenchment is more frequent than epistemic imbalance— yea and nay-saying precedes questioning. Moreover, questions seem singularly recalcitrant to hard-and-fast formalization, for their soul is indeterminacy, and as far as proof is concerned they seem to be *hors de combat*.

Perhaps not altogether. There are erotetic inferences which show that questions have certain logical features analogous to (assertoric) propositions.[43] For example, from "Who raised a question?" one can infer that someone raised a question, a logical property called analycity in a proposition, because the inference follows from its mere analysis. Again, from the same question one can infer that someone uttered, a logical property called entailment because questions trail along utterances. So one may expect that erotetic logic will be piggy-backed onto propositional logic, at least in the semantic sense that a way is found for questions to have truth values just like propositions—though truth values are what a question would at first seem egregiously to lack. Husserl,[44] who weighs very even-handedly the question whether questions are, in an important sense, judgments, furnishes one pretty telling argument against this possibility: If the proposition "S–P" is pragmatized (my term), so that it becomes "I think S–P," then the latter may be false though the former is true. But if one does the same to the question "Is S–P?" then, sincerity aside, the mere utterance of this question makes "I ask whether S–P" true. This shows, as has indeed been intimated in item 2 on p. 310, that the only linguistic way any one knows of turning a question into a proposition really does not chiefly preserve the question but rather the questioning experience. Consequently truth values will have to come some other way, the one hinted at by Cohen: Questions derive their truth from the values of their answers.[45] The following brief and necessarily imprecise exposition is largely derived from Belnap and Steel.[46]

The first step is to separate the logical essence of questions from their many appearances, and this, in turn, permits one to fix the interrogative form which "puts" the standard elementary question types. This stripped-down interrogative displays the two parts of a question: its *request,* R, and its *subject,* $(A_1 \ldots A_n)$. Thus, to take the simpler example, the "whether" question: It makes a request concerning its subject, namely the set of alternative answers. These, the wish to be told and the range of answers, are conjoined by the *interrogative function* $?$, which takes both the request and the subject as its arguments and produces a question as its value: $?R(A_1 \ldots A_n)$. For "what" questions, this formula is modified so as to express the fact that its indefinitely many alternative answers are presented by reference to a matrix (see item 2 on p. 308).

Now answers come in numerous modes: They may be possible or actual, sincere or deceitful, candid or evasive, responsive or rejecting. For logical purposes a type of reply called "direct" is defined. It is that piece of language which answers the question completely but just completely. It may be true or it may be false, but it must supply no less and no more than was asked for. (As a crucial result of the formalism it becomes "effectively decidable" whether a piece of language is in fact a direct answer.) A direct answer has three properties: (1) it selects a specific subset from the alternatives presented by the question; (2) it claims completeness, considering implicitly all the alternatives and denying those not chosen; and (3) it presents all the chosen alternatives as really distinct.

Now a question may be said to be true according as its "presupposition" is true. A question, Q, is said to presuppose a statement, A, if and only if A is a logically necessary condition for there being some true answer to Q. Thus the infamous "double" question, "Has he stopped beating his wife?" has as its presupposition the positive answer to a prior question, "Was he ever a wife-beater?" If he never was, then the question has no true answer. Similarly, "Hobson's choice" questions, like "Are you unintelligent or are you stupid?" or paradox questions such as "Can you hear me back there?" can be analyzed by seeing how their presuppositions make it impossible to fulfill the criteria of a direct answer. Moreover the "Hauptsatz" of erotetic semantics, which is that foolish questions get foolish answers, is now elucidated: Foolish questions are those to which every direct answer is false (like most questions on true-or-false exams).

So in this usage a question is true or false according as it has answerability or not. Answerability descends to a question originally through the truth of its presuppositions, which in turn begets the existence of a true answer. So the motives for identifying the essence of a question with the set of direct answers becomes clear: The set of answers tells whether a question has meaning, and the true answer tells what that meaning is. Of course I am stopping short here of the main fruit of these logical and semantic formalizations, namely the question calculus they yield.

At the same time it is obvious that the pragmatic side, the unfixed, off-balance character of questions, is largely lost in erotetic logic. The formalized question is a clear but also a denatured object.

VI. Using Questions

It is the pragmatic analysis of questions which particularly brings out their eminently practical nature: They are useful, instrumental. Many questions have an imperative cast (see item 1, page 314) and are therefore meant to be productive of information and behavior. But the pragmatic conditions, the communicative intentions of questions, are far more complex, far more variously constrained than those of brute commands. Who has the authority to ask whom to do or tell what, where, when, and in what spirit and with what expectations—these are subtle matters. Yet it is precisely the pragmatic complexity of questions which is responsible for their practical pervasiveness. They move the world in a multitude of approaches. In the immortal words of Russell Hoban's intrepid tale, *The Mouse and His Child:* "Why times how makes what"—the examination of ends compounded with the search for means puts substance into the world.

So a rehearsal of some five uses to which questions can be put, a mere sampling of the possibilities, might be opportune. They rise from the most specifically instrumental to the most encompassingly practical sphere.

1. The most mundane and narrowly utilitarian uses of questions are the zillions of informational queries, running the gamut from completely spontaneous to carefully contrived, which are issued in the course of life's business. The contrived queries bring into play all the techniques for gathering information or eliciting states of mind: questionnaires, opinion polls, lie detectors, monitored interrogations. This whole huge enterprise has given new legal urgency to the old pragmatic problem mentioned above: Who may ask—and then tell—whom what. For such data-collecting techniques may be too powerful for our purposes. They may invade civil rights.[47]

2. There is that large class of questions, alluded to above, which are by intention manipulatory and have the illocutionary force of commands. In democratic societies, to be sure, the iron fist tends to wear a velvet glove, and questions are often used as a civil guise for directives: "May I see your driver's license?" Since civility makes an egalitarian world go round, this use is not to be despised.

3. Another use of questions characteristic of democracies is in what might be called "erotetic rebellion." There is a general understanding that "the habit of questioning," a kind of reflex-like initial resistance to authority, is a healthy frame of mind for a citizen. Consequently there is near-universal formulaic approval for "questioning"—our priorities, our values, our society, you name it. There is something slightly curious, and something more than slightly questionable about the public establishment of this questioning mode.[48] The Germans, who are newer to it than we, have coined a worthy neologism for it: *Infragestellung*—"putting-in-question." For responsible questioning of traditional ways requires appreciative awareness of their presumptions. In the analysis of questions, such contextual "presumptions" are distinguished from logical "presuppositions." Presuppositions are the immediate conditions of erotetic validity (see section V); presumptions pertain to the larger setting, the communal basis, such as the frame of rights and obligations, which makes any questioning, including the questioning of authority itself, possible. In short, democratic "putting-in-question" runs a perpetual danger of cutting the ground from under its own feet. And yet—and here is the paradox—as an ingrained habit it really is also the most useful of political dispositions in a democracy.

4. The most voluminous recent literature concerning the use of questions is in the field of education. Much of it concerns narrow problems such as the positioning of questions in textbooks, the devising of examination questions, and the plotting of interrogative strategies for teachers.[49] The last of these, however, has deeper and older dimensions.

No pedagogic issue is more interesting than that of teachers' questions. It is an article of American educational faith—not unrelated to the approval of the "questioning mind" described above—that questions in classrooms are a good thing. Yet teacher questions tend toward fact and detail, not inference and integration, and they are more apt to forestall than to elicit students' questions and questioning. For this sort of pedagogic questioning ends abruptly when the answer is pronounced correct or incorrect, while students' questions are apt to be punished by counter questions.[50] In the terms of this essay (see section II), the pragmatic pole of the pedagogic question is flawed: it is, and is perceived to be, a pretend question. For the teacher neither truly asks but knows the answer beforehand, nor truly listens, but is intent on hearing a correct formula or on catching the student out. In such interrogations the question is subverted and its subject displaced. Naturally such dogmatical persecutions are provably not conducive to learning.[51] Experience in fact shows that on occasion a candidly aggressive statement of opinion is more useful in rousing mental activity than are such interrogations. For open assertions at least leave teachers somewhat exposed to the students' response, while leading questions are protective cover.

It must be said that even dialectically artful teachers, who bring both cunning and candor to the task, cannot escape the deeper quandary of pedagogic, that is, *applied* questioning: how to use a question to prod the student's intellect into activity and to elicit its contents without betraying the very question nature of a question, the asker's desire to know.

Finally, the Teacher's Quandary is not the only deep difficulty which the use of questions raises. When we come to those great frameless questions which have no discernible immediate utility and are not asked much in classrooms—philosophical questions, to come right out with it—we find that philosophers hold three widely diverse opinions about their practicality. (I here distinguish practicality from utility: Practicality pertains to full-blown human action, utility to narrower manipulations.) There are first those, like Wittgenstein, who think that the pursuit of such questions is a bad fever which philosophy ought not to encourage but to cure—though there are always new people ready and eager to be infected.[52] There are secondly those, like Heidegger, who take a grim pride in the pure impracticality of such questions: Philosophy poses precisely those questions "with which one can do nothing," the kind which true servant girls laugh at—though Lord knows what being truly a servant girl has to do with it, in Thales's time or in ours.[53] Finally there are some, like Socrates, who think that nothing but the asking and the provisional answering of such questions is practical—not distantly but immediately applicable to life: for the "unquestioned life is insupportable." Nothing marks a philosophy as does the claim or the denial that its first questions are practical.

VII. Ordering Questions

Who would deny that normal questions can be shuffled into some sort of defensible order according to their topical acuteness, practical importance, or theoretical interest?

Moreover, it has been intimated above (see item 7 in section III), that there might also be a class of not-so-normal questions that are of a higher order altogether, though their pursuit will resolve no immediate crisis, will solve no immediate problem, and will, very likely, run retrograde to the progress of science. These are the philosophical questions just mentioned. Those who have affirmed the possibility of such higher-order questions, questions out of the ordinary order, have usually believed that these questions themselves form a hierarchy, whose grandeur as a whole depends on the fact that it is headed by a first question, *the* first question—one which is recognized "first as the widest, then as the deepest, and finally as the most aboriginal question."[54] It might be posed as a "what" question, such as "What is the ultimate, encompassing whole?" or "What is Being?" or "What is intelligibility?" Or perhaps it might be formulated as a "whether" question, such as "Is there a whole?" or "Is there Being?" or "Is there intelligibility?" I do not, of course, pretend here to begin to establish such a question or its form.

There does, however, arise a last pertinent question to which I do want to venture the beginning of an answer: Is what I have called the second power of questions, the question of questions—"What is a question?"—itself possibly a first question?

The grand understanding of questions was that they are a kind of openness to what is knowable in the world (see item 3, page 316). If that is so, then erotetic receptivity and responsive being are correlatives, or as Heidegger says, "cor-respondences," and the question concerning questions is necessarily implicit in questions about the world.[55] The plenitude of the answer to the question "What is a question?" will then depend on how formative the erotetic openness is taken to be, how far questions are thought to shape the world.

If, on the other hand, we understand questions in a more restricted way, as linguistic events under peculiarly powerful pragmatic and practical conditions, then the reflection on them does not rise to any philosophical ultimacy but remains a workaday inquiry—a more modest but perhaps a more prosperous fate.

I would like to conclude by undertaking a slightly quixotic task, namely that of making a sort of inventory of the marks which distinguish questions belonging to the higher erotetic order—if only to thicken the likelihood that there is such a hierarchy.

1. There is curiosity, doubt, and a third thing, wonder. Traditionally scientists cherish curiosity, philosophers despise it,[56] and theologians suspect it.[57] For curiosity—in German *Neugier* or "news-greed"—gets enmeshed in the just-now, the changeable,

the sensuous. Some philosophers, like Descartes, deal in doubt, namely the systematic "putting-into-question" of the ordinary world. However, that doubt is only a device for achieving certainty. Neither curiosity nor doubt are the impulse behind the sort of philosophical questions I mean, but rather wonder. There is no grief in doubt resolved or in curiosity slaked, but the fading of wonder is an erotetic calamity. For directed desire or focused openness is the heart of any true question.

2. Since our desire is indefinite and our capacity for satisfying it finite, "the range of possible questions is larger than the range of possible answers."[58] In other words, the very test of validity in ordinary questions, that they have direct answers (see section V), fails in extraordinary questions, some of which are necessarily marked by our inability to furnish an answer matrix.

3. Philosophical questions are described sometimes as strange and deranged (see item 7 in section IV) and again as most common and ordinary. The reason is that they train their light on the everyday world, but it is a weird and confounding light. Philosophical perplexities are wonder given formulation.

4. A philosophical question impregnates its answer. There are, to be sure, dialectical fossils, bits of petrified thought, answers to defunct questions. These shopworn intellectual goods even have a certain utility, but they are no longer truly answers. To speak in metaphor: A philosophical answer has yet upon it the blush of having been desired, because a question is the kind of desire which does not fail with its fulfillment.

5. A philosophical question is consequently not degraded or annihilated by its answer. Hence it is not a "problem" in either of the two strangely contrary strong senses of that old word: It is not, as for Aristotle, a rhetorically posed, undecidable opposition of alternatives, either of which have a clutch of unweighty opinions in their favor, such as render the question otiose. Nor is it a formula in which the answer is implicit and which loses all interest simultaneously with the solution.[59] More generally, a question is not to be attacked methodically: "The primary effort

of method is repeatedly to complete its instances, of query to deepen each instance."[60] Call it "query" or "inquiry," the search started by a true question is not constrained by rational decision procedures but is more akin to (purposeful) play.[61]

6. Just as the most long-lived erotetic classification into dialectical questions on the one hand, and "what" (or "why") questions on the other, comes from the Greeks, so does the understanding of their use in philosophy: The dialectical questions have a stronger illocutionary direction and a more constrained set of answers. They require the addressee to choose among well-defined alternatives; they predefine a perplexity. The "what" or "why" questions (which might be said to represent the epitome of the Greek legacy to philosophy[62]) are more open both pragmatically (see section VI) and with respect to their subject. For a response to a "what" question requires not only a free and fresh focus on the object proposed in the question-subject, but also a choice of levels: "What is that?" may be treated as anything from a request for a mere nominal identification ("A plane tree") to a deep inquiry into its essence—as anything from the most ordinary reply to the most extraordinary response. Hence the "what" questions are the philosophical questions par excellence.

7. Such questions, finally, are most extraordinary with respect to their pragmatic pole. This fact shows up best when they are posed in truly engaged conversation—the more seriously they preoccupy the asker, the less are they addressed to the partner, to a you. For the true respondent, that of which the question is actually asked, is whatever it was that invited the question to begin with: something in the nature of things. One might next wish to say that such questions, even in a community of inquiry, are addressed primarily by myself to me, that they belong to that "conversation of the soul with itself" anciently spoken of by Plato.[63] But even that is not quite right in the end. The extraordinary questions, can, of course, be eventually formulated in the first person, but just as they are not ultimately asked of you, so they

are not originally posed as mine. In sum, the asking of first questions reveals a human capacity beyond that of being a self, a capacity for selfless absorption in whatever happens to be.

All critical reason relies, I think, on questions, but not all questions are critical. It appears that there are questions that are asked not in order to elicit correct distinctions and just discriminations, not in order to engage a subject matter in rational battle, but in a spirit of letting be and allowing what there is to emerge. It does, however, seem to be the experience of our whole tradition of thought that such questions cannot shape themselves unless some hard critical questioning has already taken place. Critical reason is evidently the necessary means—if not the end—of reflection.

Notes

1. Ludwig Wittgenstein, *Philosophical Investigations*, I (1947–1949), trans. by G. E. M. Anscombe. (New York: Macmillan Company, 1953), 12.

2. James T. Dillon, "The Multidisciplinary Study of Questioning," *Journal of Educational Psychology* 74 (1982): 150.

3. Nuel D. Belnap and Thomas B. Steel, *The Logic of Questions and Answers* (New Haven: Yale University Press, 1976), 1.

4. Arthur C. Graesser and John B. Black, eds., *The Psychology of Questions,* (Hillsdale, N.J.: Lawrence Erlbaum Associates, 1985).

5. Plato, *Meno,* 80d ff. A brilliant book, devoted to the Meno paradox and the possibility of inquiry, that is, the discovery of truth by rational, progressive questioning, appeared too late for inclusion in this essay: Stewart Umphrey's *Zetetic Skepticism* (Wakefield, N.H.: Longwood Academic, 1990).

6. Aristotle, *Metaphysics,* 995a ff.

7. Aristotle, *Sophistical Refutations,* V, XII, XXX.

8. Aristotle, *On Interpretation,* XI.

9. John Searle, *Intentionality* (Cambridge: Cambridge University Press, 1983), 191.

10. Aristotle, *Topics*, VIII, 2, 4.

11. Henry Hiz, ed., *Questions* (Boston: D. Reidel Publishing, 1978), xii.

12. Aristotle, *Categories*, IV.

13. Aristotle, *Physics*, II, 3.

14. Jean Piaget, *The Language and Thought of the Child* (New York: Meridian Books, 1955), 233.

15. Bernard J. F. Lonergan, *Insight* (New York: The Philosophical Library, 1958), 272.

16. Otto Jesperson, *Essentials of English Grammar* (London: George Allen and Unwin, 1933), 304.

17. Belnap and Steel, *Logic of Questions*, 19.

18. J. J. Katz, "The Logic of Questions," in J. F. Staal and B. van Rootselaur, eds., *Logic, Methodology, and Philosophy of Science* (Amsterdam: North-Holland Publishing Co., 1968), 470.

19. Belnap and Steel, *Logic of Questions*, 19.

20. *Thinking* 6 (1)(1985): 28.

21. Hiz, *Questions*, 307.

22. Jacob Klein, "The Idea of Liberal Education," W. Weatherford, ed., *The Goals of Higher Education*, (Cambridge: Harvard University Press, 1960), 160.

23. Martin Heidegger, *Being and Time* (1927), John Macquarrie and Edward Robinson, tr., (New York: Harper and Row, 1962), 24–25.

24. Edmund Husserl, *Logical Investigations* (1900), vol. 2, J. N. Findlay, tr., (London: Routledge and Kegan Paul, 1976), 839–49.

25. Hiz, *Questions*, 171.

26. Belnap and Steel, *Logic of Questions*, 35.

27. Felix Cohen, "What Is a Question?" *Monist* 39(1929): 353.

28. Eva Brann, "The Student's Problem," *Liberal Education* (October 1969): 369 ff.

29. R. G. Collingwood, *An Autobiography* (Oxford: Oxford University Press, 1939), 31.

30. Hans-Georg Gadamer, *Truth and Method,* edited by Donald G. Marshall and Joel C. Weinsheimer (New York: Continuum Publishing Co., 1988). Errol Harris, *Hypothesis and Perception* (New York: Humanities Press, 1970), 293 ff.

31. Katz, "Logic of Questions," 467.

32. Hiz, *Questions,* 313.

33. Dillon, *Multidisciplinary Study,* 152.

34. Hiz, *Questions,* 101.

35. Donald M. MacKay, *Information, Mechanism and Meaning* (Cambridge: M.I.T. Press, 1969), 36, 100.

36. Harris, *Hypothesis and Perception,* 301.

37. Edmund Husserl, *Experience and Judgment,* revised and edited by Ludwig Landgrebe, trans. by James S. Churchill and Karl Ameriks (Evanston, Ill.: Northwestern University Press, 1973).

38. Klein, "Idea of Liberal Education," 162.

39. Gadamer, Truth and Method, pt. 2, IIc.

40. Eva Brann, *Paradoxes of Education in a Republic* (Chicago: The University of Chicago Press, 1979), 142 ff.

41. Heidegger, *Being and Time,* 24–25.

42. Jon Lenkowski, "Meno's Paradox and the Zetetic Circle," (Lecture, St. John's College, 1989), 20.

43. Katz, "Logic of Questions," 465.

44. Husserl, *Logical Investigations,* par. 68–69.

45. Cohen, "What is a Question?," 359 ff.

46. Belnap and Steel, *Logic of Questions,* 3, 5, 20, 35, 68, 109, 116, 131.

47. Ibid., 146.

48. Eva Brann, "A Way to Philosophy," *Metaphilosophy* 6 (1975): 366.

49. Graesser and Black, *Psychology of Questions,* nos. 10, 12.

50. Dillon, *Multidisciplinary Study,* 159.

51. Graesser and Black, *Psychology of Questions,* 278.

52. Wittgenstein, *Philosophical Investigations,* 91.

53. Martin Heidegger, *What is a Thing?* trans. by W. B. Barton, Jr. and Vera Deutsch (Washington, D.C.: Regnery Gateway, 1968).

54. Martin Heidegger, *An Introduction to Metaphysics* (1953), trans. by Ralph Manheim. (New Haven: Yale University Press, 1959), 1 ff.

55. Martin Heidegger, *What is Philosophy?* (1955), trans. by Eva T. H. Brann. (Annapolis: St. John's College Bookstore, 1991).

56. Jon Lenkowski, "The Origin of Philosophy," *The St. John's Review* 37 (Spring 1986): 81–92. See also Plato, *Republic* 475–76; Heidegger, *Being and Time*, 346–47.

57. Hans Blumenberg, *The Legitimacy of the Modern Age* (Cambridge: M.I.T. Press, 1983), 309 ff.

58. Lonergan, *Insight*, 639.

59. Brann, "The Student's Problem," 377.

60. Justus Buchler, *The Concept of Method* (New York: Columbia University Press, 1979), 114, 142.

61. Brann, *Paradoxes*, 142.

62. Heidegger, *What is Philosophy?*, 34.

63. Plato, *Sophist*, 263–64.

14 Theology and Critical Reasoning: Ignatius' Understanding of the Jesuit University

MICHAEL J. BUCKLEY, SJ

Prisoner as I am to the homiletic tradition of the Society of Jesus, I should like to introduce my reflections with two citations from the texts of others. The first is from Peter-Hans Kolvenbach, the general superior of the Society of Jesus, and the second is from a distinguished alumnus of a Jesuit University, Archbishop John Foley.

Addressing the presidents of Jesuit Universities in November of 1985, Father Kolvenbach joined the contemporary direction of the Jesuits with the goals of their universities (and by "university" I am including all institutions of higher learning): "The option for the poor, or the promotion of justice in the name of the gospel, is not in conflict with the educational apostolate. Our universities, if they are truly Catholic, must bear witness to this priority. . . . All of us need to dedicate ourselves to the search, both loyal and creative, for those elements that specify the Catholic nature of our institutions."[1]

Addressing these same presidents, Archbishop Foley referred to what he considered the scandal inherent in the presence on Jesuit university faculties of those who do not reflect authentic Catholic teaching. When he has complained to the news media

333

about their choice of such persons as university representatives for their programs, he has met with the response: "How can we be faulted for selecting for our program those who appear to have the Church's seal of approval because they hold positions on the faculties of Catholic universities?" The archbishop comments: "I know the demands of academic freedom—and I also know its purpose: to pursue truth fearlessly and without pressure. May I suggest, however, that a truth already possessed may sometimes be compromised in the face of other fears and other pressures by the officials of Catholic universities: the pressures of government regulation, the allure of public funds, the fear of faculty reaction, the unwillingness to endure apparently bad publicity."[2] Unless I misread the archbishop, he is saying that the administrators of Catholic universities periodically compromise the Catholic character of these institutions because of the desire for money and the fear of trouble. His is by no means an isolated opinion, and his willingness to discuss it openly does credit both to the archbishop and to the presidents who listened.

If the general of the Society of Jesus sets out the project for my reflections, the archbishop exhibits something of its problematic. For the general asks for a continual inquiry into the elements that specify a Catholic university, while the archbishop's remark would raise the question for some Americans whether there can be such a thing at all. But can any institution be both Catholic and a university? Bernard Shaw's dictum is well known: a Catholic university is a contradiction in terms. Having set out something of the problem for these reflections, let me say a word about their method.

Any attempt to deal with the distinctive Catholic character of a university entails a series of options. One can simply describe what is taking place: these institutions are called Catholic; so this is what a Catholic university must be. Sociologists can do this with the present or historians with the past. Under this rubric, a Jesuit university is called a university in which Jesuits teach—and this is presented as an effective rejoinder to a question overly eager in its enthusiasms and naive in its expectations. But these simply descriptive definitions provide nothing of educational goals which remain to be realized, of the initial vision which was the originating dynamism of such institutions, and of the criteria by which growth or decline can be measured.

The alternative is a prescriptive definition. The determination of a Catholic university is taken from normative documents and these documents are used to indicate what a Catholic university should be. If descriptive discourse indicates what is (with little attention to final ends), prescriptive discourse fairly bristles with finality, goals, and objectives—and it can delimit an institution that never was and never will be.

Hans-Georg Gadamer suggests a third possibility: that the present de facto situation and the canonical statements of origins and purpose can be combined in a "fusion of horizons"—as though a conversation were taking place, one in which these statements from the past are presented to the questions that emerge from the present, and (at the same time) the present situation is opened by the questions that great and classic articulations of purpose pose.[3] The fusion of the past and the present in a continuous dialogue brings out virtualities in a text that its author may never have realised. Simultaneously, this "fusion of horizons" submits a contemporary practice and its unspoken assumptions to the searching examination of a classic. "This is just what the word *classical* means, that the duration of the power of a work to speak directly is fundamentally unlimited."[4] Our definitional inquiry, then, proposes to be neither descriptive nor prescriptive; it is dialogic.

Now the text or the classic that I propose for conversation is a section from one of the greatest works of Ignatius of Loyola, the founder of the Jesuits, *The Constitutions of the Society of Jesus*. One need not apologize too vigorously for not knowing this document; many Jesuits do not know it well either! Yet it is the document upon which Ignatius spent the greatest portion of his life, and it does uniquely specify the Society of Jesus. The *Spiritual*

Exercises are for the entire Church; the *Constitutions* are specifically and definitially for the enterprises and life of the Society of Jesus.[5]

In the fourth part of the *Constitutions*, Ignatius elaborated the meaning and structure of Jesuit education. Originally the society had no intention of engaging in educational institutions. What residences there were for academic work initially were envisaged almost exclusively for the education of Jesuit students for the priesthood, various kinds of houses of studies attached to major universities. But experience taught the founder of the Jesuits what it had taught Plato before him and John Dewey afterwards: that all substantial or permanent changes in a culture result from institutions; even the prophetic voice will perish unless it reaches institutional embodiment. And the most telling, or influential, institutions are educational. Hence, at the end of his life, Ignatius amplified the earlier drafts of the fourth part of the *Constitutions* with two additions, the last great changes he would make in this document: (1) a seventh chapter which dealt with colleges for non-Jesuits—more like the contemporary secondary school; and (2) an additional fasicule which became chapters eleven to seventeen, chapters that outline the Jesuit universities or institutions of higher learning—the Roman College, for example, would have fitted the prescriptions for the universities. The very first Jesuit university, so named, was begun in 1547 at Gandia, with what would become typical practice over the four hundred years to follow: a few Jesuits, a few students, and some financial support. Ignatius only added to the *Constitutions* his prescriptions for a Jesuit university over the years 1553 and 1554.[6] He was to die two years later. Jesuit universities just got in at the last act!

Now if one looks at those chapters—not to copy them but to dialogue with them—one gets a startling view of what a university is. It is composed of at least three faculties: humanities and languages; arts (i.e., philosophy) and sciences; and theology.

Ganss maintains that an ideal student—say, Bellarmine, or Corneille, or Calderon—would study the humane letters from ages 10–13; arts and sciences from 14–16; and theology from 17–21, or 23 (one should add) if he were to take the doctorate.[7] Frequently the age was older. If so short a course of studies would raise an eyebrow anywhere, it would raise it at the university of Paris, the academic institution Ignatius evaluated as supreme in Europe. But notice how he changed its demands. At Paris a student would begin rudimentary arts between 13 and 15, and finish the arts curriculum in some five years. Only after acquiring the M.A. at 21 or older, could he begin the theological curriculum, a course which would demand something between thirteen and fifteen more years of studies, as he moved through the stages of *studens, cursor, baccalarius* or *sententiarius, baccalarius formatus, licentiatus,* to reach the giddy heights of *doctor* (or *magister*) sometime after his 35th birthday.[8]

Ignatius cut that course down ruthlessly. What is surprising almost by counterpoint is the premier place he gave to theology. It became no longer one professional or graduate school among those of medicine and law, but the one which dominates and justifies everything else in these universities of his. Graduate or professional education in the middle ages and Renaissance included faculties of theology, medicine, and law. But the *Constitutions* make this change: "The study of medicine and law, being more remote from our Institute, will not be treated in the universities of the Society, or at least the Society will not undertake this teaching through its own members" (452). And this elimination or at least demotion of other professional schools is balanced by the place given theology. The justification of the humane letters begins: "Since both the learning of theology and the use of it require (especially in these times) knowledge of humane letters and of . . . languages . . . " (447). Philosophy and sciences have a similar legitimation: "Likewise, since the arts or natural sciences dispose the intellectual powers for theology, and are useful for the perfect understanding and employment of it, and also by their own nature help towards the same ends, they should be treated with fitting diligence and by learned professors" (450).

Let me point out what is being said and not being said in these critical paragraphs. Ignatius is not saying that a Jesuit university is a university in which Jesuits teach, or in which the majority of instructors are Jesuits, or in which the *Exercises* permeate the curriculum.[9] This may be somewhat true or somewhat false, but it is not his point. Further: Ignatius is not saying that what characterizes the universities of the Society is value-centered education (the same could be said of those in the Soviet Union) or the active presence of a vital campus ministry or the interest taken by the faculty in the students. These do mark a Jesuit university—as they do many others—but they are not his point here. What he is saying—and saying in contradistinction with the practice of the great medieval universities and the splendid *Idea of a University* by Cardinal Newman and even the contemporary usages of Jesuit universities and houses of study—is this: that theology is essentially a university discipline; that it draws into itself—as the apex of a cone draws the lines of a cone—all of those studies which we designate as liberal or scientific or philosophy; that it is theology which specifies the curriculum.

It is not merely that theology is present as one branch of knowledge among others. The bare presence of Catholic theology does not mean that a university is *Catholic*—and this is Newman's point. Its means that it is a *university*, an institution which embodies the universality of human discourse and knowledge. What makes a university Catholic for Ignatius is the organic relationship between the other disciplines and theology. Please notice that what is at issue here is theology, not necessarily the theology department. Theology constitutes the ultimate justification for the presence of other learning, as wisdom constitutes the ultimate justification for the arts and sciences. I am not trying to argue Ignatius' theory of education at this juncture; I

am simply trying to point out that he is saying something—
something significant and something different. For Newman,
what should emerge from a university education is that integration of knowledge which he called the philosophic habit of mind.
For Ignatius, what should emerge from a Catholic university education was the integration of knowledge into a theological wisdom—the highest achievement of critical reasoning. These are
not contradictory ideals, but neither are they simply identical.
And their differences may indicate something intrinsic and important about the Catholic nature of Jesuit education. Let me say
a word about each of the three faculties.

In its understanding of the humanities, the *Constitutions*
exhibits a synthesis of the medieval liberal arts of words—grammar, rhetoric, and logic—and the Renaissance humanities—literature (philology), history, and philosophy. The medievals
numbered the three arts of words (*sermocinales*) among the liberal arts because, as John of Salisbury wrote: "They are called
'liberal' either because the ancients took care to have their children (*liberos*) instructed in them or because their object is to
effect the liberation (*libertatem*) of the human person."[10] Grammar, rhetoric, and logic were not subject matters to be studied so
much as universal skills to be acquired—skills of interpretation,
argumentation, and creativity to be developed which could be
brought to bear upon any subject matter. When the Renaissance
revolted against medieval kinds of education as too abstract, it reformulated the liberal arts in terms of subjects to be mastered, or
great works to be assimilated, because one became like what one
studied. Interestingly enough, the *Constitutions* combined both
understandings of humanistic development under *Letras de Hu-
manidad*, subsuming under that title both the disciplines of
grammar and rhetoric (from the middle ages and transformed in
this new Renaissance world) and the subject matter of poetry and
history (from the Renaissance) (448).[11] The focus was upon
linguistic skills and literary texts, combined with the mastery
of various languages: Latin, Greek, and Hebrew—the classical

languages of Western civilization—and Chaldaic, Arabic, and Indian, indicating something of the movement of modernity towards global inculturation.

Secondly, there were the arts and the natural sciences. The middle ages had fielded three liberal arts of words (grammar, rhetoric, and logic), but four liberal arts that were brought to bear upon things (arithmetic, geometry, astronomy, and music). This quadrivium opened up the faculty of arts to the philosophy of the high middle ages and the natural sciences of the Renaissance. As the focus of the humane letters was linguistic—books or languages—so the focus of the arts and natural sciences were things. Linguistic competence was obviously necessary for theology, but the relationship between theology and the arts and natural sciences was more complex. Competence here enters into theology in three ways. It develops the *ingenios* of the students, that is, their natural intellectual capacities, so that they can study theology. Secondly, theology demands this kind of knowledge intrinsically both for reaching its own completion and for its exercise. Lastly, this mathematical, scientific, and philosophic knowledge by itself contributes to the same finality as theology (450). The relationship envisaged between mathematics or science or philosophy on one hand and theology on the other, between those disciplines that investigated directly some aspect of nature and theology, was never posed antagonistically. These disciplines developed a level of critical reasoning necessary for theological study; they entered into that study to bring it to its completion and into practice; and they supplemented that study with their own natural development and inherent purposes. Not a bad understanding of the relationship between science and theology!

Finally, theology itself. It consisted both of the mastery of the evidence for theological assertions—sacred scripture—and that positive theology contained in conciliar decrees; mastery of the canonical legislation of Christian practice, of the patristic tradition (446, 464, 467), and of the more theoretical or synthetic scholastic theology. In theology, the principal author among the great books was St. Thomas, allowing also for the *Sentences* of

Peter Lombard. The choice of *Summa theologiae* for the Jesuit university confirmed that theology would not be one discipline among others. The *Summa* is an enormously synthetic work, containing prolonged discussions that are cosmological and psychological, legal, philosophic, and humanistic, within a theological setting. One can understand Ignatius' strictures that theological studies demand both a humanistic and a scientific education, capacities for critical reasoning in a variety of manners, if one also understands that the theology he was stipulating was a synthetic and thoroughly methodological discipline. All other human knowledge did not simply prepare for theology and leave off once one had crossed into the temple. The temple was much more a town! Humanistic skills such as grammar and rhetoric, even poetry and history, found their place within it. Much more so did philosophy and science—there is a constant discussion between them within such a theology. All contributed to the ongoing enterprise of theology itself and brought it to a completion.

Ignatius, however, was not wedded to the *Summa;* the work itself is not mentioned, though the "scholastic doctrine of St. Thomas" is explicitly given primacy. He allows for someone to write another *summa* "better adapted to our times" (446). Yet Thomas's *Summa* represented the kind of theology that Ignatius wanted, a theology precise in its rationality and in some vital contact with the humanities and arts, the natural sciences and philosophy, scripture and the church's tradition. For it was this kind of theology that would draw the other disciplines and habits of learning into integration and wisdom. A Jesuit university institutionalizes critical thinking precisely through, rather than in spite of, theology.

I submit that it was this kind of theology which specified the Catholic university for Ignatius: *"In hanc potissimum Societatis universitates incumbent"* ("On this should the universities of the society put their principle emphasis") (446). Now I further suggest that up until twenty or twenty-five years ago this is precisely what the Jesuit universities had not done. Religion was taught in Jesuit universities, demanded of all the students, but in no sense did the university follow the Ignatian strictures that (a) theology should be "treated by highly capable professors," or (b) that it would be a kind of theology which would necessitate the other disciplines by its nature or integrate them by its influence and character. This question must be honestly asked: What contribution did American Jesuit universities make to the theology that prepared for and finally constituted the Second Vatican Council? I would not be surprised if the answer is: virtually none. If one were to focus the question upon recent decades, some twenty-five years after the council, and investigate the contemporary quality, and consequent influence, of theology at some major Jesuit universities upon contemporary theological discussions in the United States, the answer would be far more positive.

If my central thesis is correct, then in this critical and specific area, Jesuits are much closer now to having what Ignatius called the "universities of the Society" than they were then. If a vital theology rather than ubiquitous Jesuit presence or control is what is *potissimum* in the specification of such a university, then there is no doubt that the last twenty years have developed more positively in the Ignatian direction than is commonly credited. There are obviously many other characteristics that make a university both Catholic and Jesuit, but here is the central one, the *potissimum*. And even more: The *Constitutions* do not seem so conceived that *Jesuit* is distinguished from *Catholic* or constitutes a subspecies of *Catholic*. A Jesuit university should be a peculiarly efficacious way of being Catholic, just as their Catholic character should constitute an increased incentive to the entertaining of those questions and growing in that knowledge that bespeaks a university.

The history of philosophy supplies a term which may be applied to the Ignatian understanding of the function of theology within a Catholic university as the specifier and integrator of wisdom. It is a term whose origins lie with the division of the sciences in Aristotle, but which achieved its modern prominence in

Kant. The term is *architectonic,* and it designates a kind of knowledge which brings order into the vast assemblage of human sciences and disciplines, subject matters and activities.[12] In the *Constitutions* the order of these disciplines emerges both as developing stages toward that theology for which they prepare and as interlocutors with the same theology, in which they are vitally located while preserving their own integrity and autonomy.

The architectonic nature of theology does not lie—as does that of the philosophy of science and of education—in the analysis of the foundations, axioms, and methods of the various sciences. This analysis of presuppositions is essentially the work of philosophy. Theology does not so much analyze the presuppositions as it synthetically reflects upon the conclusions, which are both the sciences established and the conclusions accepted within them. Theology, then, must not be seen as one science among others, self-contained in its own integrity and adjacent to the other forms of disciplined human knowledge. It is much more like a place, a place within which the critical thought and developed habits of reasoning in the arts and sciences are encouraged and their ineluctable movement toward questions of ultimacy taken very seriously. (Such questions are not simply of interlocking content but are even of the absolute commitments entailed by serious teaching and inquiry themselves.) This is theology as an architectonic wisdom rather than as a particular science, and though I think that some Catholic universities are closer to such an Ignatian vision than they were twenty years ago, its articulation can still leave us feeling "like some watcher of the skies / When a new planet swings into his ken." Or with this question about such a programmatic in education: "Was it a vision or a waking dream?"[13]

One can parallel the simile or respond to the question of John Keats perhaps best with a concrete example. Santa Clara University has constituted an annual institute in the winter quarter which brings some courses in the arts and sciences and professional schools together around a single topic. The first such topic was suggested by the American bishops' recent pastoral letter on the challenge of peace, and it dealt with the issues of war and peace. Courses were offered in literature ranging from Homer to Hemingway, in history, in economics and political science, in biology and military science, in philosophic ethics and theology. More technical courses were offered by seminars in engineering and in international law. All of these courses were supplemented by a series of lectures ranging from James Redfield's analysis of war in the Homeric heroic ethos to Helen Caldicott's description of the medical horrors inherent in atomic war to the panel discussion of the ethical and Christian issues raised by American nuclear deterrence. Over a thousand students took at least one of these courses; all of them were responsible for the common lectures. Such an institute gave the university an integration of its various schools which it had never possessed before. The integrative function of theology was twofold: to raise in critical Socratic fashion a question of common and urgent importance; and to contribute to a common effort that both traced something of war's pervasive presence within every aspect of human experience and moved to the resolution of some of its many issues. In this way theology provided for common critical reflection among all the university disciplines, accomplishing a collaborative reflection unachievable by any of these disciplines taken separately.

So successful was this initial effort that Santa Clara has continued this academic integrating institute every winter quarter with advancing success. A few years ago, the common topic, again following the episcopal lead, was poverty. The following year, echoing the influence of its location in Silicon Valley, the topic was technology in world culture. My point is this: if theology is vital, it must engage the other disciplines, and this engagement will constitute the university both as Catholic and as a university. *One* way of doing this is the raising of a subject of common university interest, one which brings the various kinds of knowledge into discussion with the inquiries that are properly theological.

And this brings me back to the comments of Archbishop Foley. The theological discussion which constitutes a university as Catholic must be free. In no way does a simple appointment to the faculty constitute what the archbishop called "the Church's seal of approval" of a particular member of the faculty. Nor should it be seen as such. What it does or should indicate is that such a person can represent part of the universe of discourse which a university embodies and with which Catholic theology must be in contact if it is to be a vital part of American culture. What the archbishop calls "truth already possessed" can be more deeply understood, purified from its cultural accretions and misconstruals, and steadied in its assertions of the message of Christ, only if its reflections occur in an atmosphere in which its questions and its evidence are taken seriously and challenged by the questions of others with academic care and freedom. No other institution except the Catholic university can offer this service to the church. These institutions in their essential function will be destroyed if the freedom of these interchanges is inhibited under the impression that orthodoxy can only be protected by restraining honest, considered disagreement. Academic freedom, with all of its attendant challenges and abrasive moments, is essential not only if a university is to be a university, but essential also for its theology to be sound. It was the great Cardinal Newman who wrote: "That is no intellectual triumph of any truth of Religion which has not been preceded by a full statement of what can be said against it. . . . Great minds need elbow-room, not indeed in the domain of faith, but of thought. And so indeed do lesser minds, and all minds."[14]

The difference between a Catholic university and one of another designation cannot and must not be that in the latter, serious and responsible discussion ranges freely while in the former it is circumscribed. That would simply mean that one is a university and the other a custodial institution of some stamp or other. The special character to the education given in a particular university—among many other factors—lies much more with the questions to which priority is given, the knowledge that is considered most worth having, and the spirit that pervades the academic life of interchange that is a university. It is imperative that there be a strong Catholic voice in Jesuit universities, one that represents the richness and disciplined reflection of the Catholic intellectual tradition in various disciplines, and one that urges both the importance of certain questions and the kind of knowledge that embody this tradition. But if the discussion is not responsible and free, or if the Catholic is the only voice, one does not have a university. One has at best, perhaps, a seminary. On the other hand, that voice should not be so overwhelmed by an ecclectic and chaotic multiplicity that there is no conversation between Catholic thought and the universe of knowledge. In such a situation, the questions and knowledge considered critical by a Catholic culture will never be engaged with the depth and the steadiness that gives the university its Catholic character. But whatever passes as serious knowledge must also be present on that campus, insofar as this is possible. If the Catholic tradition is not in continual and serious contact with that pluralism which represents the universe of knowledge, it will possess neither a university nor a significant theology. I repeat: No other institution in contemporary culture can offer this continual and dialogic academic reflection to the Church.

Academic freedom in no way inhibits the serious responsibility of the bishop to teach what is of Catholic faith and to characterize as such what is its negation, what is opposed to it—whether this takes place within a university or outside of it. The bishops have their obligations; the university has its. Granted the complexity of each issue, the freedom of the university professor to speak does not of itself touch the freedom and the inescapable duty of the bishops to make their own judgments about the coordination between the Catholic university's curriculum and the teaching of the church, whether they deal with statements made in a university or in any other environment. Academic freedom as such is in no way contradictory to the freedom of the magisterium. On the other hand, the presence of a diversity and disagreement within the university is not only essential to its nature as a university but to the soundness and vitality of Catholic theology. There is no need to choose between the presence of an open, responsible discussion representing the world of serious knowledge or reflection and the vital presence of a Catholic orthodoxy with its fidelity to the gospel and to the *paradosis* through which this gospel has come into the twentieth century.

In summary, my argument is as follows. The Ignatian idea of a Catholic or a Jesuit university is one in which theology functions as an integrating, an architectonic, wisdom. This vision will be realized differently from its embodiment in the sixteenth century as our present culture stands in contrast with that of the Catholic Reformation. In many ways Jesuits are closer to that ideal now than they were twenty years ago because theology has begun to rise in the seriousness of its teaching and scholarship. Now there are creative new possibilities by which theology can bring into integration the various schools and departments which constitute a university. Finally, these advances demand a faithful academic freedom within a university that encourages serious discussion, freedom which would be significantly inhibited if it were condemned as a compromise of the Catholic character of the university.

Notes

1. Peter-Hans Kolvenbach, "The Jesuit University Today," Address to the Presidents and Rectors of Jesuit Universities and Other Institutions of Higher Education, given at their meeting in Frascati, Italy, November 5, 1985 (photocopy), p. 5.

2. John Foley, "Archbishop Foley Challenges Presidents," *National Jesuit News* (December 1985): 14.

3. Hans-Georg Gadamer, *Truth and Method* (New York: Seabury Press, 1975), p. 320.

4. Gadamer, *Truth and Method*, p. 258.

5. For the text of the *Constitutions*, see *Monumenta Historica Societatis Iesu, Monumenta Ignatiana*, series tertia, Sancti Ignatii de Loyola, *Constitutiones Societatis Iesu* (Rome: Gregoriana, 1936, 1938). The Spanish text is found in the second volume, the Latin in the third.

6. George E. Ganss, SJ, *Saint Ignatius' Idea of a Jesuit University* (Milwaukee: Marquette University Press, 1954), pp. 33–39. The translation of the *Constitutions of the Society of Jesus* used here is also that of George E. Ganss, SJ (St. Louis: Institute of Jesuit Sources, 1970); see p. 210.

7. Ganss, *Saint Ignatius' Idea*, pp. 46–51, 68–73.

8. John K. Farge, *Orthodoxy and Reform in Early Reformation France: The Faculty of Theology of Paris 1500–1543* (Leiden: E. J. Brill, 1985), pp. 13ff.

9. The "Spiritual Exercises" can denote either a thirty-day structured period of solitary prayer, meditation, and contemplation of the mysteries of the life of Christ, made in order to find the direction of God in one's life, or the book in which this structure is delineated. The *Exercises* came out of Ignatius' own religious development and articulate that experience programmatically. Both the *Exercises* and the themes that emerge from it have exercised a profound influence upon the members of the Society of Jesus.

10. John of Salisbury, *The Metalogicon*, bk. 1, ch. 12, Daniel B. McGarry, tr., (Berkeley: University of California Press, 1955), pp. 36–37. For a discussion of the differences between the liberal arts of the middle ages and the humanities of the Renaissance, see Michael J. Buckley, SJ, "The University and the Concern for Justice: The Search for a New Humanism," *Thought* 57 (June 1982): 225–29.

11. For a perceptive comparison of the influences of the scholastic and humanistic traditions upon the schools of the Society of Jesus, see John W. O'Malley, SJ, "The Jesuit Enterprise in Historical Perspective" (photocopy). I am grateful to Father O'Malley also for calling my attention to the study done by Farge.

12. Aristotle, *Metaphysics*, V, 1, 1013a14; *Ethics*, I, 1, 1094a14, 27; VI, 8, 1141b22, 25; *Physics*, II, 2, 194b2; *Politics*, III, 11, 1282a3; *Poetics*, 19, 1456b11. Immanuel Kant, *The Critique of Pure Reason*, II, "Tran-

scendental Doctrine of Method," chap. iii, "The Architectonic of Pure Reason," A 832/B 860.

13. John Keats, "On First Looking into Chapman's Homer," and "Ode to a Nightingale."

14. John Henry Cardinal Newman, "Christianity and Scientific Investigation: A Lecture Written for the School of Science," with an introduction and notes by Martin J. Svaglic (New York: Holt, Rinehart, Winston, 1966), p. 358. For the importance of academic freedom and liberty of discussion within a Catholic university, see Michael J. Buckley, SJ, "The Catholic University as a Pluralistic Forum," *Thought* 46 (June 1971): 181.

▐▐▐█ The Problem
of Values

15 Evaluation and Critical Reasoning: Logic's Last Frontier?

MICHAEL SCRIVEN

Speaking commonsensically, it's clear that critical thinking is to a large extent an application of evaluation. It involves the systematic evaluation of arguments, presentations, interpretations, and so on. The term creeps into some chapter headings in the new generation of texts, and lately even into the title of one or two.[1] But it does not get substantial treatment *as a topic and procedure in itself* in any that I have been able to locate. That is a loss, because evaluation is not only the correct name for much of what we talk about in teaching critical thinking, but it is also the name for much of the most important thinking we do outside that area. It is a type of thinking which needs to be brought under the umbrella of critical thinking so that it can be studied, improved, and taught. Yet it is scarcely ever discussed, in critical thinking or logical courses, or elsewhere in the humanities.

The twin aims of this paper are to examine the cultural context that led to this curious omission, and take a step toward remedying it by setting out some of the basic logic of practical evaluation.

The intellectual process of evaluation has a good claim to be the most important of all the cognitive skills, on the grounds that

353

the most important things we do and decide—individually, in our disciplines, and as a society—depend on evaluation. Its importance is also recognized by its position at the top of most hierarchies of intellectual skills. Whether or not evaluation is the most important skill, it seems likely that it is the least studied of the cognitive skills, whether by psychologists, logicians, research methodologists, or philosophers. Granted that it is more difficult to analyze than, say, observation and classification, but it is not so difficult as to be beyond the abilities of logicians and philosophers. So there is a sin of omission here.

The reason for this omission is presumably to be found in the cultural context of the academy, in the taboo on evaluation (i.e., on the objectivity of evaluative claims) that has pervaded society and the disciplines during most of the twentieth century. Lately, of course, it has become fashionable to reject the value-free doctrine, but we can hardly take that shift seriously, since the reasons given for it are as shoddy as those which were given for the adoption of the original position. The usual reason for "accepting the legitimacy of values" is the observation that scientists select areas of work on the basis of their own values, or that scientists are sometimes subject to bias (i.e., are sometimes inappropriately influenced by values). Since the proponents of the value-free doctrine never denied either of these claims and were not mentally deficient, it should be obvious that appealing to these reasons can only destroy a straw man. Thus, the critics simply confuse a descriptive thesis (scientists are sometimes biased) with a normative one (it's acceptable to be biased), showing how little they understand the point of the distinction between descriptive and normative. (The distinction has faults, indeed, but not at this superficial level.) It is in fact part of the mystery that wide acceptance should have been given to spurious reasons for "abandoning" the position. It seems that the whole issue, not just one point of view about it, contaminates efforts at reasonable thought about it.

The value-free position and its rejection was, as we shall see, supported by such bad reasons, and was so inconsistent with scientific practice, that we have to conclude it was a position adopted for causes rather than reasons. The reasons offered must, however, be addressed. Let us try to begin at the beginning again, and ask why something with the obvious practical importance of the process of evaluation should have escaped serious analysis— and in fact, should have been denied legitimacy and even existence—by those whose job involves doing such analyses, particularly the philosophers, the logicians—formal and informal—and the methodologists.

The Ultimate Treason of the Intellectuals

It seems likely, albeit demeaning, that the main cause of the avoidance of evaluation as a legitimate intellectual discipline is the same as the main cause of objections to critical thinking and to frank discussion of controversial issues in the classroom, namely fear. Despite all the insulation that tenure and the ivory tower's other defenses provide, fear crosses the drawbridge quite easily, as we saw in the McCarthy period. Indeed, it is already inside the castle, raging in those who should have mastered it long since. For the paradox is that, although evaluation is in some sense taboo, it is in some other sense the heart and soul of scholarly inquiry. Every article refereed is evaluated; every book review is an evaluation; every survey of the literature involves many evaluations; every thesis supervised and examined is scholarly work under evaluation; every choice of method and hypothesis and conclusion depends on critical evaluation of the alternatives. Every scholar has learned to deal with some level of critical thinking and evaluation in order to become a scholar. Yet many of them live in fear of such reviews of their own work, and sometimes operate in such a way as to minimize the chance of it, surrounding themselves with disciples and sycophantic colleagues, conspiring against—rather than arguing against—those who reject their point of view, creating mores of editorial or convention practice which censor criticism. Thus, in many scholars, the fearsome thing is only caged, and the suggestion that we should openly confront and deal with the monster itself is more than most scholars—and teachers or administrators—can handle. Yet that is what true scholarship requires, for the harshest criticism is sometimes right, the paradigm must sometimes be overthrown. The weaker approach is the mark of fear.

The fear of treating evaluation—and to some extent critical thinking (CT)—as a discipline is thus the fear of turning the caged wolf loose, the fear that liberating evaluation from the close confines of standard practice (where it is often disguised under another name or controlled by contextual redefinition[2]) will turn it loose on its guardians. That fear quickly generates bad arguments. It is a sorry spectacle to watch a college faculty arguing against the introduction of serious faculty evaluation—or the evaluation of teaching—when some of them have been turning in student grades for thirty years, and every argument they produce against being evaluated themselves can be perfectly matched by an argument against grading students. Of course it would be overwhelmed by arguments they would immediately produce about the need or obligation to do it, and the relative care and objectivity with which it is done—arguments which equally apply to the evaluation of teaching or overall faculty contribution.

Those in power, in politics or the professions, are never very good at handling evaluation, not willing to admit how they are using it on others while denying its applicability to themselves. This is the typical response, from those who have made it to the castle, to the cries from beyond the walls; but one should expect better from scholars, whose intelligence and calling should make the hypocrisy intolerable.

The continuing existence of this situation in the academy is an implicit criticism of the monitoring disciplines, particularly philosophy and the philosophy of science. Rather than identify the crime, philosophers have collaborated in it. It will surely become one of the great embarrassments in the history of philosophy that the profession gave such acclaim (or tolerance, or implicit support by providing no thorough alternative account) to the emotive theory of the meaning of evaluative claims. It is highly embarrassing that the suggestion that evaluative claims have *no propositional status at all*, that they are to be classified with grunts of approval or disapproval, came from those whose professional life crucially consists in justifying evaluative judgments about philosophy, philosophers, philosophy students.[3]

But the philosophers of science had even less excuse for their position because their judgments did not have to be self-condemnatory. They could have simply blamed the social scientists for inconsistency between their theory and their practice, given that the value-free doctrine originated there. Little of this occurred; the philosophers of science were largely in the grip of the postpositivist approach and its anti-evaluative stand, just as the social scientists were in the grip of the corresponding influences. Even looking for the essential logic of the physical sciences, regardless of considering metadoctrines like the value-free view, philosophers of science should have come to see the essentially evaluative nature of all science, but did not. Of course, the scientists missed the point, too. The essence of the physical sciences, as seen by physical scientists, was laid out time and again in the texts and syllabi of the post-Sputnik era. It was usually encapsulated in lists of the key intellectual skills that make up scientific method—observation, classification, quantification, measurement, hypothesizing, testing, generalizing, explaining, predicting, etc. Comparing these lists with scientific practice is exactly the task of a philosopher of science. Doing so reveals that there is only one intellectual activity which is *always* an essential part of scientific activity, namely evaluation; but it is *always missing* from these lists. Every one of the other items on these lists is missing from one or more sciences; but none can avoid evaluation, since it is what we use to distinguish good hypotheses from bad ones, good evidence from bad evidence, and thus in the end, science from nonscience.[4]

There was, and is, a third specific reason why the failure of philosophy of science to consider evaluation requires a remarkably strong explanation. It is that a whole discipline of evaluation has emerged over the past twenty-five years, essentially as a branch of the social sciences, a discipline which was originally based on program evaluation, but has now expanded substantially. Its principal professional association has a membership of several thousand and a literature of many journals, books, and articles.[5] The related discipline of policy studies, although smaller, has enough importance and standing to deserve some recognition by philosophy of science in its role of metascience.

There is, all in all, more than enough basis for work on evaluation theory to match that on explanation theory, which has long been an important part of philosophy of science. Instead, evaluation theory is a nonevent in philosophy of science. The omission must qualify as one of the most extraordinary examples in the history of thought of prejudice triumphing over evidence.

Informal logic, throwing off the bonds of formalism which were so closely tied to the positivist's fixation on unrealistic paradigms of abstract science and mathematics, was at least emotionally equipped to accept the legitimacy and deal directly with evaluation. That it did not is no doubt due in part to the professional training that most of its practitioners received in disciplines dominated by the value-free paradigm or its philosophical godfather, positivist epistemology. Then again, informal logic, unlike philosophy of science, is a very young subject, and would surely repair this omission in due course.

So the proximate cause for these oversights—in informal logic, in the philosophy of science, in philosophy, and in science education—is the lingering influence of the positivists in philosophy of science. The fact that scientists themselves continue to deny the legitimacy of evaluation as a scientific activity while practicing it constantly is also partly because of the influence of positivism, just as scientists influenced by Popper continue to insist on the impropriety of induction while employing it continually. Of course, all that such considerations show is that scientists are not very sophisticated about the philosophy of science. Intelligence is a remarkably general capacity, but it is no substitute for field experience. Listening to physical scientists pronouncing about what they see as the essential incompetence of social scientists makes it clear that expertise in scientific method does not readily generalize across the realms of science, let alone into the world of human relations, stock market investments, or politics. The same is true of evaluation: expert informal logicians have mastered one application of it—the evaluation of arguments—but are not thereby able to do any better at program or personnel evaluation, at least until they uncover and understand the *latent general logic*.

Evaluation: The Practice and the Theory

The practice of evaluation is arguably as old as intelligent thought (by definition), certainly as old as stone artifacts. Evaluation as a field-limited specialty goes back at least to the Japanese sword-testing families of the samurai era. This kind of specialized evaluation, still with negligible explicit discussion of evaluation methodology (as opposed to measurement methodology) was extended to modern technologies by the road tests of the British automobile magazines in the thirties, and from there to the more general field of product evaluation by Consumer Research. But an intellectual discipline of evaluation has only been around for about a quarter of a century and that was still field-restricted, albeit to another fairly general field—program evaluation.[6] The general logic of evaluation, like personnel evaluation, is still in its infancy. The fact that we practice evaluation in a field called informal logic is no grounds for thinking that we have learned anything about its logic, except implicitly and in that one domain: knowing *how* is not knowing *that*. Following the sword testers and the road testers we are just argument testers. It's a skill we can teach without developing a general logic of evaluation. But much more is needed.

We need to teach students how to do evaluation better in other domains that are important to them—for example, in product and personnel evaluation—and to do that we need to expose and refine the general logic of the process. This process of theory development is the one followed by probability theory as it moved from the rules learned by and implicit in the practice of gamblers to a full discipline whose principles could be taught and thus applied to other fields. It is close to the process followed in every case of science developing out of skill, for example in the development of genetics from plant breeding, metallurgy from smithing, and thermodynamics from steam engine design and experience.

While the methodologists proclaimed the impossibility of scientific evaluation, consumer publications and business consultants were simply doing it, and doing it very well indeed. They used variations on an intuitive model which many of us employ when it comes to making decisions between complex alternatives where the cost of error is high—for example, in selecting colleges or careers or in buying cars or houses. In this chapter, we begin with some clarification of this intuitive approach to practical evaluation. We argue that there are problems inherent in it which ensure that it will give the wrong results for many important evaluations, and we develop what seems to be a better approach.

These problems have not ruined consumer product evaluation because much of it is a matter of making measurements which we can then interpret according to our own needs; that is, the fact-gathering part of product evaluation is so useful that its contribution is greater than the analytical part. If you want to know the best fast computer to buy in a certain price range, the throughput measurements and discussions in *PC Magazine* (the most sophisticated in the business) will tell you. But the analytical part is often important, and in many of the respected computer magazines—*InfoWorld* is a good example—as well as in many of the *Consumer Reports* evaluations, these are the key to the conclusions and are obtained by using their own algorithms—versions of the intuitive approach—which are often fallacious.

This first step—if indeed it is that—will no doubt need much improvement, but it may do something to fill the vacuum caused by the value-free bias in recent and contemporary intellectual culture.[7] While this is at most a first step, the arguments above show why one might think of it as the start of an assault on a last frontier. Indeed, it is hard to believe that another unanalyzed tool of the size and importance of evaluation can still be found in our kit of intellectual and scientific methods. In the years ahead, no doubt some will read that remark and smile.

The Epistemologic of Evaluation

Evaluation is to measurement as painting is to drawing, or as the talkies were to silent film. The incorporation of color or sound requires a more complex and difficult process—conceptually as well as technologically—which for most observers brings us a step nearer to providing a full picture of reality. Nevertheless, like any representation, photography included, a serious painting and a complex or sophisticated evaluation are more than mirrors as well as less; they carry with them a maker's mark. This is not to say that the representation is arbitrary, any more than a good scientific theory or a clever proof is arbitrary. To be distinctive is not to be arbitrary, in the epistemologically important sense, or else science could not be said to discover truths about the world. One may, if one wishes, describe this situation by saying that evaluation, or science, is subjective; but that way of putting it is certain to be misleading, especially with simple, straightforward evaluations. They are like passport photos: no signature, no great feat, not the whole story, but solid stuff. Much evaluation is like this. To identify a chemical compound as poisonous is to evaluate it; to describe a man on death row as a murderer is to evaluate him; to say that the Yugo is a very poor car is to evaluate it; but all of these are typically straightforward matters of fact, demonstrable by evidence and inference, not subjective in the sense in which that term is usually taken—that is, not matters of taste or preference *rather than* matters of fact. That dichotomy is useful enough, for many practical purposes, but it's a different one from the fact/value dichotomy.

In some domains, notably the aesthetic one, most of the value claims are essentially subjective—have no more weight to them than expressions of preference—although they are clad in the clothing of objective evaluation ("The best of the Margaret River white wines are now better than anything from Northern France").[8] But in others, including ethics, evaluative claims—suitably supported by evidence—can be matters of fact, or even true by definition ("He's a murderer," or "Murder is never justified").

In the aesthetic cases, it is crucial to bear in mind that what we loosely refer to as matters of preference are epistemologically double-faced. There are two quite different propositions involved. The evaluative claim—the claim actually made ("Oak Creek's 1990 chardonnay is absolutely outstanding")—lacks objectivity, and we say that it "is" (i.e., it boils down to) no more than an expression of taste. Of course, the speaker doesn't agree with this. He or she would point out that the claim made is much stronger (in one sense) than a mere expression of taste ("I like the Oak Creek 1990 chardonnay very much indeed"). The extra strength claimed refers to its supposed *interpersonal* validity. The claim is not, the speaker maintains, just about the speaker's preferences, but about the wine's merit, regardless of who likes it or doesn't like it. She wants to claim objectivity here that matches the objectivity in, say, an evaluative judgment about a student's answer to a question on a mathematics test. That's about the (merits of the) answer, not about the individual teacher's preferences. But this claim for objectivity fails because this teacher, and other well-trained teachers, are able *to demonstrate the truth of the answer*, not just exhibit their agreement with the first teacher.

One of the problems here is the ambiguity of the objective/subjective distinction. It can be used to refer to the *referent* of the claim (*subjective* means "referring to the claimant only"; *objective* means "referring to something external to the claimant") or to the *credentials* of the claim (where *subjective* means "unsubstantiated matter of opinion" and *objective* means "demonstrable according to validated standards"). In these terms, where agreement is not the end of the matter (since it may just show shared bias) we can't accept the view that the objectivity (demonstrable validity) of an evaluative claim about wines or modern painting can be established. But we need to be clear that the "weaker" version of the claim, the only one we'll accept, according to which it is "merely" a subjective claim—about the claimant rather than about the wine, for example—is in fact *an impregnable factual claim in its own right*.

Most of the discussion of this issue confuses the lesser interpersonal strength with lesser factual strength. But, while this kind of claim is subjective (lacking in interpersonal validity) if treated as an evaluation, that very subjectivity (purely personal reference) ensures that it is an objective matter of fact (interpersonally valid) about the person who believes it.

And therein lies the trick in getting some objectivity into the foundations of the evaluative claims. Instead of treating them as if they were these subjective assertions about the merit of wine, they are treated as—and combined with other—objective claims about the preferences of individuals and groups. Their status in that role is solid, and in that role they form the foundations of evaluations just as observations form the foundations of theoretical claims. Nor is this just an analogy, because evaluative language is in fact one case of theoretical language, values being theoretical constructs out of likings (and logic and related facts).

Let it be stressed once more that we are not using the evaluative claims in the aesthetic realm as if they had any validity—we have dismissed them as insupportable—but only their residue, the implied expression of preference, which is a matter of fact.[9]

So, reverting to our analogy about painting versus drawing, the way that we get the "color" into evaluation, the component that makes it more than measurement but still an objective process, is by bringing in the values of people. Somewhere in the ultimate logical unpacking of evaluative claims there will be some reference to likings and dislikings, just as references to observations turn up if you keep unpacking theoretical claims in the sciences. But the evaluative claim itself is no longer merely an expression or summing of those preferences, any more than a theoretical claim is a summing of observations. It is, rather, the result of an analysis of the relation of the preferences to certain properties of the items being evaluated and to a great deal of other relevant knowledge. The logic of evaluation is an analysis of those relations, just as the logic of explanation is an analysis of the relations between facts, logic and understanding.

Just as we never say that claims in special relativity theory are "congeries of observations" we can't say that claims about the virtues of a candidate or an apartment are the results of opinion surveys. The statements of preference become just some of many premises on which the evaluation is built, and it is the combination of the truth of these claims with the truth of all the other claims that come in (about the known history of the candidates, laws of nature and society, etc.) and with the validity of the often complex inferences involved, that provides the objectivity of the evaluative claim. When the doctor says to a pregnant patient that she should cut back on alcohol, the recommendation is an evaluative conclusion, and one of its premises is the belief that the patient cares about the welfare of the embryo. This "dependence on the preferences of the individual" doesn't make the remark into a mere summary of the patient's—or for that matter the doctor's—preferences. The doctor's view of what the patient's preferences are is well supported by evidence from the patient's several discussions with the doctor, and from the way she has made an effort to follow quite difficult regimes designed for the welfare of the neonate. So the preferences become part of the factual basis for the evaluative conclusion, but it is absurd to think that the conclusion has no more objective basis than an evaluative claim about the merit of chardonnays.

When we say that the Yugo is a poor car, we do so on the basis of well-supported beliefs that consumers in the automobile market place substantial value on reliability, comfort, ease of handling and control, availability of service, and safety. The evaluation does depend on these matters of preference, but its value—its objectivity and its informativeness—lies in the complex connection of these matters of preference to the results of thorough testing—a great deal of general knowledge about cars— via valid inference. We do not dismiss the evaluation because of its dependence on preference; we accept it because (when) the preference data and the road-testing is factually sound and because of the carefully wrought linkage to other facts and logic. The situation is no different in the sciences; what makes a good theory naturally depends on what we find valuable in theories. If we did not find simplicity and fertility and coherence valuable, what we call good theories would not be good. But that scarcely makes the truth and utility of thermodynamics or relativity theory a subjective matter.[10]

So, evaluation involves the *integration* of data about a number of *independent* aspects or dimensions of performance (that is, ones which can be independently measured or observed or inferred), with data about the relevant *field of inquiry* (e.g., automobiles, houses, people), with data about the related *needs and values* of clients, consumers, and society, and with any relevant *validated standards of merit or worth*. The "color" comes from bringing in values and standards of value, and from the integration of the multiple dimensions of merit, or worth. It should by now be clear why evaluation is one of the highest-level cognitive skills, and how far from the mark is the claim that evaluations are simply expressions of preference.

Of course, one must distinguish between wants and needs, between the valued and the valuable, in the usual ways but at a practical level—children may not want but do need a reasonably balanced diet, etc. It is almost always irrelevant to get into the philosophical issues about ultimate values. Just as science works very well, most of the time, without running into trouble about the ultimate nature of knowledge, so evaluation runs very well most of the time without trouble about the ultimate source of value. These ultimate questions are completely nonthreatening to ninety-five percent of science and evaluation, just as problems in the foundations of mathematics are nonthreatening to ninety-five percent of mathematics. Where the deep epistemological questions do lead to serious rethinking of science or mathematics, as with the uncertainty principle and relativity theory, or computer theorem proving, even then most of what is affected is metascience or metamathematics. The term *foundations* is a grandiose metaphor, and what it refers to could equally well, perhaps better, be called the "stratosphere" of the subject, the last level before moving into pure philosophy.

Thus performance on its independent dimensions—weight, speed, effects, costs, process, etc.—can usually be *measured*, but overall quality, merit, and worth can only be *evaluated*, and that process involves *synthesizing* or *integrating* the performance data, unconsciously (as when judging the quality of fruit at the market) or explicitly (in professional program evaluation). This integration step is obviously crucial to the whole process of evaluation and it is the source of much error and the focus of much of the rest of this article. It has no general algorithm—although cost-benefit analysis provides a locally useful one in the rare cases where all considerations have money equivalents—and this fact often leads scientists with a simpleminded notion of their own practice (and of their own instruction) to say that the evaluation process is subjective or arbitrary. If that were so, little science would be possible, since scientists are constantly evaluating explanations and hypotheses by integrating considerations of simplicity, fertility, consistency, generalizability, testability, etc. The process of synthesis can be rational or irrational, subjective or biased, just as the process of inductive inference can be sound or flawed. Nevertheless, both deserve to be made as explicit as possible, and then discussed and modeled, since doing so often leads to the discovery of assumptions and alternatives that need to be dealt with. Both are teachable to some degree, matters of inspiration to some degree, and evaluable to a high degree. Courts as well as scientific journals and philosophers of science are entirely accustomed to passing judgment on the objectivity, plausibility, and accuracy of inductive inferences, using the everyday testimony of ordinary witnesses and that of experts. Thus they are using evaluation to rate induction—the unspeakable in pursuit of the unmentionable. Of course, induction itself also *involves* evaluation, the evaluation of alternative explanations, no doubt one of the reasons why the later neopositivists were keen to keep it at bay.

The procedure or device we discuss here is an aid to systematic evaluation and assists in this process of integration and in managing the whole process. The preferred version was developed in the context of product evaluation, but applies easily and usefully to personnel, plan, policy, and program evaluation, among other types. Those familiar with explanation theory or dialogue analysis will see certain analogies with the interactive process of explanation or communication, in which one tries to estimate—or determine by trial and error or by questioning—the level of understanding of the audience, in order to get a map of the cognitive territory through which one has to guide the audience. Here, one tries to build on the set of accepted and acceptable client/societal/professional values in order to generate an answer to the evaluation problem, a bootstrap process.

Evaluation Algorithms and Heuristics

Even though there appears to be no general algorithm for combining the multiple dimensions of relevant considerations into an evaluative conclusion, we might still be able to come up with a heuristic that is nearly an algorithm. The cost-benefit algorithm fails because one can rarely convert all benefits and costs into money terms; if one could, then one would have reduced the multidimensional evaluation problem to a unidimensional measurement problem. But there is an intuitive and widely used algorithm which avoids that conversion problem by going straight to the common currency of utility, and is widely used in making major buying or career decisions. We'll call this the "numerical weight and sum" approach (the "numerical" approach, for short). Unfortunately, it also involves some assumptions which are rarely true. In its place we'll suggest a "qualitative grading and comparison" approach (the "qualitative" approach, for short). None of the discussion here will be highly technical, apart from a quick listing of the technical problems with the numerical approach.[11]

The reason why one needs some kind of tool—it can also be called a system, model, method, or approach—for these complex evaluations is partly because of their complexity and partly because of the fact that we get very little practice in doing them. When there is a very large number of relevant features to juggle in one's head, one can only acquire a worthwhile level of skill by doing a very large number of training examples under supervision. Most of us make few of these major decisions (house purchase or lease, car purchase, career or graduate school choice, personnel selection), and usually with nonexpert supervision— you are in fact usually up against someone, the sales person, who is much more experienced than you and motivated to hinder you. For such decisions, the list of valuable features often runs from 40 to as many as 120 items. It is a major attraction of the numerical model that it will handle very large numbers of criteria just as well as small numbers; and the same is true of the substitute we'll propose, the qualitative model. Of course, so will the impressionistic approach; it just handles them inconsistently.

The first of these models is at the formal end of the methodological spectrum and it is sometimes said to provide a—or the—paradigm of scientific evaluation in circles where that is not a contradiction in terms. For example, it is built into the five "decision support" programs currently available on microcomputers. Its faults lie in the very quantifying which gives it the appearance of science, because it is based on the assumption that values can be given a more precise kind of measurement than is realistic. One might suppose that the worst penalty for such an assumption is a result which is only approximately true, but the actual penalty is far more serious: the procedure will often lead to a completely wrong answer.

The qualitative approach, like the numerical one, involves—as any such approach must—giving differential importance to the criteria of merit (e.g., desirable features and low cost)—but it only allocates *qualitative* weights and only *three categories* of these, which increases the reliability with which distinctions can be made. And it has a procedure for combining the weights with the performance ratings and for aggregating the results—as any such procedure must—but it does so without arithmetic beyond counting. Most versions of the numerical model assume interval scales of merit,[12] the linear distribution of utility across performance scales,[13] the legitimacy of multiplying weights by performance ratings (which assumes a ratio scale), and the reliability of ratings of utility on scales with five or more points. Technically speaking, using the analogy with statistical method, the qualitative approach is a move towards nonparametric evaluation procedures, that is, toward procedures which are more robust in the sense of depending on fewer assumptions about the way the world works and how people cope with it.

The other distinctive feature of the qualitative approach suggested here is its stepwise functioning; it does not pretend to give reliable answers from one pass—although in very fortunate cases that may occur—and involves a process here called "refocusing" which may occur many times before a solid result emerges. The qualitative approach is in fact a process of successive clarification rather than successive approximation, since one may discard early conclusions in the process of refocusing.

It was mentioned earlier that it is possible to implement the qualitative evaluation process proposed here on a microcomputer. With complex evaluations, the use of a computer provides a very large improvement indeed. As mentioned, there are a number of programs available for doing this. However, since they all involve erroneous methodology—along with some nice features—that approach is undesirable. One can instead use any of three applications programs in their state-of-the-art versions—a spreadsheet, a table-maker, or an outliner which most computer users already possess.[14]

The example in this chapter is from product evaluation for several reasons. First, we are all familiar with the *practice* of product evaluation and hence it provides understandable examples. Second, the product evaluation field has received much less attention from evaluation theorists than has program evaluation, and we still have something to learn from it about the general logic of evaluation. Third, product evaluation is one of the most influential fields of evaluation in terms of the size and range of its impact on the quality of life of a large number of people, and it needs improvement.[15] Finally, a focus on product evaluation keeps us away from a number of radical disagreements about the nature of program and personnel evaluation.[16]

The fact that the qualitative model has a wide range of applications also makes it useful in providing a language for discussing certain types of methodological difficulties in whatever field of evaluation they arise, that is, it facilitates interfield suggestions and comparisons.

The proposed approach is presented in two versions. The partial version, which is easy to explain, still involves one assumption about additivity which is not always true. But it is often near enough to being true, and it is clearly better to make just this one assumption rather than add to it the three or four others involved in the numerical alternatives. The full version of the qualitative approach is somewhat more complex, and here we'll just indicate how it works in broad outline. The partial qualitative approach is less complex to apply than one common version of the numerical approach, albeit slightly more complex than one other. The full qualitative approach is about as complex to use as the most complex numerical method. It also involves more reconsideration cycles, but they are essential to making it more accurate. Of course, any analytic approach to evaluating complex technology (or programs, personnel, etc.) will take a substantial amount of time simply because many facts have to be ascertained, criteria identified and weighed, and the two combined.

It is possible that the most influential reason for the widespread use of an impressionistic approach is simply that it's fast, much faster than the ones considered here. However, when a considerable amount of your money—or the taxpayer's money—is at stake, the time spent on a qualitative evaluation usually provides extremely handsome returns. Moreover, it has other potential benefits besides cost savings, such as improved quality of explanation and justification to others, and reduced stress over the decision.

Product Evaluation Methodology

Product evaluation has some distinctive features. In the first place—unlike the usual situation with program or curriculum evaluation—it's often done by individuals for their own benefit, and is often highly determined by their particular needs. Of course, that doesn't mean that it's subjective in the derogatory sense of the term, for the reasons given above, but the possibility is increased of personal bias triumphing over reason. With this double personal flavor, it's easy to see why individuals often think that evaluating things for their own use or purchase is something which only they are in a position to do. The fact of the matter, however, is that there is often such an entity as "the best product for Jones, with his present needs, and with his present resources," although Jones does not know enough, or does not process his information well enough, to identify it correctly.

In the second place, it is usual for product evaluations to be mainly comparative, since the principal need they service is the need to buy/rent/lease the best available product. But they must also help you to answer an absolute question: is this product worth to you what it will cost? This double requirement has several consequences for the design of the evaluation. In the jargon, both ranking and grading are required.

The Numerical Weight and Sum Approach

This approach can conveniently be broken up into nine steps.

1. Identifying the considerations which are valued or valuable (here called the *"criteria of merit"*: each of these identifies a *dimension of performance* on which measurement occurs).

2. Expressing their importance by weighting them, for example, on a 1–5 or 1–10 or 1–100 *weighting scale.*

3. Identifying the *candidates.*

4. Determining the *raw performance* of each candidate on each of the criteria (or using indicators to infer this).

5. Discovering *side-effects*, that is, valued or disvalued performance on dimensions not part of the standard dimensions of performance for this kind of product.

6. Converting the raw performance into some kind of *standardized performance scale*, for example, a 1–10 or 1–100 scale (this step is often called "normalizing" the data), or into a ranking (first, second, etc., of the candidates).

7. Calculating the product of the weighting by the normalized performance score, for each candidate on each dimension (the *performance values*).

8. Summing these products for each candidate.

9. Identifying the candidate with the largest score, which is then declared to be the winner.

Errors in any analytic approach like this are possible at every step, for example: missing some relevant criteria, candidates,[17] or side-effects; defining criteria that overlap[18] or are circular[19]; or making measurement errors.[20] The errors that are methodologically distinctive of the numerical approach come in where measurement or decision-making procedures are introduced—at steps 2, 6, and 9. The other steps are acceptable or simply arithmetical, although 4 involves unnecessary work.

In what follows, we begin with a brief analysis of the errors in the standard numerical approach and in an attractive improvement on it which is sometimes used by *Consumer Reports*, among others. In the process, we begin to work out how to fix these errors through modifications of the procedure. In the following section, on the proposed qualitative alternative, there is some amplification of the acceptable steps common to both approaches, some attention to "working smart" considerations (e.g., whittling the field down before doing unnecessary research), and the provision of replacement procedures for the three incorrect ones.

The most serious *distinctive* source of error in the numerical approach is that the selection of weighting or performance scales does not have, and cannot be given, the significance that the user thinks it has. This is because its de facto importance is heavily controlled by a third variable—the number of criteria involved. Suppose you give weights from the range 1–5 and scale the performance on a 1–10 scale. Then your most important criterion can only contribute a maximum of 50 points to a candidate's total score. But that amount can be completely swamped by an accumulation of only five minor considerations, each weighted only 1 but scoring 10 on the performance scale for a total of 10. Typically, that is a result you had no intention of allowing. There are usually some "most important" criteria which you meant not to be offset by *any* number of minor features. For example, "back seat comfort for three adults" may be far more important for your purposes than an extensive range of auxiliary instruments, fog lights, and other doodads, even though each of them is worth something to you. Very well, you say, I chose the numbers wrong. Let's give the top weights a rating of 20, and restrict the performance range to 5 instead of 10. But now, if it turns out that there are very few criteria, this will only get you out of the frying pan into the fire.

One problem is that you can't tell how many criteria you will finish up with in advance of an evaluation. So, if you use the numerical approach, you will have to adjust the weights and performance ranges after you have settled on a number of criteria. This is a bad arrangement since it precludes the acquisition of skill through practice with a standard set of ranges. Moreover, serious evaluation involves many iterations and reconceptualizations of the analytic process—we call this "refocusing"—and you will find that just when you thought the number of criteria was settled you will have to start a round of revisions of that number. But that's not the worst news.

The real problem is that there's no rule for selecting the weighting and performance ranges so as to get the effect you want, even when it is clear how many criteria are involved. This means that this free-form version of the numerical approach is fatally flawed. It has other problems, too. The allocation of the standardized performance scores tends to cause trouble; nearly all users want to allocate according to the utility of that performance level, but others do it, or recommend doing it, as a purely numerical transformation. If you do the latter, the weights will give the wrong result for most scores, since they can only (be guaranteed to) reflect the value of the performance at one point.

Now, Consumers Union appears to use an interesting twist on the interactive weighting approach, which avoids some of its problems. (Since they do not make their procedures explicit, what follows is an inference from the traces they leave.) They allocate a fixed total number of points for the weights, specifically 100 points (*Consumer Reports*, September, 1989, p. 566). In an evaluation of laptop computers they might allot 25 points for the readability of the display, 20 points for speed, 20 points for portability, etc. If they add or subtract criteria, they then have to alter the weights of the others. This at least partially avoids the problem of the dilution of weights by the number of criteria; you get to redo all weighting when you add criteria. However, the impression given by their occasional remarks is that they do not think refocusing is a major activity, which suggests excessive preordination of criteria and weights. It's not clear whether they then use these weights to multiply standardized scores, or directly award some part of them to each candidate (the preferable approach). The main problem is how they could justify the allocation of these very large weights. If large weights are to any degree arbitrary, the differences between them will wipe out major differences in performance values.

Various cues suggest that Consumers Union may base their weights on a general sense of what the market wants, which might or might not be based on surveys and/or needs assessments. Unfortunately, the survey designers and the market tend to lack sophistication in this area, particularly in one crucial respect. They commonly fail to distinguish two completely different senses in which a criterion may be important or very important. We can see this by contrasting the importance of two considerations which come into the evaluation of laptop computers: the readability of the screen and access to a particular operating system (and hence to the software written for that operating system). In the first sense of *very important,* which applies to readability, a criterion is important if there is some level of performance on its dimension which is *absolutely essential* for the product to be of any use at all. (If the screen isn't readable without serious eyestrain, the machine is an expensive paperweight.) In the second sense, we might consider the situation of a Macintosh enthusiast, who would regard it as a marvelous advantage (i.e., as very important) if a machine runs Mac software, but who needs a portable badly enough to put up with other operating systems. This evaluator will award many points to a Mac-compatible portable, but will not eliminate one which lacks it. Now, simply giving a large weighting to readability will not cover both these situations: *no* weighting will represent both these conceptions of *very important,* since they are contradictory. One of them means "essential, a necessary condition" and the other means "not essential, but nothing besides the essential criteria is (significantly) more important."

The solution is to *split the performance range.* A certain level of readability is rated as essential; readability beyond that is rated important (or very important or of minor importance, depending on how you or users in general feel about it). Note that this approach, which is built into the qualitative model, does not automatically result in very high weightings of very important features that appear on the list of criteria. Instead, an essential feature (or level of performance) works differently from other weightings. It acts as a filter on the candidates, precluding the listing of those which lack it. It cannot be traded off against other features, so there's no point in listing the candidate for analysis of the other features. So one normally sees very little of the operation of essential features. Either they prevented the listing of a candidate, or, if it was listed before we discovered the missing necessity, they act as a stopper on further evaluation when we discover that absence. An essential feature can be thought of as one whose absence is weighted minus infinity.

Of course, *readability* may still appear on the listing of criteria of merit; but it is "surplus" readability, readability above the minimum level, and it will be given whatever weight seems appropriate to the consumer(s) for whom the evaluation is being done.

That takes care of one error in the revised numerical approach, the error of high weighting to cover essential features.

But that is not the only problem with the "distribute 100 points across all weightings" approach.

The Consumers Union approach is also virtually unworkable when dealing with complex products, because you can't *both* allocate some weight to each of a hundred-plus criteria—about the appropriate number for the laptops—*and* allocate strongly different numbers of points to the more important ones. If you try to solve this problem by moving to a total of 1000 points for weights, instead of 100, you once more face the problem of dilution/exaggeration by the number of criteria (relevant considerations). Technically, one might get around this problem by using a hierarchical procedure, and restrict the distribution of the 100 points to high-level criteria—here called dimensions. But that procedure raises the unsolved problem of justifying the allocation of weights to dimensions without looking at the number of indicators under each dimension; and if one does know them in advance, there is the problem of allocating weights to them. It's not obvious that they should be constrained to the sum allocated to the higher-order dimension—the reverse arrangement may be better. The general problem that looms larger and larger with this approach, as one begins to worry away at the loose ends, is the essential arbitrariness of the numerical allocations to weights. This often goes much further astray than in *Consumer Reports*, as one can see by looking at the procedure used for the respected evaluations in *InfoWorld*.

One might think that the details of the process do not matter for comparative evaluation since one is using the same procedure for all the applicants. There are two problems with that view: first, one always has at least one absolute evaluation to deal with (Is this worth getting at all?), and second, the kind of flaw in the evaluation procedure we've been talking about *skews* the results, it does not just add a constant value to each of them. For example, it may make the race into a race to accumulate the largest number of minor virtues. So the candidate with the best score will not really be the best candidate.

The Qualitative Approach

Preview. The trick in this approach is to work out a process that will be systematic without committing itself to inappropriate and hence error-producing quantification. The first step is to group the criteria into three operating categories of increasing importance plus two limiting categories. That many distinctions we can make with good reliability. Then we constrain the performance range in the same way, recognizing only differences that are of significance to the user. The way we do this avoids the necessity for multiplication of the scores by the weights. This leaves us with each candidate's achievements in three ranked categories of value, and we make no further assumptions about the relative magnitude of these values. We directly compare each of these packages of achievements with each other, and can give guidelines which identify a winner in most cases. In the remaining cases, we can still reduce the number of serious contestants substantially and then compare contestants in pairs to find a winner.

The discussion of the qualitative approach is formulated as an abbreviated how-to manual with annotations of interest to the logician. It is thus meant to provide a basis for a teaching module as well as some discussion of the logical details. The hope is that this will make it easier for the reader to judge the claims that practical evaluation is teachable, useful, and a skill that is likely to be significantly improved by good teaching. The reader may well be struck by the complexity of the process. A little practice reduces this impression somewhat, but the complexity has nothing to do with the qualitative approach. Most of the same complexities are involved in any serious application of the numerical approach; but people rarely do it seriously, even when the matter at stake is serious. (This is reminiscent of the infrequency with which serious argument analysis is done.) Bold face type indicates some of the principal innovations and differences from the previously described versions of the numerical approach.[21]

Identifying Criteria of Merit. Start with a list of every (available) feature/ability/quality that seems at all useful—the *criteria of merit.* For a beginner, it is best to start by just putting these down in the language that seems natural to describe them—"light weight," "high speed," etc. A sophisticated consumer can be much more specific immediately, but the beginner, too, must eventually become more precise, even in the first evaluation task undertaken, because of the need to say exactly what performance is going to be measured, and because of the need for different weighting of different parts of the range of some criteria. Still, the general criteria make a good starting point, and make it easier to check whether any have been omitted.

In many fields, there are standardized sets of criteria, usually at this very general level, which provide a start for a list and ensure that one doesn't overlook important dimensions. For example, in the evaluation of computer products the following list of ten major dimensions is useful (dimensions are paired for mnemonic reasons): cost and availability, size and weight, ease of learning and ease of use, speed and power, safety and support. This list works very well with a wide range of products. In the evaluation of programs, the ten-point "Key Evaluation Checklist" can be useful[22]; in the evaluation of teachers and other personnel, one can often use a list of duties.[23]

Enter these criteria down the left-hand column of a spreadsheet—paper or electronic. Since you will be continually revising the list and the rest of the spreadsheet, it is much better to **use an advanced electronic spreadsheet** with reasonable text capabilities, like Excel (IBM v. 1 or Macintosh v. 2.2). One can also use, with some trade-offs, a sophisticated outliner like MORE or MindWrite, a database with calculated fields, a dedicated table maker, or—although it's not nearly as good—a word processor with an integrated outliner or one with some table-making capability (Word 4.0 for the Macintosh, for example). The first two are very much better than pen and paper; even the last two are considerably better.[24]

Some of these criteria will be rather general in nature (e.g., speed), but others will be highly specific (e.g., "There is a carrying handle on the computer itself, not just on the carrying case"). Use the Drag or Cut and Paste functions on the computer program to group the more specific ones under an appropriate general heading, if you have one; and if not, create a general concept to fit any related group. For example, group the item about the carrying handle, along with weight and shape, under "Portability" which will finish up under "Ease of Use" if you are using the list mentioned earlier. Under "Speed" we'll put some more specific descriptions, to which we will attach *different* weights, as described in the next section. For criteria which do not fit under a general heading, create a "miscellaneous" heading. If operating with both general and specific headings, the more general headings are often referred to as "dimensions" and the more specific ones as "features." All are covered by the term *criteria.*

A good deal of work and logical acumen is involved in sorting out sets of criteria for particular evaluation tasks. One still sees serious errors, for example, the error of including "value for money" as one of the criteria of merit (as *InfoWorld* does). Low cost is a merit, but value for money is the ratio of cost to merit; it's circular to rate it before you have the overall rating on merit. It must be listed after the overall merit rating.

Weighting the Criteria and Setting Standards. In the first column following each feature you value, put an indication of its importance to you (the weighting). **Do not use numerical weights.** Doing so guarantees frequent errors. We suggest using an ordered but not an interval scale of weights. A well-known example is the Mohs hardness scale, but we avoid the use of numbers, since they strongly suggest that the intervals are constant, and ten is too many for consistent subjective estimation of value. One possibility is the following sequence of symbols: 0 (zero for "of no significant value"); + (a plus, signifying just-significant value, i.e., a minor consideration); # (called a "double plus" because that's one way to write it, and that name is less ambiguous when spoken than the other names for the sign[25]; this signifies substantial or considerable value); * (a star for extremely or outstandingly valuable); ** (double star, for essential, a necessary condition for consideration). There are several points to keep in mind as you allocate weights to criteria. As you do so, group them so that all the starred items are at the top of the list, the plusses at the bottom, and the double plusses in the middle. (This is not absolutely essential. It requires too-frequent rewrites with hard copy, but is extremely easy with the outliner and not hard with the spreadsheet.) The next few pages give some helpful advice for setting up your evaluation process.

Be extremely careful about defining any criterion as essential. This weight functions quite differently from the others; it is simply a filter on candidates which eliminates a number of them from the starting lineup. This means that its absence is weighted as minus infinity. (The sign we use for violating an essential requirement is 00, which is mnemonically similar to the sign for infinity.) If you rule out something you should have kept in, the cost is very high and your evaluation process will never turn up the error; if you keep in something you should have left out, that will just involve you in a little more time on the project than you would have spent ideally—the error will eventually surface.[26] Still, don't waste time with demonstrably impossible candidates: just set the Essential requirement safely high. For example, "under 14 pounds" for a laptop computer you intend to travel with extensively—by contrast with one which you want to be able to take home or away for the weekend—is extremely conservative. (After years of using a variety of portables, most experienced journalists would set their requirement at "under 7 pounds" and the hottest part of the market centers on machines which are under 2 kilograms.) When we insert our weights on a kilogram scale, the area "over 14 pounds" will therefore be rated as 00.

Commentators frequently point out, quite rightly, that new equipment leads to new uses and new distribution of effort by each worker, often in subtle (though cumulatively large) and frequently in unexpected ways. Of course, you expect the speed with which work is done to change—that's usually the reason for computerizing. But equally important is the way that work is done, the way that different people turn out to be able to cope with it or not cope with it, and hence the way work should be allocated.[27] Since the quality and the enjoyability of the work changes—up and down—the kind of work you take on should and usually will change. So do not base your list of desirable features or the associated weights too tightly on your present practices. Read about the experiences of users of the product you are considering, as a way to look for opportunities to change and extend current practices, and even if you don't see those opportunities at first, allow room for them to emerge. As you learn more about each product, from reviews and trials, and from speculative articles, you will alter your view of the existence and relative importance of features for your own use. This practice helps to uncover side effects. You will find, as you delve more deeply into the literature and experiences of yourself and others, that a number of these will surface, positive and negative. Add them to the list of criteria; they must be counted even if unintended or unexpected or undesired.

In general, this consideration means you should go for a more capable product rather than a minimally adequate one, since it is quite likely that you will find useful ways to employ the extra power. This approach provides insurance against outgrowing a product on its own turf and allows for incidental but sometimes large payoffs. A good portable computer may be useful as backup when your desktop computer has to go in for repairs; but it can only do that if it's comparable with respect to the power on which you normally depend.

You should in general **try to avoid negative weights** by defining the converse feature as a positive. If there are times when that seems too artificial, you can use a minus sign in combination with one of the previous weights and subtract it at the last stage.

Doing so somewhat increases the chances of error, especially with intermediate weights. The one exception is for essential weighting. When labeling the bands in a performance range, it's usually more convenient to label the band beyond which (or below which) the item is useless to you by employing a symbol for *the absence of* an essential characteristic and we use the double zero for this (the absence of a double star criterion).

As we've worked on clarifying a sensible procedure, it's become clear that we're moving towards a general practical recommendation. **Do not struggle to cover major features such as cost or speed with one weighting, that is with one line on the chart.** It is much better to chop the scale up into several ranges, each of different value to you. This range-splitting or banding helps to clarify your values profile. For example, under the general heading of the Cost dimension, there is always an essential item, "costs less than $NN", where NN (No-No) is the most you can possibly spend—and that includes getting a loan.[28] We translate this criterion into a minus infinity (00) weight for "costs more than NN." Now ask yourself how much of a savings—compared with NN—is just-significantly important to you. You might answer that any savings would be valuable to you: if so, mark a plus for a range beginning at NN and going down, perhaps to half of NN—which is the point where you feel the savings becomes substantially important to you, so there's a double plus on the range from there to zero or some other point at which the savings earn a star.

In all this, you are setting up standards for value to you in the context of this purchase, which you will have to apply consistently to all criteria. That is, you are asking yourself how important money is, by comparison with the other features you are about to rate. Of course, it's just a first approximation: you'll go back and adjust the weightings for consistency as you allocate weights to more and more criteria. (The process is essentially the same if you're dealing with "value to the average citizen" or "value for a sports car enthusiast," etc., except for the problem of generating and amalgamating appropriate survey data.)

Another consumer might be so keen to get a portable, or so affluent, that he would: start with a much higher cutoff point (say, twice the value of NN); not award any plus until the cost drops to *far below* that point (instead of immediately, as you did), because he does not want relatively minor savings to offset even minor features; and award no double plusses or stars on this scale at all, for the same kind of reason. Thus, splitting the range clarifies your values, which is essential for consistency.

Repeat this process for each of the criteria, thereby establishing a price list expressed in terms of the utility to you. It is convenient to enter this price list in the left column, the Criteria column, in the rows following the one with the main heading for the criterion. For example, with Cost, "over $8,000" might be the first entry, with a weight of 00 (missing an essential characteristic, so minus infinity), the next row might list "$4000–$6000," credited with a +, and so on. Note that there can be an interval between the reject point (where an essential criterion is missing) and the beginning of the first band, but usually not between the main bands. Performances in that first interval receive a zero. The result looks like this:

COST	
Over $8,000	00
$6,000–$8,000	0
$4,000–$6,000	+
$0–$4,000	#

Using an outliner, one can collapse detailed subheadings so that one can more clearly see the main dimensions; with a spreadsheet, one can put the table into a cell-linked note which can be called up with a single keystroke.

It is not easy to give precise definitions of some criteria. On occasion, it is easier to draw a diagram to illustrate the form of a feature which is to be given a certain weight, perhaps the desired floor plan of an apartment. These can be imported into the better versions of the applications software we are discussing, for example, into the cells of a spreadsheet or table maker, where they may, if desired, be hidden until called up.

People sometimes exclaim that this process of awarding similar utility values to entirely different features is requesting them to compare apples and oranges. Indeed it is, and that exact comparison is made by millions shoppers every day, on the grounds of the common currencies of quality, nutritional need, preferences, price, etc. The trick is to do this as well as is possible, since there is no alternative to doing it (the scientist does it all the time, in judging hypotheses, experimental designs, etc). The qualitative approach is a help toward doing it consistently, and toward doing it in cases that are more complex than one can handle intuitively. Most users feel that the three functioning weights (*, #, and +, with the 0 and 00 defining the outer edges) are about all they can handle with any consistency *across criteria*, but you can use one degree of further refinement, to be described shortly.

The process of defining and differentially weighting criteria is interactive with the process of learning more about the field; it is in fact the process of setting practical standards. The first consequence of this is that it will take you a while to work out what standards are appropriate in weighting the dimensions. It's possible to use standards which are only related to your *ideals*—the perfect reading program would teach students to read in a microsecond, no doubt. However, using these will cut down the discriminating power of your analysis, to no purpose. You must combine realism with idealism. It is a fallacy to score the best available as valuable: your candidates may not reach that threshold of value. But it is equally fallacious to evaluate compact sedans as if they are luxury sedans. *You need to set standards that relate to the choice you are trying to assist.* This isn't simply a process of lowering standards. The appropriate standards for the compact sedan will be *higher* in many respects—fuel consumption, turning circle, lower first cost and running/repair costs, for example—while lower in others—road and engine noise levels, for example.

The second consequence of the way you "learn on the job" in every serious evaluation concerns the phenomenon of shifting perspectives. You will frequently find yourself redefining the criteria or resetting their weights in the light of new reviews, or discussions with users, or further thought and analysis. A good example is running into some unanticipated use of a product, or problem with a feature. The possibility of using the portable computer as a back-up when the power goes out may lead you to increase your weighting of the battery-operated mode (which not all of them possess). The discovery that the most readable screens drain the battery seriously may lead you to reduce a weighting of essential for a certain level of readability. This is **a recurrent aspect of the product evaluation process which needs to be explicitly encouraged rather than treated as a human or procedural weakness.** It is here called "refocusing" and it's most easily explained in terms of the paper and pencil approach.

Refocusing is not the same as iterating, although the evaluation process is also iterative—that is, it requires multiple passes through a sequence of steps. Iteration is necessary because work on one point uncovers information that requires reformulating or reweighing of other points. Refocusing emerges from the iterations when, after you have done more research or reading to clarify points which emerge as crucial—or to learn about candidates with which you were not very familiar—you reach stage where it is no longer *appropriate* to try tidying up your original analysis. This is not because there isn't room to fit in all the extra notes (a situation which frequently occurs with hardcopy), but because you come to realize that the whole focus is no longer appropriate. This usually means that what appeared to be the most promising candidates prove unsatisfactory, and usually that's because you find you have to drop or add criteria, or redefine or reweight those you have. In the early stages, this often occurs because your initial ideals turn out to be inappropriate for one reason or another.

While it sounds as if you could do this with substantial help of an eraser, you will find that's not really practicable. Moreover, you shouldn't do it. It is important that you save the complete version and start a new one. You will frequently find yourself very glad that you did save the earlier versions, because as the focus shifts again, you will often need parts of the earlier analysis, details on a candidate which you wrongly rejected, for example. It is not unusual to find that you have to refocus as many as six times with an expensive and complex item like a microcomputer, or a word processing or CAD program.

If you are using an electronic spreadsheet or word processor it's very easy for you to just keep modifying the one version. That's an advantage as long as you can reconcile it with keeping earlier versions. File the current version of the document under a different name every fifteen to twenty-five minutes (just add a different edition number to the file name). That process leaves an audit trail which is worth having for the reason mentioned, as well as protecting you against power or machine failure. Incidentally, this is one aspect of the process where the outliner is superior to the other applications programs (spreadsheet or table maker), since it makes it possible to hide those features that are becoming less important—without losing them for later resuscitation.

Some weights interact with or are incestuously related to other factors and should only be issued a single award; otherwise you get into double-weighting of some properties, with attendant misrepresentations. For example, short battery life in a portable computer is not fatal as long as it is possible to exchange battery packs easily (without loss of data), and the packs are not too heavy or bulky. Several machines meet this requirement, so it's not unrealistic. The best way to handle these problems is by redefining the criteria, for example, by calling your category "extended battery life" and modifying the performance figure on weight to include the weight of extra battery packs.

When you have finished weighting the criteria, scan back through them for consistency, one category of weights at a time. Ask yourself whether each plus or double plus performance means about the same to you in terms of importance. You should be able to achieve this; but if you cannot, consider an adjustment of the cutting scores (the width of your performance bands) to restore parity. If there still remain cases where some criteria strike you as definitely *more* important than others in the same category—that is, if you're chafing at the restriction to three levels of importance—put a circle around them or use some other convenient mark; we'll deal with them later.

Identifying the Candidates. We've anticipated this step in some of the discussion above, but the time has come to make it explicit. List every candidate that seems even remotely possible. Enter the name or model number as a heading for a column. If it's convenient, keep the most promising ones to the left. You would typically get this list from a study of advertisements in the local papers and the national specialist magazines or professional journals, and also from suggestions by friends, salesclerks, anyone. Be very careful about dropping an item off this list just because a knowledgeable friend doesn't like it, or because you happen to see one or two critical reviews.[29] Best to keep it on until you are absolutely sure it isn't the best compromise for you. By all means demote it on the list, so that you first look hardest at the initially most promising options. That may save you time, if you strike gold early.

The candidates you choose affect your criteria. If you know a *good deal* about the field, it may be better to begin by listing candidates first, and then generating the features list from reviews of them as well as from your own wishes. Those with less knowledge of the field, however, do best to use the order given in this chapter, because they certainly begin with an idea of what characteristics they want, even if they specify them informally and have to give up on some later.

Fast Filtering. A quick check on the situation with respect to essential parameters such as cost ("under NN") and availability (and perhaps weight or screen readability) will often **narrow the field considerably at this point.** These figures are relatively easy to get from a group review or by making one or two phone calls, and the misrepresentations you will sometimes get on the phone typically produce only false positives. Months after products have been announced and reviewed, with the reviewer indicating that they are available at a certain price, you will often find that the product is not available at all (the NEC UltraLite was a good example of this), or that prices have changed radically.

In general, it is good strategy to check *all* the essential features before doing any of the others, since checking one essential characteristic has the potential to save checking all the others. This is a good time to reconsider when you really want to insist on the ** weighting. Frequently, when a beginner finds that a candidate is about to be excluded for missing one check-point, he or she decides that it makes more sense to redefine the width of the band for the ** weighting or modify it to an * weight. If the feature's absence is absolutely, positively, and irremediably fatal, you'll want to drop that column from the spreadsheet, or stop filling in the cells, but before you drop any columns, check the essential criteria for all candidates, put in the 00s where appropriate, and Save the present version of the spreadsheet. Now trash the columns of the candidates that have have a 00 somewhere. Those about which you are not absolutely sure should be folded out of sight using the Hide command on a spreadsheet, or by reducing their rank in the outliner so that they will be invisible until resurrected.

Performance Data and Normalization. In the intersection of each row, representing a criterion, and the columns of the remaining candidates—the cells of the matrix[30]—you now record the actual performance of the candidate in that respect, to the extent that these facts are readily available. For example you might record that the clock speed of a computer is 4.77MHz or 33MHz.[31] Now, that's the performance expressed as raw data, and what you are constructing with it is the first of a series of matrices—the performance matrix. You need that as a reference and will come back to it many times.

However, looking ahead to what you want to do with it, you can see that to make further progress towards an evaluation you will have to transform the raw data into some standard form, because otherwise the results won't be comparable between different criteria. You'd end up adding MHz to kilograms, which doesn't make sense. Moreover, multiplying different quantities by the criterion weight—which you want to bring in somehow—will mean that things measured in small units will come in with a much bigger number than those whose measurement is only a fraction of a unit. By accident or by choosing units, you could juggle the numbers to make different candidates into the winner. So it's necessary to standardize or normalize the figures in some way, which will give you the Normalized (performance) Matrix. The usual options are to put in a *score* (e.g., out of 10 or 100), a *rating* (e.g., a grade from A–F), or a *ranking* (from 1 to N, if there are N candidates).

Commonsense practice goes about this far, and is incorporated in procedures used by consumer publications such as *Software Digest* when they allocate overall scores or grades. Unfortunately, there are problems about each of these alternatives, and valid solutions to these problems are not generally available. If a *score* is awarded, there is the question of what the endpoints of the scale are to represent. Does the best product on the market get the 10 or 100, or should that score be reserved for an ideal or perfect performance? How should one distribute the numbers across the performance scale? Then there are the problems about what you are going to do with the scores when combination times comes around. It's not valid to say that a score of

4 out of 5 on a starred criterion results in four stars which you can equate with the four stars acquired on two other starred scales where the candidate scored 2 for performance. Then there are good reasons for bringing in sigma units (multiples of the standard deviation), to reward outstanding performance appropriately—but the whole process is then getting rather out of hand for the individual. And, at the end, one still has no answer to the absolute question, whether the product is worth what it will cost.

If one uses *ratings* (e.g., the grades A–F), an analogous version of the scale-anchoring problem arises: how to define each of the grades—relative to the market ranking or relative to some ideal. And there is a tradition of combining grades by using the translation to numbers (A = 4, B = 3, etc.), which must be avoided here. If one uses *rankings*, the problem is that very small differences in performance may result in very large differences in ranking, which is an inappropriate way to reflect utility to you; and the problem of the absolute question remains.[32] Any use of numbers is fraught with the risk of treating them as if they justify arithmetic calculations on them, which is invalid for the same reason here as with the weights. So, **do not use numbers for the normalized performance ratings.** Any use of something other than numbers, grades, for example raises the question of how to combine them, given that you should not convert them to numbers, as we do with academic grades.[33]

Thinking about these problems forces one back to looking more closely at the function of the analysis, and suggests the following procedure, which seems more soundly based and also easier to implement, a fortunate combination if it performs as claimed.

Performance Valuation. We have screened out all candidates which fail any criterion weighted as essential; the task is now to deal with the remaining criteria and their weights. What we are eventually trying to do here is to sum, for each remaining candidate, the utility to you of its multiplicity of performances and features. The traditional "numerical weight and sum" approach is just one way of doing this, and, as we have seen, it gets into some severe technical difficulties. The qualitative approach shortcuts those problems. Instead of adding a normalized score to the raw data in each cell in the performance chart and then multiplying it by the weight, you **directly insert an estimate of the utility to you of that particular performance.** We can call this the "valuation" or "valuing" of that performance. If you have by now banded the criteria and defined the value of these bands to you, this step merely involves reading the appropriate symbol off the appropriate performance interval in the left column and inserting it in the column next to the raw performance figure. If you haven't made this move toward precise definition, another good reason for doing it has now emerged. Precise definition is also very important in order to maintain consistency across candidates. (Remember that you may well be filling in these columns over a period of time, as data turns up.)

For example, if you value at the star level a machine's ability to run WordPerfect 5.1 at a reasonable speed (perhaps because it would be a tremendous advantage not to have to learn another program and to be able to transfer files to your desktop machine), then the implementation of this in a particular case can be awarded a star, or just a double plus (if it runs at somewhat less than the ideal speed), a plus (well under ideal speed but not a constant nuisance) or a zero for only marginally useable. Anything more irritating than that would get the double zero of a minus infinity and be ruled out. Similarly, something you value at the double-plus level might be rated a double plus for full implementation, a plus for less than that, or a zero for just usable. With items weighted as a plus, the only choice is a plus or a zero, but the plus may be accented if you feel you can justify the distinction.

The result from this process, whether treated as a separate matrix or superimposed on the performance matrix, is what we can call the "valuations matrix," and it replaces two steps in the usual numerical-weight-and-sum approach—the normalization of performances and the calculation of the products of the normalized scores by the weights.

The remainder of this section is a collection of helpful information concerning performance valuation.

The qualitative procedure involves losing a small amount of information because it clumps (aggregates) the data. For example, you lose the difference between the value of something at the bottom end of a valuational interval (the range over which you give the same value), and something at the top end. But: the loss is minor, and, if you prefer, you can salvage most of it at the cost of a small complication. In any event, there are large gains in validity and consistency from keeping down the number of categories of value.

The loss is minor because it is—by definition—never as large as a single unit in the merit scale, that is, never as large as the difference between, say, just significant and substantially significant. Almost no decisions rest on fractional units (which is what we're talking about here), and those that do will go through a refocusing phase which automatically increases the power of the microscope. Nevertheless, if this simplification worries you, the loss can be handled by flagging those cases which you feel have some greater value due to performance which is very close to the next cutting point. You can use a typographical variation on the valuation symbol sign; for example, adding an accent to it (an apostrophe for convenience) when you judge that the performance is very near the top end of the range. Call this a "high plus" or a "high double plus," etc.[34] Before doing this, however, ask yourself whether you shouldn't be redefining the bands into which you have divided the range of performance on this dimension; that's often a cleaner way to reflect differences.

While the merit of performances on a continuous variable often increases monotonically with its magnitude, it's also quite common for the merit to increase for a while and then decline (e.g., the size of a keyboard, since too small is unusable for touch typing and too large is hard to pack away).

You can apply the suggested procedure to customize a performance matrix or even a valuation matrix obtained from another source. For example, many consumer magazines provide performance matrices for products they are reviewing and Consumer Reports usually provides a quality rating for each of the dimensions you are likely to value. You can insert your own weights into the matrix and use the next step here to get a much more accurate evaluation in terms of your values than by doing an eyeball correction of their overall results.

Put a question mark in a cell if you are still missing the relevant data after a source has been searched for it; doing so saves redundant searches. In many cases, you'll never have to do any further research, because the weighting of the criterion, plus the valuations of the performance on this and other criteria by other candidates make it clear that no performance in this cell could make this candidate into a winner. After you've looked at that possibility, if it is still crucial to find out something, put a double question mark in the appropriate cell. That flags crucial missing data which must be found before wrap-up.

Integrating the Results: The Decision Heuristic. The decision algorithm for the basic numerical-weight-and-sum approach is attractively simple: add up the product of the weights by the performances, to get a score for each candidate, and the candidate with the largest score wins. But we can only use that approach by making false assumptions, and the errors are often very large. **The decision heuristic for the qualitative approach is not an algorithm** and it is a little more complex to spell out fully, but in most practical cases, it takes far less time to do than read about. It's just the occasional case which requires the more complex part of the procedure. In general, it replaces the assumption of a single ratio scale of utility with the use of three categories of importance; and replaces arithmetic with comparisons.

1. Add up the valuation scores of each candidate in *three currencies;* the number of stars (including high stars), of double plusses, and of plusses. List this with slashes between categories (as p/q/r). Include the appropriate number of apostrophes, if you are using that modification. Thus, candidate one might have a complete score of 6"/4'/7"". (Good spreadsheets have Count functions, which will eliminate counting errors on a very big matrix.) Subtract negatives at this point, but that will have to be reconsidered before settling on a winner.

2. Rank the candidates on stars. There are three possible situations: a clear winner, a close winner, and a tie. Your interest is only in the winner(s) and runners-up. This process should get you down to no more than four candidates; if it doesn't, run the first step or two in the following sequence which will cut the numbers quickly.

3. When you are down to four or fewer candidates, still looking at stars only, first check to see if high stars, that is, accented symbols (apostrophes for convenience), were used. They may resolve a tie, create one from a close win, or weaken a clear win to a close win or tie. If you need to, use the rule of thumb that three accents are worth one of the base scores (of course, it's not a literal truth). This step is called an "accent check." Whatever the results at this level, they go to the next level down for reversal check.

4. Next look at the double plusses. In the case of a tie at the star level, the double plusses will normally establish a prima facie winner. (It is still subject to review as

below.) If there was a winner at the star level, there is a possibility that the double plus scores can reverse it. You can use only one fact: the star is worth significantly more than the double plus. This gives us a minimum requirement for reversal, as follows. Suppose that the winner's margin on stars (ignoring accents for the moment) is S. Suppose that the winner on double plusses beats the winner on stars by a margin of D double plusses. Unless D is larger than S, there is no case for reversal. (As the star margin increases in absolute size, the double plus difference in the opposite direction has to become even bigger to get a reversal. Although there's no exact rule, a rough guide is that D needs to be double the size of S before a case for reversal exists.[35] This step is called a "reversal check." At this point, you will almost always have a clear prima facie winner. Whatever the results at this level, they go to the next step.

5. Repeat step 3, the accent check, for accented double plusses, if any. They can be used to settle ties that have carried through the two previous levels, and to reverse small margins in the double-plus level.

6. Repeat step 4, the reversal check, for the pluses.

7. Do an accent check on the pluses. At this point there should be a clear prima facie winner—or winners in the case of a tie—of whose credentials you are convinced. But one more step is essential, particularly for beginners who may be uncertain about the reliability of their own ratings at this stage.

8. If you can't decide whether the winner is a clear winner, whether the results are close, how much higher "much higher" is, whether cutting the field down to four rather than five is crucial, or whether a huge difference in plusses couldn't reverse a small star differ-

ence, then either accept the tie or run a refocus. Beginners should always run the refocus, to be safe, until they develop a good sense of the difference between real ties and well-concealed winners.

The Final Refocus. In a refocus, you reconsider the criteria and the weightings, you drop all other candidates, and you emphasize the differences. This is one situation where construction of a graphical (bar chart) profile of the remaining candidates may be illuminating, especially if you subtract the common performance and graph only the differences.

There are four or five useful procedures for resolving uncertainty at this point. The first, which you should always do, is to backtrack the result, that is, try to identify out the main factors that led to it.[36] (For example, the winner's edge may be mainly in the areas of convenience rather than power.) See if they are in accord with your current, much enlightened, judgment about the worth of various features. A refinement of this procedure is to run a "robustness check," at least visually. That is, you should look into the extent to which the result is dependent on a few performance measurements which *could* be wrong, or on a critical weighting which *could* be an exaggeration or underestimation. Do an extra check on those factors, if the doubt begins to seem serious.

Another procedure, if you have defined most of the criteria positively, is to go through a list of the *bad* features/drawbacks about each remaining candidate. It may make it clear that you haven't weighted something appropriately. Another check involves examining what happens when you apply a conversion factor to the stars and double plusses. Suppose you feel that each is worth at least twice its successor. What result will the 1:2:4 weighting give you? This exercise may make it clear that you are being overly cautious about the plusses. A final possibility is to consider what happens if you count the accents as ⅓ of the associated weight.[37] Do not get into the habit of starting up with these assumptions, however, because fixed ratios do not hold up for every rater, product, or need. However, the ones mentioned do have the advantage of being somewhat realistic, by comparison with those used by Consumers Union or *InfoWorld*.[38] You can develop your own assumptions that better match your method of weighting.

Hybrid Quantitative-Qualitative Approaches. How far wrong would you be if you used the suggested "trial balance" numerical weights of 4,2,1 and ⅓ for accents? (For convenience, we might use 12, 6, and 3, with 1 point for accents.) Much less wrong than if you use larger ratios; much less wrong than if you multiply weights by performance scores. But, unfortunately, wrong to a varying degree which is not predictable for a given rater, and which depends on your own characteristics as a rater. A few tests suggest that the results are sometimes the same and sometimes substantially but not totally different. More trials need to be done using different raters.

Suppose you went further back in the process with this approach, scoring all performances on a 12-point scale. This would eliminate the need for accents—they will simply show up as an increase of 1, 2, or 3 points, depending on the importance of the criterion. Then you run into the really serious problem of justifying that 12:1 ratio and the psychological evidence is unambiguous: the size of the errors will go up considerably. And you won't know how big they are. The backtracking also becomes more difficult.

The Absolute Question. When you are convinced about the winner, the time has come to ask the absolute question: is the best candidate good enough for you to spend what it will cost. There's no algorithm for this, but there is a good way to go about it. The winner's row on the performance chart provides a functional profile of the product. It has a certain number of outstanding advantages, some strong points, some minor attractions, some weaknesses: walk across that row, meanwhile visualizing what it will be like to own it. Ask yourself *if that combination is worth having, at its costs*—which you are now in a position to estimate quite accurately.

Loose Ends

We have not covered some refinements such as dealing with criteria which are themselves compound or indeed evaluative rather than directly measurable (e.g., design or quality of manufacture). They present no great problem, merely calling for the identification of a set of subcriteria (indicators) which will then generate the valuations in an auxiliary table. Then there is the serious question of reliable cost analysis including nonmoney costs which often represent the most important costs (psychological costs, environmental damage, space costs, expertise costs, etc.) There is the interesting question of the conditions under which it is possible to generalize across consumers, to support claims about "the best laser printer in this price bracket," not just "the best for you"; and how to handle risk and unavailability of evidence on vital criteria. But perhaps we have covered enough to indicate the existence of a reasonable procedure for product evaluation which avoids a number of serious mistakes, and a topic which deserves to be given a place in the logic of science, not discarded into the bin of "matters of taste."

Notes

1. This is reminiscent of the way that *evaluation* turns up in educational research texts, where for thirty years the only thing it referred to, although the term was never qualified, was the evaluation of *students*. There was never any recognition that teachers or curricula or administrators or schools might need evaluation, let alone that the students might play an important role as evaluators. Even today, there is a tendency to use different words without a different meaning to refer to these other processes, *assessment* or *accreditation*, for example.

2. The very number of false names may itself be an indication of unwillingness to confront the monster directly: *assessment, refereeing, reviewing, appraisal, critique, examination, rating, comment, judgment, reporting*, are some of the entries.

We have mentioned the situation in education where *evaluation* was taken to mean only the evaluation of the powerless, the students. Even more peculiar is the implicit assumption underlying much work in curriculum and program evaluation—the assumption that it has no relation worth mentioning to product evaluation or to personnel evaluation.

3. There were some exceptions to this generalization. J. O. Urmson's "On Grading" was an early and notable one, and it attracted some discussion although it is now of antiquarian interest only. The same is true of the work in axiology that enjoyed a brief vogue as the study of values and hence presumably should have been the subfield in which the practical process of evaluation would be covered; in fact, most of the effort was spent on classification of values, a small part of the process. For example, in product evaluation (as in *Consumer Reports*), the values are only rarely an issue at all; the problematic steps are those from the values on to the evaluative conclusion. Von Wright's, and other deontic logics are almost entirely tangential. The "good reasons" approach to ethics (Toulmin, Baier, and others), like the New Criticism in literature, started off on the right track, but quickly drifted away from it, too easily distracted by the attacks on utilitarianism which seemed to be—but are not—refutations of objectivity in the domain of value.

4. A counterargument of interest here would be a reductio: if what is said is true, then it would also show that logic is the one crucial skill in science. But it isn't listed either, so the argument is unsound. This won't quite do, since logic is accepted by all as a presupposition of rational discourse, including scientific inference, and on that ground not listed. That is a different position from denying its legitimacy altogether. Philosophers of science have indeed made extensive efforts at clarifying inductive logic, since they do believe it to be part of the structure of science. Interestingly, if inductive inference is inference to the *best* explanation, it, too, is evaluative.

5. As a personal note, it is partly amusing and partly sad to be greeted by old friends in the philosophy of science area with expressed regrets about my "abandoning the subject." What I did was to move from twenty years of hard work and publishing on explanation theory to twenty years of hard work and publishing on evaluation theory, a fledgling area which posed new challenges and seemed more in need of conceptual help. But that move meant dropping off the edge of the known universe, as far as the universe of science is known to philosophers of science. It is true that I also moved into evaluation *practice*, but then

philosophers from Kant to Grunbaum have never felt that role to be incompatible with—rather, healthily complementary to—metatheorizing.

There may be a serious problem of reaction time in the philosophy of science. Looking at the subject today, it is hard to avoid a sense of stasis on topics where I am in any position to judge. The discussions of claims I worked on long ago, such as the asymmetry between explanation and prediction and the reasons for it, the contrast-class approach to causation, essential weaknesses in the Turing test, etc., although continuing, seem hardly to have progressed at all. Discussion of major new issues and areas is hard to find, for example, in the failure to pick up the many philosophically important issues in computer studies outside artificial intelligence. Of course, and rightly, judgments are tremendously suspect. The undeniable fact is the failure to respond to major new scientific areas. Eventually, one supposes, philosophy of science will get around to looking at evaluation, but a quarter-century response time is unhealthy; it's too reminiscent of the lag in symbolic logic's reaction to computer programming languages, artificial languages which were for thirty years desperately in need of formal logical analysis. Those lags have cost all parties dearly; they are part of the costs of tenure.

6. Retrospective anthologies are beginning to appear.

7. An extensive search of the literature has failed to reveal previous efforts in this direction, but they may exist, and the author would much appreciate hearing about and acknowledging references to them.

8. Despite the fact that an in-group may share the opinion, there is no sense in which someone with as much experience who disagrees can be shown to be wrong. This is the domain of fashions and tastes, which change without there being any objective change to explain it, certainly no change in the merit of the products. There are limiting cases: if the wine is bad enough to have turned to vinegar, then we can say that the judgment of lack of merit is more than a matter of preference.

9. The exact relation between the evaluative claim and the preference claim is slightly more complex, since an evaluation does not strictly, but only contextually, imply a preference. But what is said here is easily expanded to cover the subtleties.

10. Note that one tends to build the criteria of merit into the concept itself, creating a kind of ideal type. Thus we might say that what we *mean* by a scientific theory is something which exhibits explanatory

power, simplicity, etc. We do the same even with cars, by subdividing them into luxury sedans, economy sedans, sports cars, antique cars, concours cars, race cars, etc. For each of these, the distinguishing characteristics are largely those which we use as the criteria of merit; "what we mean by a sports car is one that has the following characteristics, weighted in the following way. . . . " (Compare: watches as jewelry vs. watches as chronometers vs. watches as status symbols.) The normative flavor of the term *ideal type* may come from this aspect of the practice.

11. Some technical details, including details of implementing the model on a computer, will be provided in a forthcoming paper by me in *Evaluation Practice*, the journal of the American Education Association.

12. The calculation of a GPA (grade point average) involves the same kind of assumption (e.g., that the gap between the A and the B is the same as that between the D and the F). This does lead to misleading reporting, but the context of the GPA is so standardized, and a grade sheet so easily available and readable, that we minimize the damage.

13. For example, a computer with twice the throughput usually gets twice the performance score.

14. Ahmet Bektas, a virtuoso HyperCard designer/programmer, has suggested that a HyperCard stack could also be used. Charting programs might also serve some purpose, for example, in constructing comparative profiles of competing products. When there is a very large number of criteria (and often a large number of candidates), the results will be hard to read and hence not helpful in the working process; but condensed versions of the results, converted into graphical form for reports, can provide benefits (*PC Magazine* does some very nice work of this kind).

15. For example, Consumers Union (CU) makes some serious mistakes in the design of its product evaluations, including the use of the numerical approach. Given CU's vast resources and influence, it is unfortunate that it has proved impossible to get them to take seriously any attempt to improve or even discuss their methods. In fact, they seem to believe that *methods* means "measurement." But if evaluation methodologists can develop demonstrably superior methods, perhaps we can persuade CU and other product testing (i.e., product evaluation) labs and organizations to move forward.

16. For example, the dispute about when or whether program evaluation should be done without goals, and the view that personnel eval-

uation cannot legitimately employ all predictively valid indicators of merit (the opposition view is that all indirectly validated indicators must be excluded, which includes the results of many psychological tests).

17. Candidates cannot be identified reliably by using their maker's description. In the first place these are often exaggerated, but often they are candidates which are not commonly perceived or described as in the same category. The best rug cleaner, for example, is not one of the products called "rug cleaners" but a dilute solution of a good detergent.

18. Doing this means double-counting the overlapping portion of the criteria.

19. A minor example of this is to be found in current *InfoWorld* procedures, where one of the criteria of merit is value for money, and the score on this is added in to the total merit score. But one calculates value for money by comparing total merit with total cost so you can't make total merit depend on value for money.

20. These are as often conceptual as well as technical. For example, when weighing portable computers, one must include in the weight whatever one has to take with one to work at a remote site or on the way to it, even if it's an accessory rather than built in to the computer: for example, voltage converters if one will use it abroad. Otherwise, one unfairly discriminates against the candidate that has built-in voltage conversion.

21. This version of the procedure incorporates several major changes over my previous versions, e.g., "Product Evaluation," in Nick L. Smith, ed., *New Techniques for Evaluation* (Beverly Hills: Sage Publications, 1981), pp. 121–66; *The Logic of Evaluation* (Pt. Reyes, Cal.: Edgepress, 1981); and the version in *Word Magic: Evaluating and Selecting Word Processing* (Belmont, Cal.: Lifetime Learning, 1983). Some aspects of the issue are dealt with in more detail in "The Evaluation of Hardware and Software" in *Studies in Educational Evaluation* 16(1)(1990):3–40. Some of the more sophisticated versions of NWS (Numerical Weight and Sum) include some of the suggestions in bold face type in this chapter. See Michael Scriven, *Evaluation Thesaurus*, 4th edition (Beverly Hills: Sage Publications, forthcoming).

22. See, for example, Michael Scriven, *Evaluation Thesaurus*, 3d edition (Inverness, Cal.: Edgepress, 1981), "Key Evaluation Checklist."

23. See, for example, "Duties-Based Teacher Evaluation," *Journal of Personnel Evaluation in Education* 1(4)(1988):319–34.

24. The word processor-outliners are very good in helping you to organize the material in the first column (because you can grab any row and move it up and down the column and because they allow collapsing and expanding the level of subheads on display), but very laborious for juggling material in other columns when you do not wish to move the whole row, unless they have something in the way of a table maker— which is built into the spreadsheet. This is one of a number of applications for spreadsheets which make them very handy outside the domain for which they were invented. But it would be much more useful if the outliner facility were available within the spreadsheet so that subheads could be hidden.

25. E.g., pounds of weight, number, and (proofreader's mark for) space. But the name should not be taken to imply that a double plus is worth twice as much as a plus.

26. The first kind of error is said to be a "false negative" and the second kind a "false positive."

27. Computers are often said to de-skill tasks, and indeed they do that. It is less often remarked that they also up-skill them. You and I, probably incompetent typists, can put out well-typed material on a word processor, because error correction is so easy. But the highly competent typist sometimes—quite often, as it turns out—cannot make the transition to the word processor.

28. Without remortgaging the house. Don't beg the question at this point by giving a dollar value to NN as "the most you could possibly justify spending, *as it now appears*" since you aren't yet in a good position to see what you might get for the money. Leave NN undefined for the moment or put in a figure that's fifty percent more than you now think you can afford. It may be that what you get will probably save you a good deal of money, when you come to look into it closely. With a too-early definition of NN, you would have already dropped candidates that could pay off for you—false negatives.

29. This is the second place at which false negatives turn up in many analyses. One of the most common errors of this kind is to say that a micro which won't run MS-DOS is out of the mainstream and not a sensible buy. Given the size of the software pool in the Mac and

Unix areas, and the ease of data conversion at the moment, this is a serious error.

30. In the electronic versions, these are the cells of the spreadsheet, boxes of the table, or hidden text of the outliner.

31. Of course, clock speed isn't exactly the measure you want. What you really need is throughput speed on the task mix you will use, but since no one publishes measurement standards based on your task mix, you settle for a number of secondary indicators of throughput speed, such as performance (on tasks which have been benchmarked), bus width, and clock speed, which are useful within one family of processors. But as between DISC and RISC processors, or as between architectures with graphics coprocessors and those without them, they are not valid indicators. (Clock speed is also of some value in predicting compatibility with existing software.)

32. Computer magazines occasionally set out a table in which they list the order of merit of each candidate on various dimensions and then either add up the number of first places to get a winner, or award five points for a first place and some lesser number for second, etc. The procedure does not have wide acceptance, presumably because of a recognition of the weaknesses mentioned.

33. Since writing this, Consumers Union has, fortuitously, released a test of laptop computers (September, 1989). It is competent in most respects, although it is clearly not done by people who are expert in this area of the market. For example, they print the wrong photographs of two Toshibas, with possibly serious results; they omit some crucial candidates and features which would substantially alter the conclusions (e.g., the RAM disk option on the Toshiba 1000); and they have a mistaken idea of street prices (there are no desktops with software suites at $355, contrary to the suggestion on p. 564). They use a hybrid quantitative-qualitative approach, which is discussed toward the end of this chapter.

34. This corresponds quite closely with the use of plusses and minusses with letter grades. Many instructors would strongly protest their deletion, even though it's very hard to show that they have the discrimination skills required for *consistent* application of the expanded scale.

35. This depends on the absolute numbers as well, but, roughly speaking, this rule of thumb works well when the total number of stars or double pluses is small (say, 1–5) and fails safe for larger numbers. That

is, if S represents the difference between 10 and 11 stars, it will take more than a margin of 2 double pluses in the opposite direction to reverse it. This is because *each* of the 11 stars for the winner represents a substantial increment of value over a double plus, so all of those differences have to be overcome as well as the winning margin star(s).

36. This is roughly akin to what an expert system program does when asked to explain its decisions.

37. An extension of this approach is to solve the equation so as to find out what weighting for a double plus (against a star) will give you a tie between first and second. Then ask yourself if that seems appropriate; similarly for the ratio between double plus and plus. If this approach appeals, a custom function can be constructed using the scripting function of the spreadsheet, so as to give you this result with a single command.

38. *InfoWorld* uses weights with a ratio of 10:1, which means that ease of learning (40 points) is completely swamped by performance (400 points) and even by value for money (200 points).

Biographical Sketches
of Contributors

EVA T. H. BRANN is the dean of St. John's College in Annapolis, where she has been a tutor since 1957. Her doctorate is in Classics and Archaeology from Yale University, but she has taught throughout the integrated Great Books program of St. John's. Her publications include *Late Geometric and Protoattic Pottery: The Athenian Agors* (1962), *Paradoxes of Education in a Republic* (1979), and *The World of the Imagination* (1990).

MICHAEL J. BUCKLEY, SJ, is professor of philosophical theology at the University of Notre Dame. From 1986 to 1989 he was professor of systematic theology at the Jesuit School of Theology at Berkeley. He is author of *Motion and Motion's God: Thematic Variations in Aristotle, Cicero, Newton and Hegel* (1971), *At the Origins of Modern Atheism* (1987), and numerous articles on philosophy, theology, and related topics. Professor Buckley holds a Ph.D from the University of Chicago.

ROBERT H. ENNIS is professor of philosophy of education and director of the Illinois Critical Thinking Project at the University of Illinois at Urbana-Champaign. He is one of the developers of the *Cornell Critical Thinking Tests*. His publications include

Evaluating Critical Thinking, coauthored with S. P. Norris (1989), *Logic in Teaching* (1969), *Ordinary Logic* (1969), and numerous articles on critical thinking and education. Professor Ennis's doctorate is from the University of Illinois.

GERALD GRAFF has recently succeeded Wayne Booth as George M. Pullman Professor of Humanities and English at the University of Chicago. From 1966 to 1990 he taught at Northwestern University, where he chaired the English department. His writings include *Professing Literature: An Institutional History* (1987) and other works on literary theory, curriculum, and the connection between the two.

RALPH H. JOHNSON is professor of philosophy at the University of Windsor, Windsor, Ontario, where he has been teaching since 1966. He has coauthored one textbook on informal logic (*Logical Self-Defense,* 1983) and written numerous articles on informal logic and critical thinking. He is a founder and coeditor of the journal, *Informal Logic.*

LENORE LANGSDORF teaches philosophy of communication in the speech communication department of Southern Illinois University at Carbondale. Her research interests center about the organization of everyday life, with particular attention to the intrinsic presence and possible growth of rationality. She developed an NEH-funded project for integrated teaching of reading, writing, and reasoning, and writes on issues in communication theory and philosophy of the social sciences from a theoretical orientation formed by hermeneutic phenomenology, process thought, and critical theory. She received her doctorate from the State University of New York at Stony Brook.

DONALD LAZERE is professor of English at California Polytechnic State University in San Luis Obispo. He is the author of *The Unique Creation of Albert Camus* and *Composition for Critical Thinking,* and editor of *American Media and Mass Culture: Left Perspectives.* He is an associate of the Center for Critical Thinking and Moral Critique at Sonoma State University.

His articles, reviews, and columns have appeared in academic and journalistic periodicals including *New Literary History, College English, The Chronicle of Higher Education, The New York Times, The Los Angeles Times,* and *Newsday.*

JOHN E. MCPECK is professor of education at the University of Western Ontario. He is author of *Teaching Critical Thinking: Dialogue and Dialectic* (1990), *Critical Thinking and Education* (1981), and articles on philosophy, critical thinking, and education. He received his Ph.D. from the University of Western Ontario.

RICHARD W. PAUL is professor of philosophy and director of the Center for Critical Thinking at Sonoma State University. He has published over fifty articles and five books on critical thinking in the last five years. His views on critical thinking have been canvassed in *The New York Times, The Chronicle of Higher Education, Newsweek,* and *U.S. News and World Report.* He has organized ten international conferences on critical thinking and worked with many school districts and institutions of higher learning designing strategies for the reform of education. Most recently, he has produced, in cooperation with PBS, a series of eight video programs on critical thinking and educational reform.

STANLEY ROSEN is Evan Pugh Professor of Philosophy at The Pennsylvania State University. He is author of *The Ancients and the Moderns: Rethinking Modernity* (1989), *Hermeneutics as Politics* (1987), *Plato's Symposium* (1987), and other books and numerous philosophical articles. Professor Rosen received his Ph.D. from the University of Chicago.

MICHAEL SCRIVEN holds his doctorate from Oxford University. He taught in the U.S. for thirty years, twelve of them at the University of California at Berkeley, before taking up a position at the University of Western Australia in 1982. He is currently professor at the Pacific Graduate School of Psychology, professor emeritus of education at the University of Western Australia, and consulting professor at Stanford University. He is author of

Reasoning (1976) and many publications in the areas of psychology, philosophy, program/product/personnel evaluation, microcomputer applications, technology studies, and education.

HARVEY SIEGEL is professor of philosophy at the University of Miami. He specializes in epistemology, philosophy of science, and philosophy of education. He is author of *Relativism Refuted: A Critique of Contemporary Epistemological Relativism* (1987), *Educating Reason: Rationality, Critical Thinking, and Education* (1988), and many articles in philosophy of science, epistemology, and philosophy of education.

R. W. SLEEPER is professor emeritus at Queens College, the City University of New York, and a former member of the graduate faculty of the Graduate Center of the City University of New York. He currently lectures on ethics and law at Plymouth State College. His most recent publications include *The Necessity of Pragmatism: John Dewey's Conception of Philosophy* (1986); "Naturalizing Legal Positivism," in *Ethics, Science and Democracy,* edited by I. L. Horowitz and H. S. Thayer (1987); the introduction to *John Dewey: The Later Works, Volume 14,* edited by Jo Ann Boydston (1987); "John Dewey and the Founding Fathers" in *Values and Value Theory in 20th-Century America,* edited by Murray G. Murphey and Ivar Berg (1988). He is currently writing a book on the influence of pragmatism on European philosophy, philosophical logic, philosophy of science and the philosophy of law.

ROBERT J. STERNBERG is IBM Professor of Psychology and Education at Yale University. He received his B.A. summa cum laude, Phi Beta Kappa from Yale in 1972, and his Ph.D. from Stanford in 1975. He has been the winner of the Early Career Award and Boyd R. McCandless Award of the American Psychological Association, the Outstanding Book and Research Review Awards of the Society for Multivariate Experimental Psychology, and the Distinguished Scholar Award of the National Association for Gifted Children (U.S.A.). He is a past winner of NSF and Guggenheim Foundation Fellowships. Sternberg's main research interests are in intelligence, creativity, and thought processes.

RICHARD A. TALASKA is associate professor of philosophy at Xavier University. He is author of *The Emergence of the Early Modern Concept of System* (a monograph that appears in the microfiche supplement to *Philosophy Research Archives*, 1985) and articles on the philosophy of Thomas Hobbes. His interests include the history of moral and political philosophy and the importance of the study of Great Books in contemporary education as a means to critical thinking. He received his doctorate from the Catholic University of America.

Index

413